The Anatomy of an
International Monetary Regime

The Anatomy of an International Monetary Regime

The Classical Gold Standard, 1880–1914

GIULIO M. GALLAROTTI

New York   Oxford
OXFORD UNIVERSITY PRESS
1995

Oxford University Press

Oxford   New York
Athens   Aukland   Bangkok   Bombay
Calcutta   Cape Town   Dar es Salaam   Delhi
Florence   Hong Kong   Istanbul   Karachi
Kuala Lumpur   Madras   Madrid   Melbourne
Mexico City   Nairobi   Paris   Singapore
Taipei   Tokyo   Toronto

and associated companies in
Berlin   Ibadan

Copyright © 1995 by Oxford University Press, Inc.

Published by Oxford University Press, Inc.
200 Madison Avenue, New York, New York 10016

Oxford is a registered trademark of Oxford University Press

Library of Congress Cataloging-in-Publication Data
Gallarotti, Giulio M.
The anatomy of an international monetary regime : the classical
gold standard, 1880–1914 / Giulio M. Gallarotti.
p.   cm.
Includes bibliographical references (p. 323–338) and index.
ISBN 0-19-508990-1
1. Gold standard—History.   I. Title.
HG297.G3   1995
332.4'52—dc20   94-20270

9 8 7 6 5 4 3 2 1

Printed in the United States of America
on acid-free paper

Dedicated to Gem, Giulio Christian, and Alessio;
my parents Lina and Gino;
and my sister Luisa, for their love and support

Preface

It seems to be a peculiarity of history that periods of the past are more often venerated than understood. Perhaps this is not so surprising given the attractiveness of mystery. Or perhaps the intellect is also subject to the common tendency of familiarity breeding contempt. The classical gold standard, 1880–1914, as a period in economic history, is no exception. The gold standard has a long history of stimulating thoughts of the "good old days" of monetary relations among both scholars and public elites. Advocates of resuscitating gold standards in the interwar years offered the prewar gold standard and its workings as a justification for making the necessary sacrifices in reestablishing the gold links which were broken by the War. The negotiation at Bretton Woods introduced a quite different version of this regime, but kept close to several central principles such as fixed exchange rates and giving gold a central role in defining parities, this latter goal being achieved by linking the U.S. dollar to gold. For these latter-day practitioners, it was a matter of bringing back the very "best" of the good old days. More recently, those who speak of alternatives to government fiat regimes and who lament the poor workings of the international economy (i.e., volatile exchange rates, abnormal capital flows, barriers to the movement of goods and money, lack of confidence, lack of rules) also look back to an age which in their minds was both literally and figuratively a golden one.

This project took shape several years ago, with an interest in the late 19th and early 20th centuries as just such a special period in monetary relations. I found that the veneration of the period was far more extensive than the extant scholarly understanding of the period. The workings of the classical gold standard have already been subject to quite a bit of revisionist history. But even more than the need to fill in the voids left by the revisionist work which challenged the conventional wisdom about the "rules of the game" and adjustment, central questions pertaining to the foundations of the gold standard as an international monetary system or regime have been strikingly absent. In other words, the questions How did it start? and Why did it last? (i.e., besides the workings of the gold standard, the other regime dynamics of the gold standard) have generated little attention. Part of this has surely been a result of disciplinary styles, as most of the work on the gold standard has been done by economists who have pursued a more restricted analysis centering around mainstream concerns in the traditional efficiency and performance criteria of economics. And even when economists have confronted the questions of the origin and stability of the gold standard, references have been all too brief. It is common to see references to a favorable set of political and economic conditions without much analysis of these conditions. Other social scientists, whose conventional disciplinary tools are more adapted to addressing these questions, have ventured little into monetary relations before World War I. But those that have ventured into such waters have traditionally linked the regime dynamics of the gold standard to either British monetary leadership or cooperation among major monetary players in the international system, two processes which have been highly problematic owing to a dearth of empirical and historical support. While previous work on the gold standard may have addressed either its workings, its origin, or its stability, no work has as yet systematically addressed all three together.

In seeking to address these gaps, my interests became focused on analyzing what broader set of institutions and processes were responsible for creating and sustaining a specific set of relations and outcomes in the international monetary system in the late 19th and early 20th centuries—in other words, explaining the regime dynamics of the classical gold standard. Rather than having my boundaries drawn by state-of-the-art concerns in either economics or political science, my goal was to answer the following questions as best I could, irrespective of where the answers came from: How did the classical gold standard work? How did it originate? and Why did it last? My answers to these questions comprise this book: a political economy of the classical gold standard. As with any interdisciplinary venture, this book may very well risk offending the specialist who is wedded to a particular methodology. But even here I continue to be inspired by the belief that the quest for scholarly understanding has no disciplinary boundaries.

Like most books, this one was neither conceived nor produced in solitude. I owe a great debt to a variety of individuals who have contributed to the development of this project from its early stages. Mentioning their names does not suffice to express my gratitude for their input. I would like to thank William Barber, Michael Bordo, James Buchanan, Forrest Capie, John Conybeare, Barry Eichengreen, Domenico da Empoli, Ronald Findlay, Jeff Frieden, Richard Grossman, Robert Jervis, Charles Kindleberger, Stan Lebergott, Michael Lovell, Helen Milner, Donald Moggridge, Richard Nelson, Philip Pomper, Anna Schwartz, David Selover, Tom Willett, Elliot Zupnick, and the referees of Oxford University Press for their comments. David Titus and Peter Kilby made the task of finishing the book so much more bearable by their ever-present cheerfulness.

Valuable secretarial assistance was provided by Janet DeMicco, Lee Messina, and Fran Warren. Janet Morgan, Joanne Liljedahl, and Patricia Curley provided technical support in processing the various drafts. Idan Elkon, Neeraj Shah, Susanah Washburn, Maura Solomon, and Adam Wolfe proofread various chapters.

I am also grateful to Herb Addison, Mary Sutherland, Susan Hannan, Peter Grennen, and Marya Ripperger, for their highly professional and humane efforts in nurturing this project to completion.

Finally, I would like to thank my wife Gem; my sons Giulio Christian and Alessio; my parents Gino and Lina; and my sister Luisa for putting up with the negative externalities of scholarship. I hope to compensate them sufficiently in the future.

All of the chapters in the book represent previously unpublished work except for Chapter 6, which is a revised version of "The Scramble for Gold: Monetary Regime Transformation in the 1870s" in Michael D. Bordo and Forrest Capie, eds., *Monetary Regimes in Transition* (Cambridge: Cambridge University Press, 1993).

Middletown, Conn.   G. G.
April 1994

Contents

The Anatomy of an
International Monetary Regime

1

Introduction

Few periods in the history of the international monetary system evoke such positive sentiments among economic historians as the classical gold standard (1880–1914). At the same time, perhaps few periods have been as misunderstood or, until recently, neglected. It was an epoch which was not just acknowledged for a set of favorable monetary developments at both the international and domestic levels, but often venerated as a crowning achievement in monetary relations. Strange (1988, p. 97) states that "never since then has there been so long a period of financial stability, both in the credit system and in the relations of major trading currencies." Cleveland (1976, pp. 26, 27) notes, "No monetary system is likely again to prove its equal in satisfying the criterion of international monetary order." Interwar attempts to resuscitate the prewar system treated the gold standard more as an act of faith than a discretionary act of policy. Even more recently, the current problems of the international monetary "non-system" have generated a renewed interest in the study of the gold standard.[1]

The classical gold standard has heretofore been studied principally by economists who have been most interested in it as a set of monetary outcomes that had an important impact on national and international economic performance, usually with respect to some efficiency criteria. Did central banks follow rules of the game, and how closely? Was the foreign-exchange market efficient? Did exchange rates maintain purchasing power parity? What effects did the practice of gold monometallism have on the transmission of business cycles? How did prices and output behave relative to other periods? What was the nature of financial crises? How did the adjustment mechanism function? All such questions typify the mainstream economic approach to the gold standard.[2] Much less emphasis has been placed on understanding the origin and maintenance of an integrated set of institutions and processes that crystallized into an international monetary regime.

The categories presented in the work on international regimes provide a broader political-economy framework with which to describe and analyze the classical gold standard, one that is richer and more diverse than the conventional efficiency/performance concerns of economists who study the gold standard. On a general level it provides the opportunity to integrate political, economic, and ideological factors in explaining patterned behavior in international economic systems.[3] In this respect, economic regimes are seen as much more than just outcomes of the convergence of economic processes, but are in fact approached as a set of social institutions: i.e., a

3

set of relations that comprises a variety of social processes. Hence the regime approach is by nature interdisciplinary. Although the work on regimes shows quite a variety in the way scholars define and analyze these social institutions, as well as differences in emphasis placed on the importance of specific institutions,[4] the work does share a special concern for ideological factors. A pervasive question across the different contributions to the work on economic regimes is, What "norms, principles, and rules" are responsible for the order we find in specific international economic systems?[5]

The existing scholarship (both the more traditional and empirical approaches) on the classical gold standard has in fact paid very little attention to these political and ideological factors, but such factors are especially relevant to the central workings, origin, and stability of the gold standard. The gold standard exhibited properties that are highly characteristic of the mainstream regime vision. In its international manifestations (i.e., outcomes involving adjustment, exchange rates, and capital flows), the gold standard was founded on an integrated set of norms which were embedded in the prevailing classical liberal consensus of the latter 19th and early 20th centuries. These norms generated expectations and behavior that conditioned the course of monetary interdependence among the developed nations of the period. In the current regime terminology, the classical gold standard represented an aggregation of outcomes which were largely dependent on institutions around which expectations converged in a given issue area (money), and these institutions were themselves grounded in prevailing belief systems about the proper organization of economic life. It was this liberal consensus that was most crucial in maintaining the stable structure of adjustment, which in turn was most directly responsible for preserving a set of stable monetary relations in the developed world for three and a half decades before World War I. The gold standard's origin and stability also owed much to specific domestic and international political forces that prevailed in the late 19th and early 20th centuries. Understanding these ideological and political aspects of the gold standard allows us to go considerably beyond the conventional efficiency/performance and restricted operational approaches undertaken by monetary historians, and view monetary relations in that period as a broader social system.

Contributions that might have illuminated such aspects of the gold standard are scant. Ruggie (1983), Cohen (1977), and Keohane and Nye (1985) do identify and discuss the classical gold standard as an international monetary regime, but their attention is limited and considerations of how it started and why it persisted are underplayed. Eichengreen (1985b, p. 2) points out, "There exists no comprehensive accounts of the gold standard's operation as an international system." He adds that scholars have not taken a holistic approach to understanding the gold standard, having heretofore learned about the operation of the gold standard by looking at isolated parts. A holistic approach should take into consideration the political, economic, and ideological forces that were central to the workings, origin, and stability of the gold standard, something the categories of the regime approach do address.

On the origin and stability of the gold standard, rarely have scholars who have studied the period asked what forces were instrumental in moving the developed world collectively from silver and bimetallist standards to gold in the 1870s, or asked what forces were paramount in maintaining international monetary order for three and a half decades before World War I. When they have addressed such questions, the attention and the analyses have been all too limited.[6] In the definitive account on the working of the gold standard, Bloomfield (1959, p. 9) explains the highly favorable outcomes in monetary relations under the gold standard as "the product of an unusually favorable combination of historical circumstances." He goes on to say (p. 59) that the question of why the gold standard worked so well "has been excluded from the scope of [his] study." Yeager (1984, p. 662) cites the "almost uniquely favorable conditions" that made the gold standard function as smoothly as it did, but doesn't elaborate.[7]

This book attempts to provide a more comprehensive and interdisciplinary account of the gold standard as an international system than has heretofore been provided by monetary historians. As a broader study of the classical gold standard, emphasis will be placed less on monetary and economic performance with respect to some limited efficiency criteria, and more on general processes and institutions which generated and sustained an orderly set of monetary relations during the period. For the political scientist, it illuminates the manner in which non-economic factors such as norms and political developments sustain constellations of economic outcomes and relations. For the economist, the broader interdisciplinary approach to monetary systems leads to an alternative set of questions and concerns which are quite distinct from the traditional interests which have thus far guided their study of the gold standard.

The primary purpose of this book is not oriented around constructing a theory of regimes or more generally of international relations. It makes use of the categories in the regime literature principally as means of describing and analyzing the gold standard. This case study does, however, bear upon important theoretical debates in the literature on international relations, especially in the areas of hegemonic stability, cooperation, and regime theory. These implications are systematically explored in Chapter 8, and are also discussed (although less extensively) in Chapters 3, 4, and 5.

The central issues of analysis in this study of the gold standard derive from what social scientists call regime dynamics.[8] In other words, How do specific international economic regimes work?, How do these regimes originate? and How are they maintained? Specifically in the context of the classical gold standard, the three questions: How did the classical gold standard work?, How did it start? and Why did it last? have never been systematically addressed as a whole, and the latter two questions have hardly been addressed individually. Moreover, there has been little political-economic analysis of the monetary relations under the gold standard. This book addresses all three questions in a broader political-economic context, and in doing so attempts thereby to provide an understanding of monetary relations in this period which has heretofore been missing. The findings of this book also call into question many of the traditionally held interpretations of the gold standard. In this latter respect the book aspires to important revisionist contributions to the historical work on the gold standard.

With respect to how the classical gold standard worked, at the domestic level a gold standard is nothing more than a system for organizing monetary transactions. The classical gold standard, as an international regime, was simply an additive outcome of a group of nations (principally advanced-industrial nations) unilaterally adopting gold standards in the 1870s (i.e., the scramble for gold). That gold became the foundation for transactions across nations meant that it naturally acquired the properties of an international money: international medium of exchange (i.e., vehicle currency), store of value (reserve currency), and measure of value (i.e., things equal to the same thing are equal to each other). In this latter respect, a set of international parities naturally emerged as nations linked to the same numeraire (gold). Furthermore, in that nations in the gold club practiced few capital controls (according to the orthodox metallism of the period), the individual monetary systems came to be interlinked within a greater international system, or what economists would call a fairly open international monetary regime.

In its working this international regime exhibited a fairly pervasive character across the five principal properties defining an international monetary regime (liquidity/ reserves, adjustment, exchange rates, capital control, and confidence). Outcomes under the classical gold standard were principally conditioned by market processes throughout the period: i.e., outcomes were primarily the resultants of private transactions in the markets for goods and money. Unlike the international monetary regimes that would follow World War I, very little in the prewar regime was conditioned by the actions of public authorities at the international level. There was little supranational, multilateral, and/or unilateral intervention in the markets for goods and money.[9] International liquidity was the outcome of developments in national money supplies. The international supply and demand for money were conditioned by transactions among private investors in the global capital market. Very little public manipulation of international capital flows took place, as governments in the gold club practiced very few capital controls; and of the public initiatives to influence capital flows (these by central bankers), there was more reliance on market means (e.g., competing for gold by raising the buying price) than administrative (e.g., restrictions on the export of gold) means. In this respect, the adjustment process under the gold standard was very much determined by market processes rather than public intervention.[10] For such an adjustment process to work (i.e., be sufficient to maintain convertibility across nations in the gold club) depended on the confidence of private and public actors in the regime itself. Under the gold standard such confidence was very high.

In tackling the problems of how the gold standard originated and why it lasted, account first needs to be taken of the answers which scholars have given thus far. These answers revolve around the issue of management. The conventional thinking on the gold standard's stability suggests that the regime lasted because it was either managed by Great Britain and/or a group of central banks that cooperated to reduce destabilizing impulses in the international monetary system. Much less has been said in the extant scholarship about how the regime originated. But even here account must be taken about feelings that prevailed in the period about the effects of the international monetary negotiations that took place in the latter 19th century, especially the Conference of 1867, which produced a resolution recommending an international gold union. Hence, any analysis of how the regime started and why it lasted (i.e., remained stable) would have to start with an assessment of monetary cooperation and leadership (i.e., British hegemony) in the latter 19th century.

The findings of this book suggest that cooperation in the period of the classical gold standard was not a principal factor in influencing either the origin or stability of the regime. No cooperative schemes emerged from the negotiations among national governments in the period and very little cooperation took place strictly among central banks. It is interesting that so little success was achieved at the four international monetary conferences of the period, because the most powerful monetary players in the system faced consistent and great incentives to create a formal monetary regime: either a monetary union or a multilateral-price-support scheme. British intransigence was an ongoing barrier to success. In this respect, the British appear to have acted against their own best interests, since a regime appeared to carry far more benefits than the potential sacrifices Britain would have had to make (which by all accounts were in fact small). The other major barriers which manifested themselves across the conferences were moral hazard and fears of exploitation (free riding). A good deal of complacency was created by expectations that large and powerful nations would unilaterally or multilaterally build a regime. Such complacency was also evident among core nations themselves. Hence, nations systematically held back in making concessions in hope that they could benefit from a regime which was supported exclusively by other nations. Compounding this complacency were fears that if indeed such concessions were made, the cooperating nations might be exploited by free riders. This latter factor was especially important in precluding the emergence of a price-support agreement for silver.

The cooperation among central banks was primarily in the form of ad hoc bilateral arrangements to transfer liquidity in need. The motives for the transfers were a combination of concerns for the creditors' own domestic monetary and economic systems (avoiding financial and economic spillover) and normal private business incentives (lending at penalty rates). Hence, whatever process can be said to have characterized transactions between central banks was configured more by domestic monetary concerns and individualistic norms of good business than by international norms regarding commitments to stabilizing some kind of international monetary community. While this cooperation was stabilizing, it is not clear that central bank relations in general were stabilizing, given the elements of competition among them. Central bankers competed before they accommodated in times of liquidity shortages. Hence, perhaps the cooperative schemes did nothing more than neutralize the distress which the banks themselves caused through competition (i.e., the cooperation would not have been necessary if competitive appreciation of rates did not occur). While cooperation made convertibility easier to maintain, competition made it harder to maintain, leaving the net effects difficult to assess. This competitiveness had at least one stabilizing consequence for the gold standard in that it encouraged greater conformity in discount rates.

If the origin and stability of the gold standard were not the results of cooperation, were they in fact (as most of the extant scholarship on the period suggests with respect to stability) the products of British hegemony? In other words, was either the British state or the Bank of England the leader of the gold standard? The findings with respect to the behavior of the British state in the area of monetary relations during the period suggest that the state itself was far from a hegemonic actor in the global monetary system. It carried on very limited contacts with international banking and investment, as it was an ongoing priority of the British state to stay clear of transactions in private markets for goods and money. This laissez-faire ethic was all the more pronounced in matters of finance. Furthermore, the foreign policy of Great Britain during the period, which was both relatively passive and defensive in nature, was poorly adapted to any goals of shaping international outcomes in a significant way. Moreover, foreign policy itself was little concerned with economic relations. The British state carried on limited control over and contact with the only viable agent for British monetary hegemony: the Bank of England. Aside from some informal-overview functions, the British state had very little to do with the operations of the Bank.

The behavior of British delegations at the four international conferences violated all common visions of appropriate action by monetary hegemons. Time and time again Britain had an opportunity to bring about a regime which was in its interest, and time and time again it failed to do so. In all four conferences Britain occupied an influential position in deciding whether some regime would be constructed. In all cases, building a regime would have been beneficial to both Britain and the world. But Britain never mobilized any significant support for a regime. Had it exercised even the most minimal hegemony, something might have been consummated at any one of the conferences. But it didn't. In fact, its actions more often served as an obstacle to cooperation. It never made it easier for cooperative nations to start a regime. Furthermore, it proved to be an extremely poor bargainer, as British delegates failed to take advantage of strategic opportunities to further British national interests. When Britain did act hegemonically, it did so in a very inconsistent way. In 1867 it was against union around the franc, but never pushed for union around the pound. In subsequent conferences, it sought to free ride (more consistent with coercive hegemony) on the cooperation of others, but never used even limited commitments to encourage others to build a regime.

If the British state did not hegemonically manage the gold standard, can we find such functions in the Bank of England? The Bank itself may have engaged in either direct or indirect stabilization functions for the international monetary system in the period. And its indirect hegemony may have been of either a strong or weak form. The search for both direct and indirect hegemony, and for both strong and weak hegemony, however, fails to yield satisfying results for those proponents of the Bank of England's hegemonic leadership under the gold standard. Not only can we say that the Bank did not manage the international monetary system, but it is questionable whether it even managed the British monetary system. The Bank acknowledged little responsibility for the British monetary system itself. In fact, the Bank's own private goals often worked to the detriment of the British financial system (i.e., it was a source of destabilizing impulses for British finance). In the role of British central banker (as a lender of last resort, manager of the reserve and the British economy, and manager of crises) it consistently showed itself to be a poor guardian of the monetary system. Its reserves were historically low relative to the level of liquidity in the British system, it did little to manage British finance and the business cycle as its own power over the financial community was limited, and its behavior in crises suggests that it may have more often compounded financial distress than mitigated it.

These outcomes are all the more visible at the international level. The Bank was even less of an international than domestic central banker. Acknowledgments of international responsibility were less visible than acknowledgments of domestic responsibility. In turbulent periods at the international level (i.e., crises, shortages of liquidity) the Bank hardly distinguished itself. In fact, the Bank of England was more often the recipient of liquidity than the provider of liquidity. It was quite common for the Bank of France to come to the aid of the Bank of England and British finance in times of liquidity shortages and crises. In this respect, the Bank of France was a better candidate for international monetary hegemony than the Bank of England. If the Bank of England was weak relative to British finance, it was all the more weak relative to the global financial system. And these weaknesses grew as these two financial systems became larger and more complex. Perhaps it is enough to wonder how the Bank was able to defend its own convertibility. Central banks of nations that were successful in maintaining convertibility did so either by running up excess gold reserves or through long-term borrowing. The Bank of England did neither. It is therefore not surprising that the Bank so often avoided concerted efforts to stabilize the British and world economies. That the Bank persisted in what might be called a false splendor during the gold standard is also the reason why the international system under the gold standard remained fairly stable. Neither the system nor the Bank experienced frequent or severe shocks, as both political and financial crises were limited during the period (see Chapter 7). The few times the system and the Bank's resources were tested, sufficient external support was forthcoming to place both the system and the Bank back on a calm path. Hence, we can say that the gold standard was stable for the same reason that the Bank of England remained solvent: neither was ever severely tested by international conditions during the three and a half decades demarcating the classical gold standard period.

If the origin and stability of the gold standard were not the outcomes of British monetary hegemony or cooperation, how can we account for them? The findings show that both the origin and stability of the regime were in fact outcomes of a more diffuse or decentralized process than the conventional thinking on the gold standard suggests. With respect to the origin of the gold standard, the explanation of why nations made legal changes in their monetary standards in the 1870s and linked to gold revolves around three factors or causes: structural, proximate, and permissive. As the 19th century progressed, three sets of structural forces increasingly compelled national monetary authorities toward gold and away from silver as central monetary metals: (1) ideology (i.e., the status of gold), (2) industrialization and economic development, and (3) the politics of gold. First, nations came to see monetary standards as economic and political status symbols. Gold monometallism came to confer high status, while silver and bimetallism came to confer low status. Much of the status of gold was conferred on the metal because it was a characteristic of advanced-industrial nations in the 19th century that their economies were able to keep more gold in circulation relative to less advanced economies. The status was compounded by the fact that Britain had been practicing a gold standard (de facto from 1717 and de jure from 1821). The example of Britain was especially compelling because elites were drawing associations between Britain's monetary practices and its industrial successes. Second, industrialization, economic development, and the growth of international trade encouraged the greater use of the more convenient metal (gold). The greater number and size of domestic and international transactions which resulted from economies undergoing an industrial revolution gave an advantage to gold over silver. Since the value per bulk of gold was roughly 15 times greater than that of silver, gold would naturally become more important as a medium of exchange in environments where the size and frequency of transactions and incomes were growing. The greater internationalization of economies in Europe and the U.S. made the standard which was practiced by Britain all the more compelling, since the international capital market and the international market for commercial debt (i.e., bills) were dominated by sterling. Finally, the spectrum of domestic politics changed significantly in the developed world in the 19th century. The rise of political liberalism was a manifestation of the political rise of an urban-industrial class and a challenge to the traditional dominance of an agricultural class. With the shift in the political balance of power came a concomitant shift in monetary preferences from a standard oriented around a bulky and inflationary metal (i.e., silver) to one oriented around a light and non-inflationary metal (i.e., gold). The victory of gold over silver in gold-club nations was coterminous with the political victory of a new class of urban industry over the more traditional classes connected with the land.

Although these three structural factors predisposed advanced-industrial nations toward gold and away from silver over the course of the 19th century, the actual legal changes that demonetized silver and formed the nucleus of the gold club came about in the early to mid 1870s. Once Germany made the shift from silver to gold, the rest of the gold club (with the exceptions of Austria, Russia, and Japan, whose legal transitions were delayed) followed suit in a fairly rapid fashion (i.e., the scramble for gold). The timing and rapidness of this transformation make the gold standard fairly unique in monetary history, since it is the first time such a large number of nations made fairly contemporaneous changes in their monetary standards. The timing and rapidness of this regime transformation can be explained by several more proximate factors relating to developments in the international market for precious metals and the structure of economic interdependence among gold-club nations. Legal changes before the 1870s in the monetary standards of those nations that eventually fell into the gold club were unnecessary, because supply and demand conditions in the market for metals through the 1850s and much of the 1860s were such that abundant gold was being maintained in circulation (i.e., the cheap gold created by the strikes of the mid-century meant that the mint value of gold was high relative to its intrinsic [bullion] value). In essence, irrespective of their legal standards, these nations were practicing de facto gold standards. Once conditions in the market for metals changed in the late 1860s and early 1870s in a way that significantly raised the bullion value of gold relative to that of silver (i.e., made it more profitable to hold gold as bullion, and silver as money), nations moved to demonetize silver so as to keep gold in circulation. The rapidness of the transition was the result of the high level of trade and financial interdependence among nations which served to link them together into a kind of monetary chain gang: transition in any one or several important nations meant that the others were compelled to follow along. This interdependence manifested itself both at a broader (i.e., across the gold club) and regional (within the two economic blocs on the Continent: the franc bloc and the German–Northern European bloc) level. At the broader level, growing interdependence encouraged a conformity in standards, and any significant lags in keeping up with silver demonetizations in other nations exposed laggard nations to destabilizing developments in their systems of circulation (i.e., drained of gold and flooded with cheap silver). These kinds of pressures were all the more compelling within the two existing economic blocs on the Continent.

That nations felt both a structural and proximate compellence to make a formal transition to a gold standard did not in fact suffice to assure such a transition, nor did it assure that nations that made the gold link could necessarily maintain it. In this respect, the formation of the gold club depended on permissive conditions that made possible what structural and proximate forces encouraged. Those that had the greatest success in instituting and maintaining gold standards in this period were also nations that had fairly developed public (i.e., central banks) and private (capital markets) financial institutions, and that experienced fairly favorable macroeconomic outcomes (i.e., low inflation and low budget deficits). Those nations that did not ultimately fall into the gold club, delayed their entrance, or fell in but had eventually to suspend convertibility, on a whole, exhibited financial institutions and macroeconomic outcomes that were less favorable relative to early gold-club nations.

With respect to the stability of the gold standard, the stable structure of adjustment, which represented the very basis of regime stability under the gold standard, was the result of a two-tier process. Most directly it was founded on a set of political, economic, and social-psychological conditions (tier 1). First, monetary relations were embedded in a stable set of relations in the greater international political system. That the period of the gold standard was also relatively free from political turmoil (wars, domestic unrest), especially among gold-club nations, eliminated a major source of instability. Moreover, the little international violence that did take place did not translate itself into economic warfare. Second, the greater international economy also nurtured the regime: financial crises were few; economic growth remained favorable; trade grew into multilateral networks; and factors, goods, and money moved freely. A third factor accounting for the state of adjustment under the gold standard was the behavior of the four monetary core nations: Britain, Germany, France, and the U.S. These nations consistently behaved in ways that facilitated adjustment in other nations. Core nations, which had the greatest capacity to generate surpluses (i.e., attract international investment and export goods), continued to export the means of adjustment by importing goods and imposing few controls on capital exports. Hence, the core of the system was quite adept at recycling liquidity through the regime. Great Britain, as the most important player in the international regime (the very core of the core itself), was especially prone to such recycling as it continued to practice the most liberal policies in the world with respect to the flow of goods and capital. A fourth factor proved to be a convergence of macroeconomic performance across gold-club nations. As a fixed-exchange-rate regime, adjustment was disproportionately affected by the structure of macroeconomic outcomes across the member nations. That interest rates, prices, and business cycles paralleled among gold-club nations averted conditions which created biases in the adjustment process (e.g., low-growth nations running up surpluses against high-growth nations). Finally, that adjustment under the gold standard could continue to be principally dependent on private short-term capital flows made confidence in the regime essential. For these flows to remain elastic (i.e., responsive to the demand for international liquidity), investors had to perceive exchange risk and convertibility risk as low (i.e., maintain inelastic expectations). This in fact was the case under the gold standard. In this respect, convertibility owed a great deal to a process of self-fulfilling prophecy, which in this specific case manifested itself in stabilizing speculation in capital markets. When exchange rates or convertibility were threatened (i.e., adjustment needed to take place), investors readily responded to the higher returns offered in markets in need of liquidity.

These five proximate factors which directly impacted on the adjustment process (tier 1) were themselves dependent upon a set of compelling norms about the management of money, the macroeconomy, and international economic exchanges (tier 2: the normative factors accounting for the stability of the gold standard). The compelling norms, which were essentially of a domestic nature, were themselves embedded in a greater normative superstructure (classical liberalism) which configured the economic philosophies and policies of the day. The mobility of factors, goods, and money dictated by liberal norms was essential to the adjustment process. Such mobility also created a favorable (i.e., nurturing) international economy in which the regime was embedded. The mobility of people lowered the social costs of adjustment. The mobility of goods and money encouraged the growth of global financial and trade networks. The stabilizing actions of core nations were a direct result of following liberal policies with respect to trans-border flow of goods, factors, and money. Core nations emerged as the most prolific recyclers of liquidity because they continued to resist capital controls and maintained fairly free trade. Furthermore, this freedom of exchange and mobility, as well as limited government intervention in international economic relations, was essential to the synchronous nature of macroeconomies: there was a greater tendency toward the law of one price in the markets for money and goods. Synchronous macroeconomies were reinforced by a liberal orthodoxy which was oriented around fiscal restraint and stable money. But most directly, norms of stable money and balanced budgets reduced the possibilities for two outcomes most inimical to maintaining convertibility: inflation and fiscal deficits. Confidence in the international investment environment was enhanced to the extent that capital could flow freely across borders. The lack of controls kept the perceptions of convertibility and exchange risk low as investors were assured that nations whose exchanges or gold stocks were under pressure could attract the necessary liquidity to preserve the exchange rate and gold link. Liquidity could always be pulled with the right rate because creditor nations allowed their economic agents the freedom of transferring their wealth out of the country. This was especially important during periods of financial distress when nations required capital to avoid suspensions of convertibility or changes in the exchange rate. Confidence was enhanced all the more by credibility in the norms governing the metallist orthodoxy which was embedded in liberalism: i.e., that authorities would pursue low inflation, fiscal restraint, and resist suspensions of convertibility. In this latter respect, the adjustment process once again exhibited elements of self-fulfilling prophecy.

Finally, the lack of political manipulation of economic processes dictated by liberal norms had a central impact on the adjustment mechanism both at the international and domestic levels. Internationally, it kept political rivalries from spilling over into the international economy. On a domestic level, adjustment was not subject to the vagaries of politics (i.e., the political business cycle). First, manipulating the macroeconomy to generate specific outcomes violated norms of non-involvement. Second, unlike the period following World War I, manipulating the business cycle produced little political utility because governments were not as culpable for adverse outcomes in their economies.

Hence, the stable structure of adjustment was the final manifestation (in the causal chain explaining the maintenance of the gold standard) of a chain of forces, each set of forces embedded in another set, all of which sprang forth from the prevailing economic ideology of the day: classical liberalism. The regime proved only as strong as the norms upon which it was founded. When this classical liberal consensus withered away with the coming of World War I, so too was the regime doomed. Failed attempts to resuscitate the regime in the interwar years and the subsequent construction of the Bretton Woods regime (which was configured to be more consistent with the new set of prevailing norms based on domestic growth and full employment) demonstrated just how dependent the prewar monetary regime was on this classical liberal consensus. Any explanation, therefore, of the maintenance of the classical gold standard would have to gravitate around the norms which comprised this prewar liberalism. In this sense, the gold standard fits well into an explanatory scheme founded on regimes, since the analysis of regimes is oriented around the ways in which shared beliefs (i.e., rules, norms, prescriptions, injunctions) can configure international relations into ordered patterns. In the case of the gold standard, however, the compelling norms or shared beliefs were primarily of a domestic rather than international nature; thus the order in monetary relations was additive (an international order emanated from below—an idea of an international order was missing from the norms themselves) rather than singular (i.e., order from above—some idea of an international order being manifest in the norms themselves).

The origin and maintenance of the gold standard carry implications for the study of international order under all three principal regime structures: hegemonic, cooperative, and diffuse. Contrary to many visions of the gold standard, the regime dynamics upon which it was founded showed a strongly diffuse character. Moreover, the managerial elements that did show up were quite different from the conventional categories of hegemony and cooperation in the literature on international regimes. The nature of hegemony was much more unintentional and non-state than prevailing theories of hegemonic regimes can account for. The behavior of the British state and Bank of England fell far short of the expectations of proponents of British hegemony under the gold standard. If anything, Great Britain acted more like a weak than a strong nation, and France behaved more hegemonically than Great Britain. But even here the overly domestic orientation of the Bank of France rendered its actions quite distinct from mainstream visions of hegemony. Cooperation, too, fails to explain the origin and stability of the regime. In fact, it was a failure to cooperate that led to the emergence of the regime in the 1870s. The present literature on cooperation has paid very little attention to such default or residual regimes. Interbank lending did emerge as a stabilizing force under the gold standard, but the infrequency of such initiatives and the limited transfers involved are more of a testament to the stability that existed in the regime for other reasons. Furthermore, central bank relations in the period exhibited significant destabilizing elements as well. Moreover, it is not clear that more cooperation would have produced a more stable regime. The lack of cooperative schemes effectively limited the degree to which authorities could allow their macroeconomies to arrive at conditions that would have threatened convertibility (i.e., moral hazard and adverse substitution leading to inflation and fiscal deficits).

In that monetary relations under the gold standard were highly consistent with prevailing national interests, the regime showed a harmonious and self-enforcing nature. The regime remained stable void of significant management because it featured elements that either limited the need for management or that substituted for such management. That the regime formed among a fairly homogeneous and limited set of members, and that it was embedded in a greater international political economy which was itself stable, limited the need for management. In this respect, the gold standard suggests that the state of relations in specific regimes will depend on outcomes in other regimes, and that stability in one regime may be achieved by exporting its problems to other regimes. Both, in turn, suggest that diffuse regimes may be more vulnerable than managed regimes because these interdependencies cannot be manipulated to avert shocks under the former, while they can be manipulated in the latter. In terms of substitution, it was an interlocking set of domestic norms that effectively substituted for international management. In that behavior according to these domestic norms, and the general belief in the sanctity of these norms (i.e., credibility), directly and indirectly protected convertibility suggests the importance of credible rules for the successful functioning of diffuse regimes. To the extent that such credible rules create stable and desirable sets of relations among nations, they may function as a sufficient substitute for cooperation and hegemony in the international political economy.

The Organization of This Book

Chapter 2 addresses the question of how the classical gold standard worked. Here the workings of the gold standard are explored in the context of the five most important properties of an international monetary regime: liquidity/reserves, adjustment, exchange rates, capital controls, and confidence. This chapter draws upon the existing scholarship on the period, but also confronts some traditional interpretations (especially existing interpretations of the nature of liquidity and adjustment under the gold standard) and moves beyond the prevailing scholarship by providing an institutional synthesis of these five properties.

Chapters 3 to 7 address questions relating to the regime's origin and stability. What forces led the developed world to converge on a common set of monetary practices (gold monometallism) in the 1870s? Furthermore, what forces were responsible for maintaining this set of practices through the latter 19th and early 20th centuries? When the decade began, only two countries of note (Britain and Portugal) were legally on gold standards. Virtually every other major country in the developed world was either on a silver or bimetallist standard. By the end of the decade, all major countries were practicing, to differing degrees, de jure gold standards. There has been scant attention paid to the regime transformation from silver-based currencies to gold in the developed world at the time, even among monetary historians, outside of specific single-country case studies. Moreover, existing explanations of the stability of the classical gold standard have generated at best only scant references to the fortuitous convergence of "favorable conditions."

In keeping with Young's (1983) typology of international regimes, three sources of origin and stability will be considered: hegemonic, cooperative, and diffuse. The three sources of order differ in degree of centralization and management: from the most centralized (hegemonic), where the international regime is created and maintained by one or a few powerful nations, to the least centralized (diffuse), where a regime crystallizes from the independent actions of nations pursuing domestic goals with few international concerns (i.e., limited international consciousness) and little direct negotiation. The intermediate source (cooperative) characterizes a group of nations (usually more numerous, with nations being individually less powerful, than hegemons) intentionally coordinating their policies to arrive at agreed-upon international outcomes. The hegemonic and cooperative (i.e., contractarian or managerial) sources of order are managed at a high level, while diffuse regimes are managed at low levels. This specific categorization of regime types reflects a concern with introducing, to quote Young (1986, p. 111), "clear analytic distinctions among negotiation, imposition, and spontaneous processes in thinking about the emergence of regimes or institutional structures."

Chapters 3 to 5 are responses to the prevailing scholarship on the period which suggests that the origin and stability of the gold standard were the results of cooperation or British hegemony. Traditionally, monetary historians have explained the order in monetary relations before World War I as the outcome either of cooperation among leading financial actors or British hegemony. Chapter 3 explores the extent to which the origin and stability of the gold standard emanated from cooperation among national governments or among central banks. Chapters 4 and 5 explore the extent to which the origin and stability of the regime were dependent upon British hegemony. Chapter 4 explores the extent to which the British state acted as a monetary hegemon, while Chapter 5 explores the extent of monetary hegemony by the Bank of England. The findings in these chapters suggest that neither cooperation nor British hegemony was essential to the origin and maintenance of the regime.

Chapters 6 and 7 account for the origin and stability of the gold standard respectively. The findings of these chapters suggest that both the origin and maintenance of this regime were the products of a more decentralized or diffuse process than traditional work on the gold standard admits.

Chapter 8 considers the theoretical implications which the study of the gold standard has for three types of regimes: hegemonic, cooperative, and diffuse. These implications bear upon central theoretical debates in international political economy.

2

The Classical Gold Standard
as an International Monetary Regime

Economic historians have identified a definitive set of monetary relations among the world's more advanced nations in the last four decades before World War I. The most commonly used name for this set of relations has been the classical gold standard.[1] As a set of norms around which expectations converged in the issue-area of international monetary relations, the classical gold standard exactly fits the most widely used definition of an international monetary regime.[2] The mainstream literature on regimes, in fact, has not hesitated to call it an international monetary regime.[3] It is the purpose of this chapter to describe the workings of this regime.

The general enterprise of describing any regime is extremely problematic by nature. This is a normal function of the complex and heterogeneous character of regime theory. The theoretical construct offers many definitions, although most are closely related, and various competing typologies for classifying structures of international relations across different issue areas. This complex and heterogeneous character is as evident in the context of the specific issue area of monetary relations as it is at a general level of regime classification. Cohen (1983, p. 317), for example, notes that the possibilities for aggregating or disaggregating regime classification in monetary relations are endless. Do we look at the relations specific to balance-of-payments financing as an independent regime, or part of a greater regime of adjustment? Is adjustment itself a viable regime, or should it be understood as a component of a greater regime comprising monetary relations? In other words, what are the properties (the specific issues themselves) and what are the regimes (the issue areas)? Even when scholars have converged on similar levels of analysis, the categories for describing the workings of monetary regimes and the criteria for evaluating their performance have shown commensurate diversity within the general regime analysis.[4] Hence, any attempt to describe the gold standard qua regime here is likely to produce a subjective set of descriptive and evaluational categories.

With respect to the general and specific descriptions of the gold standard, rather than focusing on a single typology, I have been most concerned with explaining the principal historical developments that characterized monetary practices and relations in the context of some of the more commonly used categories.[5] In the general description of the gold standard (the first and third sections), these categories are: scope or jurisdictional boundary, nature of norms, conditions for operation, consequences of operation or regime outcomes, instrumentalities and functions, and allocation mode.[6] In the specific description (the second section), the literature on monetary regimes has emphasized a number of properties through which the institutional character or organizational form of monetary relations in particular can be understood: 1) liquidity/reserves, 2) adjustment, 3) exchange rates, 4) capital controls, and 5) confidence.[7]

The description of the workings of the classical gold standard is divided into three sections. The first section gives a general descriptive overview of the classical gold standard. The second section considers the institutional characteristics of the gold standard within the context of the five specific properties for describing international monetary regimes. Finally, I consider the more pervasive characteristics of these five specific properties defining the gold standard in the third section.

At the domestic level a gold standard is nothing more than a system for organizing monetary transactions. The classical gold standard, as an international regime, was simply an additive outcome of a group of nations (principally advanced-industrial nations) unilaterally adopting gold standards in the 1870s (i.e., the scramble for gold). That gold became the foundation for transactions across nations meant that it naturally acquired the properties of an international money: international medium of exchange (i.e., vehicle currency), store of value (reserve currency), and measure of value (i.e., things equal to the same thing are equal to each other). In this latter respect, a set of international parities naturally emerged as nations linked to the same numeraire (gold). Furthermore, in that nations in the gold club practiced few capital controls (according to the orthodox metallism of the period), the individual monetary systems came to be interlinked within a greater international system, or what economists would call a fairly open international monetary regime.

In its workings this international regime exhibited a fairly pervasive character across the five principal properties for defining an international monetary regime (liquidity/reserves, adjustment, exchange rates, capital control, and confidence). Outcomes under the classical gold standard were principally conditioned by market processes throughout the period: i.e., outcomes were primarily the resultants of private transactions in the markets for goods and money. Unlike the international monetary regimes that would follow World War I, very little in the prewar regime was conditioned by the actions of public authorities at the international level. There was little supranational, multilateral, and/or unilateral intervention in the markets for goods and money.[8] International liquidity was the outcome of developments in national money supplies. The international supply and demand for money were conditioned by transactions among private investors in the global capital market. Very little public manipulation of international capital flows took place as governments in the gold club practiced very few capital controls; and of the public initiatives to influence capital flows (these by central bankers), there was more reliance on market means (e.g., competing for gold by raising the buying price) than administrative (e.g., restrictions on the export of gold) means. In this respect, the adjustment process under the gold standard was very much determined by market processes rather than public intervention.[9] That such an adjustment process could work (i.e., be sufficient to maintain convertibility across nations in the gold club) depended on the confidence of private and public actors in the regime itself. Under the gold standard such confidence was very high.

General Overview of the Gold Standard

Like other periods in international monetary history, the classical gold standard has generated an ample amount of debate with respect to questions relating to how it worked. Was the classical gold standard founded on an impersonal, automatic adjustment mechanism that the common textbook view of this international regime has attributed to monetary authorities blindly following the "rules of the game" (i.e., authorities allowing domestic money supplies to be determined by external gold flows)? Did it really function as a gold standard or a sterling standard? There has even been some disagreement on the time period demarcating the regime.[10]

There is far less disagreement among scholars, however, on the question of regime outcomes.[11] One is struck by the near consensus in the historiography on the gold standard that the period produced international regime outcomes which were highly desirable. Kenwood and Lougheed (1983, pp. 129, 130) state that "one cannot help being impressed by the relatively smooth functioning of the nineteenth-century gold standard." They add that its external adjustment mechanism "worked with a higher degree of efficiency than that of any subsequent international system." Ford (1989, p. 197) calls it "a system more stable perhaps than anything seen since." Cohen (1977, p. 78) sees it as an international monetary regime that marks the "Golden Age" in the history of monetary relations. He emphasizes how "enormously successful" it was "in reconciling tensions between economic and political values." Beyen (1949, p. 25) underscores the extent to which it has become perceived as "one of the world's most prosperous and 'normal' periods." Cleveland (1976, p. 5) offers extensive praise of the relative performance of this regime, calling it a period of unmatched "harmony" in monetary relations. Keynes ([1931] 1952, p. 88) noted that "the remarkable feature of this long period was the relative *stability* of the price level."[12] Triffin (1964, p. 2) points out the gold standard "provided a remarkably efficient mechanism of mutual adjustment of national monetary and credit policies to one another." Maier (1978, p. 47) calls it a "smoothly running" system. Strange (1988, p. 97) refers to it as "an island of relative order and stability." Yeager (1976, p. 308) stresses how the desirable regime outcomes of the gold standard imparted a vision on monetary relations of the period as the "good old days": something long gone but venerated nonetheless.

This high praise relates to monetary regime outcomes in the broadest sense. Among that group of nations that eventually gravitated to gold standards in the latter third of the 19th century (i.e., the gold club), abnormal capital movements (i.e., hot money flows) were uncommon, competitive manipulation of exchange rates was rare, international trade showed record growth rates, balance-of-payments problems were few, capital mobility was high (as was mobility of factors and people), few nations that ever adopted gold standards ever suspended convertibility (and of those that did, the most important returned), exchange rates stayed within their respective gold points (i.e., were extremely stable), there were few policy conflicts among nations, speculation was stabilizing (i.e., investment behavior tended to bring currencies back to equilibrium after being displaced), adjustment was quick, liquidity was abundant, public and private confidence in the international monetary system remained high, nations experienced long-term price stability (predictability) at low levels of inflation, long-term trends in industrial production and income growth were favorable, and unemployment remained fairly low. The prewar gold standard showed an array of outcomes that stands up fairly well to the diversity among economists as to what properties comprise a well-functioning and desirable international monetary regime. It supported both micro- and macroeconomic efficiency, accommodated domestic diversities (i.e., protected domestic autonomy), contributed to harmony beyond monetary relations, achieved a fairly desirable distribution of gains and burdens among gold-club nations, controlled inflation, facilitated trade and investment, maintained employment and income growth, minimized misalignments, maintained confidence, provided liquidity, and facilitated adjustment.

The scope or jurisdictional boundary of the regime was essentially limited to the developed world, with nations outside of the First World continuing domestic monetary standards centered around either silver or paper.[13] Exceptions were Chile, Costa Rica, Panama, Ecuador, Mexico, and Argentina. These cases, however, showed far shorter and more turbulent experiences under the gold standard than in developed nations. Chile (1898), Mexico (1910), and Argentina (1885) all suspended convertibility, with only Argentina (1900) returning. Suspensions among developed nations were quite rare. Of the original gold club that formed in the 1870s, only one (Italy) ever suspended convertibility, and it returned (in 1884).[14] A number of less developed nations (mainly colonial possessions) during the period came to practice gold exchange standards as well (see below). Hence, two greater monetary blocs characterized the period: a periphery (lesser-developed nations that remained outside of the industrial revolution) that persisted in the practice of silver and paper standards, and an economically developed bloc of nations that made transitions from silver standards and bimetallism to gold. But the gold club itself was composed of sub-blocs that conformed to the structure of monetary and trade dependence configured around several major powers. The Latin Monetary Union or franc bloc (Belgium, Switzerland, France, Italy) comprised nations that all used the franc as a unit of account and practiced intercirculation of currencies (e.g., French francs were legal tender in Belgium and vice versa), as well as traded extensively. The Scandinavian Union (Sweden, Norway, Denmark) comprised a fairly integrated monetary system that was trade dependent on Germany. The sterling bloc cut across both general blocs (periphery and non-periphery) in that trade and monetary relations comprised Great Britain and her Empire, as well as other peripheral nations. But sufficient use was made of sterling in the developed world (because of trade and investment interdependence) so that Britain, too, emerged as an important focal point of monetary relations in the gold club.

The emergence of an international regime oriented around gold monometallism was a piecemeal and gradual process that reached a zenith in the decade of the 1870s and was consolidated by the turn of the century. The formation of an international gold standard was a natural outcome of a growing redundance in domestic monetary standards. As more nations left silver, bimetallist, and paper standards de jure to adopt gold standards domestically, a greater gold club or bloc crystallized. In this respect, the process of regime formation was fundamentally an additive one. The famous German monetary authority of the period, Ludwig Bamberger, best expressed the dynamic rise of the international gold standard when he pointed out that "a world monetary union would be superfluous if all countries based their currencies on gold."[15]

When the decade of the 1870s began, only two nations of note were practicing de jure gold standards (Great Britain and Portugal).[16] By the time the decade had ended, virtually all of the developed world was practicing gold monometallism. The "scramble for gold," as White (1893, p. 27) called it, characterizing this decade began in Germany with the Reichstag's mandate to make the gold mark the basic unit of account and restrict the minting of territorial coins in 1871.[17] Following Germany, in December of 1872, Norway, Denmark, and Sweden signed a convention instituting a gold standard in their respective nations, with silver coins as subsidiary (i.e., token coins). By 1875 all three nations were members of the Scandinavian Monetary Union, which was oriented around the central monetary status of the gold krone. In that same year Holland continued the provisional suspension (which began in 1873) of coining silver and introduced the 10-gulden gold piece as the central coin. The ad hoc gold standard was formally institutionalized in 1877 when the coinage of silver was definitively suspended.

The U.S. mirrored the European trend in legislation against the central monetary status of silver in the 1870s.[18] The Law of 1873 demonetized the 412.5-grain silver dollar, thus leaving the gold dollar as the only central monetary unit. The Act of 1878 reinstituted the silver dollar under a policy of limited government purchase and coinage. In the following year, Austria-Hungary closed its mints to silver, although its formal adoption of a gold standard was more than a decade away.

Belgium, reacting to an enormous influx of silver in 1873, limited the coinage of 5-franc silver pieces at the Brussels mint.[19] A similar influx into France caused the coinage of 5-franc pieces to be limited at the Paris mint in the same year. In the following year, the principal members of the Latin Monetary Union (France, Belgium, Italy, and Switzerland) instituted a collective limitation of the coinage of the 5-franc piece. These limits were renewed and modified over the next two years. In 1876 both France and Belgium suspended the coinage of the piece. In 1878 the coinage of 5-franc pieces was definitively suspended over the entire Union membership. With this cessation of the coinage of the Union's central silver coin, noted Helfferich (1927, p. 181), "the fate of silver as a money metal was sealed, insofar as [economically advanced] European countries were concerned." What began as a decade which saw only two nations of note formally on gold standards, ended with the developed world firmly and legally entrenched in the practice of gold monometallism.[20] This scramble for gold in one short decade abrogated the practices of centuries (i.e., silver and bimetallic standards). By 1885 there was not a mint in either the U.S. or Europe that was open to the unlimited coinage of silver. The gold club was essentially formed by 1880 and further consolidated in the 1890s with the addition of the other principal nations: Austria-Hungary (1892), Russia (1897), and Japan (1897). By the turn of the century, the only principal economic power that had not joined the gold club was China, which remained on a silver bullion standard up until the War.[21]

In one respect, the gold standard was something new in that it was the first time many nations were simultaneously practicing gold metallism, but it was also a continuation of metallist regimes which most of the gold-club nations had traditionally practiced. Virtually all of the nations that made the transition to gold in the later 19th century had left bimetallist and silver standards, which they had been practicing for decades.[22] The bimetallist regimes that were legally in force in France, Belgium, Switzerland, Italy, and the U.S. actually ended up functioning as alternating monometallic standards. In the face of fixed legal bimetallic ratios (i.e., the official mint values at which silver could be exchanged for gold) in these nations, developments in the market for precious metals that caused the international market bimetallic ratio (i.e., the price at which silver bullion exchanged for gold bullion on the open market) to change also caused one of the metals to drive the other out of circulation.[23]

In the U.S., for instance, the period before 1834 was a de facto silver standard owing to the fact that the market bimetallic ratio was consistently greater than the legal ratio (15-to-1) that prevailed in the U.S. Reacting to a shortage of circulating gold, Congress raised the legal ratio to 16-to-1 in 1834. This now placed the legal ratio above the market ratio, which meant that it would now be profitable for individuals to take silver out of circulation (which was now the undervalued rather than overvalued metal at the mint) and bring their gold (which was now the overvalued metal) to the mints. Quite expectedly, gold now displaced silver in circulation. In 1853, the revision of the coinage laws did not alter the legal ratio so as to bring silver back into circulation. Hence, the U.S. was actually practicing a gold standard de facto from the 1830s.

Latin Union nations (i.e., the franc bloc) shared a similar experience under bimetallism. From the 1820s to the 1840s these nations found themselves essentially on de facto silver standards, as gold was more valuable than silver at the prevailing legal ratio of 15½ to 1. The situation reversed itself after 1850 as the great gold discoveries made gold the relatively cheaper metal at the prevailing legal ratio, and thus speculation in metals caused gold to drive silver out of circulation. That a majority of transactions still relied on the lower-value silver as opposed to higher-value gold coins caused problems in circulation, to which nations responded with monetary commissions and laws trying to limit the disappearance of silver. The French Monetary Commission of 1857, for example, encouraged the institution of rules which limited the dealings in silver coins and placed a tax on silver exports. In Switzerland, the Act of 1860 reduced the fineness of silver coins so as to reduce the incentives to melt them down and sell them in bullion form.

In Western European nations practicing bimetallism and the U.S., gold had actually come to displace silver in circulation in the 1850s as the great gold discoveries of that particular period caused the market value of gold to decline significantly vis-à-vis silver. In the decades of the 1850s and 1860s, bimetallist nations found themselves practicing de facto monometallic gold standards because developments in the market for precious metals rendered silver relatively undervalued at the mints. When the gold club was forming in the 1870s, nations were really doing nothing more than legalizing practices which they had been indulging in since the 1850s when gold drove silver out of circulation.[24]

The gold standard as a domestic organization of money is essentially a metallist system that gives central monetary status to gold. It is oriented around several fundamental norms. First, a nation's money is strictly defined with respect to some fixed amount of gold.[25] In 1879, for example, when the U.S. resumed convertibility, it did so by defining a dollar as 23.22 grains of fine gold. Given that one fine ounce was equal to 480 grains, one fine ounce of gold would then be equal to 20.67 dollars. All denominations of money are defined in fractions or multiples of the central unit (in this case the dollar); hence all monetary denominations have clear correspondence to some quantity of gold.[26] It has been common in metallist regimes for authorities to attempt to keep this domestic par value fixed over time. In this respect, the practice of gold monometallism is partly what has become known in monetary economics as a rule for regulating domestic money supplies. This is in contrast to a discretionary management of money supplies where authorities are free to choose growth targets at random. Under a gold standard, authorities maintain a stable value of a currency (i.e., a check on inflation) by defending the value of gold vis-à-vis the currency itself. When gold goes to a premium vis-à-vis notes (rises above the par value), it means the money supply is too large (i.e., too many notes chasing a limited amount of gold) and therefore must be held in check.[27] When the value of gold drops below par, it means that the money supply needs to be increased. The defense of par, as a rule, is dependent on another rule linking the growth in the money supply to a nation's gold stock. If the two grow in proportion, then it is expected they will also maintain their value relative to one another. More recently, a variety of nonmetallist monetary rules have been proposed as a means of controlling inflation: defending the GNP deflator (Barro [1986]), a constant-growth-rate rule for monetary aggregates (Friedman [1960]), pegging nominal interest rates (Sargent and Wallace [1975] and McCallum [1984]), a constitutional amendment regulating the money supply (Buchanan [1989]), and stabilizing nominal GNP (Hall [1980] and Taylor [1985]).[28]

Second, there is perfect interconvertibility between notes (i.e., paper money) and gold at legally determined rates. This has become known as the norm of domestic convertibility. Notes, in fact, represent claims upon metal which are the ultimate responsibility of issuing banks, and are therefore considered legal tender along with their corresponding monetary-gold equivalent. In the case of public issue (i.e., central bank or Treasury notes), monetary authorities commit central banking institutions to exchange gold for notes and vice versa at the legal rates, usually to unlimited amounts. Mints are committed to the unlimited coinage of the central monetary metal (which in this case is gold). Normally, mints impose a surcharge (mint seigniorage) on bullion brought to them for coinage.[29]

Third, coins other than the central monetary metal under a monometallist regime (i.e., a regime that confers central status to one rather than several metals) can only circulate as token money.[30] As token money, these coins normally lack full legal tender (i.e., can only liquidate debts and make purchases up to limited amounts) and are given a nominal or legal face value which is normally greater than their intrinsic value. This subsidiary status assures that they remain in circulation, since they maintain a higher value in monetary than non-monetary use.

Fourth, reserves in the public and private banking systems must have a disproportionate gold component. This follows naturally from the metallist norm of convertibility. Since credit in the banking system is determined by the availability of gold, it stands that banks themselves would organize their business (deposits, loans, discounting, issuing notes) based on their gold holdings. Gold also makes up a significant proportion of circulating money, with the rest being accounted for by notes and subsidiary coin. This reserve norm holds both for domestic and international reserves, especially the latter. Under a pure gold standard the ultimate means of clearing international payments is gold itself. Hence, in a system of nations practicing gold standards, gold becomes the principal international currency.

Fifth, private citizens are free to hold gold in whatever form they wish: coin or bullion. Individuals can have their bullion coined—by bringing it to the mint—or they can hold the metal in bullion form. If they wish, they have the right to melt coins down into bullion.

Sixth, whatever metal citizens possess is normally free of international restrictions. Under a pure gold standard individuals are free to import and export gold as they wish, in whatever form they wish.

Finally, authorities institute some rule linking the creation of paper money to a nation's gold stock. Commonly, central banks are required to create banknotes in some proportion to increases in their gold stocks: either in direct or partial proportion. This represents the principal "rule" linking the money supplies to national gold stocks.

It is interesting that the "rule" of gold monometallism that has been most talked about in the historiography (i.e., the "rules of the game") was one that was widely violated.[31] Bloomfield's (1959) now famous findings suggest that even that nation most faithful to the "rules" (Great Britain) was as likely to sterilize external gold flows as not to sterilize.[32] And the other leading nations of the day were more likely to sterilize gold flows as not. This suggests that on a domestic level the classical gold standard was not as automatic (i.e., central bankers reacting like automatons to external gold flows) as conventional visions of the regime suggest: the behavior of central bankers was more discretionary than the rules of the game suggest. Moreover, it is questionable whether the international orientation (i.e., accentuating price movements to equilibrate current accounts) attributed to such rules ever occupied the inner sanctum of the metallist norms. Metallist orthodoxy was dominated by a domestic orientation.[33]

The nations that came to join the gold club in the latter third of the 19th century practiced variants of this system, with Great Britain (the first to make the gold link, in 1717 de facto) practicing what was closest to a pure gold standard. Some nations expressed their central monetary units in several different ways, even with respect to gold, while others retained a less complex expression of their units. There were differing degrees of convertibility, as some nations maintained greater influence over the internal demand for gold. Governments also differed with respect to the extent that they allowed the free flow of metals across their borders. As with internal conversion, the transnational flow of metals was also primarily influenced through gold devices. Mint charges varied quite a bit from nation to nation and mints showed differing levels of public management and scrutiny.

All nations practicing gold standards were fairly liberal in their willingness to coin gold, but differed significantly in their willingness to coin subsidiary metals. Some nations, like Germany, France, Great Britain, and the U.S., had large circulations of gold money, while other nations, like Holland, Sweden, Denmark, Norway, Belgium,

Switzerland, and Austria-Hungary, circulated relatively less gold and more notes. Foreign coin circulated (its value being dictated either by its intrinsic value or legal-tender status) in the various gold-club nations in differing degrees. Some nations, such as Switzerland, coined little of their own money and relied primarily on Belgian and French coins for their metallic circulation. The Portuguese relied heavily on the circulation of British sovereigns. There were also significant differences in the proportion of private (i.e., issued by private banks) to public (i.e., issued by central banks or treasuries) notes in circulation.

The laws dictating the management of gold reserves and the creation of notes differed across gold nations as well. Some nations, like the U.S., had specific legal-reserve requirements for their banking communities, while others, like Canada, France, and Great Britain, had no such legal requirements. Some central banks showed a greater predilection to amass reserves, like the Banks of France, Russia, and the Reichsbank, while others, like the Banks of Belgium and England, held relatively low levels of gold reserves over the period of the classical gold standard. Some central banking authorities preferred to hold a larger gold component in their international reserves (Britain, Germany, and the U.S.), while others, such as Russia, held a higher proportion of foreign exchange. With respect to the creation of notes, some nations (Great Britain, Finland, Norway, and Russia) practiced a fiduciary system in which public banknotes enjoyed 100% gold backing after some fiduciary amount backed normally by government securities, while others (Belgium, Holland, and Switzerland) featured fractional or proportional systems where central banks maintained a gold backing to public notes that was fixed at some level less than 100%. Others (Germany, Italy, Austria-Hungary, and Sweden) practiced still other systems which mixed elements of the two. Some nations, like Germany, Holland, and Great Britain, practiced a monopolized issue of public notes where the issue of such notes was centralized in one central banking institution. Other nations, such as the U.S., Italy, and Sweden (before 1903), distributed the duty over several public and semipublic banking institutions.

There were some differences over the regulation of banks, but in general banking (central banking included), within the gold club especially, continued to be viewed as private industry. Aside from being subject to general company laws, private banks were typically subject to minimal regulation (i.e., laws usually having to do with reserves). During the gold standard period, extensive banking codes existed only in Japan and Sweden, and even in Sweden commercial banks of issue were not required to hold base money (gold and Riksbank notes) against their own notes, although the notes were ultimately redeemable. Similarly, there was a significant degree of institutional homogeneity with respect to the private nature of central banking under the gold standard. The banks dealt in all of the common banking practices of the time: taking deposits, discounting, advances, and dealing in securities. Interestingly, this generated a competitive relationship between central banks and their respective banking communities, a relationship which sometimes led to a situation where central bankers were behaving in a way that made their financial communities less rather than more secure. The testimonies of central bankers to the U.S. National Monetary Commission show that the banks carried on in a state of relatively high independence from the public domain.[34]

Most of the differences in following the injunctions of gold monometallism were, however, more of degree than of kind, as nations remained broadly faithful to the general norms of gold standard orthodoxy. Both domestic and international convertibility were consistently respected, even if not invariably practiced in an automatic way. Nations found that their domestic parities remained stable over time. Mints remained open and continued to coin gold in an unrestricted manner. Gold continued to play a major role in both circulation as well as public (i.e., central bank) and private reserves, even though the use of credit instruments (e.g., checks, drafts), notes, and foreign exchange grew as the period progressed. Furthermore, controls on domestic and international gold transactions remained minimal.[35]

The monetary orthodoxy of the gold standard represented a set of norms about the organization of national monetary systems; as such the orientation of the gold standard was domestic rather than international.[36] As de Cecco (1974, p. 60) points out, "In none of the cases . . . did those who implemented monetary reform have the slightest intention of linking their countries to an international monetary system." Whether intended or not, as with any constellation of domestic monetary practices, the collective convergence onto similar domestic monetary regimes generated a set of definitive international outcomes with respect to the major properties for defining an international monetary regime (capital mobility, exchange rates, liquidity/reserves, adjustment, and confidence) across the membership of the gold club: i.e., the various domestic regimes crystallized into a greater international monetary regime.[37]

The "additive" nature of the international regime was manifest in the following processes. To the extent that domestic par values of currencies were maintained, a fixed exchange-rate bloc was formed across the gold club. The preservation of international parities was an automatic outcome of stable domestic parities: things equal to the same thing are equal to each other, and remain so as long as the common metallic numeraire continues to maintain a fixed value vis-à-vis the currencies of two or more nations. Exchange rates will likely be more stable in a regime in which nations are practicing the same standard, *ceteris paribus*, since any changes in the relative values among different precious metals will not affect exchange rates. In a regime with multiple standards, nations on depreciating standards (i.e., using metals that are depreciating in non-monetary value relative to others) will find their currencies depreciating against currencies linked to metals that are increasing in value. History, in fact, shows that exchange rates and domestic parities among gold-club nations under the classical gold standard were extremely stable over the period.[38] But the norms behind maintaining national par values had more to do with domestic monetary orthodoxy (i.e., the metallist norm of maintaining the value of a currency with respect to some commodity) than international objectives (i.e., maintain the value of currencies with respect to each other).

Norms calling for domestic convertibility which were operationalized through a domestic monetary anchor (i.e., credit creation was consistently controlled according to metallist norms) eventually translated into international convertibility because the metallist norm of free-capital flows held. Since authorities and banks honored claims on gold denominated in national currency, the commitment to convertibility was indifferent to nationality.[39] Hence, international transactions that required a transfer of claims or funds denominated in a national currency were ultimately founded on gold. And to the extent that confidence was maintained in the influence of domestic norms of convertibility, international confidence was maintained as well: the international monetary system comprising the regime was seen as one in which liquidity was abundant because convertibility was perceived as robust.

That gold became the ultimate foundation for real (i.e., trade) and financial transactions meant that it filled the role of a principal international money. There was little disagreement on this fact, given the number of nations practicing gold monometallism. Under a more diversified regime (with nations practicing silver standards, bimetallism, paper [fiat] standards, and gold standards), questions of the status over international liquidity would have been much more pronounced. This suggests that under one pervasive standard potential political problems with respect to prestige (i.e., whose standard will assume a central role) were reduced.[40]

To the extent that the domestic monetary anchor worked (i.e., nations remained fairly faithful to norms governing the management of money supplies), nations in the gold club that were pursuing stable money found their inflation rates converging at low levels over time. This generated several consequences at the international level. First, global inflation was restrained.[41] Second, price trends were fairly synchronous across gold-club nations, and to the extent that interest rates and growth themselves moved with price trends, macroeconomic performances were also fairly synchronous across nations. Synchronous macroeconomies, in turn, had important implications for adjustment. Since macroeconomic developments had a tendency to parallel, biases in the structure of adjustment were limited.[42] And the adjustment that took place between these nations had to be attained through smaller divergences in the macroeconomic variables themselves: capital flows had to take place in response to smaller differences in interest rates.

To the extent that nations remained faithful to the injunctions of metallist orthodoxy, there emerged a fairly integrated monetary system among them. Financial transactions were facilitated by the common monetary standard (i.e., transaction costs of accounting and converting across standards were reduced) and capital moved freely, as it was a fundamental injunction of orthodox metallism to allow individuals to export and import gold as they wished. As long as the mobility of metals was not hindered, controls on non-metal money were ineffective since international transactions would be executed through metals rather than credit instruments. The high mobility of international capital which characterized the international regime had very important implications for adjustment. Adjustment was attainable relatively quickly and easily through short-term capital movements.[43] The integration of capital markets also served to enhance whatever synchronous element in macroeconomies was encouraged by collective adherence to similar rules of money-supply management. The law of one price with respect to interest rates was more compelling as open capital markets allowed for competition among money centers. To the extent that prices and growth were linked to trends in interest rates, nations found prices, business cycles, and interest rates converging toward greater conformity.[44] This imposed on the international monetary regime a structure of adjustment that was more symmetrical among nations.

The Component Parts:
The Institutional Character of the Gold Standard

Liquidity and Reserves

Questions regarding the nature of liquidity and reserves in an international monetary regime essentially center on the issue of the nature of international money. Reserves are those forms of money that effect international transactions (both real and financial). We come to know the institutional character of a monetary regime partly through knowing the principal form(s) of money which is (are) acceptable for clearing international payments. The specific issue of liquidity, on the other hand, is commonly viewed as centering around the access to this international money (i.e., do members of the regime have the capacity to obtain the money in need, and how does the money flow?).[45] In a restricted sense, the issue of international liquidity is oriented around the ability of nations to attract the necessary capital to finance temporary balance-of-payments deficits (i.e., strictly a macroeconomic issue). In a broader sense, the issue covers the general demand for money (both on a micro- and macroeconomic level) and the structure of capital flows (supply) in response to those demands. It is in this broader sense of the issue that we will be concerned. Liquidity in an international monetary regime in both senses is defined in terms of the nature of international money (i.e., the reserve question, or the composition of international money, and the manner in which it flows). Hence, the term liquidity as it is used here encompasses the broader issue of how money is held and how it moves in an international regime.

Under the classical gold standard, international liquidity was fundamentally coterminous with domestic liquidity, unlike subsequent international monetary regimes.[46] This owed primarily to the fact that the transfers of capital during the period had a disproportionately higher microeconomic component compared to periods after World War I. In fact, direct public transfers were relatively rare under the gold standard. The images of consortiums of central banks forming lending pools (e.g., General Agreement to Borrow) were quite the exception, and institutionalized international liquidity pools (IMF, IBRD) were nonexistent. Whatever inter-central-bank accommodations emerged tended to be limited, bilateral, ad hoc, and of short duration. In this respect, the dominant mode of allocating liquidity under the gold standard was extremely decentralized (emanating from a plethora of private investors) rather than centralized (coming from a small number of lending institutions or international consortiums). Balance-of-payment financing was of a different character when compared to practices of the interwar period onward. Formal inter-central-bank accommodations were more responsive to speculative drains caused by impending financial distress than to the ongoing structure of balance-of-payments positions. Capital flows took the form of private investment and the payment for goods, rather than the public (official) transfers that became a mainstay of the Bretton Woods period. These private flows ultimately maintained balance-of-payments positions among gold-club nations. In this respect, the gold standard was an unusual regime in that the principal constellation of relations with respect to the structure of liquidity was among private citizens and banks, not nations and public monetary institutions (i.e., central banks). The main regime actors or protagonists were subnational actors rather than nations and supranational institutions.

Macroeconomic imperatives (e.g., deficits) manifested themselves fairly well in the private market for capital. If a deficit created a shortage of savings, for example, the relative shortage of domestic liquidity in that nation would drive interest rates up. The higher interest rates attracted investment from abroad, which in turn financed the deficit. In this case, short-term capital flows responding to differentials in international returns to investment played the role that in a more publicly managed system of adjustment may have been played by a loan from an international organization or a transfer from a foreign government. That capital flows could serve such a function effectively relied on the absence of impediments to investment and the general confidence of investors in the international system.

To the extent that the international supply of money was coterminous with domestic money supplies, the state of international liquidity was an outcome of the overall state of domestic money supplies among the gold club. Given the adherence among monetary officials in gold-club nations to metallist norms, the classical gold standard featured a stronger element of global inflation control relative to subsequent periods.[47] Although both the private (i.e., private banks of issue) and public creation of money varied quite a bit with respect to practices and laws, the compelling nature of metallist norms about preserving the gold link (i.e., convertibility of notes into gold) kept the variations within certain stable-money parameters.[48] Hence the stable-money orientation of the international regime was very much an additive process: where international liquidity depended strictly on domestic money creation (i.e., no international credit pools) among gold-club nations. As Bordo (1992, p. 7) observes, "The pledge to fix the price of gold provided a nominal anchor for the international monetary system."[49] The stable money character appeared also to be subsystem dominant, as the four core monetary powers of the regime (Germany, France, U.S., and Great Britain) generally practiced a more orthodox form of metallism with respect to convertibility than did other nations in the gold club.[50]

With respect to the composition of money, the textbook account of the classical gold standard, which suggests that national and international transactions were undertaken disproportionately in gold, overstates the use of metal as a vehicle and reserve currency during the period, but at the same time visions of the period as being a sterling or sterling-exchange standard understate the importance of gold as both a vehicle and reserve currency, and also understate the importance of other key currencies (marks and francs).[51] Credit instruments (i.e., non-specie forms of money) were important throughout the period, and continued to grow in importance across the four decades prior to the War. The variety of credit instruments was quite large: public banknotes, private banknotes, checks, transfer orders, certificates of deposits, commercial (real) bills, financial bills, drafts, storage certificates, stock market securities, T-bonds, mortgages, warehouse receipts, and clearinghouse loan certificates. With respect to both domestic and international money, non-specie instruments were growing in importance. On a domestic level, Triffin's (1964) findings suggest that over 90% of the growth in the collective money supply of his sample of 11 leading economies of the time was due to growth in credit money (currency and demand deposits).[52] At an international level, nations came to hold larger balances of foreign exchange reserves (foreign bills, balances with foreign correspondents, and foreign bonds). Most of these balances were held in the foreign branches of domestic banks. From 1899 to 1913 the amount of foreign exchange reserves in official reserve pools among leading nations grew more than fourfold.[53] For those nations that were especially protective of their public gold reserves, or had difficulty obtaining enough gold for internal (circulation and domestic reserves) and external (international reserves) use, the holding of foreign exchange reserves came to serve an important function.[54] These foreign exchange reserves came to occupy a first line of adjustment for nations, while gold reserves were held as a second line of defense.[55] Surplus nations tended to build up foreign exchange holdings, while deficit nations would allow them to run down when adjusting. Equilibration of exchange rates which reached the gold points was more often achieved through private transactions in foreign exchange markets than through gold arbitrage.[56] International payments systematically began clearing with the transfer of foreign exchange holdings: gold was normally the last thing to move when imbalances developed between nations. In this respect, since creditor nations held proportionally greater foreign exchange reserves in their official portfolios, it appears that liquidity transfer was effected to a great extent via a transfer of claims on bank deposits.[57]

The bill came to play central roles both in the international and domestic monetary systems.[58] The bill represented a principal financial instrument of the period, with most of the international financial transactions of the 19th century taking place in the market for bills. An entire submarket grew up around the buying and selling of bills, with the leading banking institutions all drawing, accepting, and/or dealing in bills: these were the large commercial banks, discount houses, merchant banks, and acceptance houses. Specifically, the bill of exchange was responsible, along with mail transfers, for financing most of the world's trade in the 19th century. In essence, any normal commercial bill functioned like a postdated check. Such a bill was a contract drawn between an importer and exporter of goods (through the intermediation of banks or financial houses) to have the former remit a payment to the latter on some specified day in the future (a common maturity period for a bill was three months). The lag in payment was originally instituted to account for the delay in shipping goods internationally.[59] As a contracted debt, the bill gained a value independent of the real transaction it originally cleared, and itself became a tradable security or means of exchange. Bills came to serve all the major functions of money in the 19th century. They were held extensively both publicly and privately as stores of value. Bills came to make up sizable portions of both domestic and international reserves.[60] Banks liked holding bills because the size of the national and international markets for bills made them very liquid financial instruments. Furthermore, they carried lower opportunity costs than did gold holdings. The holding of foreign bills was really an offshoot of the domestic practice of holding inland bills. Bills were used extensively for clearing international payments as well. In the few cases of public accommodations across financial borders (i.e., central bank lending), it was not uncommon for one central bank to aid a foreign financial center experiencing an exodus of capital by discounting large amounts of their bills. In the 19th century, bills sometimes circulated like notes. In the early part of the century, for example, bills even rivaled the circulation of banknotes in Great Britain.[61]

At the center of this rising credit-money element was sterling. Through bills and sterling balances, the national currency of Great Britain came to play an important role in the structure of international liquidity and payments. It is no surprise that sterling came to enjoy widespread use. Britain's head start in industrialization, free trade, financial innovations, and free capital markets served to internationalize sterling before other currencies. Industrialization meant greater need for and means of international exchange, while unrestricted movements of money and goods made Britain a natural focal point in international trade and finance.[62] Compounding the effects of early industrialization and the free movement of goods and money were (1) the emergence of Britain as the largest provider of trade services (merchant banking, marine insurance, and shipping), (2) the large amount of British investment in foreign securities (which meant that foreigners had to acquire sterling to service their obligations to British creditors), (3) and the fact that the British position in international trade (i.e., running surpluses with the Empire while running deficits against Europe and North America) made it a natural clearing center for international payments. With sterling in greater use, London naturally became an international financial center, as international exchange was most efficiently transacted through the intermediation of London's financial institutions.[63] The growth of the London market provided its own internal momentum as its increasing size and evolution compounded the development of the most diversified and efficient financial services in the world. (No market in the world was preferred over London in terms of floating foreign issues.) Sterling bills became a safe and liquid investment, hence highly desirable. Most banks, in fact, held sterling bills as reserves.[64] As such, sterling came to finance not only British trade, but a disproportionate amount of trade never touching British shores.[65]

Visions of the gold standard as overly dependent on the internal and external use of gold are therefore misleading. In fact, the use of foreign exchange and bills contributed a stabilizing element to the period in that it kept national gold stocks from varying more than they might have under the exclusive use of gold in national and international transactions.

Conversely, images of a "gold-plated" regime that was principally founded on British sterling are equally misleading.[66] It is important to avoid underestimating the central role of gold in terms both of its psychological importance and actual use. When considered in terms of both functions, the gold standard was still founded on the precious metal itself, with non-specie instruments occupying a secondary position of importance. Moreover, key currencies aside from sterling also came to play prominent roles.

Although notes and credit instruments came into greater use on a domestic level, gold remained an important part of circulation in all gold-club nations. Many transactions were and continued to be effected in gold. Keynes ([1913] 1971, p. 12) underscores the importance of gold coin for paying railway fares and wages in Great Britain. The use of gold as a vehicle currency was enhanced by the fact that gold-club nations tended to issue banknotes in large denominations, hence restricting their use for smaller transactions. Even in the period shortly before the War, gold-club monetary stocks still saw gold dominating notes.[67]

With respect to the international position of gold, the metal remained the largest single asset on central bank balance sheets throughout the period.[68] Even on the eve of the War, gold still dominated central bank reserve pools.[69] Although the amount of foreign exchange reserves was growing in gold-club central bank portfolios, Lindert's (1969, pp. 10–12) findings for the 35 leading nations of the period show that even by 1913 gold still made up 68.1% of official reserves, with foreign exchange making up just 15.9%. In fact, silver was more abundant in official reserve pools than foreign exchange (1,132.5 to 1,132.1 million dollars).[70]

Although foreign exchange provided a "first" reserve (the first form of money to adjust payments), gold provided the ultimate reserve. It was always clear that foreign exchange balances represented calls on gold rather than a final form of payment. Foreign exchange continued to be used and desired because of the perceived sanctity of the commitment to convertibility. The international system of credit under the gold standard worked—and was for that matter a very stabilizing element because it allowed nations to economize on the use of gold and expedited adjustment—because of confidence (both public and private) in international covertibility. The logic behind the importance of gold for the system of liquidity under the gold standard is similar to the logic attesting to the importance of nuclear weapons for the functioning of deterrence. Although neither weapons nor gold were used extensively, it was the expectations that both were in fact usable that discouraged aggression and encouraged the use of credit.[71] Gold did in fact come into greater use during periods of financial distress when investors naturally sought the safest store of value. Although cases of actual financial crisis were relatively infrequent among gold-club nations during the period of the gold standard, when gold reserves were tested, they were usually up to the task. Central banks were able to meet stochastic demands for gold when they arose, and were able to replenish gold holdings when shortages plagued either internal or external stocks. Financial distress was quickly mitigated when gold flows signaled to private investors that the credit system was once more sound. Hence, gold was required, albeit in limited use, in order to stabilize national monetary systems.

Liquidity was ultimately perceived in terms of metal; hence nations had to be fairly careful in managing their internal and external gold stocks so as to maintain faith in the credit system. And this the gold club as a whole did fairly well. At the international level, central bankers systematically manipulated discount rates and gold devices to maintain their specie reserves.[72] Nations also made systematic use of the privilege of converting their foreign exchange when they required gold in order to 1) replenish specie reserves in central banks, 2) replenish specie in circulation, or 3) to mitigate the effects of a capital exodus resulting from financial crisis.[73] Not only did nations avail themselves of their right to convert balances, but they also held "outside" or "secondary" gold reserves in large financial centers like New York and London, either on deposit or on call, which could be repatriated when gold was required.[74]

Central bankers were also quite opportunistic in the market for bullion according to their reserve needs. In years when gold production was relatively low, central banks were more active in diverting new gold into their coffers. From 1849 to 1872, for example, when gold production was relatively abundant, only 19% of new gold went into central bank reserve pools, while 81% went to private banks and the public. In the leaner years of 1873 to 1892, however, 82% of new gold became official reserves.[75] They also deftly diversified between internal and external gold stocks according to shortages that arose in each.[76] In periods when official reserves needed to be built up (external stocks), specie circulation diminished (i.e., metal diverted from internal to external use). In this respect, gold in circulation functioned as a secondary gold reserve which could be manipulated according to changes in official reserve positions.[77]

Just as the importance of foreign exchange relative to gold could be overstated, so too could the role of sterling as the leading form of liquidity during the period. Gold holdings among leading nations dwarfed sterling holdings in official reserves. In 1913, of the 7,110.8 million dollars in official reserve holdings of the 35 leading countries of the period, only 431.6 million was being held in sterling (6%). Even as a proportion of foreign exchange reserves (1,132.1 million), sterling did not make up a majority (only 38%). The other two most abundantly held currencies, francs (275.1 million dollars) and marks (152.3 million), together made up almost as much as sterling (427.4 million dollars in francs and marks versus 431.6 million dollars in sterling).[78] In fact, if we look at foreign exchange reserves held in Europe, the major site of the gold club, we find that both francs (262.1 million) and marks (115.5 million) were held in greater abundance than sterling (76.4 million). Together, francs and marks were five times greater than sterling in European reserve holdings. As a percentage of foreign exchange reserves held in Europe (663.4 million), sterling made up only 11.5%.

Overall, the composition of liquidity under the gold standard suggests a regime founded on the use of both gold and non-specie instruments (bills, notes, foreign exchange), but whose credit system was founded on stocks of monetary gold. The creation of credit, mainly with respect to note issue, and the confidence necessary to hold and use credit were both driven by gold convertibility.

With respect to the flow of liquidity, the period saw the greatest international flows of capital relative to the size of economies in history. Neither before nor since have similar proportions of domestic savings been taken up by foreign investment. Foreign investment in Great Britain accounted for 40% of domestic savings in the period 1875–1913; for France it accounted for 33%–50% of savings in the period 1880–1913; in Germany it reached as high as 40% in the early 1870s and mid-1880s, settling into 10% of savings from 1900 to 1914; Australian, New Zealand, and Swedish foreign investment all achieved 50% in the 1870s and '80s; Canada's foreign investment reached a peak of 46.2% from 1911 to 1915; Italy and Norway peaked at 30–40% in the decades before the War.[79] With respect to GNP, net foreign investment for the three European core nations, Britain, France, and Germany, in the period 1870 to 1913 achieved levels never seen before or after: for Britain it was 5.2%, for Germany it was a bit less than 2%, and for France it was between 2% and 3%. German foreign investment reached 1/14th the size of national income in the two decades before the War. That of France reached 1/6th the size of national income on the eve of the War. For Great Britain, net foreign investment had grown to 8% of GNP by 1914.[80]

The gold standard period coincided with an explosion in foreign investment. As late as the mid-century, none of the four core nations was investing any more than 1% of its GNP overseas. Thus, the gold standard period enjoyed highly abundant capital flows as compared to periods before and since. These international flows of money were almost exclusively coterminous with private transactions in international capital markets: very few of the capital flows represented public transfers (i.e., inter-governmental and inter-central-bank transfers). Hence, official balance-of-payments financing during the period was rare compared to subsequent periods. Payments cleared through transactions in private capital markets. These capital flows were disproportionately composed of short-term capital flows and longer-term indirect (portfolio) investments. Very little direct foreign investment took place in the period, and of the portfolio investment that took place, a far greater proportion was taken up by bonds than by stocks.[81] Capital flows actually increased across the period, especially after 1900.[82]

The gold club was neatly divided into creditors and debtors. Nations in the core of the system (Germany, Great Britain, France, and the U.S.) were the major capital exporters. Although the U.S. was a consistent net capital importer from the 1870s to the mid '90s, from the mid 1890s to 1905 it was consistently a net exporter, with the period 1898–1902 seeing an average yearly net export of more than 250 million dollars. Net exports reached as high as 296.4 million dollars in 1900. After 1905, the U.S. reverted once more to being a net importer, but at a level well below the levels reached in the 1870s and '80s. Britain was the period's largest net exporter of capital. Britain in fact was a net exporter of capital in every single year from 1860 to the War. British net exports in the four decades before the War followed a cyclical pattern. They increased from a trough of 13.1 and 16.9 million pounds in the years 1877 and 1878 to a peak in the years 1887–90, when they averaged over 90 million pounds yearly. They declined again in the later 1890s and early 20th century to levels between 30 and 40 million, and thereafter achieved record heights just before the War, averaging over 160 million pounds yearly. Both France and Germany were consistently net exporters after 1880. There were in fact only two years of net inflow: France in the years 1880 and 1881. France saw a strong secular rise in her net exports from 55 million francs in 1883 to 1,748 million francs in 1906. Net exports reached over 1,900 million francs in 1909 and 1910. The net exports for Germany were somewhat more stable from 1880 to 1909, being most often between 500 to 600 million marks yearly, with record levels being achieved from 1909 on. In the two years before the War, net exports surpassed the 1,000-million-mark level in 1912 and the 2,000 level in 1913.[83] Hence, under the gold standard, a large proportion of the burden of liquidity flow fell on the most powerful monetary players (the core) in the regime.[84]

The more visible debtors of the gold club were Norway, Sweden, and Italy. Norway actually began as a net capital exporter in the 1880s, but turned into a consistent net importer after 1890. Net imports were higher on average in the decade and a half before the War (tending above 50 million kroner) than they were in the 1890s (tending between 20 and 40 million kroner). Sweden was a consistent net importer throughout, being a net importer 28 out of 34 years before the War. Its imports peaked in the first decade of the 20th century and surpassed the 100-million-kroner mark in 1904 and 1909. Italy began as a net importer in the 1880s, shifted to a net exporter in the

1890s and first quinquennia of the 20th century, only to revert back to a net importer for most of the years after 1906.[85]

For gold-club nations, a large proportion of foreign portfolio investment was in social overhead projects undertaken by private enterprise, especially transportation (mainly railway building). Other common projects included the building of harbors, roads, bridges, canals and other waterworks, and public utilities like gas pipes, sewers, and electrical plants.[86] The geographic structure of foreign investment in the period shows a fair amount of dispersion. The pattern of investment suggests that the initial spurt in foreign investment among gold-club nations tended to be in Europe, with proportionally more going to areas of recent settlement as the century progressed. But Europe remained a major target for portfolio investment throughout the period. Among the core, France and Germany kept most of their foreign investment in Europe throughout the period. As late as 1913, France still had over 60% of its foreign investment in Europe. By 1900, Germany had more invested in Europe (12.5 billion marks) than outside of Europe (11 billion marks).[87] Britain, from the mid-century on, continued to diversify away from Europe such that by the end of the century its non-European investment dwarfed its European investment.[88] The U.S. ended the period with a strong bias for North American investment, with Canada and Mexico holding 30% and 40% of U.S. foreign investment respectively by 1913.[89]

In sum, liquidity under the gold standard comprised both national credit money (non-specie money and financial instruments) and commodity money (gold), with the latter remaining the ultimate expression and foundation of international money. With respect to the composition of liquidity, international money under the gold standard was much more diversified than simple visions of a sterling standard suggest. Marks and francs enjoyed a use, especially on the European Continent, that rivaled or surpassed that of sterling.

The allocation mode of liquidity was extremely diffuse. Little central management of liquidity took place, as capital flows were coterminous with private transactions. And these flows were abundant and fairly dispersed geographically, with core nations of the gold club emerging as the largest net capital exporters of the period. Although these nations shouldered a significant amount of the burden of liquidity transfer, they did not manage it as nation-states.[90] Under the gold standard, liquidity proved abundant (with foreign exchange increasingly supplementing gold), elastic (because of limited capital controls), and geographically dispersed. One would have to conclude that in terms of regime outcomes, liquidity under the gold standard remained in a fairly favorable state throughout the period.

Adjustment

No single specific monetary regime property has received as much attention in the context of the gold standard as adjustment. In fact, we normally first come to know the gold standard in the study of international trade as an automatic means by which international payments between nations are balanced. Scammell ([1965] 1985) calls a gold standard a system of balance-of-payments adjustment whose success must be measured in light of its ability to eradicate short-term deficits and surpluses without being overly damaging to other domestic economic goals.

According to the conventional, textbook models of the gold standard, the balance of payments was adjusted according to the Humian price-specie-flow mechanism.[91] According to this vision, balance of payments was a "real" phenomenon in that it was effected by changes in trade balances, and these trade balances were stimulated by changes in prices, which in turn resulted from gold flows between nations. Assume that two nations, A and B, are trading. Nation B runs up a balance-of-payments surplus against A. Under a classic Humian process, the debt incurred by A will be eradicated through gold flows (i.e., under a Humian vision, gold is the exclusive international medium of exchange). These gold flows will produce several effects on the respective domestic monetary systems. First, the gold stock of B will be augmented by an increase in external reserves, while the gold stock of Nation A will be reduced by an equal amount as a result of a decrease in external reserves. Second, the changes in gold stocks will have the effect of pushing domestic prices down in the nation that is losing gold (A), and push domestic prices up in the nation receiving gold (B). In the receiving nation, the excess supply of gold stimulates increased demand for consumer goods, and prices must rise to restore equilibrium in the market. In the nation losing gold (A), a smaller pool of gold decreases the demand for consumer goods, and therefore domestic prices must fall to clear the market. In both cases, there occur relative price changes in consumer goods which alter consumption incentives between home and foreign goods. The lower prices in Nation A and the higher prices in Nation B will divert home and foreign demand toward A's goods and away from B's goods.[92] This will reduce the imports of A and increase the imports of B (in a bilateral context, this amounts to an increase in A's net exports and a decline in B's net exports). In turn, this will reverse the original trade imbalance that had B running a surplus against A, as gold will now flow toward the latter, thus bringing external positions back into equilibrium.[93]

The empirical research on adjustment-related outcomes under the gold standard has shown numerous inconsistencies with the conventional models of adjustment.[94] Evidence suggests prices were much more stable and convergent across nations than the classical model would have expected.[95] Wages, in fact, were found to be rigid downward in developed nations, thus suggesting a lack of flexibility in prices in the gold club. All of this cuts against the expectations of the conventional vision which sees adjustment as based on the flexibility and divergence in prices across nations. The fact that business cycles tended to converge, as well as prices, placed the role of trade in adjustment in an even more dubious position, given that nations were facing contemporaneous consumption patterns in their demand for foreign goods deriving from changes in income.[96] Price behavior in gold-club nations was consistent with Bloomfield's (1959) findings that central bankers frequently sterilized external gold flows. That domestic assets of central banks and their discount rates moved in an accommodating fashion meant that prices were stabilized rather than their movements positively reinforced. This casts doubts on traditional visions of the adjustment mechanism under the gold standard which held that the domestic economy was sacrificed on the altar of external balance. Bloomfield's work suggests that the conventional vision of central bankers as automatons which blindly followed rules oriented around external adjustment (i.e., following the rules of the game which dictated compounding price changes stimulated by external gold flows) is dubious.[97] Rather than a purely automatic process, it appears that central bankers of the period had significant discretion in how they chose to react to external gold flows.[98] The central banker of the period actually had a far more complex utility function than that posited by the conventional vision of rules of the game. Concerns over economic growth, domestic convertibility, circulation, and international convertibility were leading factors accounting for the frequency of sterilization. Central bankers often refrained from reducing discount rates in response to a gold inflow because of the fear that higher rates in foreign nations would cause a significant gold drain, thus endangering internal and external convertibility or adversely affecting circulation. Conversely, central bankers were reluctant to compound the effects of a gold outflow by raising the rate out of fear of the effects on domestic economic growth.[99] The Bank of England, for example, followed a rule of thumb that made the 4% level a threshold for its discount rate. Rate increases were much smaller and made with greater reluctance when the rate was already at or above 4%. Alternatively, rate decreases were much larger and quicker when the rate was above this threshold.[100]

In other empirical tests over selected nations, a variety of findings are equally inconsistent with the conventional vision of adjustment under the gold standard. It was found that exports and imports covaried positively rather than negatively, terms of trade were more stable than would be expected, there was little relation between international reserves and trade flows, gold flows were far smaller than trade flows, the prices of imports and exports did not move inversely, gold flows were more sensitive to changes in discount rates than to changes in prices, money stocks varied procyclically, there was a negative rather than positive relation between trade surpluses and gold inflows, the prices of traded goods differed less between nations than within nations, adjustment occurred more rapidly than would be expected from changes in trade flows, exports often increased when their prices did not fall, the quantity of imports often declined along with their prices, there was less sensitivity of prices to money supplies and balance-of-payments positions than would be expected, and gold was usually the last thing to flow when adjustment took place.[101]

The revisionist historiography on the period is of a consensus that adjustment took place principally through short-term capital flows that were driven by interest rate differentials across nations.[102] As Polanyi (1957, p. 206) noted, external accounts were "kept liquid" by fairly elastic short-term capital flows that "flitted over the globe." These flows filled in gaps in external accounts pending longer-term adjustment in real variables. That the gold standard exhibited short-term balancing through capital flows rather than trade flows was stabilizing for the regime, since the former were a much more efficient means of adjustment in the short run. Money could move quickly across borders when opportunities for profitable investment presented themselves, while changes in trade flows were subject to lags because prices responded slowly to changes in money supplies.

As with liquidity under the gold standard, the regime allocation mode by which adjustment took place was very much a microeconomic (i.e., decentralized) phenomenon. The capital flows that equilibrated payments were disproportionately of a private nature: i.e., private bank loans, individuals investing in foreign securities, and banks and houses discounting in the international market for bills. Governments were very much absent from the balance-of-payments process. Official balance-of-payments financing (i.e., advances from international lending agencies and consortiums of central banks) was rare, and nations allowed fairly unrestricted movement of the capital flows that financed deficits (capital controls being few). Whatever public manipulation of capital flows occurred—the use of gold devices and discount rates to attract gold to central banks—indirectly impacted on adjustment. The principal public goal of central bankers was to maintain sufficient public gold stocks to preserve national and international convertibility. Moreover, it was the market price for investment that stimulated the equilibrating flows rather than the central bank discount rate per se, and Bloomfield (1959, pp. 44–46) found that market and central bank discount rates frequently diverged.

Adjustment in less developed nations (i.e., outside of the gold club) was characterized by a proportionally greater real (vis-à-vis a monetary) element because their trade sectors were larger relative to their capital markets (in gold-club nations trade sectors tended to be much smaller relative to their capital markets). Furthermore, less developed nations were at a competitive disadvantage in attracting foreign capital (see below). Hence, nations outside of the gold club relied much more on real adjustment than nations in the gold club.[103]

In terms of the long-run structure of adjustment, the current accounts in the gold club under the gold standard were fairly favorable throughout the period.[104] Hence the short-term capital flows that filled in temporary gaps in external accounts were an effective tool for adjustment, since real variables (prices, incomes, productivity) did not create structural difficulties in long-term external positions. In fact, the movement of both short-term and long-term capital under the gold standard tended to move in a way that was compatible with current account positions: long-term debtors (i.e., those that ran deficits on current account) tended to be net capital importers, while long-term creditors (those tending toward surplus in current account) were net capital exporters.[105] Moreover, the capital flows themselves exhibited a stabilizing compatibility. Long-term and short-term capital flows tended to move in an offsetting manner, hence stimulating a stabilizing circular flow of liquidity. The drain which the London market experienced from investments in Australian railroad bonds, for example, was replenished by Australian investors who wanted to take short positions in London. Finally, long-term adjustment was promoted by the growth of multilateral payments networks and the relatively low level of trade protection in the period, and real biases in the structure of adjustment within the gold club were limited by paralleling business cycles and prices. In this sense, long-term balances of payments in the gold club appeared to have a highly stable structure. As in the case of liquidity under the gold standard, therefore, adjustment appears to have exhibited fairly favorable regime outcomes as well.

That short-term and long-term adjustment within the gold club exhibited no fundamental defects is not to say that the capacity to adjust within the gold club was perfectly symmetrical, nor is it to say that nations outside of the gold club (i.e., the less developed world) found the adjustment mechanism as favorable. The revisionist historiography on the gold standard has underscored how stability within the gold standard was achieved partly by shifting the burden of adjustment onto nations outside of the gold club.[106] This argument has two dimensions: real and monetary. On the real side, the argument is embodied in the so-called Triffin (1964, p. 6) effect, and relates principally to Great Britain and the primary-goods-exporting economies in the periphery of the international monetary system. The argument holds that when Great Britain's external payments were moving in an adverse direction, discount rates in the London market would naturally rise. Given the greater returns in the London market, primary-goods exporters would have an incentive to quickly liquidate their stocks of raw materials so that they could acquire the requisite funds to invest in London. With a large quantity of such goods being thrown upon the market, the price of raw materials would fall relative to the price of manufactures; hence Great Britain (which imported the former and exported the latter) would enjoy a favorable shift in its terms of trade. This effect should have given the developed world (the gold club, in fact) a natural advantage in real adjustment over the periphery, since nations in the former tended to export manufactures and import raw materials, while the trade structure of the latter nations featured just the opposite tendencies.

Empirical research on the validity of the Triffin effect, however, has produced findings which are not highly supportive of the logic. Tests on Great Britain, for which the effect was supposedly most compelling, show that British trade did not respond as expected to developments in the London financial market. The prices of British imports, for example, did not respond in the predicted way to changes in discount rates. Furthermore, it was found that the drawing of commercial bills on London was fairly insensitive to changes in rates.[107]

On the monetary side, arguments purporting an asymmetrical burden of adjustment under the gold standard propose that the capacity to attract short-term capital (what will be referred to as pulling power) favored the gold club (developed world) over the periphery (less developed world). When adjustment needed to take place over a multitude of nations, it would first take place in gold-club nations because they possessed a competitive advantage at attracting short-term capital flows: i.e., given an equal rise in interest rates across nations, capital would flow disproportionately to developed nations. In actuality, the structure of pulling power was much more of a multi-layered phenomenon within the purported blocs. In fact, the financial markets of the core nations in the gold club (London, Berlin, Paris, New York) tended to enjoy a competitive advantage in pulling power over the financial centers in other gold-club nations. Hence, we can identify two blocs within the gold club itself.

The structure of capital pulling power did indeed reveal a pattern that was highly beneficial to the gold club, especially the core, at the expense of non-core nations. International capital was most sensitive to changes in the financial markets of core nations, which gave these nations a greater capacity to attract foreign investment. This greater interest elasticity of capital going to the core conferred lower adjustment costs onto the core relative to non-core nations. These non-core nations required relatively higher interest rates if they desired to divert international capital away from core nations. This meant having to accept the burden of tighter credit conditions in terms of domestic economic growth and employment forgone. The resulting movement of international capital created a structure of international adjustment in which core nations had the capacity to redistribute the burden of adjustment onto non-core nations, and the non-core nations in the gold club that suffered a capital exodus to core financial markets had the capacity to redistribute their burden to the periphery by pulling capital away from the latter's financial markets. In this sense, the periphery functioned as a kind of stabilizing force or safety valve for adjustment in the gold club: it was a vent for surplus capital when gold-club external positions were strong, and a source of capital when external positions turned in an adverse direction.[108]

The differentials in pulling power imposed especially difficult monetary conditions onto the periphery in periods of widespread financial distress. Monetary systems in the periphery were quite sensitive to developments in monetary systems in the gold club, especially the core in crisis. Capital would be siphoned off as gold-club nations experienced a shortage of liquidity, the effect being extreme credit crunches in those peripheral monetary systems as inferior financial markets short on liquidity had to make relatively higher bids to pull capital away from more attractive (i.e., more established, less risky) markets in the developed world.[109] Conversely, in boom periods of speculation, the credit systems of peripheral nations were likely to be overexpanded. Hence, there existed a situation in which the monetary systems in peripheral nations showed fairly significant variability in response to developments in international capital markets. This condition set the periphery apart from the gold club or developed world, which experienced more stable domestic credit conditions in the face of external capital flows, the reason being a greater propensity on the part of developed nations (relative to peripheral nations) to sterilize external gold flows. This in turn was largely a result of institutional differences: peripheral nations were less likely to sterilize external gold flows because of the underdevelopment or complete lack of central banking institutions, a condition that was not true of developed nations of the period. In addition, of course, peripheral nations were much more dependent on real adjustment.

Lindert's (1969) findings on the sensitivity of exchange rates to central bank discount rates offer some insight into the structure of pulling power with respect to short-term capital in the international monetary system under the gold standard (see Figure 2.1).[110] Here we see the four core markets situated at the top rung in the structure of pulling power. New York, London, Paris, and Berlin tended to dominate the other gold-club financial centers, the only inconsistency being the domination of Amsterdam over Berlin. It is also interesting that Paris and New York dominated most of the other gold-club nations through the Berlin market. London, in turn, appears to have dominated capital flows within the core.[111] And the gold club, as a bloc, stood atop the international monetary system, as it had a competitive advantage in pulling power over the periphery. Hence, the structure of pulling power suggests that given equality in interest rates, money would flow from the periphery into the developed world, and once in the developed world it would make its way toward core financial markets. This essentially amounted to a three-tier bloc structure of pulling power: periphery to developed world to the core.[112]

The structure of pulling power can be accounted for by several factors. First, given perfectly equal returns to capital (net of transaction costs), nations with more developed financial markets were relatively more attractive to foreign investors. The greater variety of investment opportunities and services, as well as the greater confidence that comes with well-established and strong financial institutions generated a competitive advantage in attracting and keeping funds. Second, nations with relatively superior pulling power also tended to be characterized by greater fiscal restraint and stable money. This naturally made them a safer target relative to nations experienc-

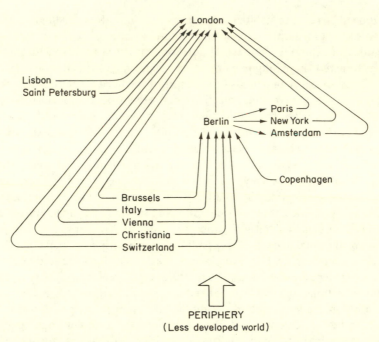

Fig. 2.1 The structure of pulling power under the gold standard. (Lindert, Peter H. *Key Currencies and Gold 1900–1913*, Princeton Studies in International Finance No. 24, August 1969. Copyright © 1969. Adapted and reproduced by permission of the International Finance Section of Princeton University.)

ing high inflation and budget deficits, given that deficits and inflation increased exchange and convertibility risk.[113] Hence peripheral nations required a premium (returns to convertibility and exchange risk) to compete with developed nations in the market for investment. Finally, it was easier for nations at the top rungs of international pulling power to adjust because they tended to be creditor nations, while nations at lower rungs were debtors. It was easier to adjust in the short run by keeping investment from flowing out (i.e., in the creditors' position) than by attracting investment from foreign markets.[114]

However, one should not readily infer too biased a structure of adjustment from the hierarchy of pulling power under the gold standard. In fact, there were several factors mitigating the burdens imposed by the structure of adjustment, both within the gold club as well as between the gold club and periphery. In this respect, the literature on the asymmetrical structure of short-term adjustment under the gold standard gives a misleading impression. First, the effects of differential pulling power were most severe during financial crises, and the period of the gold standard had relatively few crises. Those that occurred were geographically restricted and of short duration. Worst-case scenarios for nations with inferior pulling power, therefore, were rarely realized. Second, nations with superior pulling power (i.e., the core) tended also to be the largest net capital exporters, while those with inferior pulling power were net capital importers. Nations with the greatest capacity to attract short-term funds were willing to allow those funds to flow back to where demand was greatest. Hence, the flow of international short-term capital was circular rather than unidirectional (going to and staying in the core), thus assuring that the means of adjustment were generally available. This willingness of surplus nations, who were enjoying relatively superior performance in their current accounts, to adjust kept the supply of liquidity abundant under the gold standard. Third, within key currency blocs, peripheral nations found inferior pulling power mitigated by preferential access to their associate core financial centers. India and New Zealand, for example, found that crisis periods within their financial systems could be averted or controlled more easily because of their favorable access to the London market. Fourth, insofar as capital controls were practiced, the structure of capital controls in the international system compensated for the differential pulling power. Those nations that were inferior in their command over international capital flows were more likely to indulge in capital controls than nations that were superior at attracting capital. Peripheral nations practiced more extensive controls than advanced nations, while within the gold club, core nations tended to feature the fewest restrictions.[115] Thus, actual adjustment capacity was more equalized through a conformity between the management of capital flows and the structure of pulling power. Finally, the flow of private investment generated positive externalities with respect to the real adjustment capacity of nations with inferior pulling power. Since a great proportion of private investment during the gold standard went to building transportation infrastructures in export-oriented economies in the periphery, real adjustment in these nations was enhanced.[116] Hence, with respect to regime outcomes or the consequences of the workings of the gold standard, although the capacity to adjust in the short term favored the more developed nations in the international system, this advantage did not manifest itself in a structure of adjustment as skewed as the potential to attract foreign investment might suggest. Nations that attracted capital were quite willing to see it redistributed back into the system. In fact, such redistribution carried benefits for the creditor nations as capital flows increased the demand for their exports.

In sum, the process of adjustment under the gold standard was actually quite different from conventional visions of trade flows shifting according to the effects of gold flows on prices (inflation/deflation). What in fact we witnessed, within the gold club specifically, was a group of nations with fairly strong long-term external positions (i.e., current accounts) that were easily able to adjust for temporary disequilibria in their international exchanges by attracting short-term capital. Hence, the principal means of adjustment under the gold standard were short-term capital flows rather than shifts in trade (i.e., adjustment was a monetary rather than real phenomenon in the short run). Nations over the entire international monetary system showed quite different capacities to attract these funds, and these differences allowed more developed nations to redistribute some of the burden of adjustment to less developed nations in the system. But this potential to shift the burden of adjustment did not lead to outcomes that were fully commensurate with differential capacities to influence the movement of international investment, a condition which rendered the process of adjustment under the gold standard much less skewed than the literature on the period suggests.

Exchange Rates

One of the distinctive properties of the gold standard, and one which fits the text-book vision of both the classical gold standard and the general idea of a gold standard, was the stability of exchange rates between gold-club nations. This was, of course, not the case between gold nations and peripheral nations, nor between peripheral nations, given the fact that the latter remained on depreciating paper or silver standards well into the period. The stability of exchange rates was especially striking within the core (i.e., among key currencies).[117] Parities between core (key) currencies were immovable over the period 1879–1914.[118] Movements of exchange rates among gold-club nations tended to remain within the gold points, with inner-point movements showing a fairly balanced distribution around parities.[119] Among core nations, mean exchange rates tended to stay very close to par (see Table 2.1). The small standard deviations attest to the proximity of average movements to par, and the fact that the differences between mean and par rates tended to be significantly less than standard deviations suggests that average deviations tended to be fairly symmetrically distributed around par. Movements of exchange rates among core nations violated the gold points with great infrequency. The worst performance among core currencies was 88.7% in the mark-franc exchange rate. The mark-pound and mark-dollar exchange rates experienced over 95% of their fluctuations within median gold points.[120]

This was far from the case in the periphery. The Chilean peso, for example, depreciated by 66% from 1878 to 1894. The premium on sterling rose to 132% by 1908. The Argentine paper peso faced two severe periods of depreciation in the 1860s and the last quarter of the century.[121] Brazil found its exchanges deteriorating severely in the period 1883–1896. Nations that remained oriented around silver after the 1870s found the sharp and secular fall in the value of silver on the world market for bullion manifesting itself in secularly deteriorating exchanges with gold nations. In India, for example, the pound was worth 60% more in rupees in 1893 (16) than it was in 1871 (10). As with India, similar outcomes befell Shanghai, Mexico, the Philippines, Siam, and the Straits Settlements. A common response to this deterioration of exchanges in these nations was the institution of gold-exchange standards around some key currency. India linked its gold-exchange standard to sterling in 1893.[122]

The stability of exchange rates within the gold club was an outcome of processes that seem quite strange to modern visions of fixed exchange-rate regimes. Deviations, even significant ones, from par were not eradicated by central bankers intervening in the market for foreign exchange. Such occurrences occasionally did take place, but infrequently.[123] The mechanics by which rates in the gold club were able to gravitate around their parities was more consistent with what we have come to attribute to free-floating regimes. Exchange rates were primarily subject to private transaction in the market for foreign exchange.

Deviations from par in gold-club currencies toward gold points tended to be self-correcting during the period because of fairly inelastic expectations about exchange rates.[124] Movements from par generated stabilizing speculation, as investors who expected currencies to revert back to their international parities effected transactions that hastened the expected outcome. Depreciating currencies would, therefore, be-

Table 2.1 Exchange Rates among Core Nations, 1876–1914*

Francs per pound[1]		*Marks per pound[1]*	
Par	25.225	Par	20.430
Mean Exchange Rate	25.220	Mean Exchange Rate	20.431
Standard Deviation	.0644	Standard Deviation	.0487
Percentage of Exchange Rates Falling Within Median Gold Points	90.6%	Percentage Falling Within Median Gold Points	95.7%
Percentage Falling Outside of Median Gold Points	9.4%	Percentage Falling Outside of Median Gold Points	4.3%
Marks per franc[2]		*Francs per dollar[3]*	
Par	81.00	Par	5.183
Mean Exchange Rate	81.01	Mean Exchange Rate	5.178
Standard Deviation	.2525	Standard Deviation	.0224
Percentage Falling Within Median Gold Points	88.7%	Percentage Falling Within Median Gold Points	93.3%
Percentage Falling Outside of Median Gold Points	11.3%	Percentage Falling Outside of Median Gold Points	6.7%
Dollars per pound[3]		*Marks per dollar[4]*	
Par	4.8660	Par	419.8
Mean Exchange Rate	4.8687	Mean Exchange Rate	419.3
Standard Deviation	.01648	Standard Deviation	1.27
Percentage Falling Within Median Gold Points	89.2%	Percentage Falling Within Median Gold Points	96%
Percentage Falling Outside of Median Gold Points	10.8%	Percentage Falling Outside of Gold Points	4%

1. Estimates from October 1877 to July 1914.
2. Estimates from January 1876 to July 1914.
3. Estimates from January 1879 to July 1914.
4. Estimates from March 1887 to July 1914.
Source: Morgenstern (1959, pp. 193–205, 253–63)

come more attractive as speculators saw an opportunity to profit from the expected reversion back to par, while appreciating currencies were faced with a declining demand as speculators were hesitant to take positions in currencies that were expected to soon depreciate in value. In this respect, if we can identify a prevalent mode by which exchange rates functioned, it would be consistent with the decentralized character of the regime allocation mode governing liquidity and adjustment under the gold standard. Exchange rates, like liquidity and adjustment, were the outcomes of a myriad of transactions in private markets for currencies and securities. Governments and official organizations (i.e., official intervention) behaving in an international context were not fundamental to the maintenance of exchange rates.

Whatever the stability of exchange rates owed to purposive actions by central monetary authorities was an outcome of monetary developments at the domestic level.

The international market processes by which exchange rates equilibrated were very much dependent on the management of national money supplies, which in turn was essentially coterminous with monetary authorities remaining faithful to the prevailing stable-money orthodoxy embodied in metallist norms.[125] Exchange rates under the gold standard were therefore managed only in a very indirect sense. The establishment of parities, for one thing, was a natural outcome of multiple nations linking to the same standard: things equal to the same thing are equal to each other. The international parities among gold-club nations were a resultant of setting domestic gold parities. The outcome was a purely additive one. As Ford (1989, p. 198) points out, any international gold standard is merely the "sum of individual monetary authorities' efforts to maintain the fixity of the link between their domestic currencies and gold." In making the gold link monetary authorities were essentially indulging in a domestic monetary phenomenon: establishing a domestic parity in keeping with some desired value of the national unit of account. Even when international concerns, like stabilizing exchanges with principal trading partners, were a strong motivation for establishing convertibility, the norms of metallism were oriented around the specie value of the domestic currency. International outcomes were essentially seen as derivatives of adherence to domestic orthodoxy.

The maintenance of international parities was therefore never far removed from defending domestic parities. Any metallist regime is fundamentally a domestic system of organizing money. The central component of the regime is the preservation of the purchasing power of the central unit of account over time through the maintenance of convertibility. An external target could be used as a means of creating such an outcome indirectly. Targeting an exchange rate could give indications of the state of the link: a depreciating rate might signal too large a money supply to defend convertibility, while an appreciating rate might signal too small a money supply (i.e., the unit of account would rise in value vis-à-vis gold).[126] But the principal rule under metallism is the defense of the domestic mint par; hence whatever international outcomes arise in the exchanges would be primarily configured by developments at the level of domestic money.

Under such conditions (i.e., stable parities), stable international money was linked to stable money at the national level. Nations essentially preserved domestic pars by controlling inflation, and the stable domestic pars collectively manifested themselves at the international level as a set of stable exchange rates among gold-club nations. It is indicative of the importance of inflation control that nations with the best performances at maintaining the purchasing power of their currencies also found greatest stability in their exchange rates. Highly inflationary regimes which prevailed outside of the gold club, on the other hand, found it necessary to resort to capital controls to stabilize their exchanges.[127] Moreover, it was the successful management of convertibility (which was founded on stable money) at the domestic level that contributed to inelastic expectations among investors that drove the stabilizing speculation in the market for foreign exchange, which, in turn, brought rates back to their international parities. Investors maintained confidence in currencies as they expected that the growth of money supplies would be circumscribed. In fact, investors would be much more willing to take long positions without hedging in currencies whose nations were perceived as the least likely to suspend convertibility.[128] Hence, developments in international markets for bills and foreign exchange were inextricably tied to the management of money supplies at the domestic level.

In sum, the stability of exchange rates under the gold standard was indicative of the regime's collective inflation control. In the absence of official intervention, the ability to maintain parities within the bloc was founded on the success of individual members of the bloc in pursuing convergent stable-money paths. Under the gold standard, the collective convergence on a stable-money path was driven both by normative and political factors. On a normative level, stable money was fundamental to the monetary orthodoxy that was so compelling among authorities in developed nations. Moreover, the fiscal restraint necessary to pursue stable money also was normatively compelling. Both fiscal restraint and stable money, which were really part of the greater normative superstructure of liberalism (see Chapter 7), were in turn made more resilient by underlying political conditions of the period. The gold club was experiencing a political transformation that empowered stable-money groups and concomitantly purged political-power hierarchies of pro-inflation landed interests.[129] Furthermore, the kinds of political and financial crises that make stable money, stable exchanges, and fiscal restraint difficult (wars, revolutions, civil war) were generally absent in the gold club during the last four decades before World War I. None of these conditions was visible in peripheral nations.

Stable money limited the fluctuations of exchange rates (i.e., convergent around par) in the gold club. But once displaced, private transactions in the market for exchange tended to encourage exchange rates to revert back toward their parities (i.e., stabilizing speculation). The confidence that currencies would revert back to par, the most important factor driving the speculation, was enhanced by fiscal and monetary outcomes (low inflation and low deficits) in gold-club nations, as well as by perceptions of the compelling nature of the norms embodied in metallist orthodoxy.[130] In this respect, the norms that had the greatest impact on exchange rates under the gold standard were of a domestic nature. The exchange rate mechanism was founded on authorities following central injunctions of metallism, which in turn impacted on the behavior of national money supplies (i.e., stable money), as well as on the effects of this adherence on private transactions in international capital markets (stabilizing speculation).

Capital Controls

Every international monetary regime can be ranked according to a continuum with respect to openness. Highly open regimes are characterized by few restrictions on the movement of capital across their members' borders. Individuals can import capital and obtain access to foreign currencies with relative ease, they can hold money in different forms (e.g., specie, foreign bonds, foreign exchange), and they are free to export capital without restrictions. Regimes on the other end of the continuum are closed. Individuals face severe restrictions in their foreign dealings and the forms in which they can hold money at home.[131]

Nations in the gold club during the period of the prewar gold standard featured a management of international capital flows that gravitated closer to the open end of the continuum. In fact, the prevalent means and speed of adjustment under the gold standard depended on the openness of borders to capital flows. Furthermore, central bankers facing what they perceived as inadequate reserves had little trouble entering into the private market for gold.[132] A far different picture was evident in the periphery, where nations more commonly resorted to restrictions on international capital transactions. This was one way through which these nations responded to the relatively superior pulling power of the developed world. The more advanced financial markets and superior monetary/fiscal performance in developed nations made peripheral authorities much more inclined to institute restrictions on specie and foreign exchange, especially in periods of impending capital flight. Peripheral nations trying their hands (most often unsuccessfully) at metallist regimes invariably featured quite guarded international specie transactions.[133]

With respect to the organization of international capital movements, the gold club (especially the core) fundamentally followed a laissez-faire course. The 19th century as a whole, however, did not show such a consistent track record, even in the developed world. Nations systematically resorted to capital controls (both on foreign exchange and gold) in times of financial and political crises. In the first seven decades of the 19th century, capital mobility was often limited because of the intermittent arrival of crisis periods in the international political and economic systems. Wars and financial crises made it difficult to stay faithful to the injunctions of the metallist orthodoxy.[134] The Napoleonic Wars saw the use of widespread controls on foreign exchange and metal transactions. France used exchange controls to prevent the depreciation of assignats. Great Britain maintained a ban on the export of British coin: bullion exporters had to assure British officials that bullion to be exported was not melted from domestic coins.[135] Given that the gold standard years showed a fair-weather history in this respect, crisis controls were not a prevalent feature of the period. But even in normal times, the flow of money was never absolutely unimpeded. This was evident from the fact that sometimes even London, the most advanced financial market in the world, had difficulty pulling sufficient capital from the Continent when its interest rates went beyond those in Continental markets.[136]

Like peripheral nations, nations within the gold club sometimes adjusted to the asymmetrical structure of pulling power through the use of capital controls, especially in periods of impending capital flight.[137] Most often the controls were on the movement of specie as opposed to foreign exchange. Swedish central bankers, for example, were known to impose legal obstacles on commercial banks trying to obtain gold for export. The German Reichsbank would indulge from time to time in partial suspensions of convertibility. Central banks might also, on occasion, intervene in financial markets in order to orchestrate desired gold flows: when gold was desired they would nudge their exchange rate past the gold import point, and when gold was abundant they might bring the rate beyond the export point. The Bank of Italy and the Austro-Hungarian Bank were especially noted for such practices.[138] But even foreign exchange was guarded closely from time to time. Russia did so repeatedly even after 1850. In periods of restriction, Russian buyers of foreign exchange had to show evidence that the funds would go to buying imports. In 1895 the U.S. instituted informal rationing of foreign exchange in response to the financial crises of that period. Those same crises often led central bankers in other nations during the 1890s to discriminate against American bills.[139]

In securities markets, the French and German governments maintained some control over foreign issues.[140] In France the Minister of Finance had veto power over foreign issues, and foreign borrowers had to issue numerous documents to the Ministry and the representatives of the Paris Stock exchange before they could be considered for floating their issues. Usually it took some strong expression of government favor before a large foreign issue could be floated in Paris. In Germany, foreign borrowers were screened by Boards of Admission on which government representatives sat. And it was understood that the state had the power to intervene at any time, although this privilege was not extensively used. One common means by which the German government practiced capital controls was by specifying which foreign securities could be used for collateral against loans. Two of the major concerns driving the German government's interest in the market for securities were with maintaining the price of domestic issues and geostrategic imperatives.[141]

To the extent that central authorities in the gold club engaged in orchestrating capital movements, their efforts were primarily centered upon influencing gold flows via very subtle forms of capital controls which have become known as gold devices. These differed from more conventional capital controls in that they worked through a market mechanism in influencing the supply and demand for gold by manipulating its price (i.e., influencing international arbitrage by manipulating the gold points), rather than managing supply and demand through administrative mechanisms (i.e., rationing specie, preventing individuals from exporting specie).[142] Central bankers' principal goal in using these devices was to maintain sufficient levels of metallic reserves.[143]

Central bankers employed gold devices in varying degrees, usually as a supplement to the official discount rate as means of managing gold flows. Evidence suggests that the Bank of England relied a bit more heavily on its discount rate relative to gold devices in maintaining its public reserves, while France and Germany relied relatively more on gold devices. This is consistent with the greater stability in the German and French discount rates during the period (see Figures A.1–A.3 in Statistical Appendix).[144] All gold-club nations, however, made at least some use of such means, and often quite ingeniously. All central banks had legal obligations with respect to convertibility, but these obligations were neither so extensive nor so specific that they covered all possible specie transactions. Central bankers used whatever discretion was created by these loopholes and lack of specification to effect goals relating to their gold holdings. The Bank of England, for example, was legally obligated to buy gold bars at a minimum price of 3p 17s and 9d per fine ounce, and to give gold sovereigns in return for notes at a minimum price of 3p 17s and 10½d.[145] But the Bank had the leeway to structure a variety of transactions according to the state of the gold stock. When gold was scarce, the Bank used a number of strategies to attract and keep gold. The Bank often purchased gold bullion at a price greater than the legal minimum. In converting notes into coin, it could (and did) give out worn coin instead of new coins, so as to reduce returns to the export of gold (i.e., specie exporters intending to melt British coin and sell gold bullion in the international market would get a smaller quantity of bullion at a given price). The Bank might give out gold only in the form of British coins, which would reduce the incentive to export gold because specie dealers trading it on international markets would have to incur the costs of melting it down. Conversely, the Bank might accept payment in foreign coins so as to save bullion dealers the costs of melting them down before selling them to the Bank. The Bank sometimes gave interest-free loans to gold importers, hence reducing the costs of bringing gold into Britain. These loans normally had short periods of maturity and had to be paid back in gold. On occasion, the Bank incurred broker's charges when individuals or institutions were paying gold to the Bank (i.e., a reward for paying in gold). The Bank also had discretion over transactions in foreign coins, which it also used to influence the British gold stock. When gold was scarce (e.g., reacting to an outflow of gold), it systematically resorted to raising the price of foreign coin or refused to sell such coin outright. In some cases, the Bank might even discriminate against bills that were believed to be discounted for the purpose of financing the export of gold.[146]

When, instead, gold was abundant, and the Bank did not object to its export, it might alter the structure of its specie transactions so as to change incentives in a direction that favored the outflow of gold. In such cases the Bank would no longer offer a premium over its legal buying price, as well as discontinue covering broker's charges for gold transactions, discontinue interest-free loans to gold importers, and discontinue discriminating against bills which financed gold exports. The Bank might also change its form of payment to encourage exports by giving out bullion or foreign coins rather than British sovereigns, thus saving dealers intent on exporting gold the costs of melting the specie.[147]

Both French and German central bankers were even more likely to engage in such devices relative to other means of managing gold flows. The Bank of France was legally obliged to convert notes into specie, but it could select whether that specie was silver or gold.[148] In times of shortage, the Bank would often avail itself of its privilege to withhold gold and give out silver. If it did pay out gold, it might be in the form of worn 10-franc gold pieces which essentially reduced the return to French notes. One common ploy was to charge a 1% premium on the gold it gave out, and concomitantly pay a 1% premium on gold deposits. The Bank, in times of scarcity, generally gave out gold only to those who had originally made deposits in gold. On occasion the Bank might resort to the most subtle form of manipulating the price of gold: geographic diversification of transactions. This was used throughout Europe and the applications were often ingenious. In times of scarcity, the Bank would buy gold at the borders through its branches, but convert only at the central branch in Paris, thus lowering the transaction costs which individuals and institutions would bear in giving up gold, and raising the transaction costs of acquiring gold.[149]

German central bankers, too, practiced geographic discrimination in conversion: when gold was scarce the Reichsbank would invoke its legal right to redeem notes only at the main branch, but collect at port towns like Hamburg. Unlike the Bank of England, the Reichsbank rarely changed the formal buying and selling prices of gold, but did issue interest-free loans to importers of gold when gold was scarce. The Reichsbank might also close the accounts of gold exporters and stop discounting their bills. In more severe times, it resorted to a partial suspension of convertibility and charged a 3/4% premium on gold earmarked for export. But perhaps the Bank's most frequently used and effective weapon was suasion. Disseminating messages that exporting gold was simply not the patriotic thing to do abated many gold outflows.[150] Individuals and institutions were often sufficiently moved by a "frown from the Director of the Reichsbank" to refrain from exercising their legal right to collect gold in exchange for notes and/or export gold in scarce times.[151]

The idea of central bankers managing gold stocks at a domestic level is quite foreign to the conventional view of the gold standard as embodying an automatic mechanism in which bankers solely reacted to changes in the gold stock. Such a deviation from the textbook vision was in fact stabilizing for the regime. The use of gold devices kept official gold stocks more stable than they might have otherwise been under a specie-flow process, thus reducing the uncertainty of maintaining convertibility, which in turn fed back in a favorable way to the adjustment mechanism by maintaining the high elasticity of short-term capital (i.e., low convertibility and exchange risk maintained low obstacles to private investment) and keeping macroeconomic performance in a convergent structure (thus reducing biases in the long- and short-term adjustment processes). Moreover, the more stable behavior of prices resulting from the stable gold stocks kept domestic economic performance in a more favorable state, thus mitigating domestic sources of instability in monetary relations (i.e., inflation- or deficit-led growth). As in the cases of liquidity and adjustment, the actual gold standard again generated regime outcomes that were more stable than the mythical gold standard. With respect to gold stocks, management at the domestic level was stabilizing in an additive sense: all central bankers guarding gold stocks added up to a regime in which collective convertibility was more robust. Individual suspensions that had the potential to initiate destabilizing chain reactions (i.e., each member of the gold club pulling from an inferior financial market) were averted.

That public intervention in international capital markets took the form of gold devices during the period also carried stabilizing consequences. Since central bankers influenced gold flows through market rather than administrative means (i.e., tried to bid gold away from alternative uses rather than controlling it by law), access to gold in the international system was never significantly limited. Central banks that required gold to maintain convertibility could always get it at a price. Hence, the means of maintaining convertibility were always available, as opposed to systems where gold was controlled via administrative quotas.[152]

In sum, the classical gold standard represented a fairly open international monetary regime with respect to the flow of capital. Capital controls were few. Furthermore, the principal capital controls used by central bankers (gold devices) were more consistent with market principles than administrative in nature. That the regime could remain stable (i.e., the collective gold link maintained) over time with limited and subtle forms of capital controls attests to the prevalence of other factors making the collective gold link stable. Political and financial crises were few, adjustment was fast, liquidity was abundant, and short- and long-term biases in adjustment were limited. In other words, both the nature of the adjustment mechanism and the lack of destabilizing exogenous factors (political and financial crises) rendered the need for more extensive capital controls less necessary.[153]

Confidence

The final specific property of the institutional structure of the gold standard to be considered is confidence. The "confidence problem," as it has been generally labeled, is complex and can be discussed in as many contexts as there are types of money (assets) and monetary actors (both public and private) in an international monetary regime. Cohen (1977, pp. 37, 38) decomposes the problem into two separate issues: official (i.e., public) confidence and private confidence. The successful working of any international monetary regime is dependent on overcoming problems at both levels. The former concerns the kinds of monies held by central monetary authorities, and the impact which the management and the use of these assets has on international monetary relations. The latter concerns the types of monies held by private individuals and institutions, and the impact of these actions on international monetary relations.

When confidence in a money or monies among central monetary authorities is widespread, these monies come to serve all the major functions of central monetary units on an international level: stores of value (i.e., they are stored as official reserves), units of account (i.e., both commercial and financial transactions are denominated in these assets), and means of exchange which are internationally acceptable (i.e., become the principal vehicle currencies through which transactions are effected). Transactions and official holdings will become dominated by monies in which central authorities have the most confidence. This confidence has two dimensions under a metallist regime: authorities must be assured that the monies will maintain a stable international value over time (i.e., exchange risk is low), and they must be assured that the monies will always be convertible (i.e., convertibility risk is low). The first requires that the monies maintain their purchasing power with respect to a global market for goods and capital, which means maintaining a stable exchange rate over time. The second assures the widespread acceptability as a medium of exchange for goods. Where monies in which authorities have this confidence are abundant, official reserve positions will be secure, and trade and financial markets will function more smoothly (because of the abundance and acceptability of money). Where such assets are scarce (i.e., confidence lacking), the regime is prone to generate less favorable outcomes.

On a private level, individuals and institutions, like authorities, prefer to hold and use monies in which they have confidence. This means that goods can be acquired anywhere and at any time, holdings will not depreciate, and foreign holdings will be ultimately redeemable into domestic assets (whether directly, or through acquiring gold first).

The confidence on both levels (private and public) impacts upon all of the other four major institutional properties of an international monetary regime. Confidence dictates the level of liquidity in a regime as well as the composition and state of official reserves. Where confidence is widespread, liquidity will be more abundant and reserve positions more secure. Both on a private and public level, confidence is a principal determinant of the structure of adjustment. Nations will find it easier to adjust where confidence is high because individuals, institutions, and central authorities will more readily accept and hold fiduciary assets (e.g., officials can make short-term adjustments by running down foreign exchange reserves, and equilibrating short-term capital flows can be attracted from private financial markets by a rise in interest rates). Exchange rates can be better maintained if confidence is high, because external imbalances could be temporarily financed through the use of foreign exchange, thus taking pressure off the exchange rate as a means of adjustment. Finally, where confidence generates an abundance of international liquidity, capital controls will likely be lower because officials will have greater access to liquidity, and consequently reserves need not be protected to the same extent.[154]

In any metallist regime, both private and official confidence in fiduciary assets (securities, bills, foreign exchange) is predicated on the ability of nations to maintain the link between these assets and the central monetary metal. This bears directly on convertibility by assuring that private and public actors can always obtain metal in return for notes and credit instruments (i.e., low convertibility risk). Maintaining the link also serves indirectly to reduce exchange risk. Preserving the metallic link requires controlling the growth in money supplies, which has an impact on exchange rates. Controlled growth constrains the supply of national currencies which, if excessive, could reduce the international value of these currencies. The link also has a fiscal impact that bears upon the exchange rate. Since authorities know that they cannot excessively engage in monetizing internal deficits, they will be compelled toward restrained government spending, thus following fiscal practices that are more conducive to keeping inflation under control, which in turn impacts on exchange rates.

Under the gold standard, private and public actors exhibited sufficiently widespread confidence in the currencies and credit instruments of gold-club nations that fiduciary assets became an important source of both public and private money. On an official level, the confidence was somewhat less asymmetrical than the revisionist literature on the importance of sterling suggests. On the Continent, central banks tended to hold more francs and marks than sterling. However, as far as official holdings were concerned, reserves were dominated by gold even by the end of the period. On a private level, the pervasiveness of stabilizing speculation in the gold club suggests that investors were readily willing to take positions in various currencies when adjustment was required. That international capital was sensitive to small shifts in exchange and interest rates (as noted, exchange rate movements tended to remain within gold points and interest rates tended to parallel among gold-club nations), and that these flows facilitated adjustment (were stabilizing) rather than compounded a state of disequilibrium (were destabilizing), meant that external positions in the gold club were self-correcting as long as market signals remained unimpeded by administrative controls.[155]

The whole short-term adjustment process under the gold standard was dependent upon perceptions of convertibility and exchange risk. On a public level, monetary authorities were comfortable clearing payments through shifting claims on foreign exchange. This comfort level was linked to expectations that the foreign exchange would maintain its value and remain convertible. On a private level, since returns to investments were limited because of the limited spread in interest rates and limited movement of exchange rates, the perceptions of such risk had to be small indeed in order to encourage foreign investment. Hence, private actors, like monetary officials holding foreign fiduciary assets, had to be certain that currencies in which they took positions would maintain their international purchasing power as well as remain convertible into gold.

Confidence in the gold club in the last four decades before the War was probably greater than at any other period. As Bloomfield (1963, p. 26) notes, "The continued convertibility into gold of sterling and nearly all of the other leading gold currencies was never seriously in question." With respect to exchange risk, Machlup (1964, p. 294) points out how the world financial community rarely discussed possibilities of the devaluation of gold currencies. The confidence in the stability of exchange rates was visible in the structure of foreign exchange dealings: transactions in currencies on a firm gold basis were generally not hedged against exchange risk because of expectations that rates would stay within the gold points.[156] The inelastic expectations about adverse developments in gold-club currencies were essentially founded on past performances, the strength of the norms of metallism and perceptions of this strength, and on the fact that few exogenous (political and economic crises) events emerged to break the faith in the maintenance of parities and convertibility.

Confidence under the gold standard actually owes much to the previous experience of gold-club nations with metallism. Nations which fell into the gold club after the 1870s were actually practicing metallism long before. Although on silver or bimetallist standards, these nations had been fairly successful at maintaining links between national monies and central monetary metals, and had also enjoyed fairly stable exchanges with other metallist nations, especially those on similar standards. When links became fragile and exchanges unstable, it was almost invariably the result of exogenous political (wars, revolutions) and financial (crises) events. In normal times, it was quite the expectation that nations on metallist standards, especially those on the same standard, failed to maintain stable exchanges or suspend convertibility. Much of the differentials in pulling power can, in fact, be accounted for by different historical track records under metallist experiences before the gold-standard period. The core generated greater attractiveness to foreign investors not only because of more advanced financial markets and central monetary institutions, but because their former metallist regimes had performed well with respect to both stable exchanges and convertibility. Great Britain maintained the gold link since 1717, with the only interruption coming in the period of the Napoleonic Wars (the paper pound, 1797–1821). After the Wars, all of the core nations settled into quite stable experiences with metallism. The U.S. remained legally on bimetallism (which in fact turned into alternating monometallism as legal and market bimetallic ratios diverged), with a break during the years surrounding the Civil War (the Greenback Period). France too found difficulty with years of domestic political instability (1830 and 1848) and war (1871), but otherwise mirrored the U.S. experience under bimetallism (i.e., de jure bimetallism, but de facto alternating monometallism). The German states had a fairly robust experience with silver standards, but there was much more heterogeneity in German practices given the political separation between them before 1871.

Nations in the second tier on the hierarchy of pulling power had similar experiences after the difficult years of the Napoleonic Wars: metallic links in normal times appeared fairly robust. But even within the gold club, especially at the lower tiers, differentials in confidence (as was evident from capital flows and risk premiums) were apparently linked to more specific experiences under metallism. Conditions in Italy, for example, generated significant concern about transacting in and holding Italian francs. Russia and Austria-Hungary, both late additions to the gold club in the 1890s, showed great difficulty circulating gold and maintaining international obligations in gold. It is no surprise that dealings in their currencies were hedged more frequently in futures markets relative to other gold currencies. In all three cases, conditions suggested erratic money supplies, lack of fiscal restraint, as well as internal and external political instability.[157]

On the other hand, the monetary experiences of peripheral nations were at least as turbulent before the gold-standard period as during. Few nations were able to successfully maintain a stable metallic circulation (without its being hoarded) and practice both domestic and international convertibility on a sustained basis. That investors and public actors were most nervous about holding such currencies was perfectly consistent with perceptions of high risk generated by these nations' historical track records. Compounding this lack of confidence was the fact that the kind of exogenous events (political and financial) that endangered convertibility and stable exchanges were all the more prevalent in peripheral nations.[158] Confidence in the gold club was maintained because such events were relatively few.

The inelastic expectations about currencies in the gold club cannot be seen as independent of the compelling nature of the norms of metallist orthodoxy among monetary authorities. Both central bankers and private investors acknowledged the sanctity of the norm of convertibility. Beliefs that public and private bankers were normatively committed to the gold link was a major reason investors expected currencies to remain convertible and exchange rates to revert back toward their parities. Perceptions of low risk, in turn, encouraged public (i.e., willingness to hold fiduciary assets) and private (stabilizing speculation) actions that made convertibility and exchange rates easier to maintain. Moreover, the relative lack of serious political and financial crises during the period meant that these perceptions would not be shaken by exogenous events, since a gold standard was traditionally seen as a contingent rule. Hence convertibility and exchange rates in the gold club were subject to a self-correcting mechanism in the form of a self-fulfilling prophecy. Belief in the sanctity of exchange parities and convertibility (behind which were perceptions of the compelling commitment to metallist norms among banking communities) led to behavior that enhanced their resilience (i.e., stabilizing speculation). Their continuing stability (i.e., continuity of a successful track record) in turn enhanced beliefs in their sanctity. In this respect, historical experiences with metallism and perceptions of the normative strength of metallism combined and interacted to maintain the two central properties of the regime itself: convertibility and stable exchange rates.

As was the case with the other major institutional properties of the gold standard, confidence was also an outcome of a decentralized rather than centralized process. Perceptions of low convertibility and exchange risk in gold-club currencies resulted from individual historical experiences under metallism and perceptions regarding the strength of metallist norms in official circles in these nations, rather than commitments from international underwriters (i.e., great monetary powers, consortiums of central banks) that publicly announced their readiness to intervene in order to maintain exchange rates and convertibility. In essence, the resilience of convertibility and exchange rates continued to be seen in a domestic, as opposed to international, context: each nation individually dictated its own capacity to preserve its gold link and international parity. This made the gold standard a fairly unique period in monetary history. In periods after, nations either aspired to or constructed multilateral schemes (Bretton Woods, Tripartite Agreement, World Economic Conferences, General Agreement to Borrow, Plaza and Louvre Accords), unilateral schemes (U.S. hegemony after World War II), and institutions (IMF, IBRD) that used a more centralized allocation mode to impart confidence onto international monetary relations among nations.

In sum, the gold standard period can be characterized as a period of fairly high confidence, and this confidence was principally restricted to the currencies of nations that were practicing gold monometallism. These nations featured fairly successful historical experiences with metallism even before the 1870s, and people remained convinced of the influence of the central norms of metallism on their banking communities. Both of these factors served to encourage actions among public and private actors that kept exchange and convertibility risk low. In this respect, success in maintaining convertibility and international parities had a self-generating element (i.e., self-fulfilling prophecy). These outcomes were not visible in the periphery, as both past experiences and official commitments to metallism were not perceived as favorably; hence self-sustaining convertibility and exchange rates were less likely there. Finally, confidence under the gold standard was the result of a decentralized process in that it derived from the sum of individual national experiences with metallism and perceptions of these experiences, rather than any centralized processes of management at the international level.

Institutional Synthesis of the Gold Standard

In trying to construct a synthesis of the workings of any regime, one looks for elements that permeate those workings. Under the gold standard, these elements were apparent in the major institutional components of the regime: we saw them in the actors, norms, and principal properties. The most pervasive element in the workings of the gold standard was the liberal (i.e., decentralized) nature of the regime.

With respect to actors, governments were generally in the background of domestic and international finance throughout the period. This was part of a greater tendency on the part of governments during the period to remain detached from matters of private business. Banks and financial institutions enjoyed a great deal of freedom from government overview and intervention. Even central banks themselves were essentially private banks which competed in both domestic and international financial markets. Central bankers in gold-club nations tended not to be state representatives, but agents of shareholders which were themselves private citizens. Their intervention in the gold market to secure reserves did serve a public function (maintaining national and international convertibility), but this was perfectly in keeping with the dictates of good private banking: maintaining their own solvency (i.e., their obligations to convert fiduciary assets into gold) under a metallist regime. The management of money supplies itself was a decentralized and indirect process whereby the state of national credit was the additive outcome of convertibility management across national banking systems (which included the especially influential actions of central banks). In general, the actors that mattered most in the workings of the international monetary system were subnational rather than national actors. This was fairly consistent with international economic relations throughout the period of laissez-faire, as governments were not as engaged in the role of transnational economic agents as they would become after the War. As Kenwood and Lougheed (1983, p. 36) point out of the period, "only rarely were dealings conducted among countries acting as a whole."

Liquidity under the gold standard was essentially allocated through private (i.e., investment) rather than public (i.e., official transfers) means. Adjustment, both long and short term, was the outcome of transactions in the international markets for goods and investment. In the short term, private capital flows sensitized to shifts in exchange rates and differentials in interest rates preserved the equilibrium between the demand and supply of liquidity in the gold club. In the longer term, trade was allowed to shift with few impediments (i.e., protection was modest and restricted to tariffs) according to changes in income, prices, and productivity.[159] Exchange rates themselves were very stable over the period, thus restricting public use of rates as a means of adjustment. Shifts within and outside the gold points were normally caused and later corrected by developments in international markets for foreign exchange and securities. Capital controls were rare in the developed world. Public attempts to influence gold flows were consistent with market principles (i.e., over- or underbidding for gold depending on the state of the reserve) and did not violate the private imperatives of central banks. Confidence was the outcome of a set of individual national experiences under domestic metallist regimes as well as public and private perceptions of the compelling nature of monetary norms. The private short-term capital flows that were central to the adjustment system under the gold standard were driven by these perceptions of low convertibility and exchange risk. These inelastic expectations which were central to the adjustment process were generated by outcomes at the national level (maintaining stable money, fiscal prudence, and convertibility), rather than at the international level as was the case in later periods (i.e., multilateral lending schemes, international organizations). Hence, the gold standard was a regime which featured private actors as the central protagonists, and its principal processes with respect to the properties defining monetary regimes tended to be of a liberal nature (i.e., the regime allocation mode that permeated the properties was decentralized or market based).

The nature of the metallist norms upon which the gold standard was founded was consistent with this liberal character as well. The free movement of capital across borders and the liberty with which individuals could hold and manipulate their wealth were quite consistent with broad liberal tenets regarding the freedom of exchange and individual discretion over the management and pursuit of wealth. Under orthodox metallism, a single international gold market emerged as a result of the norm that individuals should be perfectly free to import and export their precious metals without government intervention. This unhindered privilege of moving gold was enhanced by a freedom to hold gold in any form (domestic coin, foreign coin, or bullion), which served to reduce transaction costs of specie exchange.[160]

At the very heart of the metallist orthodoxy lay a strong laissez-faire ethic, and this was embodied in the central injunctions calling for the preservation of the purchasing power of the national monetary unit through some rule dictating money creation. It was this metallist injunction, by which inflation was to be controlled, that gave the preference for stable money a liberal character. The alternative to a metallist rule was a discretionary manipulation of the money supply.[161] This made the purchasing power of money subject to the idiosyncrasies and whims of public authorities. There was no certainty that these authorities would use this discretion in a capricious manner, but similarly there was no guarantee against it. Metallist rules essentially effected a fundamental liberal objective: removing economic processes from central, public, discretionary manipulation. Moreover, that growth in the money supply was dictated by changes in the stock of gold fundamentally subjected the value of money to market processes: the supply and demand for metal. This in turn prevented any artificial elements from influencing the purchasing power of money, since the value of one set of commodities (i.e., consumable goods) was indexed to the value of another set of commodities (metal). Hence money creation was to be an outcome of the impersonal forces of the market, and whatever outcomes (good or bad) resulted from these forces were deemed preferable to outcomes deriving from central management under a fiat regime where the value of money was established by the decree of some central authority (i.e., had an artificial or contrived value).

In sum, the classical gold standard, as an international regime, was simply an additive outcome of a group of nations (principally advanced-industrial nations) unilaterally adopting gold standards in the 1870s (i.e., the scramble for gold). That gold became the foundation for transactions across nations meant that it naturally acquired the properties of an international money: international medium of exchange (i.e., vehicle currency), store of value (reserve currency), and measure of value (i.e., things equal to the same thing are equal to each other). In this latter respect, a set of international parities naturally emerged as nations linked to the same numeraire (gold). Furthermore, in that nations in the gold club practiced few capital controls (according to the orthodox metallism of the period), the individual monetary systems came to be interlinked within a greater international system, what economists would call a fairly open international monetary regime.

In its workings this international regime exhibited a fairly pervasive character across the five principal properties for defining an international monetary regime (liquidity/reserves, adjustment, exchange rates, capital control, and confidence). Outcomes under the classical gold standard were principally conditioned by market processes throughout the period: i.e., outcomes were primarily the resultants of private transactions in the markets for goods and money. Unlike the international monetary regimes that would follow World War I, very little in the prewar regime was conditioned by the actions of public authorities at the international level. There was little supranational, multilateral, and/or unilateral intervention in the markets for goods and money. In fact, there was little public intervention at the domestic level as well.

It is interesting to observe just how much the actual workings of the gold standard deviated from the more conventional, textbook vision of the period. It is even more interesting that the favorable outcomes of the regime were attributed to these mythical workings. In actuality, the mythical gold standard probably would have generated inferior outcomes to those that were in fact created by quite different conditions. Adjustment was faster and subject to more favorable domestic macroeconomic effects under the actual workings of the gold standard. In the more conventional vision, adjustment was brought about through shifts in trade flows (a slower form of adjustment relative to capital flows), which in turn were dictated by changes in the terms of trade (shifting terms creating potentially more unstable growth and price behavior at the domestic level). Furthermore, adjustment through gold flows was not only slower and less efficient relative to adjustment from shifts in fiduciary assets, but the greater use of substitutes for gold in investment and clearing activities created more stable stocks of gold within nations. This better protected the underlying source of confidence in the regime while expanding international liquidity.

3

Cooperation under the Gold Standard

How much were both the origins and stability of the gold standard a product of co-operation? What form did cooperation take? Did the cooperation take place between central banks or was it diplomatic in nature (i.e., between nations themselves)? These questions have yet to be adequately answered as an integrated set. In other words, there has yet to be a detailed analysis of cooperation under the gold standard that encompasses all the possible forms of cooperation. Events and historiography on the period lead us to wonder about the role of cooperation. First, the International Monetary Conference of 1867, called originally by the French to consider the extension of the Latin Monetary Union into a global bimetallist regime, actually turned into a discussion on creating a monetary union based on a gold standard and the French franc. The conference ended with a unanimous call, among the twenty most industrially advanced nations in the world, for a gold union based on French currency. The conference adjourned with the delegates bringing an international consensus to their legislatures to institute an international monetary union based on gold. The agreement specified: 1) a single gold standard, 2) coins of equal weight, diameter, and quality (9/10ths fine), 3) the 5-franc piece would be the main unit of account, 4) the British sovereign and the U.S. half-eagle would conform to the weight and value of a French 25-franc piece, and 5) the emblems of coins would be left to national discretion.[1] Monetary elites from the period made references to nations following the dictates of this conference later in the 1870s, this in turn leading to a precipitous decline in the value of silver.[2] These scattered references suggest that some cooperation among nations may have been relevant to the start of the international scramble for gold in the 1870s, which itself represented an international monetary regime transformation.

There have been more numerous references (mostly scholarly) to central bank cooperation as a principal reason for the stability of the gold standard. The historiography on the gold standard that takes this perspective argues that there was some kind of "international orchestra" among central banks which coordinated their actions so as to stabilize the international system. The term comes from Keynes's *Treatise on Money* (1930), where this view of the stability of the classical gold standard was first articulated.[3] Scammell ([1965] 1985, p. 105) extended the analysis, but fundamentally agreed that the classical gold standard was far more stable than the interwar standard because the former was essentially run by an "international financial fraternity" which expressed itself in a cooperative scheme among the great central banks. More recently, Eichengreen (1992, p. 31) argues that "central bank cooperation was essential for the stability of the [gold standard]."[4]

This chapter assesses the extent and effectiveness of cooperation under the gold standard. Cooperation among national governments is assessed in the first section, followed by an assessment of cooperation among central banks in the second section.

In the period of the classical gold standard no cooperative schemes emerged from the negotiations among national governments and very little cooperation took place strictly among central banks. It is interesting that so little success was achieved at the four international monetary conferences of the period, because the most powerful monetary players in the system faced consistent and great incentives to create a formal monetary regime: either a monetary union or a multilateral-price-support scheme. British intransigence was an ongoing barrier to success. In this respect, the British appear to have acted against their own best interests, since a regime appeared to carry far more benefits than the potential sacrifices Britain would have had to make (which by all accounts were in fact small). The other major barriers which manifested themselves across the conferences were moral hazard and fears of exploitation (i.e., fears of free riding). A good deal of complacency was created by expectations that large and powerful nations would unilaterally or multilaterally build a regime. Such complacency was also evident among core nations themselves. Hence, nations systematically held back in making concessions in hope that they could benefit from a regime which was supported exclusively by other nations. Compounding this complacency were fears that if indeed such concessions were made, the cooperating nations might be exploited by free riders. This latter factor was especially important in precluding the emergence of a price-support agreement for silver.

The cooperation among central banks was primarily in the form of ad hoc bilateral arrangements to transfer liquidity in need. The motives for the transfers were a combination of concerns for the creditors' own domestic monetary and economic systems (avoiding financial and economic spillover) and normal private business incentives (lending at penalty rates). Hence, whatever process can be said to have characterized transactions between central banks was configured more by domestic monetary concerns and individualistic norms of good business than by international norms regarding commitments to stabilizing some kind of international monetary community. While this cooperation was stabilizing, it is not clear that central bank relations in general were stabilizing, given the elements of competition among them. Central bankers competed before they accommodated in times of liquidity shortages. Hence, perhaps the cooperative schemes did nothing more than neutralize the distress which the banks themselves caused through competition (i.e., the cooperation would not have been necessary if competitive appreciation of rates did not occur). While cooperation made convertibility easier to maintain, competition made it harder to maintain, leaving the net effects difficult to assess. This competitiveness had at least one stabilizing consequence for the gold standard in that it encouraged greater conformity in discount rates.

Cooperation among National Governments under the Gold Standard

Cooperation of any kind among national governments before the 20th century was actually the exception rather than the rule. Trends in the growth of international organization suggest a very limited amount of cooperation among governments. By the turn of the 20th century there were no more than 25 international governmental organizations of any kind in existence. Early international organizations tended to be formed around specific mandates (both technical coordination as in the ITU, and economic regulation of regional waterways like the Commission on the Rhine), with regional memberships and concerns. None had anything to do with regulating monetary relations.[5]

Cooperation among governments on monetary or coinage issues before the 20th century was even rarer than cooperation in general. Willis (1901, p. 71) in his classic study of the Latin Monetary Union noted that the founding of the Union in 1865 represents the first major attempt at intergovernmental monetary cooperation.[6] Before this, there were actually a handful of monetary treaties, exclusively among Germanic states, usually governing the reciprocal acceptance of coin among monetary systems which featured a high degree of commercial and monetary interdependence.[7] The most extensive of these was the Vienna Monetary Union, which lasted from 1857 to 1866. The Union made the thaler common legal tender in Austria and southern and northern German states, all of which found that trade dependence and the infusion of each other's coins made some standardization essential.[8]

The Latin Monetary Union was originally instituted among Western European nations on franc standards: Belgium, Switzerland, Italy, and France (Greece and Romania joined later on). The initial impetus to standardize coinage among franc users came essentially because differing finenesses among small coins caused problems in circulation among these states. The problem originated with the new Italian Coinage Law of 1862, which kept the prevailing (in franc nations) .900 fineness in larger coins but reduced the fineness of smaller coin (coin of denominations smaller than 5 francs) to .835, and the Swiss Coinage Law of 1860, which reduced the fineness of small Swiss coin to .800. This created predictable problems in other franc systems that kept the .900 fineness for small coin, as differing finenesses created opportunities for arbitrage, and Gresham's Law caused small Italian and Swiss coin to drive out national coins of other franc countries (of course, Swiss coin drove out Italian coin). The bad money (coins of lowest fineness) drove out good money (coins of higher fineness). This led to destabilizing shortages in small coin, which made some kind of coordination of coinage laws necessary.

A more fundamental and political dimension of the creation of the Union was Napoleon III's conviction that the creation of a Union founded on French monetary practices would heighten the international political status of France, a necessary condition for France's ultimate reacquisition of the international dominance which ended with the Napoleonic Wars in 1815. This explains why Napoleon issued an open invitation to any nation that wished to join the Union at any time thereafter.

The Union treaty, signed in 1865, standardized coinage practices among the franc-bloc countries based on French coinage practices instituted in the early 19th century: bimetallism at a legal ratio of 15½ to 1, large coins at a fineness of .900, and smaller coins at a fineness of .835. The standardization of weights and fineness took care of the immediate problem of coinage shortages, and the replication of French monetary law conferred onto France the status that Napoleon desired: hegemony over a monetary bloc.[9]

The only other significant formal monetary agreement of the period was that instituting the Scandinavian Monetary Union in 1873. This union was for the purpose of avoiding any unfavorable developments in member monetary systems after Germany's shift from a silver to gold standard in 1871. These nations found the German transformation compelling given a pronounced trade dependence on German states; hence once Germany made the switch, they decided that their monetary systems would have to follow along.[10] Given their own monetary interdependence, each recognizing the monies of the others as legal tender, the move to gold would best be instituted en bloc. Sweden and Denmark initiated the Union in May of 1873, later to be joined by Norway in 1875. The Union called for standardization based on the krone and the gold standard. All legal-tender and subsidiary coin from any member was acceptable within the economies of the other members.[11]

These schemes can essentially be labeled as relatively low-level cooperative attempts which looked to maintain stable systems of domestic circulation of coin, with some international overtones couched in trade dependence. They were quite different from the kind of monetary cooperation which we have seen arise in the 20th century. All of these cooperative initiatives were between a limited number of nations. They tended to be regional, encompassing blocs that found themselves in some kind of monetary and/or trade interdependence. None really extended, aside from the Latin Union, to nations with which the other members had limited monetary and commercial transactions. All of them were oriented around actual or prospective problems specifically relevant to the circulation of coin: usually reactions to overabundance or shortages of coin for circulation. None were for the more general purposes we usually equate with international monetary cooperation: collective maintenance of convertibility, the coordination of inflation rates or economic growth, or management of balance of payments. The Scandinavian Union did exhibit concern for stabilizing exchange rates among trade-interdependent nations, but this as well as the other schemes were strongly driven by circulation concerns. Finally, they were configured around the monetary hegemony of a regionally dominant economy. Early Germanic schemes as well as the Austrian and Scandinavian Unions typically centered around Austria and Prussia, mainly Prussia.[12] The Latin Union centered around France.

Even this acknowledgment and concern for the interdependence among national currency systems, however, was the exception in this period. As Hawtrey (1947, p. 83) observed: "Governments have been too prone to modify their currency systems without regard to the reactions they might cause in the world market for precious metals, and therefore in the currency systems of their neighbors."

The period from the 1860s to World War I saw four major attempts to construct an international monetary regime among developed nations. These attempts took the form of international monetary conferences in the years 1867, 1878, 1881, and 1892. It was at these conferences that the leading economies of the world met to discuss the prospects for cooperative schemes which attended to principal domestic goals as well as pressing developments in the international monetary system. Each conference took place in a period when both national incentives and international developments strongly favored the collective construction of an international monetary regime.

The Conference of 1867

After the signing of the Latin Monetary Treaty in 1865 Napoleon set his sights on extending the union to as many nations as would care to join, with special attention to advanced-industrial nations. Waiting until the Austro-Prussian War concluded, Napoleon sent invitations to European nations and the U.S. to consider joining the Union. The responses to outright membership generally met with some reservation, and Napoleon followed up by issuing invitations to consider monetary unification at a general meeting of all advanced nations in Paris in 1867. The momentum and incentives characterizing the international monetary system at the time suggested great prospects for success. The franc union was growing. The Papal States had joined the Latin Union in 1866, with Romania and Greece coming on board the following year. But more generally, the 1860s saw a pronounced popular and public momentum for unification of weights and measures, monetary standardization being seen as a subset of the general initiative for international standardization in a shrinking world. There had been numerous international meetings on the general subject, with the Postal Congress in Paris (1863) being the first such meeting which extended the desire for standardization to money. Such meetings were especially visible among chambers of commerce in Germanic states. The Paris monetary conference of 1867 was directly preceded by the Conference Relative to the Establishment of an International System of Measures, Weights, and Coins in 1866. The sentiment by national representatives was clearly strong, arrangements being made for further meetings and an institutional framework to increase public support for standardization. Both through publicity reaching business classes and growing support among government officials, the period directly preceding the Conference of 1867 was one in which a clear "sentiment" for union was pervasive in public and private circles.[13]

On the eve of the first session of the Conference of 1867 it appeared that the structure of monetary incentives and burdens pointed to the consummation of monetary union. Virtually all monetary diplomats at the conference and their superiors were in agreement with the Austrian diplomat Baron de Hock on the universal unification of coinage:

> It cannot be doubted that the universal unification of coins, by creating a common medium of circulation, constitutes one of the most effective means for the development of general commerce. Such a medium, adopted by every state and individual, saves the loss of time and the trouble caused by the computation to which it is constantly necessary to resort to ascertain the precise value of the different coins; it reduces to a minimum the rate of exchange, that painful burden to commerce; it obviates the losses from exchange of money, to which the arts and manufactures and not less travellers are subject; it increases the utility of money, and thereby even its value; it diminishes the needs of circulation, and tends finally to an immediate and radical cure of the crises which sprang up in commerce by the accumulation of money at one point and its absence at another.[14]

Beside France, the other dominant bimetallist nation in the world, the U.S., whose support for the Latin Union would create compelling international momentum for unification based on the French system, showed a low estimation of the specific costs of such support as well as domestic legislative momentum in that direction. American monetary officials made it clear in 1866 that American conformity to French coinage standards would entail minimal sacrifice. "Our gold dollar is equal to 517 centimes. A reduction of 17 centimes (3½ cents) would leave it an exact multiple of the French unit, or franc, and the equivalent of five francs."[15] Everyone agreed that the reduction of value in the dollar was trivial. And monetary officials tended to see such trivial sacrifices as representing a minimal obstacle to an international union. On this point they were in agreement with John Sherman. "Certainly, each commercial nation should be willing to yield a little to secure a gold coin of equal value.... As the gold 5-franc piece is now in use by over 60,000,000 of people ..., and is of convenient form and size."[16] Furthermore, in July of that year Congress had passed a law making the metric system, which was the preferred system of measure at all of these international meetings, legal and optional in the U.S. As Sherman noted, it was a period when Congress was disposed to "adopt any practical measure" that would bring about uniform monetary practices among nations.[17]

During preliminary discussions between U.S. delegate Ruggles and French Finance Minister Parieu, it seemed that agreement between the two nations was imminent. The biggest potential roadblock in early negotiations appeared to be French reluctance to coin a new 25-franc piece, which the U.S. desired because it conformed to the half-eagle. Parieu noted his reservations but made it clear that if the U.S. insistence was strong, France would drop its objections on this issue. It appeared that the U.S., the largest producer of precious metals and one of the largest economies in the world, was primed to come into union with the franc bloc on the Continent.

Strictly with respect to coinage weights and finenesses, conformity to the French system seemed roughly as trivial for Great Britain as it was for the U.S. In order to make the sovereign conform exactly to the new 25-franc piece, Great Britain would have to reduce the fineness of gold coin to 9/10ths (from 11/12ths), an act which would also bring them into the decimal system of measure. This amounted to a reduction of value of about twopence (or four cents in U.S. money). The famous monetary authority Feer-Herzog, a representative of Switzerland at the conference, in fact, noted that this difference was so "trifling" that the two coins could actually circulate concurrently without any alteration in the sovereign.[18] John Sherman perceived the changes as "so slight . . . that an enlightened self-interest will soon induce them to make it."[19] And in Britain too, as in Germany, France, and the U.S., there was much agitation among commercial classes as manifest in chambers-of-commerce meetings for monetary unification.

Any effective monetary regime on a global scale would have to have the U.S., France, and Great Britain as members. The U.S. had a principal effect on the market for metals, being the largest producer of precious metals in the world, as well as a leading financial center. Since the intrinsic value of coin depended on conditions in the market for metals, any regime that was to stabilize national money supplies in terms of inflation and circulation would have to have the cooperation of the U.S. France was the center of the Latin Monetary Union, which meant that its currency practices would automatically be exported to its Latin allies. French cooperation would assure Continental cooperation. Great Britain, of course, featured the world's leading financial center in London, and it also housed the world's largest market for precious metals. Given the influence of London on national and international monetary developments, British membership was a principal condition for successful monetary union.

Delegates at the conference were quite outspoken about the importance of tripartite cooperation among these nations for the success of an international agreement.[20] They were also optimistic about the likelihood of such cooperation, because they perceived the interests of these three core nations to be perfectly served by such a formal union. Mind-sets gravitated around the following principles as comprising the most likely regime to emerge at the conference. First, the standard would be monometallic and based on gold rather than silver. Early prompts from Napoleon III to nations about the possibility of a bimetallist union were met with general displeasure. The consensus reaction which Napoleon received from nations was that they would only consider union based on gold. This, of course, was perfectly consistent with British interests. Great Britain was committed to keeping its own standard, and its commerce would benefit greatly from increasing stability in exchange rates with its trading partners. Second, the standardization of weights and finenesses was essential to maintaining stable circulation in nations with low restrictions on international capital flows (which included transactions in precious metals). Certainly the three major monetary players all desired stable systems of circulation. Third, the franc seemed a most efficient central monetary unit, with the 5-franc piece being the central international coin. A very important group of nations on the Continent already had domestic regimes that conformed to the franc system, while the U.S. and Great Britain had only to make "trifling" adjustments to their coins to bring about conformity in coinage.[21] Upon this set of rules, noted Russell (1898, p. 86), there appeared "apparent unanimity . . . as to the desirability of monetary union."

What started as seemingly perfunctory diplomacy on an already resolved issue, however, took on an extremely uncooperative character. The British delegation issued a statement that would become the trademark of British monetary diplomacy for the rest of the century. They kindly thanked France for the invitation, but made it quite clear that they would consider no resolutions that caused the British to change any of their present currency practices. Moreover, they declared that the British delegates should not be seen as issuing binding opinions on their government: they were there strictly to listen to the arguments, study the issues, and report back to their government.[22] Compounding the de facto withdrawal of one of the three essential monetary actors in the world from the most reasonable cooperative scheme, the other two (U.S. and France) came to an impasse over the use of specific national coins. The French came to insist on the franc as the exclusive numeraire. The U.S. preferred concurrent circulation of francs and dollars. U.S. representative Ruggles averred that it was impossible to eliminate the idea of the dollar in his country. Moreover, there was strong concern over the consequences of concurrent circulation, as both British and U.S. delegates expressed fears that the 25-franc piece might very well displace their half-eagles and sovereigns in circulation.[23] National prestige was essentially at the root of this impasse, each nation seeing the displacement of its numeraire by that of another as a sign of international economic inferiority. It appears that it was the status-consciousness of the French that was most obstructive to agreement on universal coinage, since the U.S. was somewhat more willing to discuss concurrent circulation while the French were not.[24]

France's intransigence also snuffed out whatever possibility there was to forge an agreement that would have some chance of British support. In fact, the Chancellor of the Exchequer himself made it clear that Britain might consider union with France if France would consider bringing seigniorage charges into conformity. This seemed quite reasonable, since any large discrepancy in seigniorage charges in a common currency area would cause one nation (the one with the lowest seigniorage charges) to obtain all the monetary metal. The most reasonable solution, therefore, would have dictated concurrent circulation with equal seigniorage charges, but France was being unreasonable.[25] This was curious behavior for a nation so intent on being the orchestrator of monetary union.

Another major roadblock to forging an international monetary union was that no agreement governing transition from bimetallism to gold could be reached. Such an agreement was vital to the immediate functioning of the union, since it was impossible to make a speedy transition to full monometallism. There would have to be some common legal bimetallic ratio instituted among nations in transition; otherwise arbitrage opportunities would disturb their domestic circulations.[26] Furthermore, the burden of converting silver into gold would have to be allocated among nations in a way that was perceived as fair and didn't create shortages of gold. Some kind of time frame for transition would also have to be administered. None of these issues generated agreement, as it was decided to leave transition up to the discretion of the monetary authorities of each nation.[27]

Unlike all three future conferences, however, this one did produce a resolution which delegates could bring to their legislatures. And the agreement did produce more than vague guidelines for action, but never resolved the most contentious issues. It called for nations to move to gold, with the 5-franc piece being the common denominator of the union, but coins of various nations would have legal tender throughout the union. As for rules of coinage, the kilogram was established as the common weight, common methods of assay were to be instituted, coins of similar values should have similar diameters, worn coin should be promptly removed from circulation, and nations should pursue a similar enforcement of monetary laws. Finally, future conferences were called for to hammer out more specific details and attend to unresolved issues. The conference adjourned with some optimism that national legislatures would ratify the resolution. But none of the legislatures did. Differences over fundamental issues allowed a watered-down resolution in Paris, but the differences proved too strong for legislators intent on adopting an international regime that would benefit their nations. The single most promising opportunity to build a formal international regime based on gold in the 19th century fell by the wayside. It is perhaps indicative of the failure of the resolution to generate support that a French monetary commission appointed in 1867 to study the question of monetary reform in France came out for continuing the French bimetallic standard that already existed.[28]

The Conference of 1878

The next international monetary conference would take 11 years to arrive, and this one found its origin in silver agitation in the United States. The 1870s had seen a large depreciation in the value of silver bullion (see Table 6.3 in Chapter 6). In 1867 the price of silver in London was $60^9/_{16}$ pence per ounce and the market bimetallic ratio was 15.57 to 1. By 1878 these figures stood at $52^9/_{16}$ and 17.92 to 1, respectively. In the U.S., much of the depreciation was blamed on the demonetization of the silver dollar in 1873, but in actuality broader supply-and-demand trends in the international market for metals were to blame.[29] The effects of depreciation were also evident in other nations, as nations practicing bimetallic standards found it necessary to limit or suspend the coinage of silver at their mints.

Agitation in the U.S. to resuscitate the use of silver so as to stop its depreciation was headed by Congressman Richard Bland of Missouri. His own draft of a silver bill (the Bland Bill) failed to get Congressional support in 1877, but the bill was amended into the Bland-Allison Bill, which did pass Congress in 1878. The principal features of the bill were the revival of the silver dollar and a commitment on the part of the government to purchase between 2 and 4 million dollars' worth of silver per year for coinage. The bill also called for the U.S. government to invite other governments to an international conference to discuss the possibility of instituting an international bimetallist union. With both the remonetization of silver in the U.S. and the world, it was hoped that depreciation of silver in the U.S. would be abated.

International negotiation, therefore, was no longer oriented around building a gold regime as in 1867, but for the purpose of increasing the monetary use of silver through international bimetallism. In fact, no other international conference for the rest of the century would ever consider union around gold again, but a greater monetary use for silver. This was, of course, understandable given that the precipitous fall in the value of silver created extremely difficult conditions both monetarily and commercially. It was these conditions which made monetary cooperation in the late 1870s seem rather desirable. Just as the Conference of 1867 opened on what seemed to be a favorable set of incentives and momentum, the Conference of 1878 opened under conditions which strongly dictated the creation of some kind of international monetary regime to stabilize the price of silver.

By the late 1870s many nations, certainly all the most advanced monetary powers, had already made the transition to gold monometallism unilaterally. These nations found their trade with nations remaining on silver to be greatly disturbed by the continuing fall in the value of silver. An appreciating exchange rate made their exports less competitive in the markets of silver-using nations, and trade clearing with these nations became more difficult as silver nations found it increasingly hard to pay out in gold without threatening convertibility.[30] Silver nations also found it increasingly difficult to attract capital, as investors from gold nations exhibited growing reluctance to invest in silver nations because of exchange risk. Also, all the advanced nations that made the transition to gold in this decade did so with a limp. The large store of silver that remained in monetary use in these nations found its fate linked to the international value of silver bullion. As this value declined, an enormous burden was thrown on these limping nations; a sizable portion of their money stock was losing value. This also made gold convertibility more difficult to maintain, as this silver could now fetch less gold on the international market, and gold became the primary metallic means of international clearing. Finally, the many creditors, both private and public, in gold nations that had contracted debt with silver nations naturally found the real value of debt declining in proportion to the value of silver.

The four core nations of the international monetary system all found themselves with strong compulsion to create a regime because the depreciation of silver placed great burdens on all of their economies. With India being on a silver standard in this period, one cannot overstate the concern which the depreciation of silver generated for Britain.[31] India had become the most important link in the British balance of payments. Exports to India were increasingly making up for British deficits with other nations. With India on a silver standard, British industries found it more difficult to export and found it more difficult to compete with Indian exports to Britain. Furthermore, British creditors faced the burden of receiving debt payments from India and other silver nations in depreciated silver.[32] There was also the monetary turmoil which a leading colony of Great Britain had to face because of a depreciated currency (i.e., inflation, loss of reserves). Holland was in a similar situation, as its Eastern colonies remained on silver through the period of depreciation, and all of the problems relevant to Indian-British relations also pertained to Dutch-colonial relations.[33]

More generally, every nation that made a transition to gold in the 1870s had sizable stocks of monetary silver, both in public and private possession. Germany, the U.S., and France had especially large stocks. This was a function of an inability to purge their systems of excess monetary silver. For many of these nations, in fact, public holdings of silver actually remained greater than public holdings of gold until well into the 1880s.[34] This imposed several large burdens. Further depreciation might create problems in circulation. Moreover, depreciation would impose heavy losses in the value of central bank reserves, thus threatening metallic convertibility (i.e., people and nations increasingly resisted silver in payment of debts, and the world monetary gold supply was somewhat scarce). Investors in these nations also made sizable loans denominated in silver.[35] In the Latin Union the depreciation of silver was especially threatening because the Union was founded on the agreement that should the Union end, coins would have to be redeemed by their respective governments. Belgium and France had issued very large amounts of silver 5-franc pieces and were extremely reluctant to have them returned en masse for conversion.[36] There was also a group of nations on fiat (paper) standards, principally Italy, Russia, and Austria-Hungary, that found the gold link impossible to make given the depreciated state of their paper currencies, but strongly supported an international bimetallic regime which provided a more viable form of metallic standard for them in the short run. Since gold was scarce and their paper depreciated, resuming exclusively on gold would have been impossible, as the premium on gold would drive it from circulation.

Perhaps the most pressing and pervasive development of all was the fact that the world was in depression. Prices had taken an unprecedented fall, and this was in the face of declining gold production. It was not difficult for supporters of bimetallism to make a case against the evils of monometallism, especially given the fact that most monetary authorities sympathized with the quantity theory of money. Weary monetary authorities appeared ready to accept an expansion of their metallic monetary bases that would come with the expanded use of silver.

On the eve of the Conference of 1878, the incentives which faced nations dictated some kind of regime that would make greater monetary use of silver. There was little disagreement among monetary authorities of the period that the growing demonetization of silver across the globe carried "the most fatal consequences."[37] Once the conference began it was perceived as all the more important that some regime be forged, because as one British authority stated, "if the propositions of the American delegates should be simply rejected, rejection might be erroneously interpreted by the public, who might see in such a declaration a verdict given against the use of silver as money," which would surely compound the depreciation and with it the undesirable consequences of such depreciation.[38]

The conference began in a period which generated other reasons for optimism about the monetary resuscitation of silver. The U.S. Congress had shifted to a soft-money (Democratic) majority for the first time since the Civil War. President Hayes and his advisors wanted to see the creation of some international regime to support the price of silver so as to quiet political agitation for silver legislation at home. France, the central cog in the Latin Monetary Union, had been reluctant to suspend the coining of the 5-franc silver piece indefinitely in the hope that an opportunity would arise where an international bimetallic regime could be constructed. Here was such an opportunity. And by the late 1870s gold had become extremely scarce owing to expanded use and a declining supply, while silver was extremely abundant. There had been quite a change over one decade: in 1867 nations were calling unequivocally for a gold union. Now it appeared that a bimetallic union was in great demand.[39]

The conference opened with a shock, however. Germany, absolutely committed to its gold standard, refused even to attend. The significance of this event cannot be overstated. Germany had emerged by the late 1870s as one of the four dominant monetary powers in the world. More important, it was in an ongoing process of trying to liquidate its excess silver stock so as to add to its official monetary gold stock. The pattern throughout the 1870s suggests that German officials sold silver when its price moved up and refrained from public liquidation when the price was declining. No one, except German officials, knew exactly how much excess silver was still to be liquidated, but international perceptions suggest that it still had quite a mass to liquidate, judging from estimates in public documents.[40] German officials did not abate fears at all with their taciturn style in international meetings.[41] Even with the great incentives nations had to come to some sort of agreement on a regime to support the price of silver, it would have been expecting a great deal for nations to contribute to the public good of a high price for silver when the possibility of a sinister Germany (waiting for a high price to liquidate its mass of excess silver) lurked on the horizon. In this case, the game became a pure Prisoner's Dilemma, with nations extremely reluctant to cooperate unless they could get some assurances that Germany would not impose a sucker's payoff onto the rest of them. In this specific game the sucker's outcome represented other nations acquiring silver so as to maintain some floor price, and when this price was reached Germany would dump its hoards of silver on the market. Hence, nations would lose gold to Germany (making their own convertibility difficult to maintain) and in return would gain silver which was again likely to depreciate after Germany liquidated its public holdings and the regime fell apart.

The German decision not to attend put one of the other core nations, France, immediately on the defensive. Along with the U.S., France's cooperation was absolutely essential to the viability of a bimetallist union, because it was the center of the Latin Union, which was still, at least marginally, a de jure bimetallist union, and any comprehensive regime would have to coalesce around it. The French delegates immediately proclaimed that France would adopt an "expectant attitude," which meant their decision to cooperate in a bimetallic union would be contingent on developments in the other two great silver-using nations: the U.S. and Germany.[42]

The German reluctance also froze Holland, Norway, Sweden, and Denmark. As trade and monetary satellites of Germany (in fact, they had promptly followed Germany onto gold in the early 1870s out of trade dependence), they could not adopt any standard which was significantly different from Germany's. Their cooperation was therefore also contingent on German cooperation.[43]

The U.S. was still strongly pursuing some kind of agreement. As the largest producer of silver in the world, it still had hopes of building a regime, as it felt that other nations should be willing to cooperate with a nation with such influence over conditions in the market for metals. In fact, so anxious was the U.S. to initiate a regime that they raised the sights of the conference (placating early requests by Great Britain, Norway, and Sweden) by including the adoption of a universal coin on the conference agenda.[44] But even this commitment to building a regime did not fully move European nations, some of which even harbored fears that the U.S. itself might be a candidate for exploiting the cooperation of other nations.[45]

The French delegate Say further raised pessimism at the conference by voicing serious concern over the future of the silver market. Asian demand, he argued, could never keep up with the world supply. Hence, any price-support scheme would have to invoke especially large commitments to buy silver. He also speculated on the effects on the market in the case of a mass German liquidation. With some commitment from Germany now seen as crucial, the delegates again implored Germany to attend the conference. Germany once again refused. The refusal generated more rhetoric about the risk of sucker's payoffs for nations that contributed to supporting the price of silver. Belgian delegate Pirmez cited cooperating nations as targets for those loath enough to take advantage of a high price of silver. He added that even under full cooperation, a bimetallic regime was difficult to maintain. When the market ratio came to diverge significantly from the legal ratio prevailing in the regime, the regime would become a de facto monometallic union, as Gresham's Law would cause the undervalued metal to be driven out by the overvalued metal. History supported Pirmez. The highly respected Swiss monetary authority Charles Feer-Herzog joined Pirmez in theoretical diatribes against the viability of bimetallism. With the second and third most dominant monetary powers in the Latin Union now voicing reluctance alongside of France on the question of international bimetallism, it appeared that the dominant silver bloc in the world would not be a leading force in the creation of an international regime.[46] Italy, the one member of the Union that was unrelenting in its encouragement for such a regime, had suspended convertibility in 1866 and would not resume until 1884. In fact, its own support for bimetallism was really as a transitional state of metallism: Italy looked forward to an exclusive gold link in the future, but its currency was too depreciated to support pure gold convertibility at this moment.[47]

As with the Conference of 1867, it was a fairly well-accepted fact in 1878 that an international regime could be forged out of cooperation among the four core nations of the international monetary system. In fact, most delegates believed that any viable regime really didn't require more than these nations in cooperation. With the French wavering, the U.S. might still bring the leading monetary power (Great Britain) into supportership and put pressure on France to cooperate. With the three core nations in cooperation, a regime might still be possible in some form. But as in the Conference of 1867, Great Britain once more opted out of any initiative for building an international regime. If Britain would not support a gold regime in 1867, it certainly would not support a bimetallic regime in 1878, especially given its commitment to a gold standard. And like the conference of 11 years prior, British delegates once more issued the caveat that the British government was not bound by any resolutions passed at the conference. Furthermore, the British delegate Goschen pointed out all of the reasons that further deliberations on the creation of an international bimetallic regime were pointless: Germany, Britain, and Norway would not shift from gold; Latin nations would not change their legal ratio from 15½-to-1 nor would they open their mints to silver; and the support of Italy, Austria-Hungary, and Russia was insufficient to build a metallist regime since none of these nations practiced convertibility (all being on fiat standards).[48]

Great Britain followed up these comments (stated in the third session of the negotiations) with a joint response (along with France) to a last-ditch exhortation from the U.S. for nations to consider international bimetallism. The response was drawn up on behalf of all of the other nations at the conference and submitted at the fourth session. The response essentially made three points: (1) that both silver and gold should be maintained in monetary use, but that each nation should be allowed to determine the specific way in which this was to be done, (2) nations should be free to use silver coin as they saw fit, and (3) nations could not agree on an international legal ratio for gold and silver.[49] The response received general support from the group of nations, and it essentially said that the community of nations agreed to disagree on the question of the appropriate monetary use of silver. So vacuous was the response that it generated support from both those theoretically in favor and those against bimetallism.

With the other three core nations reluctant to support the U.S. in an initiative to build a regime, and other nations (including their monetary satellites) in a holding pattern, the only other option for the U.S. was neither a viable nor a desirable one. Actually, it was suggested by the Dutch delegate Mees. He noted the possibility of looking for allies in the less developed world, where nations were still adhering to non-gold standards. Once this union acquired enough members, Europe might be induced to join. In actuality, the monetary systems of less developed nations were not stable enough to support an international agreement. Secondly, it appears that the U.S. delegates took offense at the suggestion that they might be in a cooperative scheme with less developed economies. In any case, nothing more was said about this alternative.[50]

The U.S. delegation might have been able to build some kind of price-support scheme for silver, even if not formal international bimetallism, if it had been more willing to consider major propositions separately. But they continued to present the agenda as an integrated set of rules governing a prospective regime. The British later stated that they would have been ready to vote in the affirmative on a proposition that sought to maintain some floor price for silver (perhaps a regime which strictly regulated subsidiary coinage). In fact, the British government clearly desired a price-support scheme for silver throughout the period of silver's decline. It was, for example, strongly advocated by the Gold and Silver Commission.[51] But under pressure to consider this as part of an international bimetallic union, the British refused to support the U.S. plan.[52]

In retrospect, the failure to build a regime at the conference appears very much a manifestation of typically collective action problems and moral hazard. The German refusal to attend may have doomed the conference from the beginning, as its silver stock would have essentially held the regime hostage. Fear of exploitation by free riders and rule breakers, however, were not only focalized around Germany, but were generalized even to those who would have joined the regime. Pessimism over the prospects of building a successful regime were "intensified by a sense of the precarious nature of the arrangement, by apprehensions that other nations would depart from it, and by the desire on the part of each nation to protect itself from the mischievous consequences which would result from such departures."[53] Fears of obtaining the sucker's payoff were manifest in the pervasiveness of an expectant attitude over the conference, which also mirrored economic interdependence among those nations.

Another aspect of collective failure was not so much the fear of free riding from others, but a disposition toward complacency because of perceptions that the U.S. would unilaterally shoulder the burden of a bimetallist regime (i.e., make a commitment to buy a disproportionate amount of silver). Developments in the U.S. (the passage of the Bland-Allison Act and the new soft-money Democratic majority in Congress) made other nations more optimistic about the possibility for strong unilateral action on the part of the U.S. to abate the fall of silver. These expectations were strong even before the political developments in the U.S., given the fact that the U.S. was perceived as having the biggest stake in a regime resuscitating silver: it was traditionally bimetallist by law, and was the biggest producer of silver in the world. The recent political developments heightened the optimism.[54] This created a moral hazard which reduced the urgency to forge an agreement on the U.S.'s terms, since nations felt the U.S. would accept a disproportionate burden in maintaining the price of silver. As Russell (1898, p. 224) noted, other nations became optimistic about the U.S. "pulling their chestnuts out of the fire." This seriously undermined the U.S. bargaining position, as other nations still expected a regime to be forged irrespective of their support.[55] As one monetary treatise of the period noted: "As long as [the U.S.] continues the purchase of silver and its coinage, [Europe will not feel] compelled to resort to some means to secure the use of silver as money."[56]

In general, then, the price of silver was seen as a public good. As such, nations were extremely concerned with free riders, given the perceived benefits of such action. Cooperation itself, however, became perceived as less than urgent since the U.S. was expected to contribute disproportionately to maintaining the price of silver, thus providing some free-riding opportunities for other nations. Notwithstanding the favorable incentives and strong potential for regime building in the late 1870s, these obstacles proved too formidable to overcome.

The Conference of 1881

Another conference was orchestrated three years later, with both the French and the U.S. sharing the initiative of bringing the advanced nations of the world together once more to discuss the possibility of an international bimetallic union. The time for regime building in this period was certainly not any less propitious than in periods preceding the other two conferences. When invitations were sent out in February of 1881, the world was once again primed for some kind of regime which would end the problem of depreciating silver. Although business and prices had recovered a bit from the crash of the 1870s, Europe found itself in dire straits. Europe had a bad harvest while the U.S. had a good one; this put pressure on European payments as agricultural trade moved in favor of the U.S. The resulting loss in gold forced interest rates up, and Europe found itself with sluggish economies. Distinguished European scholars, including Giffen, were in fact blaming the woes of the 1870s and early '80s on the relative appreciation of gold (i.e., there was a relation between the premium that developed on gold over paper and the deflations which nations were experiencing).[57] It was also, argued Russell (1898, p. 323), a time when the general doctrine of bimetallism had reached a peak in its perceived feasibility.

Latin Union nations still wanted some kind of protection against the Union's ending, which meant that they would have to redeem their own silver coins which were held in other Latin nations. France was especially burdened by the depreciation of silver. Most of the Latin Union silver was moving into France. Furthermore, France was losing more gold than ever. It was losing 400% more gold in 1880 than it was in 1876.[58] The Reichsbank still had large silver holdings, with two-thirds of the metallic holdings of the Bank being held in silver. More generally, German officials were making an issue of the increasing public costs of redeeming their silver into gold. This was especially troubling because the budget deficit was rather large at the end of the 1870s, and a continuation of absorbing the increasing costs of conversion would seriously disturb the public accounts. The German government did not want to resort to the option of raising taxes, because the Conservative German ruling regime was feeling intense political pressure from the socialists, and such an unpopular move could undermine the support of the Conservative state. But it did want to complete the limp as fast as possible, given the agitation of German creditors (principally bondholders), who were increasingly complaining of having to accept payment in legal-tender silver.[59]

Political agitation for silver in the U.S. made the U.S. especially willing to build an international regime. A. J. Warner's bill calling for unlimited coinage of silver passed the House of Representatives in May of 1879 by a vote of 114–97. Although the bill was killed in the Senate Finance Committee, there was no question that there was a great political schism in the U.S. which had to be cured. An international regime appeared just the medicine.[60]

The year 1881 seemed all the more favorable a period than 1878 to build a regime which solved the silver problem. The two largest silver users in the world, France and the U.S., were more anxious than ever for a regime to materialize. And this time Germany found the silver problem too compelling not to participate in multilateral talks. Considering the importance of German cooperation, given its excess silver stock, a German commitment was a necessary condition for any viable regime. With three of the four core nations apparently primed for cooperation, and the world acknowledging the importance of an international solution to the problem, the conference was awaited in an air of optimism.

The optimism even heightened as the conference began its toils. The joint invitation on the part of the U.S. and France once again proposed an international bimetallic union, to be practiced with a common legal bimetallic ratio between gold and silver. Germany announced it was prepared to limit its sales of silver abroad if a bimetallist union was formed. Moreover, it would enlarge its use of silver at home, and allow nations to discriminate against German silver in the event they felt overburdened with the metal. The French delegation was especially supportive of the theory and practice of bimetallism.[61] For the very first time Great Britain allowed representatives of British India to attend an international monetary conference. This was significant because it was the Indian problem that most compelled the British government to do something about the international depreciation of silver. Also, the leading theoretical voice against bimetallism and for gold monometallism in past conferences, Charles Feer-Herzog of Switzerland, had died shortly before the conference.

Once the formal agenda was presented, however, in a set of questions regarding the optimal method of stabilizing the price of silver through bimetallism, nations surprisingly made rather lukewarm responses. By the second session, 12 of the 18 nations that attended issued statements that made others dubious about the extent of their willingness to cooperate. Germany curiously followed up its preliminary promise of cooperation by Thielmann's statement that the resolutions of the conference would not be binding on the German government, but only serve as a basis for future negotiations. Great Britain, as usual, made its *pro forma* disclaimer: it would not consider any international regime that threatened the practice of gold monometallism in Britain. They were joined in this disclaimer by Portugal (which, of course, had to stay close to British practices), Sweden, Norway, and Denmark. Greece and Russia proclaimed it impossible to change their present systems; Russia could not foresee resuming convertibility. The delegations of Russia, Austria-Hungary, Sweden, Norway, Switzerland, British India, and Canada disclaimed any responsibility aside from informing their governments of the outcomes of deliberations. The Swedish delegate Forssell noted how this "monometallist inertia" led by Germany and Britain was putting a damper on the proceedings.[62] Support for a bimetallist regime would be principally marshaled behind a bridgehead of six nations: France, the U.S., Holland, Italy, Austria-Hungary, and Russia. Holland still had a ruler who was sympathetic to bimetallism, and the latter three nations thought convertibility would be best resumed under bimetallism rather than a pure gold standard.

Debate resumed with Belgium, as in past conferences, coming out strongly against bimetallism and for a gold standard. Much of the early debate was on theoretical issues of the viability of differing standards. This kind of debate had led nowhere in previous conferences, and was apparently leading nowhere now. It not only diluted, but also limited, substantive debate. One of the biggest supporters of a bimetallist regime at the conference, Italy, had a delegation head (Count Rusconi) who showed a penchant for trying to resolve highly problematic theoretical issues before moving on to policy prescriptions. At this point the Russian delegate Thoener presented what seemed like a reasonable compromise between those wanting a comprehensive union and those wanting just a price-support scheme for silver. He actually revived an earlier proposal of the Danish delegate Levy. The plan simply called for a regime which regulated small coin. It required nations to replace small non-silver coin and notes with silver, thus assuring an increased demand for silver in the future. Such a possibility was much discussed, but never gained enough support because nations remained unconvinced of its effects on the market for metals.[63]

Things reached a confrontational peak at the tenth session as the German representative Schraut blamed the precipitous fall of silver on the Latin Monetary Union's suspension of the 5-franc piece. Cernuschi of France responded with a statement that mirrored the feelings of many delegates: that Germany was making token concessions in order to goad the community of nations to raise the price of silver, and when the price was sufficiently high, Germany would convert its mass of silver into gold. These perceptions of the sinister, free-riding motives of Germany were something that plagued every effort at international cooperation from 1878 on. It was something no amount of German promises or commitments could ever fully destroy.[64]

At the following session, the Dutch delegate Pierson's comments summed up the general feeling at the conference. He stated that Holland would consider joining a bimetallist union that included all of Europe and the U.S., but would be reluctant to join any regime founded on some smaller subset of these nations.[65] As with the conference three years earlier, cooperation would have to be marshaled on comprehensive support or not at all, but such support did not appear to be forthcoming. From this point on, any substantive agreement seemed slim. The U.S. and France tried to save the negotiations by reissuing a joint statement of the objectives of the conference at the thirteenth session, but based on the substance of previous statements, delegates felt a positive response could not be justified. Forssell's comment was also quite representative. He noted that as long as the U.S. and France would not start the ball rolling with a bipartite regime, and as long as Great Britain and Germany refused to provide substantive concessions, cooperation was undesirable for his nation, Sweden.[66] The conference adjourned with all the perfunctory optimism about points of agreement and the possibility of exploring these further in the future.

Again, as with the Conference of 1878, nations could not overcome the collective action problems which neutralized some very favorable predispositions toward building a regime. Moreover, the moral hazard generated by expectations of unilateral action on the part of the U.S. proved once more to be an obstructing factor. It is indicative of the influence of political developments in the U.S. that right after Warner's bill passed the House, Germany immediately stopped selling silver. Perhaps German monetary authorities found it advantageous to await a rise in the price of silver resulting from U.S. legislation.[67] Secretary of State Folger, in fact, stated in a 1882 report that the most effective way of bringing about international cooperation on the silver question in this period was for the U.S. to suspend further coinage of silver dollars.[68]

Unlike three years before, however, moral hazard appeared to have more diversified sources in 1881. Nations began perceiving more pervasive possibilities for unilateral actions. The years of 1879 and '80 gave birth to rumors that Bismarck was turning to bimetallism and would remonetize silver in Germany. Rumors were vindicated when in 1880 Bismarck laid a bill before the Federal Council which called for a 20% increase in the coinage of imperial silver. One U.S. diplomat in Germany (White) wrote back to the Secretary of State that Germany was embarking on an extensive use of silver.[69] France was still strongly in the picture, given its co-orchestration of the conference with the U.S. and the fact that the Latin Union was still marginally in existence legally, even though the nations were practicing gold standards except for Italy. Some optimism even came to target Great Britain as a positive source of some significant unilateral initiative. The U.S., for one, expected something to come out of the British delegation, given the Indian problem (after all, this conference was attended by a representative of British India).

With each of the core nations expecting unilateral actions from the others, a debilitating holding pattern of moral hazard emerged among those nations that were most capable of building a regime. The U.S. and France were waiting for the Germans and British to end their bargaining ploys embodied in weak concessions, and make major commitments to buy silver on the international market. The British and Germans maintained the perception that France and the U.S. had too much at stake to let a regime slip out of their grasp. In fact, a major reason for the reluctance to make substantive British and German concessions was their belief in the inevitability of a U.S.-French regime. And, of course, within each of these pairs existed reciprocal expectations of unilateral initiatives. Britain and Germany appeared to be playing a waiting game, thinking that the other would be first to make a substantive concession.[70] The U.S. and France continued to see each other as being compelled by irresistible domestic and regional pressures.

As with moral hazard, the perceptions of prospective free riding also became more pervasive. Even though some nations saw Germany as a possible initiator of a regime, others still considered her the central protagonist with respect to perceived potential rule breakers, but the U.S. and Great Britain were also thrown into the role (the latter more in terms of a failure to contribute than any perceived attempt to liquidate silver at higher prices). Delegates were cautious about Britain's "surreptitious" attempts to goad other nations into cooperation with its flimsy concessions on the purchase of silver. Such was also the view of the German concessions.[71] It is certainly clear that both Germany and Britain desired some regime to be built by the Latin Union and the U.S., with themselves preferably making nominal concessions for cooperation. Some fears also appeared among European nations that the U.S. was trying to increase the price of silver so it could liquidate its silver stock. At one point, in fact, a U.S. delegate (Howe) was compelled to assure the other delegates that the U.S. had no such ulterior motives for building a regime. But no statement could eliminate all the fears.[72]

The reluctance of the Germans and the British to move beyond nominal support for a regime, and French and U.S. hesitancy in taking a substantive initiative, combined to limit prospects for any kind of agreement. Furthermore, the French and Americans, more generally, had a base of support that was founded on relatively weak monetary powers. Of the other four major supporters of a bimetallist regime (Italy, Russia, Austria-Hungary, and Holland), all but one (Holland) were operating on depreciated fiat (paper) standards, and Holland's metallic holdings were relatively small.

The demise of these negotiations did not bring down the final curtain on monetary cooperation. The U.S. remained a driving force through the next decade in exploring possibilities for some kind of international regime to solve the silver problem. By the late 1880s and early 1890s, the U.S. felt it once more a propitious time to initiate another conference. This time the initiative was unilateral (U.S.) rather than a joint initiative with France.

The Conference of 1892

The early 1890s was a period which appeared less favorable to international bimetallism, as the most advanced nations had now been practicing a gold standard for at least a decade, and were apparently quite comfortable with it. In fact, in a preliminary U.S. communiqué with Great Britain, the British government stated that it would not consider discussing the possibility of international bimetallism (which it did discuss at previous conferences), but would only attend a new conference whose objective was somewhat more restricted to a regime which was limited to increasing the monetary use of silver (i.e., a pure price-support scheme). France was now somewhat less animated about pursuing an international bimetallic regime, since the Bank of France had accumulated so large a gold stock that monometallic convertibility was no longer as difficult to maintain. In fact, it even refused to host the conference; Brussels was chosen as an alternative site. Furthermore, Austria-Hungary was preparing to make the link to gold in 1892. Hence the U.S. lost some support from its erstwhile allies on the international silver question. Moreover, Great Britain was resolved to link India to gold should this next conference fail.

However, virtually all the incentives which made nations want to support the price of silver a decade ago were still in existence in the early 1890s. And since gold was still relatively scarce, greater use of silver was certainly still desirable. Furthermore, since the U.S. delegation was now planning to set its sights a little lower and push for a price-support scheme rather than an international bimetallic union, prospects for a substantive agreement appeared more promising. When the conference finally took shape in 1892, once again the attendance represented all economically advanced nations in the world.

The initial signals appeared mixed. Spain, Holland, Mexico, Denmark, and Great Britain accepted the U.S.'s vague resolution calling for increased monetary use of silver. This was especially exciting for the U.S., since it was unusual for the British delegation to vote on anything, given its historic behavior at international monetary conferences. It appeared that the British delegation was unusually supportive of some kind of regime at early negotiations.[73] But reactions from other nations seemed less promising. Delegates from Germany, Russia, and Austria-Hungary made statements to the effect that their governments precluded them from voting on resolutions. They were just there to observe and report. Germany voiced satisfaction with its present system, although it was perturbed by developments in the silver market. France was somewhat inconsistent in its initial reaction to the U.S. proposal. On one hand it criticized the U.S. for lowering its goals on the silver issue, but also questioned why France should be willing to make greater use of silver when its own system was overflowing with the metal. Romania, Greece, Portugal, and Turkey expressed outright reservations on the U.S. proposal.[74]

Early statements by both India and the U.S. raised the urgency of reaching some kind of agreement. Molesworth, the delegate of British India, averred that if the conference failed to produce a solution to the silver problem, India would make a shift to a gold standard. He further argued that an effective price-support regime could be built around India, the U.S., and Latin Union nations alone. McCreary of the U.S. followed up this statement with his own: if indeed the conference failed, the U.S. would surely repeal the Sherman Act.[75]

The one concrete plan to emerge from the early sessions came, surprisingly, from a British delegate (Rothschild). The Rothschild Plan was essentially a price-support scheme that targeted a floor price for silver at 43 pence per ounce. Unfortunately, the plan proved to be as contentious as it was beneficial for Europe. The plan drew the immediate vehemence of the U.S., as no proposal in the history of monetary negotiations in the 19th century was ever a more blatant attempt to free ride. Rothschild called for the U.S. government to continue its present level of silver purchases into the future. Europe and Great Britain would only commit to buying silver if the price of silver dropped to 43 pence per ounce (i.e., this would be the intervention price for Europe). And even then, Europe and Great Britain were not committed to buying anything more than 5 million pounds sterling of the metal. With the U.S. continuing its present level of purchases and the silver market invigorated with news of a successful conference, it was unlikely that the intervention price would ever be reached under normal conditions. And even if it were, European and British central banks stood to make a profit, as they would be buying at a floor price and could convert their excess silver when the price appreciated. This would create the regime which European nations desired all along, one where the burden of supporting the price of silver would be borne almost exclusively by the U.S. The plan was eventually modified to increase the European purchase quota, but never lost its free-riding character.

At this point a smaller committee of the whole was selected to confer over proposals which they could present to the body at large. The committee resuscitated the Levy Plan, which was last marshaled by the Russian delegate Thoener at the Conference of 1881. Some saw such a plan for regulating small silver coin as a viable common denominator, while others considered it only a palliative without real substance. In any event, it was the British who spoke out strongly against this plan, insisting that it would have to be integrated into the Rothschild Plan to be acceptable. Furthermore, the British government did not want to retire the necessary amount of gold coinage called for by the Levy Plan. Interestingly, now that the British delegation was so active (unlike the previous three conferences), it was either trying to free ride on other nations or block what seemed to be the most reasonable agreements. India protested for reasons that the plan was not substantive enough to solve the silver problem. Hence, nations disliked it from extremely different vantage points: some said it asked for too much, while others insisted it didn't ask for enough.[76]

By the concluding sessions, debate had appeared to lose its focus, and arguments seemed to come full circle to the Conference of 1878 when gold supporters argued against supporters of bimetallism on the theoretical and historical grounds for each's favored standard. The proposals now seemed to be going back to more elaborate plans for international bimetallism at a point when the delegates appeared unable to reach agreement on a regime of a lower order. To its own detriment, discussion shifted to specific facets of elaborate plans, when only general principles had a chance for generating some agreement. Given the state of negotiations, the delegates thought it prudent to adjourn until next May. The conference closed its duties without voting on a proposal, not even the Levy or Rothschild Plans. This adjournment closed the curtain on international monetary cooperation in the 19th century. There would be no renewal of the conference's business in May of 1893, as nations felt attempts at regime building to solve the silver problem carried little potential for success.

As in the Conferences of 1878 and 1881, problems of collective action and moral hazard proved once more to be obstructive forces. The British attempts to free ride through the Rothschild Plan and the moral hazard created by the passage of the Sherman Act in the U.S. in 1890 (raising the silver-purchase obligations imposed by the Bland-Allison Act raised expectations that the U.S. would act unilaterally) created both confrontation and complacency, respectively. But in 1892 neither problem appeared to be as debilitating as it was in the previous two conferences. The Rothschild Plan was modified and the Sherman Act appeared doomed if the conference failed. The British were taking an initiative instead of waiting for unilateral action by France, Germany, or the U.S. Other nations were not as expectant of unilateral action from Britain, given that it was considering altering India's standard to gold. And France now was perceived as less of a source for unilateral action, as its gold holdings had increased dramatically over the decade. Germany, too, was seen as having adapted to the gold standard as excess silver problems were perceived as less pressing. What probably was most responsible for the failure of the conference was diminishing support for international bimetallism. The U.S. had maintained the initiative throughout the 1880s, but its supporting cast continued to diminish. Nations had become comfortable with gold standards, and they had preserved them through the years in which the fall in the value of silver was most precipitous. Even France had dropped out of that dynamic group of nations pushing the creation of a bimetallic regime. It was difficult enough for the U.S. without its supporting cast from the Conference of 1881. But without France providing its traditional support, any U.S. initiative was unlikely to engender the necessary cooperation for a regime.

The century closed without a single successful conference. Although the first engendered a resolution (to adopt an international monetary union founded on the franc and gold), the resolution was not ratified by legislatures.

Central Bank Cooperation under the Gold Standard

Given the failure of monetary cooperation among governments, we are driven to ask, What contributions did cooperation among the other important monetary actors of the period (i.e., central banks) make to the origin and stability of the international gold standard? Clearly, the origin of the standard had almost no relation to any links between central banks, the reason being that the selection of a national standard was not a prerogative of central bankers but of the state. Hence any cooperation among central bankers would have no direct impact on the creation of an international standard. As for the maintenance (stability) of the gold standard, cooperation among central banks (and even private banks and governments) would be relevant because such links could enhance the potential of each central bank to maintain convertibility.[77] And the maintenance of convertibility over all gold nations automatically preserved the international standard.

Careful scrutiny of the relations between central banks in the period of the classical gold standard, however, suggests a rather unimpressive picture of cooperation among central banks. It suggests that (1) central banks did not generally consider each other's policies when instituting their own policies, (2) there was little communication between them, and (3) perceptions of international monetary interdependence were less developed relative to the period after the War. Viner (1937, p. 274), for example, pointed out that "Cooperation among central banks in the management of metallic currencies was . . . exceptional rather than an established policy."[78] Ford (1989, p. 219) concurs. King (1936, p. 317) noted that such cooperation "was almost nonexistent." Bloomfield (1963, p. 33) points out that "a notable feature of international monetary arrangements before 1914 was the virtual absence of any systematic cooperation among monetary authorities." Bloomfield does acknowledge the emergence of proposals later in the period that called for such cooperation, such as a call at the Conference of 1892 for central bank cooperation over balance of payments in Europe and Luzzati's 1908 plan for a program of central bank lending and cooperation, but these initiatives "met with little response" from monetary authorities. Beyen (1949, p. 2) points out that whatever cooperation did exist among central bankers "was based on a tacit international understanding to interfere as little as possible with the free play of economic forces."[79] Even the Bank of England, which many came to see as the "conductor of the international orchestra" (i.e., the leader of a cooperative scheme among central banks), stated Viner (1945, p. 64), "never showed any interest in developing connections with other central banks and in systematically planning in advance for collaboration in case of need."[80]

Whatever rules were in fact being followed showed little international consciousness, but instead were couched in domestic monetary orthodoxy. Bloomfield (1968b, p. 27) observes:

> Certainly any such rules, if formulated at all, were never the subject of an explicit or . . . implicit understanding among central banks. . . . Monetary authorities showed little or no overt awareness of a mutual responsibility for the smooth functioning of the international gold standard.

The Bank for International Settlements (1943, p. 126) notes that in fact the international business cycle was not even on central bankers' agendas. The classic concerns of central bank coordination which began to develop in the interwar period (the international spillover of domestic monetary policies, the effects of discount rates on foreign external accounts, avoiding offsetting policies) were far more underdeveloped before World War I.[81]

Even extensive survey of the public documents, especially the studies of the National Monetary Commission which represent comprehensive records of the functions of all major central banks of the period, shows a striking absence of references (both from the authors' descriptions of functions and the statements of foreign central bankers) to central bank cooperation.[82]

The period was not without its share of cases when central banks in crises (liquidity shortages, convertibility problems) would turn to foreign commercial banks, foreign governments, and other central banks for help. This help usually took the form of advances, swaps, discounting bills, or credit arrangements. During the Baring crisis, for example, the Governor of the Bank of England asked if the Russian government would refrain from liquidating its portfolio of British securities in order to abate possibilities of a potential gold outflow. Furthermore, there was a long train of instances when the Bank of France provided liquidity to the Bank of England (1826, '32, '36, '39, '47, '90, '96, 1906, '07, '09, '10). Such links between central banks were not restricted to the period after 1880, but were visible throughout the century.[83]

The cooperation that actually did take place tended to be restricted to ad hoc bilateral arrangements and was extremely myopic—hardly the grand managerial schemes that we have come to equate with international monetary cooperation as seen after World War II. Only occasionally would larger banking syndicates arise, but they were always for transitory purposes.[84] And in all cases, the arrangements were, to quote Viner (1945, p. 64), "extemporized at the critical moment." Once the need for liquidity was over, the arrangements were promptly terminated.

The myopic nature of the arrangements consisted of their market orientation and their particularistic character. As for the former, central bank operations fit into the market for international capital. Banks, no matter what their status, that were in the market for discounts or advances were more concerned with the terms of their transactions than the source of liquidity. Central banks did not feel compelled to seek liquidity only from other central banks in times of need. Private banks were as likely to be involved in central bank transactions as were other central banks, usually from both sides of the transactions. The Bank of Finland obtained short-term credits of 10 million Finnish marks in 1892 from Swedish, German, and British commercial banks. In the face of a serious depletion of gold reserves in 1895, the U.S. Treasury signed an agreement with a syndicate of bankers headed by J. P. Morgan and August Belmont who agreed to buy government bonds up to a total of 65 million dollars.[85] In 1898 the Banks of France and England issued advances to German commercial banks.[86] In the early 1860s, the Bank of France bought gold in the London market so as to avoid having to raise its discount rate. Later, after the Franco-Prussian War, France acquired the funds for the indemnity in the private market by floating French bonds rather than through central bank advances.[87] When Hamburg found itself in need of liquidity in 1857 it turned to a variety of private banking concerns: the Barings and Hambros of London, and the Rothschilds and Fould of Paris.[88] These transactions, like most market transactions, were mutually beneficial. Central banks in great need were willing to accept penalty rates in terms of interest on advances, or discounts on bills. In either case, the lenders, public or private, found a high-price buyer for their loans or discounts. In the case the debtor was a central bank, the transaction was all the more desirable for the creditor, given the low level of risk involved in lending to central banks. Private banking consortiums created for the purpose of making advances to central banks operated under similar motives to those formed for foreign investment purposes: good business.[89] That central banks sometimes went to other central banks instead of the private market suggests nothing more than the fact that the rates offered by central banks were better, or too great an amount of liquidity may have been needed to be covered in the private market. All of this was in perfect keeping with the private nature of central banks of the period: the profit motive was important given their responsibilities to their shareholders.

Furthermore, it is not clear that transactions were any greater between countries than within countries. Central banks dealt more with their own private banks than with foreign banks. Throughout this period domestic financial transactions dominated international transactions. Banks had stronger links to domestic than to foreign institutions, whether private or public. In the 1870s, for example, the Deutsche Bank complained that direct relations with foreign financial markets were difficult to institute; these relations had to be carried on through London.[90] But even before central banks turned to their own commercial banks, they usually exhausted all of their own means of generating the required liquidity. They could raise discount rates to attract domestic and international depositors, they could employ an extensive array of gold devices to manipulate the gold points to attract and keep gold, or in the last resort they could (but rarely did) turn to more traditional forms of capital controls. In many cases, central banks even turned to their own governments, which floated bonds to cover the advances (an extremely embarrassing thing to do for central bankers of the period). The Swedish Riksbank, for example, borrowed large sums from the National Debt Office in 1899 and 1907, the Bank of Finland borrowed sizable government funds in 1890 and 1900, the Bank of Norway borrowed from the Norwegian Treasury in 1901, and the Bank of Belgium often supplemented its reserves by drawing on the foreign exchange in the Belgian Treasury. Given the embarrassment of such requests, one would presume that international or other domestic loans could not be contracted under acceptable terms.[91]

That central banks were linked more into the networks of their own major financial markets, even in the latter part of the century, was very much in keeping with their parochial dispositions. All major central banks originally thought of themselves principally as players in their own central financial markets. The Bank of France, for example, thought of itself throughout the 19th century as the Bank of Paris: its principal business was in the city and it held a monopoly over note issue in Paris. For a large part of the century, the Bank was hostile to the creation of branches in the countryside, a sure indication that it saw its principal role as a Paris rather than national bank. Similarly, the Bank of England was known for most of its early history as a London bank. Even by the early 19th century its notes hardly circulated outside of London. It did not begin branching until the second quarter of century, and even this extension of its banking operations was frequently resisted by Directors who were wedded to the imperative of doing business in London.[92]

Morgenstern's (1959, pp. 105, 346, 394, 406–10, 416, 456) findings support the idea that central banks saw their principal role within their own economies and financial systems, rather than the world system. Central bank rates were correlated more with their own domestic market rates than with each other, suggesting the primacy of conforming to domestic markets rather than coordinating rates to influence world markets. Even more reflective of the underdevelopment of central bankers as international managers was the finding that central banks generally followed rather than led market rates in their economies at periods when both rates moved in the same direction after a turning point.[93] In the case of Britain in the period 1877–1914, in only 3 out of 19 instances when rates changed together at turning points did the Bank of England rate lead the discount rate. In the case of the Reichsbank in the period 1876–1910, of 58 changes in the Bank rate, 28 were accounted for by domestic demand for money and only 13 were initiated to manage external gold flows. This latter finding suggests that the dictates of the German domestic financial system dominated those of the global economy in determining the Reichsbank's discount policies.

The typical central banker's order of priority for strategies to acquire liquidity appeared to place its own operations first (i.e., central bankers first relied on their own means of attracting liquidity), second going to the domestic capital market, and last to go either to their governments or to the international market. Furthermore, as noted, once banks did turn to the international market, there was no rule or tradition restricting them to transactions with other central banks.

It is consistent with the banks' valuation of their status that they would exhaust all their own means of attracting liquidity before turning to others. Moreover, it was quite embarrassing for central banks to have to turn to other central banks for help, especially banks (as borrowers) that occupied central places in the international monetary hierarchy. It was actually deemed prestigious to help a bank perceived as ranking higher than yours on the international hierarchy. Certainly, the Reichsbank and Bank of France's willingness to help the Bank of England found a strong motive in this.[94] Conversely, there was a loss of prestige when central banks accepted help from supposedly weaker banks. In 1836, when the Bank of England accepted loans from the Bank of France, Tooke referred to it as "almost national humiliation." The transaction was only publicly announced by the British government four years later.[95] In 1873, fresh from victory over France, Germany sought to enhance its monetary prestige by offering unsolicited aid to the Bank of England at any time the former found itself in need. Britain promptly made it clear that such aid was not necessary. The French transfers to the Bank of England in 1906–07 were especially revealing. The London financial press became extremely animated in countering French statements that the loans were solicited. The press argued that the loans were initiated unilaterally out of fear that turbulent financial conditions in London would spill out to Paris. Editorials suggested that the Bank of England would never put itself in such an embarrassing position as to ask for help in this period from France.[96]

The humiliation would be greatest if such help was asked for and then refused. This was the major reason for Governor Lidderdale's reluctance to ask Russia and France for help during the Baring crisis. Refusal was a real possibility, as there were no norms dictating that central banks had to accommodate requests from other banks.[97] There were many sources of possible refusal: from public criticism (e.g., aiding the bank of a perceived adversary) to reservations from monetary elites. In 1890, for example, the French Finance Ministry received intense criticism from legislators for helping the Bank of England. The Minister found it necessary to defend the act by pointing out the possibilities for a London crisis to spill out to Paris.[98]

As far as the international links that central banks did exhibit, it appears that these links were more visible within monetary blocs than between monetary blocs. With perhaps the exception of France, Latin Union central bankers dealt more with each other than outside of the Union's confines. Within the Scandinavian Monetary Union, when member nations made the transition to gold en bloc during the early 1870s, they set up lines of credit (allowing transfers and clearing among central banks) only among themselves. They also arranged to accept each other's notes at par.[99] This was not surprising, given that bloc memberships were more trade and monetarily dependent. We would expect credit arrangements to first spring up between their central banks.[100]

The kind of interbank lending schemes that went on never deviated from what Bloomfield (1963, p. 33) calls the "narrow self-interest" of the banks and their domestic situations. Banks lent not so much for the sake of others as to avoid the effects of foreign liquidity shortages on their own financial markets. The long history of Bank of France lending to the Bank of England was shaped by French concern over the spillover of financial distress from London to Paris. It was feared that distress in London would automatically spill out to Paris. Hence the Bank of France was always prepared to come to the aid of the Bank of England. Usually, the objective of French officials was to help alleviate tight credit conditions in London so as to avoid an increase in the Bank of England discount rate, which the French would have felt compelled to follow.[101] When the Bank of France, therefore, lent to the London market, it was not for some international objective relating to world or regional stability, but based on its own domestic concerns.[102] Patron [U.S. Senate (1910a, pp. 139, 157)], in his classic study of the Bank of France for the National Monetary Commission, referred to this strategy as the "enlightened self-interest" of cooperation. The relief of tension in London was essentially part of the Bank of France's domestic policy.[103] Patron [U.S. Senate (1910a, p. 139)] identified this as part of the Bank's general strategy of attacking financial crisis "at its source." He (p. 147), however, made it clear that the Bank looked to its cooperation with other central banks as "an exception" rather than an obligatory rule. In fact, the Bank wanted neither the role of international hegemon nor that of initiator of international cooperation, mainly because it did not want other nations to have any claim to its reserves. Even by the end of the period, Luzzati's proposals for cooperative schemes among central banks (1907, '08) failed to gain the support of the Bank of France.

For German central bankers, interviews of the National Monetary Commission show a somewhat more complex structure of self-interest underlying the Reichsbank's willingness to make foreign advances. First, it was "for the sake of such of our industries as seek a foreign market." Second, coming to the aid of foreign banks, especially in London, conferred a great deal of national status as a major monetary player on the global scene. And third, such actions improved Germany's credit standing with the world.[104]

Irrespective of the perceived roles of central banks and the infrequent amount of cooperation, the question Was this cooperation stabilizing for the maintenance of the gold standard? is still relevant. That these schemes of accommodation made the maintenance of convertibility easier cannot be disputed, but it is unclear that the overall *relations* of central banks (which included both competition and cooperation) were more stabilizing than destabilizing (i.e., the net effects of central bank relations appear much more problematic than the effects of the schemes of accommodation).[105] Viner's (1937, pp. 274, 275) assessment of central banking reactions to international crises suggests that central bankers were more likely to become "engaged in competitive increases of their discount rates and in raids on each other's reserves." Ford (1989, p. 219) notes how periods of generalized financial crisis put central bankers in a defensive mode which dictated competitive behavior so as to assure some desired level of reserves. He (p. 275) quotes a British monetary authority of the period, Robert Somers, who characterized differing central banking policies as being "conceived in hostility to one another." Tennant (1865, pp. 417, 418), in his study of the Bank of England, argued that the Bank of England and the Bank of France were most likely to get into a competition of discount rates at times when gold was scarce in both capital markets. His description essentially portrays a typical Cournot game of oligopolistic competition where the actual outcome (the Nash equilibrium) is Pareto inferior to one that could have been realized through cooperation (i.e., both banks maintained discount rates that were higher than the optimal rates). Moreover, the competition seemed to increase with the severity and pervasiveness of financial conditions. Great Britain found itself unable to attract gold through its own operations during the crisis of 1906–07 because rates on the Continent were propped up to prevent the loss of gold. Sometimes the Bank of France and the Reichsbank considered it more expedient to arrange transfers to Britain than to allow competitive appreciation of rates to achieve debilitating levels for domestic trade. Also, arranging transfers gave them greater control over how much gold they would lose.[106] In 1871 when Germany's transition to gold necessitated a large increase in its monetary gold stock, it pulled a large amount from Great Britain (about 5 million pounds sterling from July to October of 1871). The Bank of France was especially aggressive about building up its gold stocks in the mid to late 1870s when the Latin Union was subject to large gold outflows. In the years 1874–78 France imported about 3 million pounds sterling a year. In the three years prior to the resumption of convertibility (1875–78) in the U.S., the U.S. Treasury was successful in doubling the monetary gold stock.[107] Clare (1909) found some regularity in U.S.-European competition for gold, linking it to cyclical developments in the U.S. capital market. When the demand for money in the U.S. increased at harvesttime and drew liquidity from Europe, European central bankers strove to raise their own rates to abate the drain, or to make up the loss of liquidity to the U.S., to quote Clare (1909, p. 120), "at the expense of [their European] neighbors." The result, he added, was a regular "war of rates," "[a] fight for gold."

In the 1870s and '80s the competition for gold was mainly the result of nations' wanting to consolidate their newly instituted link to the gold standard. Germany was especially animated about building its gold stock for this purpose. As the period progressed and nations entered into geopolitical competition, gold stocks came to be seen as a "national war treasure" which were to be kept up in case of conflict. In effect, success at acquiring gold itself took on a geopolitical status. One major reason France did not support the Luzzati plan for central bank cooperation was that it did not want other nations having a claim on its gold reserves in turbulent political times.[108]

To the extent that central bankers preferred to exhaust all their own means of attracting gold, and as a last resort would call upon the help of other central banks, it appears that central banks tried to pull liquidity away from other central banks before asking for accommodation: i.e., a strategy of fighting them before joining them.[109] Hence, accommodation schemes may simply have smoothed over turbulent conditions which central bankers created in the first place (i.e., mitigating their own destabilizing impulses). This further suggests that whatever parallelism we find among discount rates in this period was probably more the result of competition (defensive or otherwise) between central banks for reserves than the joint management of the international credit and business cycles.[110] The most interesting aspect of this is that the paralleling of discount rates (see Figures A.1–A.3 in Statistical Appendix) emerged as one of the more stabilizing elements of the gold standard (i.e., paralleling rates minimized the pressure on external accounts).[111] Hence, if this competitive posture was a principal component in the parallelism of rates, then the stability of the gold standard owes at least something to elements of competition among central bankers.[112] Essentially, the foundation of what Brown (1940, p. 169) called the "unconscious cooperation" of the classical gold standard was itself partly the result of conscious competition. This requires qualifying the view of the classical gold standard as creating conditions in which, as Eichengreen (1986a, p. 139) says, "international policy coordination was a moot point." Certainly, conformity in credit conditions and discount rates was a function of a pervasive link to gold in domestic standards, but whatever defensive posture existed among central bankers regarding their reserves compounded the convergence of central banking practices and macroeconomic outcomes.

In sum, in the period of the classical gold standard no cooperative schemes emerged from the negotiations among national governments and very little cooperation took place strictly among central banks. It is interesting that so little success was achieved at the four international monetary conferences of the period, given that the most powerful monetary players in the system faced consistent and great incentives to create a formal monetary regime: either a monetary union or a multilateral-price-support scheme. Problems of Britain's intransigence (in the face of great potential net benefits for Great Britain from the creation of a regime), moral hazard, and fear of free-riding behavior produced a situation which prevented nations from collectively achieving desired goals.

With respect to central banks, cooperation proved to be primarily in the form of ad hoc bilateral arrangements to transfer liquidity in need. The motives for the transfers were a combination of concerns for the creditors' own domestic monetary and economic systems (avoiding financial and economic spillover) and normal private business incentives (lending at penalty rates). Whatever process can be said to have characterized transactions between central banks was configured more by domestic monetary concerns and individualistic norms of good business than by international concerns oriented around stabilizing some kind of international monetary community. While this cooperation was stabilizing, it is not clear that central bank relations in general were stabilizing, given the elements of competition among them. While cooperation made convertibility easier to maintain, competition made it harder to maintain, leaving the net effects difficult to assess. This competitiveness had at least one stabilizing consequence for the gold standard in that it encouraged greater conformity in discount rates.

4

British Hegemony
under the Gold Standard

The findings in the previous chapter suggest the regime dynamics of the classical gold standard were fundamentally founded on neither cooperation between national governments nor cooperation among central banks. If the gold standard was not, in terms of origin and stability, a cooperative or negotiated regime, was it an imposed or hegemonic regime (as, in fact, much of the economic historiography on the period says it was)?

The idea that international regimes are founded on the efforts of very powerful nations, usually referred to as hegemons, has become a fairly common one in the study of international political economy. The vision is very strongly state-centric in its orientation, in that national governments (rather than subnational actors) are seen as being mobilized in pursuit of goals that conform to some observable national interest.[1] Less commonly, such efforts may emanate from very powerful subnational (e.g., central banks) or transnational (e.g., churches) actors which are attempting to influence international relations in a way that achieves some benevolent or particularistic objectives.[2] Specifically with respect to explaining the origin and perpetuation of the international gold standard, these two visions have fixed upon the British state and the Bank of England as the leaders or managers of the regime. This chapter will assess the extent of hegemony undertaken by the British state, while the next chapter will consider hegemony on the part of the Bank.[3]

Brown (1940) was among the first to make arguments regarding the need for a leader or manager in an international monetary system. Kindleberger (1973) brought the argument its greatest notoriety. For both, the success of the prewar gold standard owed much to the expert management of Great Britain. Ford (1962, p. 19) identifies Great Britain, through its London capital market, as the center of global finance. Its primacy in the markets for short-term and long-term capital, as well as the market for gold, conferred upon it a predominant international monetary influence which it used responsibly throughout the period. Bergsten (1975, p. 34) calls Great Britain "the major manager of the pre-1914 monetary history." Skidelsky (1976, p. 162) adds, "Not only did Britain 'manage' the prewar economic system, but it is unimaginable that such a system could have developed in the nineteenth century without such management." Richardson (1936, p. 33) cites the "singleness of purpose under British monetary leadership" as the major component of stability under the gold standard. For Gilpin (1981, p. 138) the British state "desired" a global economic system organized around British industry, finance, and economic philosophy (laissez-faire). He adds, "A primary objective of British foreign policy became the creation of a world market economy based on free trade, freedom of capital movements, and a unified monetary system," and the state used the economic and political means at its disposal to create a monetary regime and manage relations within it. Cohen (1977, p. 81) calls the classical gold standard a "hegemonic regime—in the sense that Britain not only dominated the international monetary order, establishing and maintaining the prevailing rules of the game, but also gave monetary relations whatever degree of inherent stability they possessed." Krasner (1976, p. 338) concurs: "British power helped create" open and stable monetary and trade systems.

Any assessment of hegemonic behavior by the British state, irrespective of what kind of hegemony it was (wholly benevolent, coercing specific policies perceived to be of a stabilizing nature, supported by other powerful nations, etc.) would have to consider three central questions carefully. First of all, was it an explicit objective of the British government to stabilize some set of international monetary relations? Second, did the British state use its principal means of monetary hegemony (in this case the Bank of England) to effect such outcomes? The use of its principal means of hegemony is extremely important, given that the Bank of England would have had to be at the very center of any plans which the government had to influence the international monetary system. No other institution had as influential a place over the London market, which itself was the single most influential financial market in the world economy. Hence any kind of state hegemony would have had to be characterized by a principal-agent link to a Bank of England which was pursuing well-defined state goals with respect to the international system. Finally, what kind of behavior did we observe from the British state at the actual monetary negotiations that took place during the period at the four major international monetary conferences?[4]

This chapter is organized around these three major questions, each of which is addressed in a separate section. To the extent that the British state did hegemonize the gold standard, we would expect that the state itself had fairly well-specified goals with respect to international monetary relations, and we would expect that the state used the Bank of England (its most powerful means of influencing international monetary outcomes) to bring some of these goals about. Furthermore, we would also expect those cases which provided crucial opportunities for the British state to achieve some of these goals (i.e., the conferences) to be important litmus tests for monetary hegemony: we would most expect to see manifestations of leadership or international monetary management in these cases.

The behavior of the British state with respect to monetary relations during the gold standard period suggests that the state itself was far from a hegemonic actor in the global monetary system. It carried on very limited contacts with international banking and investment, as it was an ongoing priority of the British state to stay clear of transactions in private markets for goods and money. This laissez-faire ethic was all the more pronounced in matters of finance. Furthermore, the foreign policy of Great Britain during the period, which was both relatively passive and defensive in nature, was poorly adapted to any goals of shaping international outcomes in a significant way. Moreover, foreign policy itself was little concerned with monetary relations.

The British state carried on limited control over and contact with the only viable agent for British monetary hegemony: the Bank of England. Aside from some informal-overview functions, the British state had very little to do with the operations of the Bank.

Finally, the behavior of British delegations at the four international conferences violated all common visions of appropriate action by monetary hegemons. Time and again Britain had an opportunity to bring about a regime which was in its interest, and time and again it failed to do so. In all four conferences Britain occupied an influential position in deciding whether some regime would be constructed. In all cases, building a regime would have been beneficial to both Britain and the world. But Britain never mobilized any significant support for a regime. Had it exercised even the most minimal hegemony, something might have been consummated at any one of the conferences. But it didn't. In fact, its actions more often served as an obstacle to cooperation. It never made it easier for cooperative nations to start a regime. Furthermore, it proved to be an extremely poor bargainer, as British delegates failed to take advantage of strategic opportunities to further British national interests. When Britain did act hegemonically, it did so in a very inconsistent way. In 1867 it was against union around the franc, but never pushed for union around the pound. In subsequent conferences, it sought to free ride (more consistent with coercive hegemony) on the cooperation of others, but never used even limited commitments to encourage others to build a regime.

The Goals of the British State

If indeed the British state did show any hegemonic initiatives in either building or stabilizing international monetary regimes, or shaping international or regional monetary relations, these initiatives would have had to show up in one of two state organs: Parliament or the Foreign Office, most likely in the latter since this was seen as the preserve of foreign relations. But as a democratic state we would expect to see any important initiatives at monetary hegemony show up both in Parliamentary debates and the Foreign Office. The Treasury was an unlikely place to look for manifestations of monetary hegemony, since it would have had to dictate conditions in the British financial system (or at least influence developments in that system), and this it simply did not do. The national financial system at the time was perceived as a composite of private banking, and as Ziegler (1988, p. 249) notes: "To a nineteenth century Chancellor of the Exchequer, the idea that he might intervene in a matter of private business was anathema."[5] Even if it had aspirations to influence domestic and international financial markets, Treasury officials historically lacked the means to do so. During the Baring crisis, for example, Salisbury informed Rothschild that even if the Treasury wanted to help maintain Baring's solvency, it lacked the mechanisms to do so, government accounts being managed by the Banking Department of the Bank of England. If anything, the Treasury maintained surveillance over the management of the national accounts at the Bank of England, and kept itself informed on periods of crisis in British finance, but was not a player in shaping domestic financial conditions, and therefore certainly not a player in the international monetary game.

It was an institution mainly configured around the fiscal condition of the nation, and any concern over the national banking community was usually related to this principal function. Its interest in the Bank of England was mainly oriented around a client-bank relation, since the Bank managed the government accounts.[6]

In the case of Parliament, careful scrutiny of monetary debates in the period shows a striking paucity of debate centering on international issues.[7] In fact, relatively little debate took place on monetary issues at all. Consistent with the division of labor in British government, it was the Bank of England's and the Treasury's tasks to tend to matters of money, and even these in the case of the Treasury tended to be mostly in areas affecting the fiscal condition of the nation. More generally, the prevalence of laissez-faire attitudes suggests that banking matters were more a concern for the market than for MPs. This even extended to the government's banker: the Bank of England. As Bagehot ([1873] 1921, p. 43) noted: "Nine-tenths of English statesmen, if . . . asked as to the management of the Banking Department of the Bank of England, would reply that it was no business of theirs, or of Parliament at all."[8]

Parliament was little interested in international monetary matters.[9] And insofar as it was, it was usually on issues affecting the colonies.[10] The colonial questions appeared driven primarily by maintaining stable banking systems and circulations in the colonies. There was little discussion about the international conferences (the Conference of 1867 was hardly mentioned) that took place in the period: many of the comments of MPs on these conferences represented requests for information pertaining to their outcomes. There were no substantive comments of any kind from MPs in issues referring to the stability of international or regional monetary systems of any kind. When MPs did call for some kind of regime to be built, it was usually driven by Britain's own particularistic reasons. For example, MP calls for a bimetallic union were usually founded on concern over the effects of a depreciating rupee and/or the effects of depreciation in other silver currencies on British trade.[11]

The other principal international issues which arose among MPs were: whether Britain should coin money for other nations, charges on colonial minting, the importation of foreign coin by bullion dealers, foreign mint charges, problems of Latin Union coins circulating in Great Britain, and the effects of the depreciation of silver on the Eastern trade. Except for the problem of the depreciation of silver, international questions tended to be quite mundane, especially in their concerns over matters of circulation and foreign mint practices. Questions more in keeping with an aspiring monetary hegemon like concerns with world credit conditions, the state of international banking, the fiscal and monetary conditions in foreign nations, patterns in the flow of international capital, and the structure of monetary interdependence were absent. It is also quite surprising to see, irrespective of hegemonic aspirations of the state, that a great financial power like Great Britain could be so unconcerned with the state of the international monetary system on the eve of the War. Both Parliamentary debate and negotiations between the major banks of London show a surprising absence of references to the effects of the War on world finance; they were much more concerned with Britain's own ability to continue convertibility as it had been traditionally practiced.[12]

The search for manifestations of monetary hegemony does not do much better when we turn to the British Foreign Office (FO). The FO actually never made a clear statement of its official policy toward foreign monetary relations.[13] Evidence suggests, in fact, that any coherent policy was indeed lacking in the general area of economic affairs.[14] Indicative of this were complaints on the eve of World War I by *Economist* editor Francis Hirst that the FO had not even arrived at any policy rules about loans, concessions, and the Open Door by 1914.[15]

Several characteristics of the FO emerge when we scrutinize the history of foreign policy in this period. First, economic issues in general, and money specifically, were the least of the FO's concerns. Second, the FO generally kept out of relations among private and/or public financial actors. Finally, what little interest the FO took in relations over money was normally founded on the particularistic interests of the British state or British citizens, not on stabilizing international and regional monetary systems.

The FO's own acquired hierarchy gave economic matters the lowest priority. At the most general level, it was the geopolitical state on the Continent and other areas of vital British interest that most shaped the FO's agenda. Objectives related to the geostrategy of British interests were perceived as being obtainable primarily through politico-military and diplomatic means, not economic means (such as aid or trade). The latter were not seen as being essential parts of the diplomat's arsenal. In fact, diplomats looked to involvement in economic relations as a lower form of diplomacy, well below the exciting "grand diplomacy" they all aspired to.[16] The bias against involvement in matters of foreign finance was all the more reinforced by a propensity to minimize the FO's contacts with both domestic and foreign financial agents.[17]

Relations over money were essentially seen as market transactions (even if central banks were involved, given their private status), and it was not like any branch of the British state to get involved in the play of the market, especially in this period of laissez-faire.[18] Money, in fact, was considered the most private of all domains.[19] When asked for state intervention by British citizens, often to address matters of foreign default, the response from the FO was fairly consistent: "British financiers have to make their own arrangements."[20] The FO policy toward financial transactions across borders was consistent with a general philosophy about international contracts: they were seen as matters for the contracting parties to police. In the words of Palmerston, British citizens carried on transactions "at their own risk."[21]

The Foreign Office's response to foreign governments requesting aid was similar: the British government "declined to use State credit for the purpose of financing or assisting industrial or commercial undertakings overseas."[22] In some cases where the FO might itself have been predisposed to intervene in foreign finance, other constraints arose. Foreign secretaries were historically reluctant to initiate involvement in foreign financial matters because such initiatives would be brought to Parliament, where the general mood was dead set against such involvement. Even during the Crimean War, for example, the War Loan to Turkey was severely criticized in Parliament.[23] It was usually only in cases of great geostrategic importance (and most often even these were not sufficient) that the FO became involved in foreign financial matters. But even here the likely official intervention took the form of assistance and advice in bringing the grievance of British citizens to foreign authorities, or in somewhat more forceful style issuing "friendly remonstrance" against the offenders themselves.[24] In fact, the links between strategy and finance were very much underdeveloped in British foreign policymaking in this period. Baring's actions during the Crimean War would be almost unthinkable in the 20th century. The financial house kept marketing Russian bonds in London throughout the War.[25]

The only truly international goal which can be imputed to the FO and its view of international relations in the sphere of money was a preference for equal and open access in foreign markets (this was not restricted to finance either, but also pertained to trade). Lipson (1985, p. 39), in fact, calls this a "minimal statement of . . . economic hegemony." But even here, the FO observed more transgressions than it acted upon, and the ones it acted upon almost invariably involved the exclusion of British investors from foreign financial markets. The FO was most animated by equal and open access in areas extensively patronized by British citizens, like China.[26] Hence, even here what may have appeared as the global consciousness of a hegemon was nothing more than a particularistic concern for its own citizens. Moreover, irrespective of the source of intervention, when the markets appeared to offer equal access, the FO immediately disengaged from any communication or action over the matter.

Even if there were a link between strategy and finance, and economic objectives were tightly integrated into the foreign policy imperatives of the British state, one wonders just how adapted was the type of British foreign policy we saw during the period of the gold standard to the goal of shaping foreign economic relations. Any foreign policy that was hegemonic in nature would be expected to show an active and forceful character. Whether this hegemonic action came in the form of benevolently supporting the international economic system with resources, or coercing nations into bearing the hegemon's burdens, we would expect to see a foreign policy of strength rather than a passive one that allows relations to fundamentally shape themselves.[27] But the period hardly vindicates this vision of British hegemony in terms of foreign-policy styles. In fact, there was much debate in Britain in this period revolving around the optimal foreign policy: views ranged from Disraeli's "strong" foreign policy to a more passive quest for a policy of "sobriety and peace."[28] One can hardly classify British foreign policy as an uninterrupted train of support for actualizing some British world vision. Instead of unity, notes Kennedy (1981b, p. 65), one sees a series of rival perceptions about British national interest and the state of international relations.[29] Disagreements ranged over everything from the means of foreign policy to the goals of foreign policy. There never even emerged any agreement on which part of the world was most important for British interests.[30] And very often these disagreements (especially intense ones) had the effect of producing a policy of inaction—i.e., intense positions paralyzing policy, as in the case of the proposed alliance with Germany in 1898 against Russia, which seriously split the Cabinet and required some deft mediation by Salisbury to allow British policy to proceed, and the debacle over intervention in the Russo-Turkish War in 1878, which brought on sharp policy swings which ultimately gave way to inaction in the midst of numerous resignations.[31]

If anything, we see great caution in British foreign policy in the period of the gold standard. Kennedy (1981b, pp. 74–76) argues that the caution emerged from the Crimean War, which raised strong doubts about Britain's international power and its aristocratic leadership. These doubts conditioned foreign policy well into the future. Manifestations were quickly seen in a reluctance to intervene in the Polish uprising in 1863 and one year later in Schleswig-Holstein. The latter sensitized all future British administrations to the need for public support in foreign-policy initiatives.[32] With caution being the trademark of Parliamentary and popular approaches to foreign policy, it was not surprising that British policy was purged of much of its systematic resolve to forcefully shape international issues. After 1870, notes Platt (1968, p. 357), "British foreign policy . . . was perpetually on the defensive."

A predilection toward "splendid isolationism" emerged under Gladstone and Salisbury, and the style of British foreign relations forged under their administrations would fundamentally shape the essence of foreign policy until the War. Salisbury himself summarized British policy of the latter century as floating "lazily downstream, occasionally putting out a diplomatic boat-hook to avoid collisions."[33] The policy was very much in keeping with Gladstone's own personal orientation toward foreign affairs, which showed a disdain for both expansion and involvement in Continental relations because of the perceived risk of being pulled into a general confrontation. Because of the risk, Gladstone thought it inappropriate for Britain to play the part of global "judge and policeman."[34]

Salisbury's quasi-isolationist style was characterized by reluctance to enter into new agreements and enthusiasm about relinquishing old ones. Both he and Lansdowne were very concerned about the effects of overstretch, especially about how adverse effects could turn public opinion against their administrations. His policy aspired to no more than "defensive strength."[35]

Caution in foreign policy throughout the period was all the more reinforced by the potentially adverse domestic political effects which foreign relations might generate. Foreign policy entered into partisan political competition at home. The goal became to avoid foreign failures, which were much more visible when an adventuristic policy failed. A defensive position with limited interventions seemed perfectly adapted to a populace relatively well-off economically but seriously concerned with the effects of international overstretch. The embarrassing difficulty of overcoming 75,000 Boers with 300,000 British soldiers at the turn of the century compounded the insecurity in elite policymaking circles which started with the Crimean War, and further reinforced a policy style that was anti-spirited.[36]

Even the high points of Britain's so-called strong policy (especially under Disraeli) represented no more than "spasmodic aberrations."[37] The cases of imperial extension, aside from being defensive in nature, coexisted with many cases in which Britain gave way to the expansion of others in strategically vital areas.[38] Often such was done to buy neutrality from a third nation in any potential dispute Britain had with a main rival. Cases of such appeasement took place in South West Africa, Togoland, the Cameroons, New Guinea, and East Africa.[39] Even the quest for peace in the world, a visible goal of the British state in this period, suggests neither an international consciousness reflective of hegemonic aspirations, nor an uninterrupted series of successes. Peace was for the benefit of Great Britain rather than other nations. The nation most active in the international economy benefits disproportionately from world peace. But even here Great Britain hardly showed a stellar record in its direct attempts to impose peace on the Continent and elsewhere. In the mid-1860s Britain was fearful of making a unilateral initiative to stop the Austro-Prussian War, so it fell back on the Paris Protocol of 1856, which called for joint action by France, Russia, and

Britain against any aggression. Britain refused even to issue strong language (in joint opposition to the War) against the aggressors in fear that it might be perceived as a signal of a possible military intervention. Both this trilateral initiative and Britain's summoning of the Concert failed to stop the eventual hostilities. In the 1870s, Britain not only found the advent of the Franco-Prussian War unstoppable, but failed to influence a more legitimate settlement to the War—something they saw not only as vital to the future prospects for peace on the Continent, but also vital to their own particular interests in its bearing on the Eastern and Belgium questions. In the mid-1890s, Britain sought a multilateral entente in Asia to prevent the outbreak of hostilities that would affect both the strategic balance and trade in Asia, but it couldn't line up support from the U.S. and Germany. The Sino-Japanese War shortly followed, and significantly changed the Asian map. In the first and third cases, Britain sought multilateral support for peace because of its perception of weakness to effect a unilateral outcome. Moreover, in both these cases it was not even able to sell prospective allies on its prescribed plan of multilateral intervention.[40]

In sum, if the British state considered itself a hegemonic presence in the international monetary system, it did not show up in Parliament, nor in the Foreign Office, nor in the style of foreign policy it adopted.

The Principal-Agent Link: The Bank of England as an Agent of British Hegemony

If the British state had any kind of aspirations to influence developments in the world or regional monetary systems, a necessary condition for an effective influence would have to be the use of the Bank of England as an agent of hegemony (i.e., a principal-agent relationship). First, international conditions would have to be effected through manipulating the London capital market which occupied the very center of the international monetary system. Tightness in the market would automatically export itself to the global economy, since trade was cleared disproportionately in British bills. Hence, any developments in market discount rates in London, for example, would have immediate consequences for importers trying to get new credit, irrespective of nationality. A higher market rate in London would make credit difficult to get everywhere, importers would be limited in their purchases, trade would decline, and the world economy would slow down. In addition, a disproportionate amount of international investment and lending was coming out of London houses and banks, thus dictating credit conditions directly. No single institution in London had more power to influence credit conditions in London than the central bank itself: the Bank of England.[41] If market rates in London were influenced by the Bank of England rate, then we could make a plausible case for the viability of controlling international credit conditions though manipulating the Bank rate. No other monetary instrument was as likely a means of hegemony as this rate, since it was the most influential rate in London.[42]

The only other means of influencing international monetary relations would have been the use of private banks as agents, or using more conventional foreign-policy tools such as military force, the threat of intervention, or sanctions. But as discussed above, neither of these was the case. The state had little to do with private banking, and foreign policy had little concern for financial developments in the world. Moreover, even if some aspirations to influence international outcomes existed, it would have been marshaled on anything but an aggressive foreign policy.

With respect to any possible principal-agent link, the origins of the Bank are revealing. The Bank, like most other European central banks, was essentially designed to solve specific fiscal problems: it was founded as a means of providing liquidity to the state.[43] These banks were instituted through state charters which were subject to renewal periodically, but were essentially conceived as private commercial banks rather than managers of national financial markets. Lending to the state was just part of their general duties.

The Bank of England was seen by both the state and public as a private commercial bank fairly consistently throughout the 18th and 19th centuries. The following exchange between MP Wyld and the Chancellor of the Exchequer in the House of Commons is both revealing and indicative of an ongoing mind-set in British government.

> Mr. Wyld said, he would beg to ask Mr. Chancellor of the Exchequer, Whether it is expedient that the Directors of the Bank of England should exercise the power they possess by their exclusive privilege of issuing notes to compel the sale of Consols, and thereby depreciate the securities of the State upon which their own issues are mainly founded?
>
> The Chancellor of the Exchequer: Sir, I hope my honorable Friend will allow me to say that this is a question which opens a very wide field for discussion upon a matter of general policy. It amounts in reality to a question as to whether the entire position of the principal issuing body in this country should be changed, and whether issues and advances should be made on the direct responsibility of the State? . . . I must say that on the principle of the law as it stands, and viewing the Bank of England as essentially that of a commercial establishment . . . , I think it would be quite impossible to deprive the Bank of England of the discretion it is possessed of, and which it exercises with a view of making a greater or less amount of advances either on public securities or mercantile accounts.[44]

The exchange suggests that the private status of the Bank was so sacrosanct that the state had to sit idle in the face of Bank decisions that affected the fiscal health of the state (depreciating Consols) and even poor management of British credit (if its discretion over advances on securities or mercantile accounts was used in a highly inflationary manner).

As a private bank, its status put it on the very periphery of state involvement, as British law showed little regulation of the banking system. In fact, banking was probably the least-regulated sector in the British economy. The state took the attitude that it was inappropriate to inquire into affairs of private finance, any arrangements being subject to private contracts, and therefore a matter of transactors to monitor and police. The state did not even institute reserve requirements for banks, including the Bank of England. Peel himself, the author of the Bank Act of 1844, contended that "the public must rely on their own caution and discretion as a security against being injured or defrauded."[45] Even in constructing his famous Act he requested only limited revelation of banking business to the public (i.e., the periodic publication of note-issue levels by banks of issue), stating that it was improper to "pry into the affairs of each Bank."[46]

Interviews with the Directors of the Bank of England over the course of the century show little change in the relation between the British government and the Bank. Whether it was the Bank Charter Hearings of 1832 or the National Monetary Commission reports of 1910, the answers to questions of Bank management changed little. The following exchanges from the National Monetary Commission are revealing and quite representative.[47]

> Q. Has the Government any voice in the management of the bank or any interest in it through the ownership of shares?
> A. The Government has no voice in the management of the bank, nor does it own any stock.
> Q. Is either your issue or your banking department at any time examined by the Government, or in any way under its supervision?
> A. There is no actual supervision by the Government.
> Q. Have the obligations of the bank to the public or the Government been changed from time to time?
> A. No, not in any important particular.

The Government and Bank carried on what might be referred to as friendly consultation, mainly through elite contacts among the Governor and the Chancellor of the Exchequer, but the contacts were informal and ad hoc rather than systematic and institutionalized.[48] Such contacts were more likely to be expedited at meetings of the Political Economy Club or the Old Oxonians than through official Bank and Treasury stationery. Most of the concern of the government with the Bank was nothing more than the normal concern of a customer in the bank which is managing his/her money. The Bank's interest was reciprocal, given the size of the government accounts.[49] But in the event that the Bank refused some exhortation from a state representative, there was no legal means, short of requesting new Parliamentary legislation, of making the Bank act accordingly. Officially, each was in its own legal and institutional sphere.[50]

The Bank was separated from the government through a shroud of secrecy that extended even to information that was vital for both the British fiscal and financial systems. It was not uncommon in Parliamentary hearings for officials to refuse to divulge information about specific operations. Note the following exchange in Parliament:

> Mr. Labouchere (Northhampton) asked Mr. Chancellor of the Exchequer, "What is the amount of the Local Loan Stock held by the Bank of England?"
> The Chancellor: "I am not aware of the amount of different kinds of securities held by the Bank of England; nor if I were aware should I that it was open to me to make the information public."[51]

Knowledge about the securities portfolio of the Bank was crucial given that the Bank's holdings affected the market for securities, to which the fiscal health of the nation was tied. Furthermore, the Bank's dealings in securities also affected credit conditions in Britain through open market operations, although these were not frequently used in the period. Sometimes this shroud of secrecy led to adverse developments for the Bank as well as the British monetary system. Sayers (1976, V. I, p. 42) cites one incident in 1905 when a Governor of the Bank complained that the increased disbursements on behalf of the government had the effect of neutralizing a Bank attempt to raise the market discount rate by bringing money into the Bank through requests for advances.

Whatever Parliamentary overview of the Bank and the financial system existed was especially evident in financial crises. But even here state involvement in the Bank's affairs did not go beyond information gathering in post-crisis periods. It was common for Parliament to institute special committees to look into the causes of financial crises. Part of the process was to assess the causes and effects of the crises. Of concern was the behavior of the Bank, and what effect it had in mitigating or fueling the crises. Questions were asked of a plethora of experts, including the Directors of the Bank themselves. Aside from a number of similar questions asked across committees, there was no systematic way in which the inquiry would proceed, nor any understanding that the committees had special powers to reform the financial system as a result of their findings. The inquiries resulted in reports which would be considered by Parliament at large; but these reports represented only topics for discussion, which proved relatively scant when surveying the actual debates. This is somewhat surprising given the contentious nature of some of these reports.[52]

In its normal workings, Parliament was relatively uninterested in the Bank and developments therein. Compared to other matters, the questions about the Bank were few, and they also tended to be quite mundane, nothing approaching grand questions of monetary policy and central banking. Debate over the crisis of 1866 appeared to be the most extensive on any such issue, but even here the primacy of the Court over the government in determining the Bank's actions in crises was obvious. In the midst of the crisis, MPs questioned the Chancellor on whether the Bank would be issuing excess notes. The Chancellor answered that he would recommend the Bank Act of 1844 be suspended, but whether the Court chose to issue any more notes would be determined by its "usual prudent rules of administration."[53]

Even on the very eve of World War I, with the British financial system faced with the monumental task of maintaining some semblance of stability in the face of a Continental war, the British government was anything but a compelling presence in the midst of prewar meetings of the British financial community.[54] Lloyd George presided over most of the deliberations as head representative of the British state. At most his role appeared to be one of mediator with a strong opinion. The British state's strategy for actualizing its preferences was to add its voice to groups that sought similar goals: this was most apparent on the issue of convertibility when it threw its weight behind industrialists pushing to maintain gold convertibility throughout the War. It was common for Lloyd George to allow extremely sensitive questions among bankers to be resolved in private, without a government representative present. At one point, when negotiations reached an impasse between Lloyd George and the banks on the acquisition of and rate on Treasury notes, the banks asked the House of Rothschild to replace Lloyd George as mediator. He readily stepped down. Throughout, notes de Cecco (1974, p. 169), the British government was negotiating from a position of weakness: "The banks were strong enough to call all of [Lloyd George's] bluffs. As with all weak Governments, he had only the extreme measure of imposing those controls over the financial system that were theoretically available."[55]

In sum, the loose connections between the Bank and the state, and the discretion exercised by the Court of Directors over the Bank's policy, even in crises, suggest that any principal-agent link through which state hegemony was expedited was extremely weak at best. That the state did not hegemonize through the Bank is fairly certain. But given the discretion of the Court, it was possible for the Bank to manage international relations from its own initiative. In fact, the Bank would have faced few obstacles in doing so had such a thing been its intention. This possibility is explored in Chapter 5.

Great Britain and the International Monetary Conferences of 1867, '78, '81, '92

Evidence is fairly compelling on the point that the British state did not involve itself to a great extent in international monetary relations through its normal institutional means of government. But when it was intimately involved in actual negotiations among governments on questions of money, what kind of behavior did we see on the part of the British state? Did the actions of the diplomats at these four international conferences suggest any properties of leadership, management, dynamic initiative, and/or international concern which are consistent with the role of a monetary hegemon? If such hegemonic properties were to be seen at all in this period, they would have had to come at the conferences. The conferences were the largest and most important international monetary gatherings of the period, and all were invoked for the purpose of building international monetary regimes: either unions or price-support regimes for silver.[56]

At the very beginnings of domestic and international agitation for building bridges between nations so as to reduce the costs of interdependence (through standardization) in the 1850s and 1860s, the British state was reluctant to lend support to such undertakings. This reluctance was not in keeping with a minimal property of hegemony: a greater international orientation than that of other nations.[57] Standardizing weights and measures would disproportionately favor economically dominant nations: given their level of interactions with other nations, these nations disproportionately bear the costs of international transactions. Domestic agitation from the London Society for the Encouragement of Art, Industry, and Commerce, in the aftermath of the momentum built at the International Exhibition in London in the early 1850s, failed to produce the desired state initiative in calling together leading nations for the purpose of standardizing weights, measures, and money. The Statistical Congresses that followed shortly thereafter in Brussels and Paris received similar responses from the British state, notwithstanding strong support from governments of economically less powerful nations. In the mid-1850s, domestic agitation led the U.S. to initiate an invitation to Britain to harmonize their respective coinage systems through the decimal system. In January of 1859 Lord Derby issued the government's official response: it refused to take the initiative in a plan that required Parliamentary approval, but would consider and confer on any proposals. The initiative failed in 1859 and again three years later when it was revived by Secretary Samuel P. Chase in hopes that it would stem the depreciation of gold. The International Statistical Congress of 1863 in Berlin produced the first extensive international discussions on unifying differing coinage systems, but even a very zealous British delegation failed to generate any follow-up initiative on the part of their government. The Congress was hardly even discussed in Parliament. On the eve of the world's first international monetary conference (1867) among the leading nations of the world, the British state had already carved out a history of intransigence at building international bridges (monetary or other) between nations.[58]

The mid-1860s was a high point in terms of domestic-group support for standardization of coinage in Britain. Interviews from the *Report From the Royal Commission on International Coinage* (1868, pp. 63–66, 96, 118, 126, 138, 150) exhibited a strong predilection for standardization, even if British currency had to be configured to that of France. The Royal Commission itself issued a report in favor of a union around gold. Careful scrutiny of the interviews suggests that Britain had striking incentives to support some kind of union based on gold. As the leading commercial and financial actor in the international economy, its traders and financiers would benefit greatly from standardization: financial and commercial transaction costs would be reduced, and exchange rates would likely be more stable since nations were linking to the same metal. Witnesses agreed that even if Britain did not contribute significantly to building such a regime, it would be devastating for commercial and financial interests if Britain stayed out of any prospective regime. Wrigley's testimony is representative.

> If [the Latin Monetary Union agreement of 1865] were carried out, and we were excluded, we should be practically isolated from the rest of the world. . . . [Given] the increase in competition which our manufacturers have now to encounter . . . , [it becomes] extremely hazardous for us to allow our competitors any advantages.[59]

For Bagehot, the advantages for Britain were so great that the government should "take a leading part in promoting the object."[60]

Furthermore, the apparent structure of incentives in other nations produced a prospective regime-building process which was likely to impose limited sacrifices onto Britain.[61] It was clear that the other two leading economies in the world, the U.S. and France, were strongly in favor of union judging from the course of official actions they had undertaken in initiating schemes of monetary union and standardization. France had just orchestrated union among franc nations in 1865. It had called together the leading nations of the world to globalize this union in 1867. Napoleon III had even dropped his insistence of union around bimetallism to entice as large a number of nations as possible to the conference. The U.S. had prompted Britain for bilateral standardization of coinage; and just before the conference, the House of Representatives had passed a resolution empowering the President to form a special commission to forge a union between the U.S. and other nations. Moreover, no serious regime spoilers were apparent. The two major Continental monetary blocs, the Northern European–German bloc and the Latin Union, were centered around nations (Germany and France) from which cooperation could be expected.[62] And the U.S., of course, supported union.[63] With this level of apparent support and lack of regime spoilers, hegemony seemed relatively inexpensive to carry out.

The conference was sponsored by the French (who in issuing invitations acted more hegemonically than the British, who accepted an invitation). Napoleon's preferred outcome was for nations simply to accept the rules governing monetary practices under the Latin Union. The response to his first question, "By what means is it most easy to realize monetary unification?", suggested a collective reluctance to consider bimetallism as a viable standard for union. In this, Napoleon was disappointed but conceded to pressure for a gold standard. Napoleon's acceptance of this standard for the Latin Union brought the whole scheme closer to British interests. Initial discussion proved favorable, given fundamental agreement on basic principles about union. A large majority accepted the idea of union based on gold and the franc at 9/10ths fine (with the 5-franc piece being the universal coin). The delegates appeared even to be moving toward agreement on the Hock proposal, which had proved a contentious issue.[64] The conference seemed to have reached a high point with broad agreement on both the general form of union and various difficult specific issues. The French Minister of Foreign Affairs, the Marquis de Moustier, in fact, made a report to Napoleon of the great success which had been achieved at the conference, and the French press hailed the proceedings as unprecedented. There was no better time for the British government to add its weight to the momentum created by the U.S. and France and forge an irresistible coalition to consummate a proposal that MPs would find strongly favorable to British interests.[65] Instead, the British delegation did just the opposite. Mr. Rivers Wilson made the following statement on behalf of his government:

> So long as [British] public opinion has not decided in favor of a change of the present system, which offers no serious inconveniences, either in wholesale or retail trade, and until it shall be incontestably demonstrated that a new system offers advantages sufficiently commanding to justify the abandonment of that which is approved by experience and rooted in the habits of the people, the English government could not believe it to be its duty to take the initiative in assimilating its coinage with those of the countries of the continent. . . . Thus, while consenting to be represented in this conference, the English government has found it necessary to place the most careful restrictions upon its delegates; their part is simply to listen to the different arguments, to study the situation as developed in discussion, and report to their government. . . . They cannot vote for any question tending to bind their government, or express any opinion to induce the belief that Great Britain would adopt the convention of 1865.[66]

The British delegation could not have done a better job of sabotaging the regime-building scheme if it had intended.[67] With the center of the world's financial and trade markets and central market for gold reluctant to support a union, the result was predictable. The move immediately dislodged Portugal, which faced extreme monetary and trade dependence on Britain, from a preliminary commitment to organize its coinage in multiples of the franc. The Prussian delegation was now less animated about the prospects of union around Napoleon's conditions. The U.S. and French delegates still persevered strongly, but even their enthusiasm for the outcome was less visible. Although discussion continued, it did so at a lower level of momentum.

With the understanding that specific proposals on practical matters for union would be undertaken at future meetings, and that any votes taken would not be binding on national governments, the British joined in an ultimate proposal that called for union based on gold and the 5-franc piece (at ⁹/₁₀ths fine) as the common denominator. There remained some international optimism about the possibility of ratifications by national legislatures, since the principles were so broad. But the uncertainty of British commitment and its effects on the commitments of other nations proved a difficult obstacle for national lawmakers to overcome.[68]

There were several rationalizations of the British reluctance to support the regime proposed in Paris, but all seemed extremely problematic when held up to careful scrutiny, and it is therefore difficult to use them as a valid justification for Britain not to support the regime. First, there was the problem of centering the union on the franc instead of the pound. Clearly, Britain's monetary status dictated that such an action would place its currency below that of France in the international monetary hierarchy. But the proposal called for other national coins to circulate with international legal tender. One of these coins would have been the sovereign, which would have circulated at equal value to the 25-franc piece. Under free competition in national currencies, the money that wins out will be the one belonging to the nation with the dominant financial and trade sectors, which in this case was the sovereign. Hence, the regime would have evolved into a de facto sterling regime. As Jevons himself noted, when coins begin to circulate concurrently in the world "there would be some means of determining which was the most suitable unit," and that "in consequence of their leading position, and in consequence of having so many colonies in which the sovereign already circulates" the British would see sterling displacing the franc and thus attaining central monetary status.[69]

A second apparent British reservation with monetary unification around the franc was that of conforming the British system of currency to the French system: the sovereign itself would have to be devalued by about ⁹/₁₀ths of 1% (.88%). This would create equal value between the sovereign and the 25-franc piece. The British government refused this concession. It is difficult to determine just how much this was a function of status considerations versus a matter of the burden of recoinage, but both cases provide little justification. The decline in status from recoining to French standards would have been restored when the sovereign proliferated in circulation. Furthermore, by many accounts from expert testimonies on the recoinage, the burden appeared small. Aside from the size of the devaluation (what amounted to about 2 pence, or 4 U.S. cents), the inconvenience would be short run (i.e., force a one-shot reestimation of wages, prices, and debt). It was pointed out that people assimilated within 12 months to the recoinage in Ireland in the early part of the century. Moreover, as Jevons noted, a very large number of British gold coins were already below current weight and therefore a general recoinage would become a necessity under any circumstances. Hence, Britain would have had to bear the burden of recoinage anyway.[70] All other comments from the conference delegates and British monetary experts on this issue underscore the insignificance of the change.

The only kind of hegemony we can make a case for with respect to British behavior at the Conference of 1867 was that of negative hegemony: blocking the regime-building initiatives of other nations.[71] But there is no evidence in either primary or secondary documents that the British approached the conference with any such insidious intentions.[72] Also, it is apparent from the *Report From the Royal Commission on International Coinage* [Great Britain (1868)] that British society, government included, exhibited a general perception that the benefits of union outweighed the costs. Hence, it is difficult even to say the British government was very rational in pursuing the national economic interest. What emerges appears to be a general sense of apathy on the part of the government to proposed regimes that carried potential benefits for the British economy. In the theoretical literature on hegemony, hegemons are either coercive or benevolent (sometimes even malevolent), but never apathetic to international developments, especially ones that affect them.[73] The British state was not benevolent (because it was interested only in its own particularistic consequences from a potential regime), nor coercive (because it forced no nations into action), nor malevolent (it didn't try to impose a regime which was favorable only to its own interests), nor did it appear to be rational given the perceptions of benefits and costs within British society.[74] In fact, to the extent that the small burdens of recoinage caused reluctance in the British government, and to the extent that this reluctance translated itself into opposition against a regime, we would have to say that Britain acted more like a weak state (i.e., unwilling to bear even small burdens) than a strong state. The U.S. and France would have ended up bearing similar if not greater burdens (and without attaining any greater benefits than those of the British), but were willing to do so.[75] In this respect, we can say they behaved more like hegemons than Great Britain. Britain neither initiated a process of building an international monetary regime based on its own standard (France did this), nor was it willing to make minimal contributions to a process initiated and strongly supported by others.

During the decade between the late 1860s and the late 1870s, much had changed in the international market for metals, and these developments placed great pressure on both Great Britain and the world to come to the conference table once more. This time, the need was not so much for a union founded on gold (most of the advanced economies of the world had already made the transition unilaterally), but for some kind of regime that would restore and stabilize the value of silver (see Table 6.3 in Chapter 6). The depreciation of silver was a major problem for every advanced economy (see Chapter 3). If the British government were behaving hegemonically in a benevolent way, the instability caused by silver's depreciation was sufficient compulsion to incite some initiative to solve the problem. But even if Britain were a self-interested hegemon looking only after its own interests, we could have expected some initiative as well. Britain felt as much pressure as any other nation through the 1870s and '80s, given the fact that India (the vital cog in Britain's multilateral payments network) remained on a silver standard. The depreciation of silver had immediate and significant effects on British-Indian trade. The period, in fact, saw no fewer than three special committee hearings instituted to consider the effects of the depreciation of silver (1876, '86, '92). The effects of the declining pound-rupee exchange rate (see Table 4.1) bore not only on bilateral trade between Britain and her colony, but gave Indian producers an advantage over British exporters in the international market. From 1876 to 1887 Indian exports of cotton yarn increased about twelvefold, from 7.927 million to 91.804 million lb. Indian exports of cotton-piece goods

Table 4.1 Average Pound-Rupee
Exchange Rate, 1865–1890*

Year	Pounds per Rupee	
1865	1s	11.835d
1870	1	11.267
1875	1	9.625
1880	1	7.956
1885	1	6.254
1890	1	6.090

Source: Ellstaetter (1895, pp. 115, 116)

increased from 15.544 million to 53.405 million yards in the same period. India's total exports of wheat almost tripled from 1877 to 1883: 5,587 to 14,194 CTW. Conversely, from 1880 to 1887 British exports of cotton yarn to the East declined from 46.420 million to 35.345 million lb., while the exports of British cotton-piece goods in the same period rose only from 509.099 million to 618.146 million yards.[76]

The problems were even more extensive than this for both India and Great Britain. Monetary experts were always fearful of the advent of severe inflation in India.[77] The depreciation made fiscal management in India more uncertain, because it was difficult to plan for transfers to Great Britain (which also bore on Britain's fiscal state). Furthermore, India's debts with Great Britain put pressure on authorities to raise taxes, something that they wanted to avoid at all costs. Perhaps the greatest localized burden fell on British civil servants in India, who were paid in rupees and found that the real value of their remittances was depreciating significantly.[78] Bonamy Price (1878, p. 395) was actually speaking for a large cross-section of British monetary elites and society when, in the year of the new Conference of 1878, he warned that the depreciation gave the British "only too much reason for fearing calamitous consequences." With the advent of a new conference, the British appeared more motivated than a decade earlier to build some kind of regime—this time, one that would check the decline in the value of silver.

Once again, the strong support of France and the U.S. (the developed world's largest users of monetary silver) would have made a prospective regime relatively easy to construct—i.e., hegemony did not appear costly. The former held tightly to the legal vestiges of the Latin Union hoping for silver to be readily accepted once again in mints. The U.S. sought some kind of solution to the political turmoil caused by the silver movement at home, a problem which the hard-money orientation of U.S. politics would not solve domestically. For the community of nations at large, it appeared that the most severe deflation of the century (1870s) softened the hard-money orientations of monetary elites enough to allow some kind of use of even a metal that had been depreciating, and of course it was easy to entice those who believed in the quantity theory of money toward a joint standard as a solution to the problem of deflation. Hence, leadership in a scheme to bring about the greater international use of silver appeared to be a painless undertaking, one that would attract even the most cautious and parsimonious hegemon.

The invitation issued by the U.S., couched in a request to discuss a bimetallist regime with a fixed international legal ratio, however, was met with great reserve by the British government. Parliament sent a letter to the Foreign Office stating: "The question to be submitted to the conference is not an open question so far as the United Kingdom is concerned."[79] The actual response to the U.S. was that Britain could not attend if the goal of the conference was to establish a bimetallist union, but it would look favorably upon discussing the prospects for an international currency (i.e., the general acceptance of certain international coins). In one respect, the interest in an international currency was consistent with Britain's place in the international monetary power structure; but without couching it in some greater union, its effects did not promise to be as beneficial to the value of silver. Furthermore, if Britain was thinking of increasing the international use of British coin, the effect might compound the depreciation of silver, since an expansion of British coin would be mostly in gold, which would displace some of the silver in circulation and reduce that metal's demand. With prompt agreement from the U.S. to consider British interests, and some strong prodding from the Secretary of State for India, the British government sent delegates to Paris for the meetings in 1878.[80]

When the proceedings began, the British delegation hardly made an auspicious start: it failed to show up until the second session, which held up substantive negotiation. Its subsequent behavior did not appear any more promising. Delegates continued to politely refuse the proposals of the U.S., something the government (in deference to Anglo-American relations) did not want to be put in a position to do from the start, but which the delegates found inevitable given their instructions.[81] Right at the beginning of the third session (only the second substantive session), the British delegate Goschen revived the devastating rhetoric of Rivers Wilson 11 years before and stated that the British delegation was "bound . . . by instructions that did not leave them freedom of action."[82] But Goschen made things even worse by pointing out other reasons why a regime could not emerge from the deliberations. He noted that other delegations besides the British were prohibited from voting on propositions that would threaten the domestic standards already in place in their nations. Goschen mentioned Norway and Latin Union nations in this regard. He added that the likely supporters of a regime were themselves not in a position to affect the price of silver: Russia, Austria-Hungary, and Italy were all on fiat standards at the time. Finally, he averred how difficult it would be to open mints to silver when the German silver stock was hanging over the market (i.e., conversion of excess silver threatening even greater depreciation).[83] The shock waves that ensued were reminiscent of those that followed Wilson's statement in 1867: the conference proceeded, but at a lower level of enthusiasm.

The U.S. maintained its goal of international bimetallism throughout the proceedings, and at the fourth session Goschen once more recalled his assessment of the unlikelihood of agreement under the circumstances, and even added that under these conditions further deliberations on the U.S. proposals were pointless. He repeated his position at the sixth session, but he agreed to let the U.S. make one more appeal to the body at large. When it did, the body of delegates at large allowed both the French and British to respond in the name of the other delegates. The French-British joint response essentially placed the delegates in a position to agree not to agree. The proposals embodied in the joint statement called for each nation to decide its policy on silver for itself, and that the body at large looked unfavorably on an international bimetallist regime.[84] There was little to do beyond this, and the meetings ended with all the perfunctory diplomatic courtesy.

Once again, British behavior at the conference was more in keeping with a nation wishing to block a regime from emerging than one intent on seeing a regime built. This seemed to go against all British interests tied up in the value of silver, which by consensus were extreme. The argument that this was the act of a rational hegemon blocking an undesirable regime (bimetallism) so as to preserve a desirable regime (gold) is not compelling. If the British sought the preservation of gold standards in the world, why did they block possibilities for a gold regime 11 years before? Furthermore, the British had coexisted in a world of bimetallism for decades as one of only a few gold standard nations; why would Britain push for a larger gold club now when it had not historically? Furthermore, a bimetallist regime would have solved their silver problem even if they themselves made only marginal contributions. But even if the British were averse to international bimetallism, they still could have initiated or built a price-support regime for silver where nations simply made commitments to increase the circulation of token coin. Clearly Britain had the influence to do this, considering how willing the U.S. was to shape the conference agenda in order to assure Britain's attendance.

The conference essentially presented Britain with an opportunity to solve its problem through a relatively low-cost form of hegemony.[85] The two major silver nations, the U.S and France, were anxious to support a regime. Even in the face of the reluctance of Germany to participate and Germany's stock of excess silver, a strong British commitment could have made up for any fears of German liquidation: here Britain would have had to commit to the conversion of some amount of Germany's public liquidation of its excess silver stock, or extract a commitment out of Germany for a gradual liquidation.[86] Britain failed not only to take up the gauntlet, but from the beginning to the end its delegates acted in ways that made cooperation more difficult rather than easier. And if it wanted a different type of regime, there were many opportunities to initiate such things at the conference (like at the sixth session with the joint response with France), or initiate such a thing unilaterally, or even go outside of the conference and negotiate with the U.S and France. Instead, it used strategic opportunities to perpetuate the silver problem rather than solve it.[87] British behavior was quite inconsistent with the statements by the British delegation throughout the conference that the British government sought to maintain the extensive use of silver in monetary systems. This, in fact, was the truth, but the behavior of the British state was poorly adapted to its goals. Even as a nation that preferred to free ride on the cooperation of others, which in fact it attempted, its actions were poorly executed. A clever free rider in Britain's position could have issued grand supportive rhetoric, even if the real commitments were limited. A show of good intention was crucial for cooperation, since some apparent support from Britain was seen by delegates from all nations as a necessary condition for success in building a regime. Certainly it would have emboldened the powerful silver nations to build a regime. The British state appeared not only to be a poor hegemon, but also a less than astute free rider, and more generally a poor agent for the British national economic interest.

With silver continuing to depreciate and the pound-rupee exchange rate continuing to fall in the late 1870s and early '80s (see Table 4.1), agitation over the silver problem was compelling the British state toward some kind of action. Influential Commercial Boards of London were calling for some policy toward the silver problem. Representatives of the Liverpool Chamber of Commerce carried their cause directly to the office of the Chancellor. Many bankers were petitioning for some kind of bimetallist regime. Several Bank of England Directors were also joining in the chorus for silver.[88] The first response by the British government to the pressure was quite limited. It sought to work directly on the pound-rupee rate by reducing the drawing of Council Bills (which were substituting for silver shipments to India) and arranging a 10-million-pound-sterling loan from India to Britain. This actually served to advance the value of silver a bit. The advance was quickly followed by Germany's liquidation of half a million dollars of its silver stock, which served to check the increase.[89] The bilateral initiative was ineffective outside of the short run, and conditions worsened. Banks involved in Eastern business found their equity depreciating along with the fall of silver. The Banks of Australia and India saw the value of their stocks depreciate by 25%, the Banks of Hong Kong and Shanghai by 33%, and the old Oriental by 75%. Business conditions were worse than in France and the U.S. Banks and businesses continued to fail. Disraeli called it a period of depression seldom equaled in British history. And popular and public opinion were gravitating around the pound-rupee problem as central to the economic woes Britain was suffering. By the early 1880s, the British government was preparing to enter monetary negotiations with unprecedented domestic pressure to build a viable international regime to solve the silver problem.[90]

When France and the U.S., in 1881, issued a joint invitation to the community of nations (including Britain), these nations had even more incentives (as the silver problem worsened) to cooperate on building a regime than they had three years before. This time Germany did attend the conference, and the excess silver which was holding the world hostage could be placed on the agenda and controlled multilaterally. But even in the midst of this unparalleled momentum, the initial British response was all too familiar. It held that the British state could not support any bimetallist union, but out of courtesy would send delegates (to observe and report back) with the understanding that Britain would not be bound by any resolutions achieved at the conference. With some of the momentum already diminished, delegates met once more in Paris in 1881. Again the British delegation was late in arriving, this time the tardiness bearing even more on British interests as the early proceedings were laboring to select a special committee to draw up a formal questionnaire that would serve as an agenda for the conference: a strategically poor move by any nation (weak or strong) that sought to shape negotiations in their own interests. That the agenda was subject to negotiation and the fact that Germany made a preliminary statement that it would consider placing limits on its liquidation of excess silver appeared to give Britain a crucial opening. Now with the three other core economies supporting a regime, British support would prove definitive. Furthermore, Britain could shape the agenda in a way that assured its first preference: a price-support regime rather than union based on bimetallism. British delegates, however, did not work to shape the agenda; nor did the early concessions they made (to ensure the holding of a silver reserve by the Bank of England equal to $\frac{1}{4}$th its gold holdings—something already allowed by the Act of 1844) sway others into perceiving sincere British cooperation.[91]

As in the Conference of 1878, Britain followed up a preliminary lack of support in response to the invitation with a diplomatic statement early in the proceedings that compounded perceptions of British reluctance. The British delegation at this conference actually had little to say. But when Britain was actually making statements about concessions (i.e., on the Bank of England reserve) they were mistimed. One such occurrence took place when Fremantle brought up the concessions in the midst of a highly theoretical argument during the seventh session. Another occurred in the twelfth session when the proceedings were approaching a point of no return. The delegation ended its participation with as vacuous a statement of support as could be expected: the British delegation reaffirmed an interest in discovering a "means of giving its co-operation in the work undertaken by the Conference, namely, the restoration of the value of silver."[92] With the U.S. and France strongly favoring a regime, and Germany more willing than three years earlier to support one, Britain was in a crucial position to determine the success or failure of cooperation. Hence, with Britain's reluctance, the negotiations came to naught. Pierson of Holland succinctly summarized the consequences of Britain's position: "You have but to utter a word, and the thing is done. Others are hesitating only because they are afraid of failing without you."[93]

Russell (1898, p. 303) underscored how much Britain had wanted the conference to succeed. It was, however, difficult to square such a preference with the subsequent actions of the delegates. He also noted how much Britain desired for other nations to solve its silver problem for her (i.e., free ride). But even as a free rider, Britain showed no perspicacity. Obvious strategic opportunities to generate momentum that would stimulate a regime supported by others were squandered. When the proceedings moved adversely, opportunities to resuscitate momentum were missed. In most cases the actions undertaken worked more to discourage than encourage cooperation, but even as a blocking force the strategy of the delegation was inconsistent, as it continued to repeat the one concrete concession it had made in three conferences. It is difficult to find anything that is consistent with hegemonic behavior in this panoply of motives and rhetoric, as diverse as theories of hegemony are. The behavior of the British delegation suggests, once again, a disposition of apathy in the face of regime-building initiatives, with a very visible commitment not to entertain any changes in British monetary practices for the sake of solving the silver problem. But even this apathy does not square with the obvious and pressing concerns exhibited by both British society and elites about the problem in the exchanges with India. Britain acted as if it was apathetic when it was clearly not. It was most certainly immovable with respect to bearing any burdens to solve a problem which had a collective cause. And in this respect, it once more acted like a weak rather than a powerful nation.

Even outside of the sphere of the conferences, Britain's own unilateral responses to the problem with India appeared to be more characteristic of a weak rather than a strong state. The one significant undertaking it initiated (working directly on the Indian-British exchange through bilateral transfers) was quickly discontinued when

Germany began profiting from the rise in the value of silver, which counteracted the favorable movement in the exchanges. It is clear that Britain perceived Germany's power to disrupt the exchanges as greater than the power of Britain (the leading financial power in the world) and India (the leading silver market in the world) to stabilize them. There appeared a sense of low self-esteem at work here. Moreover, as two dominant players in the market for metals, there was much a bilateral initiative between India and Britain could have done to at least limit the silver problem. Seyd, for example, suggested minting corresponding coins (4-shilling silver piece for Britain) in both India and Britain. The greater demand for silver engendered by concurrent circulation would serve to help stabilize the market for silver, but moreover the 4-shilling denomination would create a common multiple which would go far in encouraging the British goal of introducing greater circulation of British currency in India.[94] And even if bilateral action were insufficient to achieve desired conditions in the market for metals, it is difficult to believe that a British request for support from the U.S. and France (in the face of concerted British action) would not evoke some cooperation, both nations being so adversely affected by the fall of silver. Both as a hegemon that worked alone, then, and as one that worked with the support of others, the expression of British hegemony in the early 1880s was less than distinguished. Britain proved to be neither a benevolent nor a coercive hegemon, nor anything in between. It acted quite the part of a weak and apathetic nation.

During the rest of the decade the pressure from British commercial interests and financial interests tied up in Eastern business continued. The Gold and Silver Commission itself came out in favor of a bimetallist regime among all other nations except Great Britain. When 1892 came, and the U.S. once more issued invitations for a conference, the British felt compelled to attend. France, which was now less intense in its support, was still willing to cooperate if not willing to initiate. The British delegation came in with the feeling that, as Houldsworth noted, "there will never be a permanent solution to this difficulty [of silver] until we have an international bimetallic agreement."[95] Rather than initiating the proceedings with a call for a bimetallist union, the U.S. delegation opted to come in at a lower-order target: a price-support scheme for silver. Since this entailed only commitments on silver purchases with a minimal likelihood to effect changes in currency laws, it seemed that the initial agenda was one that would not alienate Britain as higher-order quests for union had done in the past.

The British delegate Rothschild did not disappoint when he made the first substantive proposal (a plan to support the price of silver) ever issued by a British delegation at any of the conferences. As the points of the plan became clear, however, it also became apparent that Britain wanted the world (primarily the U.S.) to bear the burden of its own silver problem. Now that the British state had finally assumed a more dynamic posture in monetary negotiations, it was doing so in a way that was obviously exploitative.[96] Whereas before, most of the anger the British drew was for their reluctance to support mutually beneficial regimes, the ire they drew now was targeted toward their attempts at free riding. The Rothschild Plan, intended to be a deft coup by the British to sucker other nations into accepting the majority of the burden of buying silver, fooled no one. The five-year Plan called for the U.S. to continue its present level of silver purchases (54 million ounces a year), while Europe would stand ready to purchase an additional 5 million pounds sterling, but only in the event that the price of silver dipped below 44 pence per ounce. It was fairly obvious to all the other delegates that if the Plan were instituted, Europe would do little buying of silver. The price shortly before the conference had been hovering around 43 ppp. Any news of a successful international conference would immediately bring the price up. And with the U.S. maintaining its purchases, it was unlikely that there would be a large enough depreciation in five years to activate European purchases.

The Plan drew much criticism and generated antagonism, especially from the U.S. and Latin Union nations who felt targets of British exploitation. At a roadblock, the conference's labors shifted to a smaller committee which would draw up a plan for the body at large. The committee resuscitated the Levy Plan from past conferences, which called for introducing more silver into fractional use (i.e., a regime regulating the purchase of bullion for smaller coin). But here the British found it too much of a sacrifice to replace small gold coin and lower-denomination notes with silver. Other nations found the Plan too weak to form the basis of a regime. Agreement was not forthcoming, but it was again striking how reluctant Great Britain was in the face of what by most accounts was a trivial adjustment in their circulation.[97] Discussion proceeded toward more abstract and complex plans oriented around buying commitments on the part of nations. Britain might have helped the cause of silver by bringing the debate back to general points of practicality, but it merely followed along with the current of discussion. As with the previous two conferences, this one adjourned without a resolution.

British behavior at this conference did show some motives normally attributed to coercive or malevolent hegemons: that their self-interest manifests itself in regimes where others bear a disproportionate burden. Indeed the Rothschild Plan had such an intention, but coercive or malevolent hegemons expend resources to encourage other nations to cooperate. In this instance Britain did not. In fact, when it had a chance to agree to a price-support scheme (its preferred option), it refused to commit to even a small sacrifice in taking some gold coins and low-denomination paper out of circulation. Hegemons may be self-interested, but they are never overly parsimonious (i.e., they all will expend some resources in encouraging others to cooperate). Looking at the magnitude of the silver problem, it is difficult to argue that British officials could have possibly perceived the sacrifice in adjusting small coins to be greater than the benefits in arresting the decline in the value of silver. In fact, the replacement of small coins which were worn, and the disappearance in circulation of small-denomination coins, were two of Parliament's biggest monetary concerns of the period. This dictated that some additional public buying of silver by Britain to support a regime would probably carry great benefit for the British monetary system (in terms of improving circulation). Therefore, one must question the rationality of the British state. But if it were acting from motives of the other category of hegemony—benevolently—it clearly lacked the will to make even limited sacrifices to solve the world's silver problem.

Reviewing British participation in all four of the conferences of the period, one would have to say that British monetary diplomacy in the last third of the 19th century left a trail which cuts sharply against common visions of how powerful nations behave in international economic systems. In fact, if anything, British behavior was more reflective of a weak nation, one with limited monetary resources and influence.[98] Nations that were less hegemonic than Britain (with respect to monetary influence) actually acted more hegemonically than Britain. The two nations that were acting in ways most typically hegemonic were the U.S. and France, which, together or alone, initiated all the conferences of the period and proved willing to make significant sacrifices to see regimes built. This was especially true of France, both in and outside of the conferences.[99]

In all four conferences Britain occupied an influential position in deciding whether some regime would be constructed. In all cases, building a regime would have been beneficial to both Britain and the world. But Britain never mobilized any significant support for a regime. Had it exercised even the most minimal hegemony, something might have been consummated at any one of the conferences.[100] But it didn't. In fact, its actions more often served as an obstacle to cooperation.[101] It never made it easier for cooperative nations to start a regime. Furthermore, it proved to be an extremely poor bargainer: its delegates participated little in the discussions, they had a propensity for showing up late, and they failed to take advantage of strategic opportunities.

When Britain did act hegemonically, it did so in a very inconsistent way. In 1867 it was against union around the franc, but never pushed for union around the pound. In fact, its delegates voted for the resolution citing the franc as the international numeraire. In subsequent conferences, it sought to free ride (more consistent with coercive hegemony) on the cooperation of others, but never used even limited commitments to encourage others to build a regime.[102]

Time and again Britain had an opportunity to bring about a regime which was in its interest, and time and again it failed to do so. Two factors seem to stand out as crucial to explaining British behavior, but both are also quite problematic as satisfactory explanations. First, it was clear throughout that Britain would not make the smallest change in its monetary system to bring an international regime into being. Perhaps a maniacal monetary orthodoxy explains Britain's reluctance.[103] Orthodoxy in Britain was oriented around the nature of the standard; hence we would not expect Britain to change its gold standard. But there would have been no problem in manipulating the issue of small coin to raise the international demand for silver (this was consistent with a gold orthodoxy). Furthermore, Britain could have avoided any change at all merely by allowing India to take on her burden of silver purchase. All that had to be done in this case was to increase India's demand for silver. Britain had, after all, made a habit of using its colonies in the national interest, and other nations were in fact more concerned with silver demand in India than in Britain. Public documents, however, do not show any pattern of concerns consistent with such extreme fears to tinker.[104] If anything, the documents do show that the concern about the silver problem absolutely swamped any reservations about costs of tinkering. In this respect, British behavior is difficult to explain both rationally and ideologically.

A second factor appears to gravitate around moral hazard: i.e., Britain sat back because of its expectations that the U.S. and France would ultimately solve the problem. Such thoughts did make themselves apparent from time to time, but negotiations were an iterated rather than one-shot process. Britain had an opportunity to learn that without British support, neither nation felt compelled to take on the burden. Not only did the history of failed conferences tell the British this, but the conference participants were making such statements directly to the British and other delegates.

No single factor, or simple set of factors, explains what appears to be undue apathy on the part of a nation which by most accounts possessed hegemonic capabilities in the monetary area. It has been the intention of this chapter to show that the behavior of the British state was not consistent with common visions of monetary hegemony. Curiosity about the sources of actual British behavior appears to be better served in this case by looking at each individual opportunity for the British to negotiate a regime as being a point of convergence in the intersection of prevailing forces in British politics and international relations. In this case, a search for historic trends which illuminate systematic factors do not do an adequate job in explaining British behavior, irrespective of whether Britain had hegemonic power or not. Such an explanation, given British motives, would have demanded more concerted action in regime building on the part of Britain whether it was a hegemon or not.

If the conferences showed any sort of consistent hegemony on the part of the British state at all, one would have to say that the hegemony was either self-interested but incompetent (i.e., executed stupidly), or benevolent but parsimonious (i.e., they cared about the stability of the international system but were willing to make very few sacrifices to see their benevolent goals actualized). The first would lead to behavior that was not typically hegemonic, while the latter would lead to inaction (which was not typical of hegemons either). Neither of these is a category in the present hegemonic-stability literature, but both appear to be better explanations of British participation in international monetary negotiations in the latter 19th century than are the conventional hegemonic-stability categories.

In sum, the evidence on the behavior of the British state with respect to monetary relations during the gold standard period suggests that the state was far from a hegemonic actor in the global monetary system. It carried on very limited contacts with international banking and investment, and it also carried on limited control over and contact with the only viable agent for British monetary hegemony: the Bank of England. Moreover, the behavior of its delegations at international conferences violated all common visions of appropriate action by dominant monetary powers. It is fairly certain that the search for British monetary hegemony in the realm of the state, both in terms of starting and stabilizing regimes, is misplaced.

5

Hegemony and the Bank of England

That the British state did not behave hegemonically (i.e., that we cannot attribute the rise and maintenance of the gold standard to the actions of the British state) does not *prima facie* invalidate the thesis that the gold standard was somehow hegemonized. In fact, more scholars have attributed the stability of the gold standard to management on the part of the Bank of England than have attributed it to the British state. Clearly, if the Bank was a source of management, it was not in the service of the state. But the Bank itself may have taken it upon itself to stabilize the international system. The justification for such an act would have been quite apparent, and consistent with a variety of strands of hegemony, both of a benevolent and coercive nature. If behaving in the interest of the system (i.e., benevolently), the Bank may have taken up the moral duty of being a central bank for the world (managing the international business cycle and credit system, and providing liquidity in last resort). No other institution was situated in as favorable a position to affect world monetary conditions: being the central bank in the world's major financial center. From a purely self-interested point of view, on the other hand, it was rational to stabilize the international monetary system because international economic transactions were preponderantly executed by British citizens (as consumers, traders, investors, and bankers).

Fetter (1965, p. 255) observes how widespread has been the vision among 20th century economists that the stability of the gold standard relied on the "Bank of England action as managing director, or executive secretary." The vision of the Bank as a manager of the international gold standard is both a common and old one. Keynes (1930, V. II) and Scammell ([1965] 1985), and more recently Eichengreen (1986b), saw the Bank as the leader of the international orchestra of central banks, and it was to the harmonization of this orchestra under the Bank's leadership that the gold standard owed its stability. Beyen (1949, p. 14) argues that it was the Bank's policy to be an international "shock absorber." Cleveland (1976) concurs. Wood (1939, p. 139) avers that it was the Bank's special position that led her to "guide the international standard." Kindleberger (1984, p. 68) calls the Bank the "central focus of [the] management" of the classical gold standard.

All suggest the ease with which the Bank could manage the international monetary system given the influence British interest rates had over international capital flows (i.e., British rates dictated world credit conditions and the business cycle). Since British commercial bills financed a disproportionate amount of world trade, British rates would dictate the ease with which traders could obtain credit to purchase goods;

this directly impacted on foreign incomes. Also, being a dominant financial market, Britain could attract or repel investment depending on its prevailing rates.[1] These market rates were purported to be linked to the Bank rate; hence the Bank had significant power to dictate the level of liquidity in the international system, and foreign income trends. The impact of the Bank as an international monetary hegemon would, therefore, depend to a large extent (but not entirely) on its influence over, and management of, the British monetary system, especially the London financial market. What international hegemony could not be accounted for by the Bank's manipulation of the London and British markets would have to be sought in a more direct international role. This chapter will explore the extent of both: (1) hegemony through the London and British markets (indirect hegemony), and (2) direct hegemony over the international monetary system.

The search for both types of hegemony is coterminous with an exploration of the central banking functions and goals of the Bank of England. To the extent that it was a hegemon through its manipulation of the British financial system, we would expect to find some kind of significant central banking functions and/or goals directed to the British system, especially London. In other words, we should expect to find some kind of significant influence over and management of British finance. To the extent that the hegemony of the international system was direct, we should see the Bank undertaking central bank functions and/or adopting central bank goals which were applied directly to the stabilization of the international monetary system itself.

Central bank functions and goals are many and varied. Furthermore, the goals and functions have changed quite significantly over time. However, certain fundamental characteristics of conventional central banking have been fairly prevalent across time and theory: stabilizing the price level around some desired target, control over the system of credit, managing the business cycle, lending in last resort to the financial system, providing clearing functions to the banking system, supervising banknote issue, issuing notes, and maintaining convertibility. For convenience, these will be grouped into four categories, and the domestic and international functions and goals of the Bank of England will be analyzed with respect to each so as to determine the extent of its hegemony over the gold standard: (1) acknowledging public responsibility, (2) managing the reserve and standing ready as a last-resort lender, (3) managing the monetary system, and (4) managing financial crises.

This chapter first considers the extent of indirect hegemony of the Bank of England over the classical gold standard, and then considers the extent of direct hegemony by the Bank.

The search for both direct and indirect hegemony, and for both strong and weak hegemony, fails to yield satisfying results for those proponents of the Bank of England's hegemonic leadership under the gold standard. Not only can we say that the Bank did not manage the international monetary system, but it is questionable whether it even managed the British monetary system. The Bank actually acknowledged little responsibility for the British monetary system itself. In fact, the Bank's own private goals often worked to the detriment of the British financial system (i.e., was a source of destabilizing impulses for British finance). In the role of British central banker (as a lender of last resort, manager of the reserve and the British economy, and manager of crises) it consistently showed itself to be a poor guardian of the monetary system. Its reserves were historically low relative to the level of liquidity in the British system, it did little to manage British finance and the business cycle as its own power over the financial community was limited, and its behavior in crises suggests that it may have more often compounded financial distress than mitigated it.

These outcomes are all the more visible at the international level. The Bank was even less of an international than domestic central banker. Acknowledgments of international responsibility were less visible than acknowledgments of domestic responsibility. In turbulent periods at the international level (i.e., crises, shortages of liquidity) the Bank hardly distinguished itself. In fact, the Bank of England was more often the recipient of liquidity than the provider of liquidity. It was quite common for the Bank of France to come to the aid of the Bank of England and British finance in times of liquidity shortages and crises. In this respect, the Bank of France was a better candidate for international monetary hegemony than was the Bank of England. If the Bank of England was weak relative to British finance, it was all the more weak relative to the global financial system. And these weaknesses grew as these two financial systems became larger and more complex. Perhaps it is enough to wonder how the Bank was able to defend its own convertibility. Central banks of nations that were successful in maintaining convertibility did so either by running up excess gold reserves or through long-term borrowing. The Bank of England did neither. It is therefore not surprising that the Bank so often avoided concerted efforts to stabilize the British and world economies. That the Bank persisted in what might be called a false splendor during the gold standard is also the reason why the international system under the gold standard remained fairly stable. Neither the system nor the Bank experienced frequent or severe shocks, as both political and financial crises were limited during the period (see Chapter 7). The few times the system and the Bank's resources were tested, sufficient external support was forthcoming to place both the system and the Bank back on a calm path. Hence, we can say that the gold standard was stable for the same reason that the Bank of England remained solvent: neither was ever severely tested by international conditions during the three and a half decades demarcating the classical gold standard period.

Indirect Hegemony: The Bank of England and Central Banking in Great Britain

There are two fundamental ways in which we can attribute international monetary hegemony to the Bank of England insofar as its central banking functions were executed with respect to the British financial system (i.e., indirect): a weak form of hegemony and a strong form. In the weak form, international hegemony would be perfectly coterminous with domestic central banking. Since London and Great Britain comprised the very center of the world's monetary system, any conditions in the core would strongly influence international conditions in general. Therefore, a stable international monetary system could be enhanced by keeping the British system itself stable—i.e., the Bank would stabilize the international system by stabilizing the domestic system. In the other type of indirect hegemony (strong form of hegemony), the Bank would actually manipulate the domestic system (i.e., the credit cycle, the business cycle, the banking system) to effect specific conditions in the international system.

For the first to hold, we would expect to find that domestic central banking functions and goals on the part of the Bank of England were both present and effective across the four central banking categories specified. To the extent that the Bank did not exhibit effective central banking of a domestic nature, the weak form of international hegemony is less compelling. For the second to hold, not only would we expect to see effective central banking on the part of the Bank (i.e., the domestic system is managed toward specific outcomes), but we would expect the Bank to exhibit significant power over the British system.[2] We would expect the latter to be a necessary condition for strong hegemony via the domestic market, since it is inconceivable that the international system could be directed or stabilized by a domestic monetary system that was only marginally responsive to the direction of a central bank. It may, however, be the case that the domestic system exhibits some instabilities while it is manipulated in the interests of the international system (e.g., imposing deflation at home to abate international inflation). In this case, effective central banking may be absent even though a central bank is engaging in strong hegemony. But it is unlikely that such a thing could be prevalent, since instability in the domestic monetary systems of core nations can quickly proliferate internationally. Therefore, as a general rule, we should expect both effective domestic central banking and significant power over domestic finance for the strong form of hegemony to hold.

We should expect to see the acknowledgment of some public responsibility to the British monetary system in any kind of indirect hegemony, whether strong or weak. It is with this issue of public responsibility that we begin our assessment of the Bank of England's hegemony.

Acknowledging Public Responsibility

In this particular category of central banking, the origins of the Bank of England and of most early (i.e., before 1800) central banks are indicative. The modern conceptualization of central banking was foreign to the standard operation of most central banks even up until the eve of World War I.[3] The Bank of England had its specific origin in the fiscal needs of a British state which sought advances to finance its war against France in the late 17th century. In response to this need for war funds, the government invited financiers of London to subscribe to a joint-stock company which would be used by the government to manage its accounts (i.e., the government's banker as opposed to a national bank) and be called upon occasionally to lend to the government. The nature of the management and functions of the Bank of England remained fundamentally unchanged in a legal sense until after World War I.[4] Its charter and bank laws did not impose any public responsibilities on it that (aside from handling the government accounts) were in any way inconsistent with a privately owned bank of issue which carried on the standard business of the day (discounting, accepting deposits, issuing banknotes, making advances, and dealing in securities). Overlying, but fundamentally independent of, these practices were its public responsibilities to the British state: manage public debt (manage government bonds and disperse dividends), make liquidity available to the state in need, collect taxes, hold government deposits, make transfers, and hold the national reserve. Aside from these functions, the Bank operated as nothing more than a large commercial bank. In the words of Governor of the Bank Thompson Hankey (1873, p. 114), the business of the Bank did "not differ . . . from that of any well-conducted Bank in London." Its customers, in order of importance, were: the government, banks (London clearing banks, merchant banks, British overseas banks, foreign banks), discount houses, and private individuals.[5]

That the essential structure of the Bank was founded on private commercial banking created a strong profit motive.[6] The Directors, as agents of the shareholders, were entrusted with looking after the size of the dividend. Any public consciousness or responsibility held by the Court or individual Directors with respect to stabilizing the British financial system would have had to invariably come into conflict with this profit motive.[7] Of principal importance in the Bank's perceived public duties was as the chief repository for national convertibility (i.e., the holder of the nation's gold stock).[8] This came in direct conflict with the profit motive, since gold holdings were nonworking balances. Metallic reserve holdings did not generate interest earnings. Hence, as more of the Bank's resources were held in the form of gold reserves (e.g., as opposed to securities and foreign exchange), profits declined commensurately. Critics of the Bank's management of British finance, like Walter Bagehot ([1873] 1921), based many of their criticisms on this private imperative of the shareholder. The Bank's historically low level of gold holdings was repeatedly criticized as a manifestation of the Court's tendency to put the interests of the shareholders ahead of the British banking system.[9] To the extent that the profit motive of the Bank of England, therefore, was a principal goal of the Court, public responsibility of the Bank suffered.

Fetter (1965, p. 61) points out that early on (in the period 1793–1811) many of the Bank's actions and statements from Directors gave the impression that the Bank's own internal image was merely one of a commercial bank that was obliged to lend to the government, and not an underwriter of British or London finance. It was the severity of the crisis of 1793 and the reluctance of the Bank to make advances to the financial community that brought the role of the Bank into significant public debate for the first time.[10] Statements from the Directors themselves suggest that the Bank wished to impress upon the financial community a self-image of independence from any public responsibility that might restrain the discretion of the Court. It was fairly common to hear Bank Governors deny public responsibilities outright throughout the century.[11] Governor Morris stated that the Bank "is to be managed in the same way as any other bank." He noted that the only significant difference between the Bank and other commercial banks was that the Bank was "carrying on business at a much larger scale."[12] Hankey (1873, pp. xi, 114) called it a commercial bank like any other and claimed that the only duty of the Directors was to maintain their reserve at a sufficient level to meet the demands of their customers, "knowing quite well that the gold question can take care of itself."[13] Hankey and Hubbard warned financiers that when financial houses exhausted their funds, they should not count on the Bank for help.[14] In response to the suggestion that the Bank managed the banking system through leadership of a core of principal banks, Governor Gibbs adamantly retorted, "I repudiate all responsibility as the chief of a confederation of banks."[15]

The private interests of the Bank were most visible in the Court's responses to legislation which adversely affected the Bank's ledger. Such legislation was systematically met with strong protests from the Directors. When the Peel Income Tax Law of 1842 eliminated the preferential tax rate on terminable annuities, which the Bank held in large number, the Bank made strong statements of disfavor to Parliament. Similarly, when Gladstone instituted a policy of deferred payment to the Bank on securities, and when service charges levied by the Bank on the government were revised downward, the reaction from the Court was strong, unified, and swift (something generally lacking in the Court's public initiatives). One ongoing manifestation of the Bank's profit motive was the reluctance with which the Bank acceded to government pressure to increase the number of its branches. The Court did not desire to increase its branches because the existing ones had proved to be less than satisfactory in generating profits. This private concern directly conflicted with the Bank's capacity to manage the British credit system, as more branches would give the Bank greater influence over regional credit conditions.[16] The Bank also resisted for years (before succeeding in suspending) the practice of reporting bankers' balances as distinct from private deposits. The Court historically saw the need to report the balances as an infringement on any common bankers' rights to privacy (from the government and the rest of the market).[17]

It is fairly clear that whatever public responsibilities were felt by individual Directors and Governors, and were ultimately manifest in Bank policies, combined with the Bank's private imperatives to form a kind of institutional schizophrenia—an identity crisis that was as much discussed in the London financial press as it was in the Court itself.[18] Like any other group of individuals that arrive at collective decisions, it is expected that they would not function as some monolith. Although the decisions represented consensus (coerced or natural), each Director brought a different set of beliefs to bear on each decision. The public burdens which the Directors themselves respected were no doubt as varied as the opinions in the financial press about the proper public functions which the Bank should undertake. Even this set of values was dynamic rather than static. As Bank Governor Weguelin noted, "The opinion of the Court fluctuates very much."[19] Directors differed over goals, means, and expectations about the effectiveness of means. There was disagreement over what in fact was the Bank's most effective means of influencing credit in Britain: some believed it was the rate while others believed it was the manipulation of the terms under which bills were discounted.[20] As King (1936, p. 159) noted, the Directors "realized in a general way that the Bank's special position gave it special responsibilities . . . , but they had no clear idea of how that realization should be translated into practice and day-to-day policy." Hence, even when acting out of public consciousness, it was not altogether clear what paths the Court would take and what duties of central banking these conveyed.

The problem of the Bank's dual mandate (profit and public) became salient after the Bank's perceived lack of public behavior in the crisis of 1793. But even after the Bank Act of 1844, which itself was stimulated by ongoing dissatisfaction with the Bank as a public institution in the early decades of the century, there still existed a "chaotic situation as regards opinion on what the Bank was and how it was supposed to act." Fetter (1965, p. 259) adds that the problem of the Bank's responsibility was as controversial and more confused in the 1870s than it had been in 1847. And even by the 1890s, states Clapham (1944, V. II, p. 372), "the Directors . . . remained divided between two conceptions of their business." Most of the statements from Directors that acknowledged dual responsibilities were rarely specific about the actual operationalization of the dual mandate.[21] Governor Morris's statement that the Bank was "bound to consider both" was quite the norm.[22]

It was also a style of the Directors to deny that the dual mandate threatened the stability of the British monetary system. Statements that the two were perfectly compatible, and even complementary, were common responses to public concerns about the Bank's profit motive. In its boldest form this response stated that the Bank had a duty to be as profitable as possible so that it could properly shoulder its public responsibilities.[23] There are in fact some scenarios that could be conceived in which a profit motive might be compatible with fundamental dictates of central banking. Following the market rate, for example, could lead to effective countercyclical policy, i.e., reduce the demand for money when the economy was growing too fast, and increase the demand under conditions of slow growth. Following the rate could also be consistent with the maintenance of convertibility, since funds could be attracted in times of financial distress and let go when conditions normalized. Furthermore, responsible note issue and management of gold reserves was absolutely in keeping with standard operating procedure of any bank of issue: mismanagement would affect its own solvency.[24] But if we look at the historical trail of developments in British finance owing to the Bank's quest for profit, we see the compatibility between public and private imperatives as dubious at best. The concern for dividends led to actions that were often diametrically opposed to responsible central banking.[25]

Many of the open market operations, for example, that went on around periods of financial crisis were more geared toward securing the Bank's own liquidity than pumping liquidity into the economy. These operations often drained more than maintained liquidity in the banking system.[26] The Court's own concern with never deviating too far from the market (i.e., keeping some proximity between the Bank and market rates) not only inhibited the Bank from pursuing an independent role in the market (a necessary condition for management of the credit system), but often had destabilizing effects as well.[27] Conforming to market conditions when credit was tight had the effect of compounding the shortage of liquidity and its effects on the economy. Conforming to the market when credit was abundant could lead to a loss of reserves (thus affecting confidence in the financial community), fuel speculation, and compound an overheated economy. In any case, the Court's typical use of its rate to maintain desired levels of liquidity at the Bank (as opposed to using other means of attracting liquidity as a substitute for the rate) and the rate's sensitivity to prevailing market conditions effected a volatility in the rate that was often criticized as inimical to responsible central banking, which required a more stable rate (see Figure A.1 in Statistical Appendix).[28] In its normal lending operations, notes Sayers (1976, V. I, p. 45), the Bank pursued conventional private banking behavior without "any special regard for what the gold standard . . . required." The market constraint made the Bank too slow to react both to external drains and internal speculation.

The management of its reserve ratio was also strongly configured by normal banking procedures, often to the detriment of the role as the keeper of the national reserve. The reserve ratio followed a procyclical pattern: being lower in the upswing of the business cycle and rising in the downswing. This suggests that the Bank was indulging in an expansion of business when the demand for money was up, and retrenched when demand was down. Hence, its services reflected the normal price elasticity of banking. But this trend in reserves compounded the business cycle, and the Bank found itself short of reserves when demand was greatest.[29] Moreover, its bouts of aggressive discounting were an ongoing contributor to speculative fevers leading to crises throughout the century.[30]

Its own competition in the market for notes and commercial banking created a posture toward other banks, even in crisis, that was diametrically opposed to a stable banking system. It fought very hard over the course of the century to preserve as much of a monopoly on commercial banking and note issue as it could. When these monopolies were broken down in regions outside London, the Court retrenched into its own London market. In this sense, the Bank had an incentive to let banks which competed in its services fail, and much of its behavior was consistent with such an incentive.[31] The Bank was historically reluctant to set up discount accounts and offer accommodation to other banks of issue and commercial banks, even in crisis. This carried especially destabilizing potential, because these banks held a large number of bills as reserves. In the crisis of 1847, it refused accommodation to other banks of issue. The Bank restricted rediscount facilities to bill brokers after the crisis of 1857, a move the Bank rationalized by the argument that rediscounting leads to overspeculation. The financial press in London, however, issued statements that placed the move in a perfectly competitive banking context: as rivals of the Bank, the brokers should not be surprised that the Bank took this opportunity to deal them a blow. In fact, the London banking community did not take the restriction sitting down. Overend, Gurney & Co. responded with a series of actions designed to embarrass the Bank, one being the quick withdrawal of two million pounds sterling from the Bank in 1860. De Cecco (1974, p. 82) suggests that Overend's famous demise in 1866 was at least partly facilitated by the Bank of England, which, remembering Overend's actions in 1860, failed to come immediately to its rescue and instituted a 6-month dear money policy which hastened its dissolution. Aside from these isolated acts, the Bank consistently refused to allow other joint-stock banks into the clearing union in the first half of the century, it continued to offer advances at low interest to banks that gave up their own issues and used Bank of England notes, and its branches consistently competed with country banks by shaving commissions on discounts.[32]

Even toward the close of the century, the competition between the Bank and other financial institutions was still what Clapham (1944, V. II, p. 373) refers to as "bitter."[33] In the first decade of the 20th century, the Bank was still carrying on little rediscounting business with the London joint-stock banks. This mutual hostility was a major reason for the banking community and the Bank's failure to form a substantive cooperative link that would have benefited themselves and the financial community at large. When it came to the health of the British banking system, it was not always clear that the Directors of the Bank of England wished to prevent shocks, especially if that meant knocking off some erstwhile competitors.

When its position in the banking system was secure, the profit motive and its own financial position still made the Bank a less than benevolent presence, even in times of greatest need. When after the crisis of 1857 the Bank restricted rediscount facilities (rediscounts had imposed heavy drains on its reserves during the crisis), it was cutting off important intermediaries in the London financial structure from crisis liquidity in order to protect its own resources.[34] In 1858, in the face of rampant speculation and loss of reserves, the majority of the Court outvoted a public-minded minority (that desired an upward adjustment of the Bank rate) because of its concern over earnings. With World War I looming on the horizon, Governor of the Bank Cole told a weary group of representatives from the clearing banks that the Bank could not significantly increase its reserve because of its adverse effects on profits.[35]

The Court was also traditionally reserved in calling for the famous letter of indemnity which suspended the Bank Act of 1844 (thus allowing greater note issue), because the letter violated the idea of the Banking Department of the Bank of England as a profit-making institution. In this case, the Court preferred a restriction of the Bank's power to manage crisis to the implicit understanding that the Banking Department was in some way responsible for the health of British finance. Even on the eve of the War, most of the British financial community exhibited clear expectations that the Bank would look after its proprietors, irrespective of what kind of public support was required from the Bank. In considering just how much of a burden to place on the Bank with respect to holding the national gold reserve in this crucial period, a Treasury memo noted: "The Bank of England cannot be expected to endanger its modest dividends by heroic measures."[36]

In sum, looking over the century as a whole and specifically the decades of the gold standard, the Bank carried on as an institution that had an underdeveloped sense of public responsibility. This was couched in an identity crisis that often worked to the detriment of British finance. The statements from the Directors themselves suggest that the Court's vision of the Bank was more one of private/commercial bank of issue than a central bank, and the period was marked with a train of actions which attest to their commitment to the proprietors.

Managing the British Monetary System

A second major way to assess the hegemony of the Bank of England would be to determine what sort of domestic monetary manager it was. In this category both hegemonic visions (strong and weak) can be assessed. The strong form (the Bank imposed conditions onto the international system through the manipulation of the London market) would expect to find that the Bank had significant power over the London market, and that it manipulated this market accordingly. The weak form of hegemony attributed to the Bank (i.e., the Bank kept the world stable by keeping the London market stable) does not posit the same degree of control (although some control is surely assumed), but requires that the Bank engaged in some form of management to keep the private market stable.

Strong Hegemony

The search for strong hegemony fundamentally revolves around the question, Did the Bank of England have the power to effect conditions in the domestic financial market to a significant degree? Although this question is so broad that it could generate a plethora of debates over differing central banking tools used by the Bank and their effects, the historiography on the period has discussed power over the market in the context of the ability of the Bank to impose its discount rate onto British and London private banks—in the common terminology of the literature, "making the Bank's discount rate effective." To the extent that the Bank could impose its discount rate onto the market, its power to orchestrate the credit system could be considered significant, and a necessary condition of strong hegemony would be fulfilled.[37]

It is reasonable to talk of the power to effect the rate only after the first third of the 19th century. The Bank rate was not freed from the constraints of the 5% ceiling (on all short bills) until the Bank Act of 1833. Furthermore, the Bank didn't have branches, which would give it an increased regional presence, until after 1826. Its notes hardly circulated outside of London before the 19th century, and then only assumed legal tender over the Isles in 1833. Open market operations, as we know them today, were not really practiced until the 1860s. Moreover, the Court's review of the rate became regular and frequent only after the mid-century.

In looking over the views in the London financial community, both inside and outside the Court, there appears to have emerged a strong feeling that the market rate dominated the Bank rate. The century was marked by ongoing statements from the Bank Governors themselves suggesting that the Bank rate didn't *lead* the market rate, but in fact was *led by* it. Governor Hubbard stated that the Bank watches developments in the market and then follows accordingly. Weguelin said that "we never lead the way in the rate of interest."[38] Governor Hankey (1873, pp. 21, 22) noted that the idea that the Bank rate guides the market discount rate is a "belief which is perfectly erroneous as a general rule." He also underscored how any significant and sustained deviation from the market would impose intolerable losses onto the proprietors. Governor Gibbs argued,

> No arbitrary rate of the Bank of England can ever lead the market, at least in an upward direction. At the most it is a barometer, pointing to the state of the accommodation market; but even for that purpose it is . . . too much affected by other influences to be quite trustworthy.[39]

Governor Morris saw the Bank's adjustment of its rate as being driven by the same factors as those found in any other bank: with any indication that money would be dearer (e.g., excess of gold exports), "unless the Bank and all other bankers took steps to raise the rate at which they employ their money, there would be an increased demand upon their reserves."[40] Bagehot ([1873] 1921, pp. 111–14) found himself in rare agreement with these Governors on this point. Morgenstern's (1959, p. 406) data appear to support the view that the Bank followed the market during the period of the gold standard. In the years 1877–1914 Morgenstern counted 21 turning points in the Bank of England rate (i.e., cases where the rate moved in an opposite direction from its previous move). The market rate showed similar turning points in 19 of those cases. But in only 3 cases did the Bank rate precede the market rate, while the market rate preceded the Bank rate (1–3 months, on average) in 11 cases (the other 5 cases saw perfectly contemporaneous turning points).

Throughout the 19th and into the 20th centuries the weakness of the Bank rate in dictating market conditions is evident from the elaborate and frequent use made of other Bank instruments when the Governors sought to influence credit conditions. The Court almost always combined a change in the Bank rate with one or several of the following: changing the Bank's buying and selling prices for bullion and coin (i.e., the gold devices), open market operations, manipulating bankers' deposits at the Bank, borrowing on Consols, borrowing and lending in the market (including night loans), dealing at special rates, manipulating the advances rate (i.e., rate for short loans), and manipulating conditions under which it discounted bills (e.g., accepting longer bills, discriminating against bills based on type and source).[41]

Students of the Bank in the pre–World War I period see the Bank in a process of learning the art of central banking, with its influence over the market increasing to a point (at the end of the century, and immediately before the War) where the Bank rate could have some influence over the market void of other tools.[42] The fact that from the mid-century the Court shifted to a policy that kept the Bank rate under the market rate to one where the rate was maintained above has been highlighted as an indication that the Bank was increasing its sensitivity to the public at the expense of the proprietors. But even by the 1870s people in the London financial community were still talking about the existence of two rates.[43] King (1936, p. 300) and Beach (1935, p. 154) noted that the 1880s saw a similar inability on the part of the Bank to bring the two rates into convergence. In the last decade of the century, Sayers (1970, p. 5) points out that the Bank rate was still more sensitive to the market rate than vice versa. It is not clear that the instances of failure on the part of the Bank to effect desired capital flows in and out of Britain were any more numerous before the 1870s than after.[44]

Whatever increase in market power was effected by a shift to a higher-than-market rate after the mid-century appears to have been neutralized by subsequent actions on the part of the Bank. Restricting discounting facilities to brokers and discount houses in 1858 served to detach the Bank rate from the market. The link was further severed in 1878 when the Bank began offering discount facilities to customers at the market rate (i.e., below the Bank rate). This, notes Sayers (1970, p. 3), "divested [the Bank rate] of much of its meaning." There is no more striking indication than this that even in the last decades of the century the Bank was unable to impose a rate on the market; hence it made many of its own transactions at that market rate.[45]

Moreover, whatever success the Bank had in effecting its rate in the 20th century was strongly linked to the cooperation of the other major financial players in the London financial community.[46] The fact that the Bank needed the cooperation of major banks to effect its rate attests to the unilateral weakness of the Bank rate even toward the eve of the War. Faced with a gold outflow in 1906, the Bank first went to other banks asking them to keep their rates up rather than trying itself to unilaterally impose a rate. In 1906 and 1907 it asked the major joint-stock banks of London for loans (at a low rate of interest) to bolster its diminishing reserves, something we would expect to be resolved most easily by the Bank's own rate of discount (i.e., it couldn't even attract gold from banks in its own local financial system). In 1910 the joint-stock banks bought gold in the market to prevent the gold reserves of the Bank from swelling, thus avoiding a rapid decline in the Bank rate. In this latter case, it was the private banks that were making their rate effective on the Bank of England.[47]

Cooperation, however, even well into the period of the gold standard, was neither extensive nor systematic. As late as 1910 Felix Schuster of the Union of London and

Smiths Bank stated that the Bank does "not take part in the ordinary meetings that bankers have among themselves."[48] The London financial press consistently criticized the major private banks for their reluctance in following the Bank rate, especially upward. The banks were also criticized for not managing their balances at the Bank with more sensitivity toward helping stabilize London finance. The standing rule of 19th-century competition between banks, "sauve qui peut," was carried on into the 20th century.[49] Even on the eve of the War, negotiations between the Bank and the banking community showed bargaining which was as much directed toward maintaining their competitive positions in the market as it was toward stabilizing British finance in the advent of war. The major commercial banks resisted placing the onus of convertibility on the Bank in fear that their customers would transfer their accounts to the Bank (the government mediated by suggesting an agreement to discourage transfer of accounts). The Bank was upset about the possibility of the Treasury making notes available to the commercial banks at low rates when it was constrained to charge penalty rates on its own advances. An especially contentious issue was over the "spoils" represented in the distribution of the liabilities of the acceptance houses among the Bank and the commercial banks.[50]

Whatever independent influence the Bank had over the market rate, therefore, appeared to be limited and conditional. If it had any influence, it was short-run.[51] The Bank might be able to influence the rate which was quoted in any given day or week, but had quite a limited influence in dictating average rates over periods longer than three months.[52] If anything, it was more an accelerator of the market rate than a leader of the market rate. Furthermore, its influence was conditional on the seasonal structure of liquidity in the British capital market. The Bank rate grew in effectiveness when the "market was driven into the Bank," i.e., when capital shifted from the possession of private financial institutions to the Bank (as in the first quarter when tax payments were due), or liquidity in the market was at a low level. However, even in such cases, notes Morgan (1965), the Bank was often reluctant to exploit its increased influence over the market.[53]

More problematic still in averring the existence of some strong hegemony was the fact that irrespective of the power the Bank had over the market, any central bank that was trying to effect international conditions through the manipulation of its own economy would be expected to link its most powerful weapon to those economic processes that most influenced foreign transactions. Recent findings, however, show that the Bank rate had a relatively weak link to all these processes—i.e., to exports, imports, terms of trade, foreign lending, and even gold reserves.[54]

Finally, whatever experience the Bank may have acquired over the period with respect to the art of influencing the market was neutralized by the growth of the private market relative to the Bank's transactions and reserves (reserves being historically small). While at the beginning of the century its deposits and discount business were large relative to the market, these magnitudes became relatively insignificant by the end of the century. This structural transformation, notes Morgan (1965, p. 193), caused the Bank to go "from the largest lender in the market [to a state in which] the Bank was now practically out of touch with it [by the third quarter of the century]." Moreover, the century saw the rise of very large players in London finance which individually found their policies less dependent on the Bank's actions, and collectively (as London finance became more oligopolistic toward the end of the century) were a more potent force for the Bank to overcome since these big banks could more easily collude on rates.[55] On various occasions the banks themselves used their power to discipline or coerce the Bank, as in the years 1890, 1907, and 1910 when clearing banks put enormous pressure on the Bank by recalling their call loans from discount houses, thus driving the houses en masse to the Bank for liquidity.[56]

In sum, the history of the Bank in relation to the British financial system during the gold standard was one of weakness rather than strength. It had neither the power nor, evidently, the desire to impose conditions onto financial markets, even in its traditional regional domain (London). Given this weakness over private finance, any strong hegemony (i.e., imposing desired conditions onto the international monetary system) which the Bank imposed could not have come through the market. It would have had to be manifest in actions on the part of the Bank which directly influenced foreign markets and central banks. This possibility is considered in the second major section of this chapter (i.e., direct hegemony).

Weak Hegemony: Stabilizing the International System
through Domestic Stabilization

The Bank did not dominate the British monetary system. However, it is conceivable that the Bank could have imparted some kind of stability onto the international monetary system in weak form. This would be a minimum condition for the Bank's hegemony: that the Bank stabilized the international system by stabilizing British finance. Such a type of international hegemony would require a less dominant influence over the British financial system than what we would expect in the case of strong hegemony. At a minimum, the Bank might encourage specific short-term and long-term conditions in the British system without a complete manipulation of financial markets. First, the Bank could manage its reserves in a stabilizing way and function as a source of last-resort liquidity. Second, it could carry on some ongoing management of the economic system (e.g., nudge inflation and the business cycle toward desirable outcomes). Finally, it might expend its limited powers in strategic periods such as crises, so as to keep the British system stable. Any kind of weak hegemony would have to revolve around some or all of these three central bank functions.

RESERVE MANAGEMENT AND LENDER OF LAST RESORT

Given the reluctance of the Bank Directors to ever publicly accept the responsibility of lender in last resort, any confidence generated in the British monetary system would have to come from the level of reserves held by the Bank and ongoing actions affecting the availability of the Bank's liquidity. As for the first, there would be little disagreement among almost any member of the British financial community in the period or historiography on the period that the Bank was the worst central bank in the developed world at backing national and international financial liabilities. Sterling, both nationally and internationally, was propped up on a "thin film of gold."[57] Bagehot's classic *Lombard Street* can be described as a diatribe against the Bank of England's management of the national reserve. In his own words "a more miserable history [in managing a national reserve] can hardly be found."[58] The constant criticism from monetary elites and the financial press became stronger as the period progressed because other central banks (especially France, Germany, and Russia) were making concerted efforts to bolster their reserves of gold while the Bank of England complacently watched its film of gold remain relatively meager.

The big banks in the London community, in fact, lost faith in the Bank as a central bank because of the Bank's reluctance to hold larger reserves.[59] In fact, this agitation caused the big banks themselves to run up their reserves (which were deposited as bankers' balances at the Bank) toward the end of the century.[60] As agitation grew in the new century, these balances were increased, but in both instances the gold reserves of the Bank of England failed to respond.[61] In effect, the Bank of England was free riding on the publicly oriented actions of the big banks by letting them bear the burden (in terms of opportunity costs of holding reserves) of underwriting the system as holders of the reserve. This tendency toward allowing public functions to shift to private banks raised the ire of the big banks, and it served to shift national reserve management somewhat away from the Bank and toward the private banking community. The Bank actually encouraged the big banks to run up their reserves so that they would be more self-sufficient in periods of excessive demand for money. In essence, this was an attempt to avoid a last-resort borrowing scenario by redistributing the burden of absorbing demand shocks to the banking community at large.[62]

The historiography on the Bank underscores the priority which the Court gave to its responsibility of maintaining gold convertibility.[63] There is no doubt that the Bank throughout the 18th and 19th centuries (except for the period of the paper pound) always maintained the gold convertibility of sterling, and this was conducive to confidence in the British monetary system.[64] But maintaining convertibility and even discounting in periods of tightness were perfectly consistent with the Bank's private banking imperatives. Maintaining convertibility was perfectly consistent with the Bank's own private obligations, as it essentially held gold in trust for its customers, the biggest of which comprised the core of British banking (i.e., big commercial banks). Since it held obligations with respect to the big banks (qua customers), and the big banks held obligations to the British public, the Bank's responsible management of its own obligations (i.e., solvency) indirectly transferred to the British economy as a whole.[65] As Schumpeter (1954, p. 697) observed, "If the [Directors of the Bank] had been guided exclusively by the Bank's long-run profit interest and even if they had recognized no responsibility to anyone except the Proprietors (stockholders), [the Bank] would have had to do most of the things which . . . constituted the functions of a central bank." Furthermore, penalty rates in periods of distress or credit shortage (i.e., crisis lending) kept the risk-adjusted returns on the Bank's assets stable across market conditions, and the transfer of liquidity on the part of the Bank remained oriented around its customers. Historically, the Bank lent only on the best collateral, and when pressed with demands for liquidity, the Court increasingly discriminated over the collateral it would accept.

Moreover, if we look at developments in the access to Bank liquidity over the century, we hardly find a record of a magnanimous lender of last resort. In the first major tests of the Bank with respect to crisis lending, it left much to be desired. In 1793 and 1795 it found its funds inadequate for discounting in the face of excess demand, with the Court actually limiting discounts in the latter year. In fact, discounting in crisis throughout the 18th century was subject to quotas.[66] In 1825 the Court and the government each tried to pass the responsibility of crisis lender on to the other and set a precedent for the future. The government wanted the Bank to issue advances to merchants against inventories, while the Bank asked the government to take charge and issue exchequer bills to merchants.[67] Before the mid-century, one of the Court's priorities in managing the Bank rate was to limit the demands upon it as a last-resort lender.[68] The Bank Act of 1844 actually restricted the Bank's function of last-resort lender because it relieved the Banking Department of any central banking responsibility and eliminated the discretionary management of the issue of Bank notes. The Governor of the Bank at the time (Cotton) in fact declared that because of the Act, the Bank could no longer be considered a last-resort lender.[69] In their testimonies in 1848, Governor Morris and his assistant, Prescott, cited an erroneous perception that the Bank owed the financial community support in periods of distress, when in fact the Bank was limited "just as any other banking company."[70] As the century progressed, we in fact saw a trend toward shutting key players off from the Bank's resources, players that were strategically situated in the London financial community: any limitations these players experienced in access to liquidity could reverberate in a destabilizing way through the system (i.e., an unstable pyramid of finance). In 1858 when the Bank cut off rediscounting to brokers and discount houses, Morgan (1965, pp. 173, 174) calls it an act consistent with an ongoing propensity on the part of the Bank toward "shrinking of the responsibility of lender of last resort."[71] Joint-stock banks faced an historic difficulty in getting access to the Bank, given the latter's reluctance both to open accounts for them and to accept bills endorsed by these banks. Even by the 20th century, the discount business with these banks was relatively small.[72]

When it did discount, it did so in a fairly restricted way as well. It historically discriminated on the time and quality of bills, showing a preference for shorter and high-quality (i.e., prime) bills.[73] It also carried on a preference for real (i.e., commercial) over financial bills. Sometimes it made these limitations formal, as when it declared that only very short bills would be discounted. Even in periods where the Bank reversed or suspended a restriction on its discounts or advances, there was a tendency to hedge both formally and informally. When its rediscount restrictions of 1858 were loosened in 1878, it was under the condition that only the shortest bills (15-day) were acceptable, and statements of the Court still proclaimed that discounting facilities to brokers and the discount houses would continue to be limited. When the maturity of acceptable bills was extended in 1897, and again in 1910, to 3 and 4 months respectively, the Bank always maintained its de facto preference for short bills.[74] Furthermore, it was not always the case that any policies which made access to the Bank easier were in fact instituted for the purpose of enhancing last-resort functions. When the Bank made the requirements for starting accounts at the Bank less stringent (i.e., reducing the minimum deposit requirement), for example, it was mainly for the purpose of increasing business.[75] When the Bank increased its advances to jobbers in the stock exchange, it was done primarily to enhance earnings: the jobbers paid high rates and provided good collateral in the form of stocks. This latter development actually carried a destabilizing potential for British finance, because it enhanced the capacity for overspeculation in the stock market—i.e., jobbers leveraging their purchases of stocks with the advances.[76]

In general, the Court left itself sufficient discretionary power to consider each request for liquidity in turbulent times on its merits, which explains an ongoing reluctance to commit to any formal rules for discounting in crisis. This is perfectly in keeping with a greater concern for its own solvency than the stability of the British financial system (which would have benefited by such commitments). It is not surprising that the London financial community was never free of fears that at any given time the Bank might refuse access to its facilities. In his testimony to the National Monetary Commission, a British banker summed up the feeling in the London banking community regarding the perception of the Bank's commitment on crisis discounting for financial bills.

> Q: Is it the policy of the Bank of England to discriminate against finance bills in times of financial crisis?
> A: The Bank has not usually acted upon such a policy, but there is an impression in Lombard street that it might do so at any moment, and this feeling has a restraining effect upon the creation of this class of paper in bad times.[77]

That the Bank was successful in maintaining convertibility in the 19th century can hardly be attributed to an advanced practice of managing the reserve and standing as a last-resort lender. In the period before 1880, when the Bank was tested, it hardly distinguished itself, requiring that the government issue the famous letter of indemnity to restore confidence in the financial system in 1847, '57, and '66. After 1880 it really wasn't tested again until 1906–07.[78] Even in 1906–07, the Bank of England was not faced with lending in last resort alone, as it found welcome relief from the Bank of France, which stepped in to help it meet demands for liquidity.

The history of the Bank with respect to the functions of holder of the national reserve and lender of last resort in the 19th and 20th centuries reads like a novel about an escape artist. Faced with difficult situations in the period before 1880, it always found good fortune smiling in the form of a letter of indemnity from the government or help from the Bank of France. From 1880 on it was tested far less frequently, and the one significant test (1906–07) found more of the good fortune experienced in earlier decades. Hence, it appears to be more valid to say that the British monetary system during the gold standard remained stable not so much *because* of the Bank's actions as holder of the reserve and lender of last resort, but *in spite* of them. The Bank in this period was never placed in a position where its weakness in these areas was severely tested.

MANAGING THE BRITISH MONETARY SYSTEM

A search for indirect or weak British hegemony in the ongoing management of the British economy—i.e., managing the credit (inflation) and business cycles—yields results that are not dissimilar to the search for hegemony in the Bank's last-resort-lending and reserve-management functions. Viner (1937, p. 254) characterized the management of the Bank up to the mid-century as an "inexcusable degree of incompetence or unwillingness" to fulfill the requirements of a manager of the economy.

Part of this unwillingness, according to Schumpeter (1954, p. 696), emanated from fears within the Court of failure, or of adverse public reaction to the Bank's management. To quote Schumpeter,

> in the formative stage of [the Bank's] policy, it would have been madness to assume . . . the responsibilities that we now attribute to a central bank. . . . This would have meant commitments which the Bank could not have been sure of being able to fulfil.

It is interesting that Peel's Bank Act of 1844 found its origin in a quest to guard against the capriciousness of the Bank, a capriciousness which was perceived to have compounded speculative booms that led to crises in British finance. But what came out of good intentions had effects which restricted the Bank's capacity to engage in the ongoing management of the credit and business cycles. The Act limited the discretionary issue of notes, placing issue on a rigid formula of one-to-one backing of notes with gold beyond an initial fiduciary amount backed by securities. This meant that any discretionary adjustment of inflation or the business cycle would have to come in the management of the Banking Department's assets and liabilities (i.e., how much it would take in or let out through discounting and deposits). But everyone, including the Court, was under the impression that the Act relieved the Banking Department of any central banking duties.[79] With the exception of the letter of indemnity from the government in periods of crisis, the discretionary power of the Bank to manage the British economy was circumscribed. It was indicative of the change in the perceptions of the Bank's Court following the Act that the Bank rate was dropped immediately from 4% to 2½% when Gurney was charging 2% on prime bills. The Act actually increased the competitive behavior of the Bank by making the rate more sensitive to the demand for discounts than the management of the economy.[80]

When combined with the problem of managing an extremely small pool of reserves, this sensitivity to market conditions produced an erratic Bank rate that actually carried adverse consequences for British finance and business.[81] Not only did the concern for profit make the rate more variable (because the Court was sensitized to movements in the market rate), but the small reserve required more frequent changes in the rate in order to prevent excessive conditions in reserve levels, something central banks with very large reserves like the Bank of France and the Reichsbank didn't have to worry about.[82] The erratic rate was a target of criticism from both the British business and financial communities throughout the period.[83] Both sensitivity to the market and the need to manage the small reserve pool quite predictably led to a pattern of movement in the Bank rate that often compounded rather than stabilized the credit cycle in Great Britain: the Bank often fueled speculative booms and exaggerated periods of tightness.[84] Even when changes in credit were quite regular and expected, the Bank rate and reserve levels didn't adjust to stabilize the swings in the credit cycle. This is apparent in the Court's passivity in the face of seasonal variations in credit. The most predictable seasonal trends, like the first-quarter tendency of tax payments to bring money into the Bank, and the May and November tendency of Scottish banks to draw on the Bank to cover regular wage and rent payments, were allowed to influence the market unabated by the Court.[85]

Several times the banking community, dissatisfied with the Bank's performance, attempted to form a clearing union independent of the Bank, and use their pooled reserves to impose more stable conditions onto the London financial market. Plans for such an alternative to the Bank's management were visible as early as 1847, when the banking community accused the Bank of fueling the speculative bubble leading to the crisis of that year. Later, in the period of the gold standard, banks were especially perturbed by the Bank's inability to abate speculation in London. The banks wanted to use a new collective reserve pool to better discipline market rates. Though these later plans were seriously discussed, an inability to agree on the distribution of burdens in forming a clearing union doomed the negotiations to failure.[86] But even when the Bank was making concerted efforts to manage the system, the disagreement among the Directors on priorities and the effectiveness of the Bank's weapons resulted in a trail of inconsistent and often mistimed initiatives.[87] If any combination of these initiatives formed some effective and coherent plan of central banking, it most probably came about, as Pressnell (1968) argues, absentmindedly.[88]

Managing the system became more difficult as the British financial community grew. The Bank itself grew increasingly dependent on private banks in effecting desired conditions in the market.[89] As the British system "outgrew the Bank," any kind of management would have to be effected through cooperation with the big banks, but this cooperation never overcame an historic antagonism based on competition in the private market. Hence, even when the Bank did have good public intentions and the policies were potentially stabilizing, it was less and less likely that these policies could be instituted autonomously, and collective execution of the policies had to overcome an historic animosity among the major financial actors in the British system. Moreover, we would expect an active manager of the British economy to influence macroeconomic outcomes through the use of its principal weapons (the discount rate and reserves). Data (see Figures A.5–A.8, equations 14–22, and Granger tests in the Appendix), however, show little sensitivity of the various British series to the Bank of England rate. Real GNP shows little sensitivity to the Bank of England rate (see equation 16 and Granger tests on BE-GBRGNP). Real GNP does show some sensitivity to the Bank's reserves (BERES) in equation 16, but not in Granger tests. Although money aggregates MB and M3 exhibit some sensitivity to the rate and reserves in Granger tests, neither British price series (GBRP and GBPDEF) shows any such sensitivity in the Granger tests. And in equations 21 and 22, of all the coefficients of BE and BERES, only the coefficient of BERES in equation 21 is statistically significant. Furthermore, the coefficient of BE is not statistically significant in both equations 17 and 18. Moreover, that money aggregates (MB and M3) are most sensitive to the Bank's rate and reserves is hardly compelling evidence of the Bank of England's management of the British economy. Since MB and M3 include deposits at the Bank itself, a rate and reserves which are sensitized to these aggregates need mean nothing more than the fact that the Directors of the Bank of England were protecting their own solvency (i.e., manipulating the rate and reserves according to changes in their deposits).

In the ongoing management of the British economy, therefore, like the Bank's behavior as holder of the reserve and last-resort lender, the Bank was hardly a conspicuous source of indirect hegemony over the international gold standard.

MANAGING CRISES

There is general agreement in the historiography on the Bank that its public consciousness was most visible in periods surrounding crises. Sayers (1970, p. 3) notes that after 1878 the Bank rate itself became more of a "crisis" rate than a rate that managed the business and credit cycles. Clare (1909, pp. 57, 58) identified a closer relationship between the rate and the Bank's reserves during crisis periods. Viner (1945, p. 63) pointed out that although in good times the Bank pursued profit with full vigor, difficult times brought out the public concerns of the Directors. But even here, the vision of an animated central banking institution which quickly tamed speculative booms in financial markets, and one that marshaled its resources in a forceful way to impose order in crises, falls short of reality. It is not even clear that the stabilizing behavior of the Bank was substantially greater than its destabilizing behavior, especially in periods surrounding crises. The Bank of England consistently showed what Andreades (1909, p. 332) referred to as "imprudent behavior."

The Bank's actions in the years 1845–1847 were principal contributors to the crisis of 1847.[90] In the years 1845 and 1846 the Bank aggressively expanded its deposits, many of them being special railway deposits used to fuel speculation in railway securities. The Bank's deposits and reserves dropped to extremely low levels by 1847, a development which Fetter (1965, pps. 203, 204) notes was irresponsible even for a private bank. The Bank watched large grain imports during the mid 1840s lead to an exodus of gold which they finally addressed only in 1847, but the rise in the Bank rate was too little and too late. The Bank hardly redeemed itself as a crisis manager. It continued an ongoing practice of refusing accounts to other banks of issue, thus excluding important financial actors from liquidity. The Court announced that it was suspending advances on exchequer bills and public stocks, which threw the stock market and the market for government securities into a frenzy, as investors feverishly liquidated their stocks and securities for cash. Moreover, even though it did make advances against quality bills and some securities; it refused renewal of advances, discounted only short bills, and limited the number of bills it would discount.[91]

The crisis of 1857 was caused by a severe drop in the Bank's reserves, as the Court allowed the reserves to fall from over 4 million pounds sterling to less than one million in about one month. It was in this crisis that the Bank decided to deal with the problem of moral hazard (i.e., reluctance of private institutions to hold greater reserves) in the British financial community by restricting discount facilities to brokers, but such a measure was best suited for fair-weather periods rather than in the midst of a severe crisis. The Bank's policy appeared extremely shortsighted, even with respect to its own specific interests. One of the major pools of liquidity upon which British finance rested was the bankers' balances which were held at the Bank of England. Brokers were heavily in debt to banks. If brokers could not obtain liquidity from the Bank, they would not be able to service their debts to the banks; hence banks would be forced to draw down their balances at the Bank of England to meet any significant increase in the demand for money, which in turn left the Bank itself short of liquidity.[92]

In the Overend, Gurney crisis of 1866, as in the two crises before, the letter of indemnity probably did more to stabilize financial markets than any strategic actions on the part of the Bank, many of which were actually destabilizing.[93] Issuing the letter was especially important to allay fears among country banks which needed assurances that the British financial system had adequate liquidity. It is interesting that even this weapon to combat crises, which actually belonged to the government rather than the Bank, was resisted by the Court, as the letter violated the idea of the Banking Department as a private banking operation.[94]

After the Overend, Gurney episode the Bank would not be significantly tested again until 1906–07. The famous Baring incident in 1890 was more a case of crisis prevention, and the Bank's own involvement owes more to the individual perspicacity of Governor Lidderdale than any formal central banking functions in either the Court or the Governor's office. In both the cases of Baring and the years 1906–07, we saw the Bank either abating or preventing panic not by marshaling its own resources, but by asking major British financiers and foreign central banks and governments for funds or special accommodations. In seeing that Baring's liabilities had grown excessively high, Lidderdale asked a variety of banks for subscriptions to back them. Lidderdale was successful in obtaining subscriptions totaling 17,105,000 pounds sterling, with the Bank putting up only one million of its own funds. He was successful in obtaining an agreement from the Russian government not to withdraw the 2.4 million pounds sterling of deposits it held with Baring, and, of course, the Bank of France came through with its usual accommodation when developments in British finance threatened crisis in Paris. It is interesting that the Bank's best-handled crisis, 1890, was also a relatively mild one.[95]

By the time the Bank's final major test before the War came about, the actions of the Bank were ominously familiar. In 1906 it was fueling a speculative boom with loose credit, allowing its reserves once more to reach levels that were causing a stir in financial markets. The Court's initial reaction was to hint to the banking community that all banks should collectively maintain high rates to avert a drain. The hint appeared all too suspicious coming from an institution that was in competition for discounts. The speculation became excessive and the Bank responded, but in an excessive way, raising the rate to 6% and shocking markets. As Beach (1935, p. 143) observed, the Bank's early laxity forced it to act in "a more severe manner than would otherwise have been the case." In both the years 1906 and 1907 the Bank of France appears to have been an important stabilizing force for British finance, as it came forth to discount large amounts of British bills and ship American eagles to London. In 1906 France was instrumental in relieving pressure in London by discounting British bills up to 75 million francs, and it released 200,000 pounds sterling to Egypt, which was pulling gold from London (along with the U.S. and Brazil). In 1907 the gold flows from London to the U.S. were essentially mediated by the Bank of France, which sent 80 million francs' worth of American eagles to London so that London could meet the U.S. demand for gold in a form of payment attractive to Americans.[96] In 1906–07 the stabilization effect of the Bank of France was perhaps greatest. As in so many British crises before, the Bank of France was there to ease financial tensions for the Bank of England.

The search for indirect hegemony in the role of crisis manager may at least be partially vindicated. The Bank did take on a greater public consciousness during periods of financial distress, and it did frequently increase its distribution of liquidity in crisis. But the Bank's track record is hardly commendable. In many instances its actions both before and during crises compounded nervousness in British finance.[97] It is certainly not clear that it was a grand stabilizer in net terms (i.e., when you factor all of its destabilizing actions into its crisis behavior). The Bank was often too soft on credit before crises and overly restrictive during crises. Both not only shocked British finance, but increased rather than stabilized oscillations in the credit and business cycles. When the Bank did bring British finance out of crisis, it was either because of the individual perspicacity of a Governor (Lidderdale in the Baring episode 1890) or because of help it received from domestic and foreign banks. The Bank of France was especially helpful in mitigating crises in the British financial system. In this respect, any search for indirect hegemony might be better directed toward the Bank of France. By helping stabilize the British financial system, the Bank of France was partially responsible for any indirect British hegemony.

In sum, the overall record of indirect hegemony (both of a weak and strong form) by the Bank of England is rather disappointing for those who have seen the stability of the gold standard as founded on the Bank's management or manipulation of the British economy. The Bank proved to be neither a truly dominant nor overly capable managerial force. In many cases it was itself a destabilizing force in British finance. It would appear more valid to say that the British financial system remained stable *despite* the Bank of England than it is to say that it remained stable *because* of the Bank. In searching for indirect hegemony, one might be better off looking to the relations between the Bank of France and British finance.

Direct Hegemony: The Bank of England as an International Central Bank

A more direct form of international hegemony under the gold standard would entail the Bank taking actions which directly affected international monetary relations. In the context of this argument, all of the standard central bank functions become relevant, but in an international rather than a national context. Any search for such hegemony would therefore have to scrutinize the behavior of the Bank of England in all of the four fundamental categories of central banking once more, but this time with the international monetary system as the principal target for stabilization.

Acknowledging Public Responsibility

Finding expressions among statements of the Directors of the Bank that suggest the acceptance or acknowledgment of responsibility for some international system are even rarer than expressions of public responsibility for the British monetary system. Careful scrutiny of interviews and publications of the Directors, and all the major historiographical works on the Bank of England fail to produce any substantive reference to interest in stabilizing or managing the international monetary system on the part of the Bank's Directors.[98] That such an acknowledgment is lacking is very much in keeping with the private imperatives of the Directors, i.e., reserve holdings for the global monetary system would have incurred even greater opportunity costs than holdings for domestic needs. But irrespective of the public concerns of the Court, it is clear that the domestic situation dominated. One obstacle to the Bank's capacity for international management was its own identity crisis at home. As Fetter (1965, p. 255) points out, "It would be asking too much to assume that with a babel of voices telling the Bank what it should do for Lombard Street it should have any clear vision of what it was supposed to do for the world." To the extent that the banking community and public were concerned with the international system, they appeared more sensitized to the possible ways in which the international system could adversely affect the Bank and British finance than to how the Bank could stabilize the system. Fetter (1965, p. 256) points out that if someone had informed the British financial elite that they were managers of the international gold standard and lenders of last resort for the world, they would have been as surprised as the character in Molière's *Le Bourgeois Gentilhomme* who found that, unbeknownst to him, he had been speaking prose throughout his life.

Viner (1945, p. 64) underscored how the Court was principally concerned with looking after the convertibility of its notes and left the monetary affairs of other countries up to their own central bankers. He added that the Bank never showed any interest in developing ties with foreign central banks. In this respect, Viner called the behavior of the Court "completely unenterprising and unimaginative." Sayers (1976, V. I, pp. 8, 9) cites the rarity with which Bank Directors made official visits to foreign central banks, and how foreign visitors to the Bank were normally restricted to courtesy visits. As Sir Ernest Harvey, a Bank Director, pointed out, "The Bank was amazingly detached from international affairs; heard from no one; saw no one; only watched the gold and took the necessary steps automatically."[99]

The vision of an insular monetary institution is not altogether an inappropriate characterization of the Bank. It is interesting how little the Directors knew and how little they felt they needed to know about developments in foreign markets, given the Bank's prominent position in the international monetary system. When asked, for example, what practices foreign central banks undertook in backing their liabilities, Governor Palmer said he was ignorant with respect to such matters.[100] Some Directors defensively justified ignorance of foreign practices and developments by claiming that international developments would manifest themselves in domestic conditions in Great Britain. This would be true of lesser monetary powers which imported the developments of other monetary systems, but hardly true of nations (in a dominant position) which exported their developments to others.[101]

The Bank rate was more sensitive to the reserve than to global monetary conditions. As Governor Gibbs stated, "The sole principle which actuates us in fixing the rate of discount . . . is the state of our reserve, the amount which we have in our coffers, wherewith to pay our debts, and meet demands upon us."[102] The Bank remained a hesitant international actor, even when it involved the interests of British citizens. In 1891, for example, a reluctant Bank was cast in a role of mediator over a dispute between British citizens who had invested in Argentinean bonds and the government of Argentina, which found servicing its debt difficult. Quite in character, its shyness and parochial orientation were made immediately apparent when the Bank declared itself neither responsible for the state of the proceedings nor the outcomes from negotiations between the conflicting parties.

With respect to its public responsibility, then, the Bank of England had an under-developed sense of duty to the British monetary system itself, and its duty toward the international monetary system was even less visible.

International Reserve Management and Lender of Last Resort

The Directors were somewhat less vocal in denying responsibility for last-resort lending at the international level than the domestic level, because they were consistently attacked by the financial press regarding the latter but never the former. No one in the London community, whether banker or citizen, ever conceived of the Bank's responsibility as extending beyond British borders. When statements did come from the Directors regarding international lending, the response was a fairly common one. As Bank Governor Hankey (1873, p. xi) pointed out, "It is no part of the duty of the Bank to make any provision for providing gold for export." Foreign banking systems, in fact, acted as if the Bank was not *the* lender of last resort in the international system. Foreign private and public banks did not systematically go to the Bank when domestic or international conditions had created shortages of liquidity. Some of this demand for money was bloc-driven, while other parts of the demand were driven by custom. Nations in the sterling bloc went predominantly to Britain for liquidity in last resort. Nations in the franc bloc (the Latin Union), however, went to Paris, while Canada went first to the U.S. Italy and Russia were traditionally clients of Paris; the U.S. and the British Empire were clients of London; while Belgium, Holland, and Germany were clients of both London and Paris. The world monetary system was far from a state in which there was a default source of liquidity.[103]

When it did make liquidity available to foreigners in times of distress, the transfers hardly signaled a strong international concern. Foreign lending was not undertaken frequently, the goals of such transfers were usually quite restricted geographically, the transfers were carried out reluctantly, and the sums transferred were rarely large. When asked if the Bank was a source of international liquidity, Governor Palmer responded, "Very few occasions have occurred when the Bank has sent specie abroad, and those occasions have only been in times of an unfavorable exchange, and chiefly for the purpose of operating on the Paris exchange direct."[104] The reluctance was sometimes quite visible, as when the United States Bank (short of liquidity) asked the Bank for an advance in 1839. The response was an offer of only 300,000 pounds sterling in the form of stocks (the U.S. Bank wanted cash) for a period of only one month. The U.S. Bank didn't even take the loan, but instead raised 800,000 pounds in the London market. In the crisis of 1907, the Bank discouraged dealings in American bills when it conveyed to London banks that it considered American acceptances a threat to the stability of British finance. If, in fact, we look at the cases where central banks made transfers across their borders in periods of crisis, the Bank of England was much more often a receiver than a lender. Kindleberger (1978, p. 188) notes that if you take into account the demands for liquidity in crises by the Bank in the years 1873, 1890, and 1906–07, the Bank's behavior during the period of the gold standard made it more of a "borrower" than a "lender" in last resort. This was fairly unusual behavior for a supposed source of liquidity. Given the number of times transfers went across the English Channel from Paris to London, one might say that if indeed the Bank was a last-resort lender, the lender of last resort itself had a lender in the Bank of France. The international banking community well knew that "the Bank of England in times of need has always the Bank of France at its disposal."[105]

The international reluctance of the Bank was consistent with reserve holdings that by almost everyone's admission were small even for guarding domestic convertibility. Considering that London was the clearinghouse for international trade (i.e., that huge sterling balances were building up in a system committed to the convertibility of sterling), the thin film of gold appeared even more deficient. Patron [see U.S. Senate (1910a, pp. 109, 110)] mirrored a common view of the period:

> Thus the fact that [Britain] undertakes international settlements carries with it the obligation of supplying gold. Financial leadership implies monetary leadership, and such should necessitate strong reserves. Is this the case with England? . . . London has not a sufficient amount of gold to satisfy the needs of Great Britain. . . .

Bloomfield (1963, p. 27), Beach (1935, p. 39) and Clapham (1944, V. II, p. 379) note the especially precarious tendency of maintaining modest reserves in the face of greatly increasing foreign sterling balances, such foreign balances being especially unpredictable and difficult to control relative to domestic balances. Morgan (1965, pp. 167, 168) adds that with increasing foreign balances in London, the Bank became much more sensitive to conditions in foreign monetary systems, and itself was subject to more frequent and potentially more destabilizing demands because of shifts in these balances in and out of the London market.[106] The sensitivity of the Bank was compounded by the growing integration and complexity of the international monetary system, as the speed and volume of financial transactions were increasing significantly in the latter 19th century. In 1903, Warren (1903, p. 224) noted that "the financial world has outgrown London." At the domestic level, the growth of British finance made the Bank more sensitive to developments in its own market. A major component of both national and international vulnerability was the increasing bankers' balances at the Bank. But even with the growing international and national burdens, the Bank continued to run among the lowest reserve ratios in the developed world. If reserve holdings relative to foreign balances were a measure of hegemony during the period, almost every other central bank in the developed world at the time could have been considered more of a hegemon than the Bank of England. The Bank of France, in fact, held about four times as much gold as the Bank of England with far fewer foreign liabilities throughout the period.[107] (See Table 5.1.) If the reserve of the Bank of England was really a "working balance," the French reserve might be considered a "hoard."[108] As Patron [see U.S. Senate (1910a, p. 112)] pointed out, Britain may have been the "clearinghouse of the world," but the Bank of France was a better candidate than the Bank of England as the world's "general gold reservoir." In this respect, the Bank of France would have to be acknowledged once more as behaving in ways more consistent with hegemony than the Bank of England, but the Bank of France had no more public concern for the international system than did the Bank of England.

Table 5.1 Gold Stock of Leading Central Banks, 1913* (millions of dollars)

Bank of England	164.9
Bank of France	678.9
Reichsbank	278.7
U.S. Treasury	1,290.4
Austro-Hungarian Bank	251.4
Italy (3 banks of issue)	265.4
Bank of Russia	786.2
Canada	115.4

*Source: Lindert (1969, p. 10)

That the gold standard could carry on without major suspensions of convertibility, given the Bank's thin film of gold, depended on the avoidance of severe tests for the Bank. In fact, severe tests were few, and when they did appear as in the years of 1906–07, the Bank itself found international support forthcoming. It is dubious that the Bank's resources (without augmentation from outside sources) could have withstood any serious test. If the Bank was deficient as a reserve manager and lender in the domestic monetary system, then its performance at the international level might be considered criminal.

Managing the International Monetary System

Any kind of management of the international monetary system would have to be manifest in the management of global inflation and the global business cycle. One would presume that a responsible manager would want a global business cycle with limited oscillations and a similar outcome with respect to changes in international prices. Of course, the hegemon may want to impose conditions that many consider unstable along some international Phillips curve. But in any case, hegemonic management would have to reveal itself in some kind of attempts at manipulating international economic growth and prices. We would expect to find a link between the Bank's most important instruments (the rate and reserves) and global business and inflation.

The evidence on this in fact suggests that the Bank was not managing the dual cycles in the international economy.[109] Figure A.4 (see Appendix) shows that changes in the Bank's reserves were fairly erratic within differing phases of the global business cycle. The depression of the 1870s saw reserves rising sharply instead of falling. The expansion of the early 1880s saw reserves falling. The depression of the mid 1890s saw an increase, while the expansion of the late 1890s saw a decline. This procyclical pattern is exactly the opposite of what we would expect from a stabilizing international central banking policy (reserve movements in this case compounded the cycle rather than smoothed it).[110] Movements in the Bank rate over the global business cycle (Figures A.1–A.5 in the Appendix) showed that some turns in the Bank rate corresponded in an accommodating (i.e., consistent with hegemony) way to turns in global economic growth: early and late 1870s, early and late 1880s, early and mid 1890s, and 1900. And these co-movements were fairly contemporaneous. But the mid 1870s saw a sharp rise in the rate in the midst of depression, the rate moved down somewhat in the expansion of the late 1880s, there was a sharp increase in the depression of the early 1890s, and an increase took place during the downturn before 1903. Comparing both the movements in reserves and the rate across the business cycle suggests further evidence of the limited influence of the rate in attracting gold from abroad: the rising rate in some expansionary phases was less influential than foreign demand in stimulating gold flows. In this respect the reserve may have been driven more by the international demand for liquidity (running low when demand was high in expansionary phases, and running high in downturns when demand was low) than the Bank rate. Hence, even if the Bank of England might have wanted to use its instruments in a hegemonic way, it lacked the power over international capital to effect a strong kind of hegemony.

Other inconsistencies between the dictates of global central banking are evident in the behavior of the Bank rate relative to other central bank rates (see Figure A.1–A.3 in the Appendix). The Bank of England rate tended to be somewhat less stable than other rates: the variability and range of movement were generally greater than in other series. As in the domestic case, we would expect an international monetary manager to maintain a more stable rate so as to limit fluctuations in global economic growth and prices. The rate tended also to be below other rates in both upturns and downturns in the global business cycle. One can make a strong case that such a pattern encouraged an inflationary bias in global credit. What was also revealing was the spread between the Bank of England rate and various other bank rates. This suggests a limited ability to make itself fully effective in the global monetary system.[111] Furthermore, the spread tended to be fairly stable across the business cycle; certainly we would expect a central banking policy with intent to stabilize the international monetary system to make its rate more effective in crisis, as the Bank itself sought to do in its own domestic system. Moreover, French leads in co-movements between the Bank of England and Bank of France rates suggest that the Bank of France may have been more likely to influence the Bank of England than vice versa.[112]

Looking at co-movements between the Bank rate and international prices of commodities and manufactures (Figures A.1–A.3 in the Appendix), it appears that the Bank rate was moving in a more conventional-accommodating fashion, i.e., dampening the variability of global prices. But coefficients (see equations 12 and 13) and Granger tests assessing the impact of BE and BERES on global price indexes produce statistically insignificant results. Moreover, when the Bank rate moved in an accommodating fashion against global price movements and the global business cycle, it may just suggest that the rate was *responding to* rather than *leading* movements in the global economy.[113] Granger tests and equations 12 and 13 on the relation between global price indexes and British series suggest that global price movements were not determined by the British economy either (see Appendix). Although British real GNP shows a positive effect on manufactures prices in Granger tests at lag 2 and a positive contemporaneous effect on primary product prices in equation 13, the Bank of

England rate and reserves show little impact on real GNP itself (see equation 16 and Granger tests on BE-GBRGNP and BERES-GBRGNP). Hence the little sensitivity between the global and British economies did not appear strongly mediated by the tools of the Bank, as the rate and Bank reserves did not appear to be driving the British economy.

If the British economy were indeed dictating trends in the world, we would expect to see a fairly pronounced transmission of the British business cycle. Other tests suggest that such is not the case. Huffman and Lothian's (1984) data on the transmission of business cycles in the Atlantic community suggest that the transmission of the British cycle to the U.S. weakened over time. By the last half of the gold standard period, the U.S. was actually transmitting its business cycle to Great Britain. Easton's (1984) tests on real income transmission among the leading developed nations in the period of the gold standard show this Atlantic pattern to be consistent over a greater number of nations. Developments in British economic growth showed a limited influence over growth patterns in other developed nations. Considering the income series of Italy, Germany, Canada, the U.S., Denmark, Sweden, and Norway, in only the last case is there evidence that trends in British economic growth significantly affected the business cycle of another nation. Moreover, from a purely monetary capability to affect international conditions, McCloskey and Zecher (1976) question whether the Bank of England could manipulate international prices and interest rates if it wanted to. They note that if the Bank sold all the securities in its Banking Department, it would decrease world reserves by only 0.6%. If it sold all the gold in the Issue Department, it would increase the world monetary gold stock by only 0.5%.[114]

To the extent that the Court of Directors used the Bank's principal weapons to stimulate capital flows in and out of the Bank, it is clear that its objectives had more to do with its own financial solvency and domestic British conditions than foreign conditions. Directors' statements consistently show that the Bank's operations of note issue, discounting, rate and reserve management, and gold devices had little to do with foreign developments.[115] Certainly, it would be overly presumptuous to think that with the low level of reserves the Bank consistently ran, its most powerful weapon (the rate) had the luxury of fixing on foreign conditions. The low reserve levels absolutely necessitated greater sensitivity of the rate to reserves at the exclusion of other targets, both domestic and international. In this respect, the Bank operated in very orthodox private fashion, affixing its major weapons on its own solvency.[116] In fact, in targeting the rate toward maintaining a minimum viable reserve, the Bank was actually a less stabilizing force at both the domestic and international levels. Frequent variations in the rate and the reserve would be something that responsible monetary managers would avoid.[117] It is indicative of the problems caused by erratic rates that the Bank of France in the mid-1860s tried to delink its rate somewhat from the Bank of England rate because adherence was destabilizing for business conditions in France.

Even if the Bank of England did make it a priority to manage the dual international cycles (inflation and business), did it have the capacity to do so? As noted above, the Bank had an historic inability to make its rate effective even in the British monetary system. Doing so on an international level would be even more difficult given the greater transaction costs of international relative to domestic investment. In fact, effecting the Bank's rate internationally depended on the ability of the Bank to effect it domestically, since capital flows in and out of Britain were transactions carried out primarily through private institutions. Therefore, the Bank's limited ability to effect its rate domestically also limited its power to effect international capital flows. Just as the 19th century was filled with instances of a less than effective domestic rate, it also showed a less than dominant capacity to dictate the flow of international liquidity, even in and out of Britain itself.[118] That the rate was less than compelling internationally is once again (as in the domestic case) attested to by the necessity of supplementing rate changes with other means of stimulating capital flows. One of the most discreet usages of gold devices by the Bank of England for stimulating desired capital flows was the custom of giving out worn coin to those converting notes (this was a subtle way of raising the price of gold in order to discourage its export). Morgan (1965, p. 225) takes an indignant swipe at the idea of British hegemony when he refers to this practice as the "ludicrous spectacle of the most powerful monetary institution in the world picking and sorting its sovereigns so as to pay its obligations in coin of the lightest weight." Moreover, this power over international markets was decreasing through the gold standard period as foreign centers were growing and the international monetary system was evolving toward greater complexity. Foreign central banks found that they could tolerate greater differences from the Bank of England rate without fearing the loss of gold to London.

Giovannini (1988), in fact, finds that the Bank of England rate showed less than hegemonic influence over the other two European core banks. Of 104 changes by the Bank of England in the period of the gold standard which he considers (59 up and 45 down), the Reichsbank followed only 25 (11 up and 14 down) within one week, while the Bank of France followed only 3 (2 down and 1 up) within one week. Granger tests (see Appendix) suggest that Giovannini's findings are consistent with findings over a greater number of central banks in the developed world during the gold standard. The F-statistics relating the Bank of England rate to the rates of the Bank of France and Reichsbank are insignificant over three lags. Of the significant F-statistics generated in the tests, all but the 1st and 2nd lag tests on the Bank of Spain suggest that the rates of other central banks were Granger causing the rate of the Bank of England.[119] In the equations, with the exception of the Banks of Italy and Reichsbank (see equations 2–11), coefficients linking the Bank of England rate (as an independent variable) to other rates tend to be statistically insignificant.

It is not even clear that the Bank was any more of an unintending stabilizing force than the British banking community itself. If British banks were anticipating conditions in British credit by considering the effect of foreign developments on domestic conditions, the result might very well be a synchronous response in the private banking community that stabilized the global credit and business cycles. In his testimony on common banking procedure in Great Britain, Vincent Stuckey's statement is suggestive:

> I . . . see what the [foreign] exchanges are, and . . . the price of precious metals, and if I see that they are very much against [Britain], . . . I get a circular letter written to all my managers, stating that they must be very cautious in their advances. . . .[120]

It is apparent that such behavior spread over numerous British banks (and we would expect such a spread in competitive as well as oligopolized banking systems) could result in Great Britain applying a countercyclical wedge against the global economy. When foreigners were increasing their economic activity as a result of surpluses run against Britain, the British banks would initiate a policy of tight credit and bring global economic growth and inflation under control. When Britain was growing at the expense of the world economy (i.e., running surpluses against the world), British banks would initiate a loose credit policy that would limit global deflation and encourage growth.

If indeed there were some kind of ongoing influence by the British financial system over the global economy, it is more likely (given the evidence) that it was the outcome of such collective credit policies in the British banking system than any actions on the part of the Bank of England.

Managing International Crises

The management of crises that affected foreign centers is especially difficult to assess during the gold standard period, given the low number of observations. Widespread crises during the period were relatively few, and the Baring crisis was relatively mild by pre–1880 standards. But in the crises which Great Britain shared with other nations, it was not clear that the Bank of England was the institution that other banks automatically expected to act. As noted above, crisis borrowing had large components of tradition and regional monetary interdependence, which meant there might be several sources of crisis liquidity that banks could go through before reaching the Bank (also, it certainly wasn't the case that the Bank was necessarily the last stop in the global search for liquidity). In periods where crisis transfers were taking place across national boundaries, the Bank was more often the borrower than the lender. Clare (1909) identified a systematic tendency on the part of the Bank rate to undergo more gyrations during crisis periods than non-crisis periods. This suggests that the Bank was probably more interested in maintaining safe reserves in crisis than stabilizing either the world or British monetary systems, which in turn might suggest that the Bank was having difficulty insulating the British system from foreign disturbances, the rate being manipulated according to shifts in capital flows in and out of Britain resulting from conditions in foreign markets. Even if it had to impose penalty rates, a more stable rate would increase confidence during periods of distress.

The one true international test in the gold standard period, the crisis of 1906–07, hardly showed a resolute international crisis manager. The Bank's weaknesses in this crisis recalled characteristics that had been visible throughout the 19th century, especially in the Bank's dependence on external support in periods of greatest domestic and international pressures, and its reluctance to place British liquidity on the altar of international demand for money in restrictive periods. In the years 1906–07 the Bank faced problems in keeping gold from flowing out of Britain, and even high rates were sometimes unable to satisfactorily abate the flow of capital out of Britain toward the Continent and the U.S. The Bank of France took it upon itself, under its usual precaution against adverse spillover from London to Paris, to discount British bills heavily so as to keep gold in the London market.[121] The actual capital flows that went from London to the U.S. in these crisis years are somewhat misleading as indicators of the Bank's global monetary management, because the capital was recycled from the Continent, as both the Bank of France and the Reichsbank voluntarily allowed capital to flow across the Channel so Britain could send it along to the U.S. This was especially apparent in the recycling of American eagles from France to Britain to the U.S., which Patron [see U.S. Senate (1910a, pp. 143–45)] called a case of "false hegemony." The Bank of France in this case had become a kind of central bank for England, something no proud and resolute hegemon during the period would have tolerated. Given the humiliation of accepting help from a central bank lower on the monetary hierarchy, one would suspect that if the Bank of England had the unilateral power to deal with the developments in these crisis years, it would have done so. Its decision, however, was to accept the relief and then categorically deny that any such help was ever requested.[122] Perhaps the ultimate humiliation occurred when the U.S. began negotiating with the Bank of France for direct relief, allowing both to sidestep the intervention of the London market.[123]

Given the evidence, the search for direct hegemony in crises appears better directed toward the Bank of France, which showed a century-long tradition of coming to the aid of the London market when periods of financial distress arose.

In sum, the search for both direct and indirect hegemony, and for both strong and weak hegemony, fails to yield satisfying results for those proponents of the Bank of England's hegemonic leadership under the gold standard. Not only can we say that the Bank did not manage the international monetary system, but it is questionable whether it even managed the British monetary system. The institution was relatively weak not only in the face of the world banking community, but also relative to the British banking community. And these weaknesses grew as the financial systems became larger and more complex. Perhaps it is enough to wonder how it was that the Bank was able to defend its own convertibility. Central banks of nations that were successful in maintaining convertibility did so either by running up excess gold reserves or through long-term borrowing. The Bank of England did neither. It is therefore not surprising that the Bank so often avoided concerted efforts to stabilize the world economy. That the Bank persisted in what might be called a false splendor during the gold standard is also the reason why the international system under the gold standard remained fairly stable. Neither the system nor the Bank experienced frequent or severe shocks, as both political and financial crises were limited during the period. The few times the system and the Bank's resources were tested, sufficient external support was forthcoming. We can therefore say that the gold standard was stable for the same reason that the Bank of England remained solvent: neither was ever severely tested in the period of the gold standard.

6

The Origin of the Gold Standard

The previous three chapters suggest that the regime dynamics of the classical gold standard were founded on neither cooperation nor hegemonic leadership. Both the origin and stability of the gold standard, in fact, resulted from much more diffuse or decentralized processes (i.e., not managed at the international level). The next two chapters attempt to explain the origin and stability of the gold standard, and in doing so analyze these processes. This chapter considers the origin of the gold standard, while the next chapter considers the stability of the gold standard.

The regime of the classical gold standard crystallized in the decade of the 1870s as the greater part of the bloc of developed nations found themselves compelled to transform their domestic monetary standards from silver and bimetallism to gold— i.e., the scramble for gold.[1] When the decade began, only two nations of note were legally on gold standards (Great Britain and Portugal). By the end of the decade, all of the major economies in the world were effectively practicing de jure gold standards. So complete was this transformation in the developed world that by 1885 there was no longer a single mint open to the unlimited coinage of silver in either Europe or the U.S.[2]

The scramble for gold in the 1870s can be principally understood as a resultant of three types of forces: structural, proximate, and permissive. The first refers to long-term and developmental forces in the 19th century that compelled nations away from silver-based standards toward gold. Proximate forces represent critical developments in the 1860s and '70s that served as the immediate catalysts for legal changes in monetary standards. Structural forces incrementally compelled the shift to gold, but it was these critical developments that account for the timing of the transformation. Finally, permissive factors determined whether nations could follow this structural and proximate compellence, and link to gold as well as maintain convertibility.

This chapter is organized as follows: the first section discusses the structural foundations of the movement toward gold, the second section discusses the proximate foundations of the movement, and the third section discusses the permissive foundations.

As the 19th century progressed, three sets of structural forces increasingly compelled national monetary authorities toward gold and away from silver as central monetary metals: (1) ideology (i.e., the status of gold), (2) industrialization and economic development, and (3) the politics of gold. First, nations came to see monetary standards as economic and political status symbols. Gold monometallism came to confer high status, while silver and bimetallism came to confer low status. Much of the status of gold was conferred on the metal because it was a characteristic of advanced-industrial nations in the 19th century that their economies were able to keep more gold in circulation relative to less advanced economies. The status was compounded by the fact that Britain had been practicing a gold standard (de facto from 1717 and de jure from 1821). The example of Britain was especially compelling because elites were drawing associations between Britain's monetary practices and its industrial successes. Second, industrialization, economic development, and the growth of international trade encouraged the greater use of the more convenient metal (gold). The greater number and size of domestic and international transactions which resulted from economies undergoing an industrial revolution gave an advantage to gold over silver. Since the value per bulk of gold was roughly 15 times greater than that of silver, gold would naturally become more important as a medium of exchange in environments where the size and frequency of transactions and incomes were growing. The greater internationalization of economies in Europe and the U.S. made the standard which was practiced by Britain all the more compelling, since the international capital market and more specifically the international market for commercial debt (i.e., bills) were dominated by sterling. Finally, the spectrum of domestic politics changed significantly in the developed world in the 19th century. The rise of political liberalism was a manifestation of the political rise of an urban-industrial class and a challenge to the traditional dominance of an agricultural class. With the shift in the political balance of power came a concomitant shift in monetary preferences from a standard oriented around a bulky and inflationary metal (i.e., silver) to one oriented around a light and non-inflationary metal (i.e., gold). The victory of gold over silver in gold-club nations was coterminous with the political victory of a new class of urban industry over the more traditional classes connected with the land.

Although these three structural factors predisposed advanced-industrial nations toward gold and away from silver, the actual legal changes that demonetized silver and formed the nucleus of the gold club came about in the early to mid 1870s. Once Germany made the shift from silver to gold, the rest of the gold club (with the exceptions of Austria, Russia, and Japan, whose legal transitions were delayed) followed suit in a fairly rapid fashion (i.e., the scramble for gold). The timing and rapidness of this transformation make the gold standard fairly unique in monetary history, since it was the first time such a large number of nations made fairly contemporaneous changes in their monetary standards. The timing and rapidness of this regime transformation can be explained by several more proximate factors relating to developments in the international market for precious metals and the structure of economic interdependence among gold-club nations. Legal changes before the 1870s in the monetary standards of those nations that eventually fell into the gold club were unnecessary, because supply and demand conditions in the market for metals through the 1850s and much of the 1860s were such that abundant gold was being maintained in circulation (i.e., the cheap gold created by the strikes of the mid-century meant that the mint value of gold was high relative to its intrinsic [bullion] value). In essence, irrespective of their legal standards, these nations were practicing de facto gold standards. Once conditions in the market for metals changed in the late 1860s and early 1870s in a way that significantly raised the bullion value of gold relative to that of silver (i.e., made it more profitable to hold gold as bullion and silver as money), nations moved to demonetize silver so as to keep gold in circulation. The rapidness of the transition was the result of the high level of trade and financial interdependence among nations, which served to link them together into a kind of monetary chain gang: transition in any one or several important nations meant that the others were compelled to follow along. This interdependence manifested itself both at a broader (i.e., across the gold club) and regional (within the two economic blocs on the Continent: the franc bloc and the German–Northern European bloc) level. At the broader level, growing interdependence encouraged a conformity in standards, and any significant lags in keeping up with silver demonetizations in other nations exposed laggard nations to destabilizing developments in their systems of circulation (i.e., drained of gold and flooded with cheap silver). These kinds of pressures were all the more compelling within the two existing economic blocs on the Continent.

That nations felt both a structural and proximate compellence to make a formal transition to a gold standard did not in fact suffice to assure such a transition, nor did it assure that nations that made the gold link could necessarily maintain it. In this respect, the formation of the gold club depended on permissive conditions that made possible what structural and proximate forces encouraged. Those that had the greatest success in instituting and maintaining gold standards in this period were also nations that had fairly developed public (i.e., central banks) and private (capital markets) financial institutions, and that experienced fairly favorable macroeconomic outcomes (i.e., low inflation and low budget deficits). Those nations that did not ultimately fall into the gold club, delayed their entrance, or fell in but had eventually to suspend convertibility, on a whole exhibited financial institutions and macroeconomic outcomes that were less favorable relative to those of early gold-club nations.

The Structural Foundations of the Gold Standard

The Ideology of Gold

According to Joseph Schumpeter (1954, p. 770) it is difficult to explain prevalent cases in the transition from paper standards to gold standards in the last two decades of the 19th century independently of a "non-economic" factor: the quest for monetary "prestige." Italy, Austria-Hungary, and Russia shifted from a non-metallist regime where paper was depreciated in terms of silver to one in which monetary units were raised to an arbitrary gold parity. All of this occurred in decades which witnessed numerous deflationary years. Moreover, some of the dominant economic interests in those nations were opposed to fixing exchange rates.[3] This is explicable, he argued, when we realize that gold monometallism as a standard became a "symbol of sound practice and badge of honor and decency," and that national monetary authorities were compelled by the "admired example of England." In other words, gold monometallism became an ideological focal point. As a standard, it was imputed a value which was independent of purely economic advantages (e.g., non-inflationary standard, low transaction costs in exchange). What Schumpeter attributed to monetary authorities of the 1880s and 1890s can be no less attributed to authorities of earlier decades.

In the minds of monetary authorities in these decades, a gold standard was seen as the most "modern" monetary system. It was considered prestigious to establish the gold link and quite "embarrassing" to break it. Deputy Dr. Foregger of Austria reminded his colleagues about the ongoing loss of "esteem" which Austria had to tolerate as a result of being on a "scrap-of-paper economy." The Russian economist Gurjev reiterated the international political relevance of a monetary standard. "Membership in worldwide civilization is unthinkable without membership in the worldwide monetary economy."[4] The Marquis de Moustier, presiding at the International Monetary Conference of 1867, stated that "sentiments" independent of economics held sway over monetary institutions, and that such sentiments were largely based on ideological attachments to certain practices (e.g., fondness for certain coins, fear of innovation). Gold monometallism, he suggested, generated such sentiments.[5]

National monetary authorities in this period were strongly metallist. Paper rated lower on the monetary hierarchy than either silver or gold. John Sherman's (1895, p. 387) view was quite representative of monetary authorities of the period, especially those in advanced-industrial nations: an irredeemable paper currency was a "national dishonor." Even in periods where traditional metallist nations suspended convertibility, there was a popular feeling that the government was taking away people's "natural" money. Nations unable to move out of a paper standard preferred to think of their standards in potential transition to metal (i.e., aspirations dictated a link to silver or gold).[6] Even actions that seemed to disavow metallist orthodoxy were often done for metallist reasons. Nations imposing controls on exchange of currencies and metals, and who found it necessary to suspend convertibility and devalue their currencies, often did so for the purpose of protecting their metallic reserves and circulations.[7] Hence, the prevailing ideological preference ordering of the period with respect to monetary standards was: gold preferred to bimetallism preferred to silver preferred to paper. In international payments this ideological bias had been visible for a much longer period, as commercial clearing showed a strong preference for gold throughout the 19th century.[8]

The ideology of gold was quite visible early on in Great Britain, it being a principal contributor to British allegiance to the standard for many decades before other nations adopted gold de jure.[9] As early as the 1820s it was clear that in monetary circles, gold monometallism was becoming a "matter of theology rather than economic analysis."[10] In fact, monetary authorities increasingly found the question of which standard Great Britain should practice an inappropriate one, debates being reserved for mundane aspects of the standard and questions of banking practices. At the Bank Charter Committee hearings in 1832 (the most comprehensive bank hearings in British history), 5,978 questions were asked of numerous witnesses. Only two of the witnesses actually spoke out against gold. Parliamentary attempts to substitute for gold continually fell upon deaf ears in British government. In Fetter's own authoritative study of British monetary orthodoxy in the 19th century, he describes British attachment to gold using terms such as a monetary "priesthood," "dogma," "creed," and "faith." Irrespective of other structural forces which consolidated Britain's gold standard, ideology was a central factor.[11]

The ideological attachment to gold outside of Great Britain emanated primarily from a propensity on the part of monetary authorities to make associations between national monetary practices and greater achievements in the international political economy. Authorities became sensitized to a prevailing association: there emerged a fairly visible relationship between the importance which gold played in national monetary systems, and the levels of economic development and political importance which those gold-using nations achieved. By the latter 1860s it had become clear that gold was perceived as "the natural standard of the stronger and richer nations, and silver of the weaker and poorer nations."[12] Ernest Seyd of the U.S., in his letter to the U.S. Monetary Commission [see U.S. Senate (1876, V. II, p. 11)], cited the prevalence of the belief that "civilized nations" should use gold and "uncivilized nations" silver.[13] The Swiss monetary diplomat Charles Feer-Herzog went so far as to call silver the "inferior metal."[14]

The status of gold derived disproportionately from the British example. Great Britain was somewhere near the height of her financial supremacy and her methods had stood the test of time.[15] That Great Britain was not only a monetary role model but also an economic-policy role model in the 19th century is generally acknowledged in the economic historiography on the period.[16] Michel Chevalier (1859) underscored how readily French and other European authorities imitated British financial innovations.[17] On all dimensions of money, nations would "turn to England for financial wisdom."[18] The compelling nature of the British example is attributable to what Jervis (1976) would call overlearning from history—i.e., hastily attributing a cause-and-effect relationship to a simple existing association.

In explaining the attraction of gold after 1850, Edward Atkinson and William Sumner's testimonies to the U.S. Monetary Commission [see U.S. Senate (1876, V. II, pp. 274, 275, 356)] representatively conveyed the prevailing lesson.

> The tendency of opinion in Europe had been for 20 years in favor of the mono-metallic system. From the example of England it was seen that the English by the mono-metallic system of a gold standard enjoyed great advantages, and the Continental nations, especially Prussia, seeing this, decided to go into the mono-metallic system. . . .

> The prosperity of England is due largely to its monetary standard . . . [T]those [nations] who adopted gold as their standard of value have . . . been most permanently prosperous.

That the belief was fairly widespread is partially evidenced by the reactions (sometimes unfavorable) of prominent British statesmen like Disraeli and Lord Beaconsfield. The latter, addressing a group of Glascow merchants in 1895, noted,

> It is the greatest delusion in the world to attribute the commercial preponderance and prosperity of England to our having a gold standard. Our gold standard is not the cause, but the consequence of our commercial prosperity.[19]

Maleworth, a representative of British India at the International Monetary Conference of 1892, argued that the gold standard had led to many problems for Great Britain, and in no way accounted for her economic success.[20] For the U.S. monetary diplomat Dana Horton the purported causal link became a "doctrinaire propaganda" used by the advocates of gold to drive out silver. Irrespective of differences on its validity, however, the lesson was compelling. Horton noted that notwithstanding its propagandistic nature, the lesson drove nations to transform their monetary standards.[21]

Of the nations that experienced policy transformations in the 1870s, the structural effects of ideology seem to have been strongest in Germany. For Germany, ideology was certainly one of the principal factors underlying its strong predilection toward gold after 1860. The period marked, in fact, a high point in what Stolper (1940, p. 33) called Germany's "Western orientation." It was most visible in liberal-elite circles championed by Ludwig Bamberger and Delbruck, and supported strongly by Bismarck, who had venerated Western styles in policy from his early years. Bamberger, the single most important influence on German monetary unification in the early 1870s, saw the Western trend as being one characterized by the growing displacement of silver by gold. Bamberger, Camphausen, Delbruck, and other leading liberals were "dazzled by the universal sway of gold" in developed countries.[22] These men saw gold (in that it was a fundamental part of the liberal-economic-policy agenda) as a means of what one publicist of the period referred to as putting Germans "in the same position as the citizens of the great industrial states."[23]

Within this Western orientation, the British precedent was especially compelling, and it was as strong in monetary as trade policy.[24] Bismarck's banker and financial advisor, Bleichroder, noted the prevalence of a desire in certain elite circles "to tailor our [monetary practices] to the British pattern."[25] The gold mark became a symbol of the German challenge to the politico-economic hegemony of the British, as "the [gold] mark could take its place beside the pound as the mainstay of stability in the West."[26] The importance of monetary status was all the more evident by the questionable economic rationality of a sudden transformation of six Germanic monetary systems traditionally founded on silver and paper circulation (only Bremen had been on a gold standard before unification). U.S. Secretary of the Treasury McCulloch (1879, p. 16), in fact, argued that such a rapid transition to gold monometallism was a mistake. Germany, he added, paid a great price for "[placing] herself along side of Great Britain." She risked severe deflation and could not match Britain's capacity to keep gold and thus maintain convertibility. For Germany, the competition for monetary and economic status in a world overshadowed by British preeminence fit directly into a general competition alongside its scramble for colonies and the "risk" navy. It was a quest for international recognition as a dominant power.

At a lower order of prestige, less developed nations were also compelled by the ideology of gold: they too sought to modernize their monetary institutions by emulating the practices of the West. Those that found it possible to begin practicing convertibility frequently did so, but their attempts to maintain the gold link often failed quite miserably.[27] Aside from possessing underdeveloped financial markets and underdeveloped central banking institutions, these nations also found the ideological drive to emulate developed nations especially difficult to accommodate because they felt the need for monetary systems that generated abundant liquidity, something perceived as a necessary condition for viable financial sectors. But generating abundant liquidity was easiest through a large note issue, which conflicted with the conditions necessary for maintaining convertibility.[28]

Both the developed and undeveloped nations in the global monetary system, then, felt the ideological pull of gold. This was, in fact, the only structural predisposition which the developed and underdeveloped world shared. Of the developed nations that were moved by the status of gold, Germany was perhaps the most compelled.

Industrialization and Economic Development

Laughlin (1886), White (1893), and Helfferich (1927) all accounted for the scramble of the 1870s as part of a general monetary evolution that continually caused inconvenient monies to be replaced by more convenient monies. The impetus for a more convenient metal was the result of the industrial revolution. The size and amount of economic transactions grew with economic development, and growing economic activity spilled out internationally as the level of foreign trade increased proportionally. This naturally raised the burden of using silver, the metal with much higher transaction costs in exchange. O. D. Ashley at the time noted:

> [Gold] is less bulky and easier to transport, more convenient to carry upon the person, and more easily guarded against theft or destruction. Ten dollars in silver would be an uncomfortable weight in the pocket, while in gold it would make no perceptible difference. . . . If there were no other reasons than these, they seem strong enough to give gold the preference as the principal measure of value. . . .[29]

Chevalier (1859, pp. 39, 40, 94, 95) argued that just as Rome stopped using bronze when silver became sufficiently abundant, gold came to displace silver when it became available in sufficient amounts in the 1850s. For Parieu the events of the latter 19th century fit perfectly into a pattern that saw "mineralogical, industrial, and commercial circumstances" lead to metals of superior "portability and density" replacing those of inferior portability and density. It is perfectly natural, he argued, that "silver first took the place of iron and copper, and . . . silver is now displaced by gold."[30] Edward Atkinson of the U.S. called the rise of gold in the 1870s a process of "natural selection."[31]

Monetary history shows that considerations of selecting optimal mediums of exchange in optimal denominations has always been sensitive to the income level of societies.[32] "Great civilized communities," argued Chevalier (1859, p. 95), "modify the machinery of their exchanges, in proportion as commerce extends its operations and enlarges its spheres." Lord Liverpool pointed out,

> Coins should be made of metals more or less valuable . . . in proportion to the wealth and commerce of the country in which they are to be the measure of property.[33]

Laughlin (1886, pp. 168–70) identified a "one-way" trend in the evolution of monetary practices in the 19th century. Nations, he said, allowed gold to displace silver in circulation in the 1850s and '60s, but would not tolerate the opposite trend in the 1870s. Nations were more troubled by a lack of gold than a lack of silver. Russell (1898, p. 202) referred to this 19th-century bias as "the natural tendency with advancing civilization to give to gold a quality as a measure of values which it denies to silver."[34]

This suggests that there was a systematic instability in bimetallism after 1850 that would have made it difficult to sustain cyclical shortages of gold emanating from the workings of Gresham's Law. Such cyclical shortages affected both metals in bimetallist regimes throughout the 19th century, which essentially rendered the practice of bimetallism an alternating monometallist standard.[35] Under any hypothetical bimetallist regime, if the market bimetallic ratio is distributed randomly around the prevailing legal (i.e., mint) ratio over time, and divergences between the two ratios make arbitrage in metals profitable (i.e., are greater than the transaction costs of arbitrage), then Gresham's Law will produce alternating abundances in one metal (the bad money, or that money whose mint value exceeds its intrinsic value) and shortages in the other (the good money, or that money which is undervalued at the mint). It is clear that nations' one-way orientation toward media of exchange in this period would have tolerated periods of de facto gold standards more than periods of de facto silver standards. Even outspoken bimetallists of the period admitted that due to silver's inconvenience for large transactions, any bimetallist standard which led to cyclical shortages of gold was unacceptable.[36] In this respect, preferences seemed to "tip" toward gold as a central metallic medium of exchange.[37] Hence, it appears that bimetallism after the 1850s might not have been as stable as Friedman (1990a and 1990b) recently contends. Nations would have instituted restraints against recurrent shortages of gold. In the 1870s this took the form of demonetizing silver.[38]

The transformation of monetary standards was not independent of the greater evolution of financial institutions in the 19th century. Rapid industrialization and economic development after 1850 shaped financial institutions in the developed world according to new imperatives. Nowhere was this more evident than in Germany and France, where the development of banking systems capable of handling long-term industrial lending was a response to the needs of the new industrial economies on the Continent.[39] Bouvier's term for the transformation of French banking in the 19th century ("cosmopolitan") aptly fits the transformation of monetary standards. Gold was the more cosmopolitan standard and silver the more rustic, since gold was better adapted to an urban-industrial economy and silver to an agricultural economy (where transactions were fewer and smaller). As an issue of the *Economist* (1866, p. 1252) of the period pointed out, "Gold money is becoming the money of commerce. . . . The large obligations of modern times are best settled in a costly metal. Gold is . . . the wholesale money of mercantile nations." The greater transaction costs in clearing payments in silver as opposed to gold was a major reason nations preferred to receive gold in international payments, the costs of dealing in silver being an implicit tax (the size of the tax being commensurate with the difference between the spread of the gold points and the silver points). This explains why gold was the first metal to be shipped when multiple metals were used to clear payments.[40] In nations with lower incomes, the compulsion toward a less bulky coin in larger denominations did not fit the nature of transactions, as MP Barbour's statement to the Indian Currency Committee of 1892 attests. He proposed that "a gold standard with a purely gold currency of full legal tender coins would not suit India . . . , because the gold coins would in practice be of too great value to suit the vast majority of Indian transactions."[41] In fact, when the British government initiated a greater circulation of sovereigns into India in the early 1900s, they found that such high-denomination coins were infrequently used in transactions.[42] Similarly, when the British government tried to substitute British money for cowries in Nigeria, they found cowries to be exceptionally resilient in circulation due to the excessive denominations of British money. As expected, cowries were especially resilient in the poorest agricultural areas.[43]

Transactions in coin after 1850 were still sufficiently abundant to make convenience in domestic exchange an important issue. In 1856, 80% of French payments were effected in metal (50% gold and 30% silver), while only 20% were effected in banknotes. As late as 1891 France still had 160 million pounds sterling worth of coin in circulation. In Italy only 1/10th of the money in circulation represented banknotes as late as 1865. In the U.S., the proportion of gold in the money supply increased from 39% to 49% in the years 1890–1911, years that also saw an increase in note issue.[44] Even in Great Britain, the need for gold in transactions was pronounced up until World War I.[45] Since banknotes in Britain tended to be in large denominations (the minimum denomination of Bank of England notes was 5 pounds), their use in ordinary transactions was limited, so much so that even in the period 1880–1914 the most important money in circulation was still gold coin.[46] As of 1914, there was 123 million pounds sterling of such coin in circulation in Britain. Similarly, French and German notes experienced limited usage due to their large denominations. In France the minimum denomination note was 50 francs. In Germany the smaller 20-mark note came into use only after 1906. The problem of large denominations in notes was a problem which pertained to most of the leading economies. It was finally redressed after the War.[47]

Even by 1909, in only four of the 12 leading financial powers of the period was there more paper than gold in circulation (Germany, Belgium, Sweden, Finland). Of the four core nations, in only Germany was the amount of paper greater than the amount of monetary gold (see Table 6.1). Interestingly, it was in the nations where the use of credit instruments and non-metal money was most advanced that we in fact see the biggest advantage of monetary gold over paper. In Great Britain, monetary gold was more than four times greater than notes per capita. In France the advantage was more than six times greater and in the U.S. more than two times greater.

If we differentiate between the early and/or rapid industrializers of the 19th century and the late and/or slow industrializers, we see a division of actions in the monetary diplomacy of the 1860s and '70s that is roughly consistent with the expected structural preferences. The early and/or rapid industrializers (Great Britain, Germany, Sweden, Denmark, Switzerland, and Belgium) can be said, as a group, to have fought harder to attain and retain gold standards in the 1860s and '70s. The late and/or slow developers (France, US, Italy, and Holland) fought less hard.[48] Holland was the only nation at the International Monetary Conference of 1867 to oppose the overwhelming call for the international adoption of gold monometallism. The U.S. and Italy fought the hardest at the International Conference of 1878 to bring nations back to bimetallism. France, of course, supported international bimetallism at the Conferences of 1878 and 1881, and stayed de jure with a bimetallist standard through the first half of the 1870s, as other nations turned to gold.

The growth of an international economy in the 19th century compounded the effects of domestic economic development on the choice of a monetary standard. For Unger (1964, p. 331), "the strong, world-wide current for an international gold

Table 6.1 Per Capita Monetary Stock of Leading
Countries, 1909* (in dollars)

Nation	Monetary Gold	Paper
Great Britain	12.54	2.55
France	23.57	3.82
United States	18.29	8.71
Germany	3.15	5.72
Denmark	7.11	5.44
Belgium	3.05	18.27
Italy	8.37	4.29
Switzerland	18.48	7.82
Sweden	4.61	6.04
Norway	5.52	3.17
Holland	11.69	9.88
Finland	2.10	3.97

*Source: U.S. Department of Commerce (1910, p. 731).

standard [was a response to the] rational needs of a developing international economy." The enormous growth of trade in the middle decades of the century naturally conferred a greater attractiveness onto the superior trade-clearing metal.[49] Gold's importance in foreign trade had historically preceded its importance as a domestic medium of exchange. It was not uncommon for nations on standards other than gold to clear their trade payments in gold. In Sweden, for example, where the silver rix thaler was the central monetary coin, trade was cleared in gold ducats. A dual standard was also practiced in Argentina, where gold became the medium for international payments, while paper became the domestic medium of exchange.[50]

One major concern behind the attempt at an international monetary union at the Conference of 1867 was with reducing the transaction costs of foreign trade through the institution of a common gold standard. Here again, gold was part of a greater movement of the time: international standardization. Russell (1898, pp. 82, 83) talked of the consensus at the International Monetary Conference of 1867 for gold as being reflective of a "spirit of the times." Part of this spirit was a movement toward reducing the transaction costs of international interdependence by standardizing the means of transportation, communication, and exchange. Ludwig Bamberger and John Sherman argued that with the growth of commerce, nations would be increasingly compelled toward conformity in their monetary systems.[51] The complex calculations required in determining the values of foreign currencies without standardization, and the foreign-exchange charges incurred by merchants, became more burdensome as trade grew. Laughlin (1886, p. 152) underscored the pressure put on French monetary authorities to use gold as a result of the growth of trade after 1848. In Belgium, where the trade sector was quite large relative to the economy, the pressure for gold was especially acute.

The growth in trade also served to compel nations toward Great Britain's standard because most of the world's trade was cleared in London. Moreover, with the growth and internationalization of finance, the standard used by Great Britain became more compelling, as financial institutions were drawn into an international marketplace for financial services and investment dominated by London. As nations' international transactions increased, the influence of the London market grew and encouraged gold standards.[52]

For reasons both of growing domestic and international exchange, therefore, silver was increasingly perceived to be inferior to gold as a central monetary metal.

The Politics of Gold

The victory of gold over silver in the 1870s was as much a political victory as it was an economic and ideological victory. As with most economic institutions, monetary practices exhibited a consistency with ongoing political developments in the world at the time. The growing attraction of gold over silver partly reflected changing political power structures across the 19th century. A rising urban-capitalist class (professionals, business, banking) was displacing an agricultural class (farmers and landowners) in the political hierarchy. The monetary victory of gold over silver and bimetallism was coterminous with the political victory of the bourgeoisie.[53] De Cecco (1974, pp. 58, 59), in fact, sees differences in the selection of monetary standards among nations (developed nations moving toward gold and less developed nations staying with paper and silver) as attributable to different political power structures defining economic interests.[54] The victory of gold over silver mirrored the victory of industry over agriculture, and stable-money interests (importers, creditors) over inflationary interests (exporters, debtors). This transition was most visible in the developed nations in this period. In the less developed world (periphery), the transition was far less advanced as traditional groups connected with the land remained in power. It is not surprising, then, that while the practice of gold monometallism permeated the developed world, it failed to make substantial inroads into the less developed world. It is also not surprising that Great Britain was the first to go to gold, given that this political struggle was first resolved there. Monetary philosophies can be differentiated according to particular class preferences in this period. The virtues of gold were best adapted to urban-industrial interests, while silver and bimetallism were better adapted to agricultural interests. Gold was naturally the preferred metal for business interests given that its convenience most efficiently expedited transactions.[55] More generally, the nature of urban vs. rural transactions created a natural division of preferences. Urban interests, who transacted more often and in larger amounts, preferred gold, while rural dwellers, who transacted less frequently and in smaller amounts, were less burdened by the use of silver. Most all rural areas in the developed world before 1850 transacted principally in silver. Russell (1898, p. 15), in fact, noted that it was the "plain people" in America that complained of the disappearance of silver after changes in the coinage ratio in 1837.

Creditor (banking) classes would naturally favor the metal that was perceived to be historically most stable, while debtor (agriculture) classes would side with the more inflationary metal. The 19th century witnessed a widespread perception that gold was that metal which was best at maintaining its value.[56] Starting in the 1860s, silver would begin a secular and precipitous decline vis-à-vis gold, thus definitively casting pro-inflation (agricultural) interests on the side of silver, and stable-money (creditor, urban-industrial) interests on the side of gold. But even before the 1870s, many creditors had been collecting debts in gold.[57] Furthermore, stable-money interests sided with monometallism, while pro-inflation interests sided with bimetallism. First, there was the conviction that a multiple metallic standard would encourage a larger money supply.[58] Second, under bimetallism debtors had the benefit of accepting loans in an appreciating metal and liquidating in a depreciating metal.[59] To some extent, this narrowed the monetary menu to a choice between gold and silver monometallism in a period when the silver standard was the least acceptable (ideologically and economically) metallist option.[60] By the 1880s, with the consolidation of urban industry's political position in Europe and the U.S., the creation of an international bimetallist league to abate the decline of silver became politically difficult to orchestrate.[61]

The rise of the urban industrial classes on the Continent manifested itself in the rise of liberal parties. In Germany the party of note was the National Liberal Party, which came to represent, according to Stern (1977, p. 177), the interests and ideals of the German middle class (academics, industrialists, urban professionals, bankers, merchants). It crystallized from the fracture of liberal politics in the 1860s and emerged as the principal challenger to the German Conservatives, a party strongly grounded in agricultural interests (peasants and landowners). In the 1870s liberals became the dominant party in the Reichstag (they had as many as 40% of the seats in 1874). One legislator, Freytag, observed that the Reichstag had become "nothing but a great assembly of delegates for customs and trade interests."[62] This was to be expected, since the Reichstag, like the Constitution, was a manifestation of bourgeois political agitation for democracy.

The political struggle between classes, in Germany and on the Continent as a whole, was coterminous with the struggle between autocratic government and parliamentary government. In Germany it was specifically between the Crown (the conservative bases of power were the army, bureaucracy, and the Crown) and the Reichstag. Bismarck, whose own leanings dictated a conservative government in Germany, was intent on resolving this dispute in a way that would bring about unification founded on a clear conservative hierarchy which was supported by an urban-industrial class. He felt no government was sustainable without the backing of the two economic pillars of the German state (agriculture and industry).[63] To do this he would orchestrate a quid pro quo which configured domestic economic policy according to the preferences of liberals in exchange for liberal support of a conservative government. The political aspirations of the liberals would be "appeased by material concessions."[64] Having been extremely sensitive to the power of the new political classes in German society after 1850, Bismarck worked especially hard to gain their support from the 1860s on via economic reforms in a laissez-faire direction. As Hamerow (1972, p. 345) notes, "The forces of nationalism, liberalism, and industrialism rooted in the middle class formed a bulwark for the policies pursued by the government after 1866."[65]

Part of the economic reform quid was in monetary policy. Liberals sought a monetary policy adapted to the needs of an industrialized society, i.e., unification, rationalization, and standardization of German money on a gold basis. Conservative groups in government, led by the Junkers, resisted gold, fearing its deflationary consequences.[66] Bismarck saw the reforms as means to a political end, which interested him much more than monetary matters.[67] Notwithstanding Bleichroeder's pleas to the Iron Chancellor for bimetallism, Bismarck went along with the liberal monetary agenda. Monetary reform would be allowed to take place in a Reichstag dominated by liberals; and in monetary matters, the liberals were guided by Ludwig Bamberger.[68] Bamberger's own personal vision of unification was quite representative of broad liberal preferences on the Continent: stable money, unification of coinage based on simplicity and gold monometallism, and central-bank control of credit. An intellectually elite subset of the German liberals—members of the Congress of German Economists (principally Bamberger, Prince-Smith, Braun, and Grumbrecht)—were responsible for writing the laws establishing German monetary unification in 1871 and '73. The Congress leaders essentially controlled intimate elements of economic policy in the late 1860s and early '70s. Schmoller observed that it was this small group that "dominated the market, the press, and legislation" in this period.[69] By the 1880s, their economic agenda was so politically entrenched that initiatives of inflationist groups (like the Congress of German Farmers) to bring back silver were consistently falling on deaf ears.[70] President of the Reichsbank direktorium Havenstein summed up the political bias over monetary politics in Germany from the 1880s onward in his testimony to the National Monetary Commission.

> But there can be no doubt that, considering the fact that Germany has been converted from an agricultural to an industrial country, and that this transformation is going on at an accelerated rate, it must be regarded and prescribed as the chief duty of the Imperial government and of its credit and monetary institution, the Reichsbank, to look after the interests of trade and industry, however distasteful this may be to our landed gentry.[71]

The defeat of the Kanitz Plan (calling for bimetallism, a reform of the stock exchange, and the nationalization of grain imports) in the 1890s marked the last significant contestation over Germany's monetary standard before the War.

In the Latin Union and Northern European nations, there was much more continuity between real political influence and economic policy. In Germany, liberals found that the former fell far short of the latter. In France this was not the case. The Second Empire (1852–1871) saw France make major strides toward a government consistent with liberal principles.[72] Politics became inextricably tied to the preferences of the rising economic classes. Napoleon III's own power elite (appointed ministers) came disproportionately from the grand bourgeoisie (merchants, financiers, and industrialists). The legislature (Deputies) came to be dominated by former civil servants and the grand bourgeoisie, each more numerous than landowners.[73] Napoleon's political agenda was not functionally dissimilar to Bismarck's. Both men courted a broad-based coalition of political movements under a fundamentally conservative banner. Napoleon sought a union of the masses, aristocracy, and bourgeoisie under a Bonapartist bridgehead. Both courted the middle classes through economic reforms under the full realization that no French or German government could be viable void of bourgeoisie support. Napoleon, however, was personally more motivated by economic reform than Bismarck, who saw it as a means to specific political ends.

The political strength of the bourgeoisie and the pro-bourgeois economic orientation of French economic policy carried on into the Third Republic and the administrations of Thiers and MacMahon. Although Thiers denounced the liberal policies of Napoleon, he himself took a stronghold in the center-left, a position grounded in middle-class politics. MacMahon too deftly straddled the political fence between right and left, without losing a centrist-bourgeois orientation.[74] The Third Republic came to rest politically on a foundation of "businessmen, merchants, manufactures, professional classes, and petty proprietors and tradesmen: the bulwarks of bourgeois respectability."[75] It was clear by the 1880s that the mainsprings of republicanism were commerce, industry, and finance (the political rift between the latter two being mitigated by the Freycinet Plan), and it was within these elements in French society that gold found its greatest support.[76]

In Switzerland and Belgium, after many years of liberal agitation, we saw the entrenchment of liberal governments by the 1870s. Belgium's liberal constitution, founded after independence from Holland in 1830, set a European precedent. Liberals, representing large-town bourgeoisie, dominated Belgian politics from 1847 to '70. The Liberal Party took formal control of the government in 1878 under M. Frere-Orban.[77] This was particularly instrumental in consolidating gold monetary policy, since Frere-Orban and the liberal platform had strongly supported a gold link in the 1870s.[78]

Switzerland, even before federation in 1848, was dominated by liberal politics through regional control in the cantons. The constitution of a united Switzerland was, in fact, the creation of liberal forces.[79] This institutionalization of liberal politics was crucial in moving the Bundesrath in a direction that was consistent with the demands of business and banking in the mid and late 1850s. One of these demands was the monetization of gold consistent with the French system.

Italy in the 1860s and part of the '70s was dominated by a liberal elite. The political system was an extension of Piedmonte's, which had a liberal-constitutional system from the late '40s. It essentially reflected Cavour's own political and economic leanings, which were strongly configured around the English example. Up until 1876 when the left took power, leaders tended to be Cavour clones, reflecting both his political and economic agendas.[80] It was indicative of the strength of the capitalist commitment to and fight for gold that gold monometallism maintained great support even in periods when metallic convertibility was difficult to maintain.

The Scandinavian nations and Holland followed the Continental trend. Sweden saw the rise of liberal politics in the 1840s as a function of the political rise of a business class. As in France and Germany, liberals used this leverage to promote economic reforms. The general reforms of Oscar I in the 1850s were typical of the Continental trend. In Sweden the rise of liberal politics was especially pervasive, manifesting itself in the management of political, economic, judicial, and social systems.[81] Liberal politics in Denmark were also quite visible and active in the first third of the century during the reign of Frederick VI. For Denmark, like Sweden, the 1840s was a crucial period in the growth of liberalism. Liberals became a national party in 1842 and gained significant influence in state assemblies by the late 1840s. This decade saw Christian VIII undertake extensive economic reforms. By the '50s the National Liberal Party came to dominate the Royal Council and the Landsting.[82] Holland too fit the Continental model. Some, in fact, would say that Dutch society was historically bourgeois.[83] The rise of liberal politics was intense in the 1840s, with 1848 proving to be a crucial political turning point. Led by Thorbecke, liberals imposed a constitution (onto the government of William II) which reflected a middle-class political agenda. The system, consolidated under William III (1848–90), carried on a typically Continental style of economic policy.[84] Holland also showed the same political dynamics over monetary issues that France did in the 1870s: a split between a Crown or executive which sympathized with silver versus a coalition of capitalist groups pushing strongly for gold. The reluctance to relinquish silver and bimetallist regimes de jure in these nations in the 1870s can be largely explained by a liberal lag in co-opting the executive on monetary practices.[85]

Norway did not reflect the typical Continental timing in the transformation of politics, although the Norwegian political struggle was indeed typically Continental (liberal coalition versus a conservative government led by the Crown). Party politics remained relatively underdeveloped. It wasn't until the mid-1880s that liberals and conservatives formed viable political parties. Although liberals gained moderate power throughout the century, it wasn't until 1884 that they took formal control of the government.[86] Much of this is explained by the fact that Norway didn't experience the same socioeconomic transformation that other Continental nations did. It remained predominantly a small peasant farming economy throughout the 19th century.[87]

In the U.S., the politics of money after the Civil War were coterminous with the politics of inflation. In the 1860s and early '70s, the political conflict over inflation was between metallism and paper (fiat), i.e., the politics of resumption. Inflationists favored the continuation of the greenback regime put in place during the War. Stable-money interests advocated prompt resumption of convertibility. When silver began its precipitous fall in value during the late 1860s and '70s, and was therefore perceived as a metallist alternative to a fiat standard for inflationists, the politics of inflation saw a redefinition in its factions. Inflationists now saw silver as a viable substitute or complement for a fiat regime, while stable-money forces swung sharply away from bimetallism and silver to gold monometallism.[88] The monetary factions crystallized into three somewhat overlapping sets of opposing forces: by class, region, and party politics. With respect to class, the factions fundamentally mirrored the European style. Stable money was the preference of an urban-capitalist class (commercial bankers, professionals, merchants, manufacturers, gentlemen reformers, respected literati) and was confronted by an inflationist-rural-agricultural class of farmers, landowners, and miners.[89] Regionally, the issue often split along a North-East (stable money) versus South-West (inflationists) cleavage. With respect to party politics, it was the "hard-money" Republicans versus "soft-money" Democrats.[90] Regional and class politics overlapped, with an industrial North and East against a rural South and West, and a creditor East supplied the liquidity needs of a debtor

West (in farm mortgages) and South (in crop liens).[91] Partisan politics also overlapped with region: a Republican North and East against a Democratic South and West.[92]

Unlike Europe, where the shift in monetary politics in favor of stable money was incremental, the shift in the U.S. power structure emerged abruptly from the ashes of the Civil War. The War, by enhancing industrialization and regionally polarizing party politics, created rigidities favoring stable-money interests in American politics for the rest of the century. First, the War was also a "social war" in which the structure of class-political power shifted to an urban-industrial class.[93] The class grew strong both in Democratic and Republican politics, but found its ultimate partisan base in the latter.[94] As Schlesinger (1945, p. 503) points out, the party "was captured during and after the war by a boarding party of bankers and industrialists." In its identification as the "union party" or "savior of the union" during the War, and with its ongoing linkage of Democratic politics to the War (i.e., a practice termed "waving the bloody shirt"), the party was able to create voting and alignment rigidities that enhanced the power of national and regional Republican political agendas for the rest of the century.[95]

The rigidities in monetary politics manifested themselves in a stable-money policy orientation from the 1860s onward.[96] The history of crucial legislation in this period bears this out.[97] The Contraction Act of 1866 called for the retirement of greenbacks and their replacement with government bonds. The Public Credit Act of 1869 committed the Treasury to redeem bonds, both principal and interest, in gold. President Grant vetoed the Inflation Bill of 1874, which had called for a large expansion in note circulation. The Resumption Act of 1875 called for the end of the paper standard and the re-institution of convertibility in 1879. In 1877 the Bland Bill for unlimited silver coinage was voted down in Congress.

Even the supposed victories of soft money in this period were nothing more than hard-money concessions enacted for the purpose of avoiding more inflationary legislation, or for relieving economic pressures created by contractionary legislation. The Act of 1868, suspending the retirement of greenbacks, was a means of abating the sharp price decline set in motion by the Contraction Act of 1866.[98] The June Banking Act of 1874, which gave inflationists concessions on reserve requirements as well as on the issue and distribution of banknotes, was a conciliatory response to soft-money dissatisfaction with the veto of the Inflation Bill.[99] The Bland-Allison Act of 1878 was the compromise alternative to the Bland Bill of 1877, which was voted down. The act included a moderate silver-purchase agreement (2–4 million dollars per month), which fell far short of silverite preferences. For stable-money groups, limited silver purchase was seen as the lesser of two evils. Similarly, the Sherman Act of 1890 offered limited government purchase and coinage of silver instead of unlimited coinage, although the purchase clause of the act increased the Bland-Allison targets.

The politics of money, as a reflection of the greater political struggle within the developed world, showed that monetary issues were increasingly resolved in favor of stable money, which by the end of the 1860s and early '70s was equated with gold. This was not the case in the less developed world and even parts of Europe (especially Eastern Europe). Latin America was quite representative of the structure of the politics of inflation in the less developed world in this period. The ruling oligarchs were owners of large monocultural latifundia. Their income derived almost solely from agricultural exports, and they of course paid wages in domestic currencies. Depreciation of the currency was deemed favorable because it decreased their real costs (in wages) and increased their real income (in greater amounts of domestic currencies per unit of foreign currency which they received for their exports). Their export prices and the wages they paid in domestic currency were linked to the premium on gold in their economies; hence depreciation served the dual function of raising revenues and decreasing costs, thus generating a greater profit from each unit of agricultural product.[100] Moreover, landowners tended to have large mortgage debts, which of course were paid off in domestic currencies.[101] Since business and banking classes were small or nonexistent, the coalition for stable money was structurally underdeveloped. Hence, the politics of inflation saw an asymmetry which was just the opposite of that asymmetry in the developed world; there remained structural political impediments to anti-inflation laws and policies. This is an important factor in explaining why less developed nations did not jump on the gold bandwagon as readily as developed nations did in the last third of the century. They tended to remain with silver or paper.[102]

This is not to say pro-stable money groups were absent. As in the developed world, monetary and coinage laws were actually contested, albeit in asymmetrical fashion. There were various groups that provided a voice for a strong currency. Foreign indirect investors wanted a strong currency to maintain acceptable real returns. Foreign direct investors, of course, found the purchasing power of their repatriated profits declining as the currency of the host nation depreciated. Foreign creditors preferred stable-money regimes for obvious reasons. Finally, immigrant workers in less developed nations had overlapping interests with foreign direct investors: their remittances back home would decline in purchasing power to the extent that the domestic currency depreciated. In virtually all the instances of less developed nations actually making the gold link (although the link was rarely maintained for any significant period), the initiatives were results of these pro–stable-money voices making a political impact, with especially glaring cases occurring in Chile in 1892–95, Costa Rica in 1896, Panama in 1906, Ecuador in 1908, Mexico in 1905, and in Argentina's multiple attempts.[103] In Eastern European nations, agricultural groups remained strong, which is an important reason explaining why these nations made later transitions to gold in the 1890s rather than in the 1870s.[104] In these cases it took a very strong stand (driven principally by the status of gold) by political authorities to join the gold club.[105]

In general, the structural compellence toward gold tended to be consistent, with the exception of ideology, over the three factors. Developed nations were not only compelled by a pro-gold ideology, but both their levels of economic development and their political transformations encouraged the stable-money/convenient standard. In less developed nations, ideological orientations did encourage gold (i.e., the prestige of joining the gold club was pervasive), but the lack of economic development and the absence of a bourgeois political transformation abated pressure to introduce a standard that checked inflation and facilitated large transactions (both domestic and international). Furthermore, it may be the case that monetary status was a necessity for the developed world, while it was only a luxury for less developed nations. Developed nations apparently felt more pressure to conform to the practices of leading nations. Ford (1962, p. 134), for example, notes how Argentina did not feel the same shame that Great Britain would have felt in breaking the gold link, while Keynes ([1913] 1971, p. 15) observed that when the Reichsbank found it necessary to limit convertibility, it did so "covertly and with shame."

Inconsistencies in preferences over monetary standards in this period often reflected inconsistencies in structural characteristics. The U.S. experienced an especially turbulent period in the politics of inflation, and itself was often a leading voice in the international resuscitation of silver. It was, however, one of only a few major nations of the period to be simultaneously a large exporter of agricultural and manufactured commodities. It had one of the largest agricultural sectors relative to the rest of its economy in the developed world, and it was also the only core nation to be an international debtor during the period.[106] The U.S. tended to find international allies in its cause to discuss the greater use of silver among nations that experienced relatively slow or late industrial revolutions (like France, Holland, and Italy). France and Holland were also late shifting to gold relative to other Western European nations. In addition to a relatively late industrial revolution, Holland was somewhat less compelled by a pro-gold ideology, the ideology of the Crown favoring bimetallism. Italy's own vacillation in and out of the gold club (suspending and renewing several times) was in keeping with a nation in which both the Continental political and economic transformations were relatively underdeveloped. Similarly, late transition to gold in Eastern Europe was consistent with the underdevelopment of these same transformations. Spain, too, stayed off gold, which is not surprising given its agricultural economy and traditional political power structure in this period.

Inconsistencies in the less developed world appeared slightly more anomalous (i.e., the occasional success of stable money interests in shaping the monetary agenda), but the distinct pattern that emerged was that the more advanced nations of this group had a greater likelihood of going to gold.[107] This was hardly the case in greatly underdeveloped colonial possessions, but in these cases the monetary policies were determined by mother countries, which found a colonial monetary bloc consistent with their trading imperatives. Trading interests in both mother and colony found stable exchange rates paramount, but pure metallist standards were difficult for colonies to maintain. A satisfactory compromise took the form of gold exchange standards centering on key currencies, with the exchanges closely monitored by currency boards dominated by commercial imperatives.[108] In some cases, lesser-developed nations like China and Mexico stayed with silver while continuing to hope that some international effort would be made by powerful nations to stabilize the value of the metal. Both these nations, in fact, continued making diplomatic requests to the U.S. throughout the period to orchestrate a price-support scheme for silver.[109]

Determining some kind of sense as to the relative importance of each of the three structural forces compelling nations toward gold is difficult both in general as well as in specific cases. This is due to the fact that there was significant complementarity among the factors, and because outcomes were compounded by permissive (i.e., the domestic institutional and policy conditions conducive to making and maintaining a gold link) and proximate factors (trade and monetary dependence among nations).

With the exception of ideology, nations were fairly consistent in their characteristics across the factors. Nations that experienced an industrial revolution tended also to be nations that were undergoing a bourgeois political revolution. Nations that had not undergone an industrial revolution also tended to find themselves under the rule of traditional landed groups. Hence, in the case of developed nations, all three forces ran in the same direction. In less developed nations, ideology appeared to encourage gold but economic and political structural trends cut the other way.

In assessing relative impacts among structural factors, some anomalies might carry suggestive implications. Portugal, for example, made the shift to gold in the 1850s before the scramble period in the face of traditional political power structures and an agrarian economy. Notwithstanding some ideological leanings, it is clear the move was driven by extreme monetary and commercial dependence on Great Britain. Here, the influence of economic dependence appeared most important. Spain, too, had some of Portugal's characteristics in terms of its politics and economy, but it never felt British dependence as strongly as Portugal (certainly not monetary dependence as much). It stayed on a standard that revolved around silver and paper. Italy exhibited similar structural characteristics to both, but it remained legally on bimetallism through the first half of the 1870s, its monetary regime being dictated by the preferences of France which dominated monetary decisions in the Latin Monetary Union, of which Italy was a member. Hence, three nations with roughly similar structural character-istics all pursued different regime choices. Unfortunately, the interdependencies among the three sets of causes (structural, proximate, permissive) complicate even these crucial structural cases. We can say for sure, however, that those nations in which the structural preconditions appeared strongest were also the most likely to fall into the gold club, and in fact those nations that made transitions in the 1870s found themselves in this situation. Conversely, nations in which the structural pre-conditions for a gold link were weakest tended as a whole never to enter the gold club, with only a very few exceptions.

Moreover, it is difficult to identify necessary and sufficient characteristics in the three structural causes. It is not clear that ideology can be definitively labeled a nec-essary cause of gold, even though just about every nation adopting a gold standard in this period had strong elements of a gold ideology. In fact, it is almost impossible to find a nation that didn't have an ideological attraction to gold; hence there is no major variation within this property.[110] Furthermore, neither politics nor economic development can be seen as sufficient (they certainly were not necessary causes given the cases). Germany, for example, lagged behind the rest of the Continent in its poli-tical transformation from a traditional agrarian state, but was the first after Great Britain and Portugal to go to gold. Economic development was slow in Norway, yet it was one of the first on the gold bandwagon in the 1870s.

Notwithstanding limitations in determining relative effects of structural factors, structural compellence toward gold was a powerful one. The sentiment for gold pre-vailed among monetary authorities who fundamentally believed in the quantity theory of money (i.e., prices and money supplies respond to the quantity of specie) in a period (1870s and 1880s) when prices exhibited strong deflationary tendencies. This sug-gests every likelihood that gold would give way to bimetallism or silver. In fact, the three major monetary conferences after 1867 gave nations the opportunity to take this step in a stabilizing way (i.e., it had to be multilateral—nations had to revert en bloc). Yet this did not occur. Even when deflation was most severe, the gold standard never lost majority support of the governments of gold nations.[111]

The Proximate Foundations of the Gold Standard: Chain Gangs and Regime Transformation

The 1860s: A Decade of Growing Nervousness

The compelling structural changes in the developed world in the 19th century created an environment ripe for monetary regime transition after 1850.[112] It would not be until the late 1860s and early '70s, however, that a structurally predisposed developed world would encounter the proximate catalysts that would consummate the transformation of monetary standards. These catalysts represented critical events that created and compounded nervousness over future trends in the value of silver.

The policy changes of the 1870s that demonetized silver were part of a common trend in the monetary history of the 19th century which saw nations protecting their monetary systems against disturbances in the market for metals. The gold strikes in the late 1840s and '50s, for example, led to a depreciation of gold which caused Belgium, Spain, Naples, Switzerland, and Holland to protect their silver circulations by limiting gold convertibility. For similar reasons, Great Britain limited the monetary use of gold in India in the 1850s.[113] The Act of 1834 changed the legal bimetallic ratio in the U.S. from 15-to-1 to 16-to-1 in order to abate a shortage of circulating gold coin resulting from a market bimetallic ratio that undervalued gold and overvalued silver at the mint. The Act of 1853 reduced the weight of small silver coins to abate the effects of the gold discoveries on silver circulation. Like other domestic metallist monetary regimes, then, the regimes of the 1870s were subject to vagaries in the market for precious metals, but the constellation of policy responses of the 1870s was far broader on a national level, and far more pervasive on an international level, than any similar phenomena before it.

The 1870s version of this trend showed policy responses to the displacement of gold by silver in circulation owing to a depreciation of the latter metal. This reversed the pattern which prevailed in the 1850s and early '60s when the depreciation of gold led to the displacement of silver (i.e., large gold but limited silver circulation). By the late 1860s, with the movement of the market bimetallic ratio to a level which overvalued silver and undervalued gold at mints, it became profitable to import and coin silver, and melt and export gold. A continuation of this trend had two severe consequences. First, national monetary systems would be dominated by silver circulation, and gold would be scarce. Second, with the inflow of silver, nations would be on de facto standards based upon what John Sherman (1895, p. 541) pejoratively referred to as a "depreciated currency." Nations had difficulty tolerating the first, given their greater dependence on gold for larger-coin transactions. As for the second, a depreciating currency carried the possibility of several undesirable consequences. The foreign debts of nations on silver would be more difficult to service without threatening convertibility, as they would have to sell increasing amounts of silver to get the gold necessary to liquidate debts. The falling price of silver would make it difficult for nations to estimate governments' fiscal needs. Depreciation would enhance exchange risk, thus repelling foreign investors. Borrowers from silver nations would be subjected by creditors from gold nations to greater debt service costs in the form of higher interest rates to make up for such risk. This would make private and public transactions more complicated for both debtor and creditor. Depreciation also meant that silver nations would have to export an increasing amount of goods in order to continue importing any given amount of goods from gold nations. Finally, a depreciating currency encouraged inflation. The stable-money orthodoxy of the period made monetary officials especially hostile to this latter possibility. Chevalier (1859, p. 201) noted how destabilizing it was for nations to shift to a standard (i.e., silver) "at the very moment when it is impaired in value and launched in a movement of depreciation."

Like domestic metallist regimes of the past, therefore, the regimes of this period were sensitized to developments in the market for precious metals. Given the strong structural predisposition toward gold, any developments in the supply and demand for metals that suggested a secular decline in the value of silver in the face of a stable or rising gold value was the cause of grave concern. The worst-case scenarios portrayed the maintenance of silver and bimetallist standards when the decline in the value of silver was large, rapid, and secular. The nervousness over the market for metals became significant in the 1860s when the expressions of the preferability of gold over silver and bimetallist standards became pronounced, thus suggesting that major shifts in the demand for gold (whose value promised to rise) and silver (whose value would decline) were on the horizon. The expressions became more intense and international, thus more visible, as the decade progressed. With this visibility came a higher level of apprehension.[114]

At the national level, the calls for a legal gold standard were widespread. The Congress of German Economists and Chambers of Commerce (Handelstag) had been advocating a gold standard in German states throughout the 1860s. Toward the end of the decade Prussian legislators, the German Customs Parliament, and various business groups (trade congresses) were calling for German membership in an international union based on gold. In 1869 a strong movement in Belgium arose to demonetize silver. Norway in 1869 began transforming its reserves from silver to gold. In Sweden, a specially formed monetary commission in 1869 unanimously called for monetary union among Scandinavian nations based on a gold standard. French Chambers of Commerce and public opinion advocated a gold standard in France. Similarly, in Switzerland, commercial and banking groups, along with the various canton administrations and economists, strongly supported the move to gold. The Swiss National Council, in fact, interpreted the Act of 1860, which monetized gold in Switzerland, as reflecting an intention to institute a gold standard in that country.[115]

At the international level, there were two major gatherings of nations considering monetary union: the Latin Monetary meeting in 1865 and the International Monetary Conference of 1867. The Latin meeting, which was originally called in response to disturbances in subsidiary silver circulation among the franc-bloc nations, ended up consummating a broader monetary union among France, Belgium, Switzerland, and Italy. The delegates of all four nations originally advocated union based on gold monometallism, with the French delegates eventually changing their preference to bimetallism after strict instructions from the French government. The Latin Union was founded on de jure bimetallism, but in actuality maintained a de facto gold standard by instituting a legal bimetallic ratio of 15½-to-1.[116] While the Latin meeting was regional, that of 1867 was truly international (inviting 20 nations that represented the developed world at the time) and unanimously proclaimed gold monometallism as the only appropriate standard for economically developed nations.[117] The conference proved to be one of the more crucial events in convincing nations that a major disturbance in the market for metals was imminent. Monetary experts of the period and historians have identified the conference as a fundamental turning point in the scramble for gold. According to Feer-Herzog, the conference "sowed precious seed . . . which the future would cause to germinate."[118] For the U.S. monetary diplomat Francis A. Walker, "The Conference of 1867, in proclaiming the crusade against silver . . . did [initiate the demonetization of silver], the consequences of which are even yet only half unfolded."[119] As a direct consequence of the conference, the Bank of Norway was authorized to change its reserves from silver to gold.[120] The conference also proved to be a principal catalyst of Germany's movement to gold. Its proclamation of an impending monetary transformation in the developed world made a German transformation seem ever more necessary in the Reichstag because of the large amount of silver in German states which would have to be liquidated.[121]

In addition to the proliferation of appeals for a legal gold standard, developments in India also bode poorly for the future value of silver. India had emerged as one of the principal silver markets in the world. Aside from extensive monetary use of silver, India being on a silver standard, the country also exhibited a large non-monetary use for silver. Silver was heavily in demand as ornaments for women, who under Hindu law could own no property except for jewelry and ornaments of precious metal. These ornaments and jewelry also traditionally served as a family reserve: households in need of liquidity resorted to pawning such possessions. Moreover, silver was also heavily used in architecture and the arts.[122]

Indian silver imports relative to world production exhibited an enormous increase after 1854. From 1855 to 1865, with the exception of the year 1860, yearly Indian net imports of silver were either greater or slightly below the entire yearly production of silver in the world (see Table 6.2). The net imports in 1865 were almost twice the world production of silver.[123] The period 1866–70 saw a decline in yearly net silver imports relative to world production to levels lower than the quinquennial imports of 1856–60.[124] Even though the price of silver showed little immediate sensitivity to shifts in Indian demand, these developments augured difficult times for silver in the future because the conditions leading to a lower demand for silver were not perceived as reversible.[125] First, with the return of U.S. cotton onto the world market, Indian exports were never again expected to reach the levels achieved in the years 1861–65. Furthermore, less silver was flowing into India because of an increasing use of council bills to clear payments, a practice which was expected to continue in the future. In the 1870s the average yearly sale of these bills was greater than 60

Table 6.2 Indian Imports and World Production of Silver, 1851–1879 (in thousands of dollars)

Year	Net Imports of Silver into India[1]	World Production of Silver[2]	Net Imports as % of World Production
	[000]	[000]	
1851	14,327	39,875	36
1852	23,025	,,	58
1853	11,529	,,	29
1854	148	,,	<1
1855	40,972	,,	103
1856	55,366	40,725	136
1857	61,095	,,	150
1858	38,641	,,	95
1859	55,738	,,	137
1860	26,640	,,	65
1861	45,432	49,550	92
1862	62,751	,,	127
1863	63,984	,,	129
1864	50,394	,,	102
1865	93,343	,,	188
1866	34,815	60,250	58
1867	27,970	,,	46
1868	43,005	,,	71
1869	36,602	,,	61
1870	4,710	,,	8
1871	32,564	88,625	37
1872	3,523	,,	4
1873	12,257	,,	14
1874	23,211	,,	26
1875	7,777	,,	9
1876	35,994	112,500	32
1877	73,382	,,	65
1878	19,853	,,	18
1879	39,349	,,	35

1. *Source*: Estimates in *Report to House of Commons* 1876 and *French Report of Conference of 1881*; reprinted in Laughlin (1886, pp. 252, 253).

2. *Source*: Soetbeer's estimates, reprinted in Laughlin (1886, p. 218).

million dollars.[126] It became apparent that the decline of one of the world's largest markets for silver might be secular rather than cyclical, given that significant changes in net silver imports before 1860 were never the resultants of the systematic uses of new financial instruments.

On the supply side, the production of silver had been secularly increasing from the second decade of the century, with especially large increases after 1850.[127] The rise of silver production in the 1860s, however, was not extraordinary when compared to the 1870s. The average yearly increases from the period 1856–60 to that of 1861–65, and from 1861–65 to 1866–70, were both 22% (see Table 6.2). Even in the latter quinquennia, the average yearly increase from the previous quinquennia was still well below the average yearly net imports of silver into India. But aside from contributing to a mild decline in the price of silver in the late 1860s, the increase added more concern about the market for metals, especially in light of the fact that the production of gold during the 1860s was declining. Gold production declined from the middle to the end of the decade, and total decadal production in the 1860s was 7% lower than production in the '50s. These differential trends in supply promised to compound the effects of prevailing demand conditions in moving the values of gold and silver in directions that would threaten national gold supplies. In fact, the latter half of the 1860s saw the price of silver dip and remain below 61ppp, and the market bimetallic ratio move from a level that was below the legal ratio in Latin Monetary nations (thus encouraging a large gold circulation because gold was overvalued at the mints) to one that was above it (thus threatening to drive gold out of circulation).[128]

In sum, the latter half of the 1860s witnessed the emergence of a nervousness over conditions prevailing in the market for metals. The principal concerns centered around supply-and-demand conditions that carried important consequences for monetary standards, and these conditions tended to be perceived as permanent rather than transitory. Gold would continue to dominate larger-coin transactions, the Indian market for silver was declining, and monetary authorities were compelled by the practice of gold monometallism. Critical events embodied in national and international proclamations of the superiority of gold monometallism as a standard for developed nations were perceived to carry important secular demand consequences. Furthermore, in the short run, the supply of precious metals showed an increase in the production of silver and a decline in the production of gold. It became commonly perceived that the world was moving toward conditions which would make it impossible to concurrently circulate silver and gold at par, and that any such attempts at concurrent circulation under the traditional practice of a fixed legal ratio would result in a scarcity of the most convenient metal: gold. Furthermore, any nation remaining on a silver standard would be faced with the possibility of a depreciated currency. In a fundamental sense, the 1860s initiated a contraction of the metallist menu in the eyes of monetary authorities. With prevailing conditions increasingly delegitimating the practices of orthodox bimetallism (i.e., with a fixed legal ratio) and silver monometallism, the choice was converging toward gold.

Already the changing supply-and-demand conditions in the market for silver (especially the falling absorption of silver on the part of India) were having an impact, although not yet debilitating, on national monetary systems.[129] The market bimetallic ratio reached and surpassed the prevailing legal ratio in Latin Monetary nations (going from 15.44 to 1 to 15.57 to 1), thus enhancing fears that bimetallic arbitrage (i.e., Gresham's Law) would lead to the disappearance of gold. And the price of silver declined from $61^1/_{16}$ to $60^7/_{16}$ (see Table 6.3). In France, legal tender silver rose from 185,000 francs in 1866 to 54 million francs in 1867. Although France's silver exports were greater than her silver imports in the years 1853–1864 (by as much as 350 million francs in one year), in the years 1865, 1866, and 1867 silver imports were greater than silver exports by 70, 40, and 180 million francs, respectively.[130]

However, as the decade ended, no significant policy initiatives were enacted that would legally eliminate silver as a central monetary unit, or significantly limit the convertibility of silver. Latin Monetary nations were still legally bimetallist, as was the U.S., which was continuing a suspension of convertibility. Sweden, Denmark, Norway, Holland, and Germany were legally on silver standards. As long as the value of silver had only depreciated slightly and mints remained open, fears of gold depletion and floods of silver were not yet overwhelming. This created a holding pattern in the late 1860s.[131] Critical developments in the 1870s, however, would turn this disposition of watchful waiting into a scramble for gold.

The Monetary Chain Gang

In terms of pervasive economic policy changes, the transition to gold in the 1870s was relatively rapid. The decision to move to gold monometallism was consummated in Germany and Scandinavian nations by the end of 1872. For members of the Latin Monetary Union, the transition was initiated in 1873–74, first with the limitation on the coinage of 5-franc silver pieces in Belgium and France in 1873, and then the institution of limits over the entire membership of the Latin Union in 1874.[132] Holland limited the purchase of silver ingots at the Netherlands Bank in 1872 and temporarily suspended the coinage of silver in 1873. The U.S. was still on a paper standard, but did legally demonetize its central silver coin in 1873 and further marginalized silver by instituting a policy of limited silver coinage with the Bland-Allison Act of 1878. Hence it took essentially three years from the time Germany moved to gold in 1871 for all these nations to eliminate silver as a central monetary metal.

This rapidness was a natural outcome of conditions that created a monetary chain gang among these nations. The movement of any one or a few nations to gold in this period of nervousness would assure that the others would follow along. The chain-gang structure of monetary policy emanated from two types of interdependence. The first I refer to as speculative interdependence. The second type of interdependence was of a monetary and trade nature.

As for speculative interdependence, conditions in the market for silver in the late 1860s and early '70s were functionally similar to conditions in markets which find themselves at the height of a speculative boom (i.e., bubble): where investors are holding assets or commodities whose values are threatened with sharp and rapid declines. The liquidation of assets or commodities in such markets at what is considered a peak is typically one of contagious liquidation or "running with the herd," where one or several significant liquidations will create an urgency for other investors to follow along.[133]

Table 6.3 Average Price of Silver in London and Market
Bimetallic Ratio Between Gold and Silver, 1860–1895

Year	Price of Silver in London[1] (pence per ounce)	Market Ratio[2] (silver/gold)
1860	61 11/16	15.29/1
1861	60 13/16	15.26
1862	61 7/16	15.35
1863	61 3/8	15.37
1864	61 3/8	15.37
1865	61 1/16	15.44
1866	61 1/8	15.43
1867	60 9/16	15.57
1868	60 1/2	15.59
1869	60 7/16	15.60
1870	60 9/16	15.57
1871	60 1/2	15.57
1872	60 5/16	15.65
1873	59 1/4	15.92
1874	58 5/16	16.17
1875	56 7/8	16.62
1876	52 3/4	17.77
1877	54 13/16	17.22
1878	52 9/16	17.92
1879	51 1/4	18.39
1880	52 1/4	18.06
1881	51 11/16	18.24
1882	51 5/8	18.27
1883	50 9/16	18.64
1884	50 5/8	18.58
1885	48 9/16	19.39
1886	45 3/8	20.78
1887	44 11/16	21.11
1888	42 7/8	21.99
1889	42 11/16	22.10
1890	47 3/4	19.77
1891	45 1/16	20.92
1892	39 3/4	23.68
1893	35 9/16	26.70
1894	28 15/16	32.57
1895	29 13/16	31.57

1. *Source*: Lauglin (1886, p. 224) and U.S. House of Representatives (1903, p. 512).
2. *Source*: Laughlin (1886, p. 223; 1931, V. I, p. 514).

Monetary experts of the period described the late 1860s and early '70s as a period of "alarm and apprehensions" and even "panic" over developments in the market for metals that would have grave consequences for national monetary systems.[134] Any compelling signs that market conditions were turning against silver, either by a sharp decline in its value or crucial events (like legal changes in monetary practices) that signaled an impending decline, created a sense of urgency to preempt others in demonetizing silver, or following closely behind the demonetization initiatives of other nations. Any lag was considered with the greatest concern. Feer-Herzog's assessment of the situation facing monetary authorities of nations on silver and bimetallist standards shortly before 1871 is representative of a common perception of the time:

> There are two milliards of silver in Germany and Austria demanding that they be converted into gold, because the states that possess them are resolved to adopt the gold standard. The state that demonetizes first will do so with but little loss, while the state which shall have hesitated and waited will undergo the losses resulting from the demonetizations which have preceded its own, and so will pay for all the rest. The German authors have perfectly understood . . . the advantages which will accrue to their country from acting speedily. . . .[135]

From the late 1860s, both France and Germany acknowledged the advantages of preempting others onto gold and the disadvantages of lagging behind. The pressure was enhanced by the fact that a large proportion of the monetary silver stock represented public holdings (i.e., central banks and financial institutions with official functions). Such balances had the potential to come onto the market for liquidation rather quickly, the speed and the amount carrying dangerous consequences for the market for metals. The silver holdings of various principal central banks were actually greater than their gold holdings well into the period. In France, defenders of gold in the French Monetary Commission of 1869 stressed that the North German states were committed to gold, and that France dare not delay its transition in a world which appeared on the verge of a scramble. Germany's own movement to gold was formulated in an environment in which monetary authorities accepted the inevitability of a global movement toward gold, and were therefore more disposed toward a strategy of early transition.[136] Sumner's assessment of the scramble of the 1870s noted that as soon as nations became convinced of the inevitability of a widespread transition to gold and away from silver (thus assuring a declining value of silver), "they seemed to be running over one another's heels as fast as they could to get rid of silver, because the one who sold first would get the best price."[137]

The chains linking the monetary standards of nations were strengthened by trade and monetary interdependencies which created greater urgency to monitor and respond to changes in the monetary practices of other nations. Nations were concerned with keeping uniformity in their standards so as not to disturb trading relations with their principal partners.[138] Holland would have found it extremely difficult to sustain a silver standard once Germany and Great Britain, its two major trading partners, were both practicing gold standards. The Dutch monetary diplomat Mees stated that as long as Holland stood between Germany and Great Britain financially and geographically, she must conform to their monetary practices.[139] In the U.S., it was acknowledged in elite monetary circles that the movement to gold by the major trading nations of the world necessitated U.S. adoption of a gold standard.[140] John Sherman (1895, pp. 470, 1190) continued to argue against central monetary status for silver on the grounds that such a practice would "detach the United States from the monetary standards of all the chief . . . nations of the world . . . with which [the U.S. had its] chief commercial and social relations." In France there was grave concern over carrying on exchanges with the "great commercial nations" in a depreciated currency.[141] As more nations made the shift to gold, so much more compulsion would be felt by trade-dependent nations to follow along, especially when this shift caused greater changes in the relative prices of metals. Trading with nations under these conditions meant exchanging goods in the face of unstable exchange rates.[142]

In the greater constellation of developed nations that made transitions to gold in the 1870s, trade and monetary dependence most visibly manifested itself in two economic "satellite" systems: (1) Germany and its Northern European satellites (Sweden, Denmark, Norway, Holland) and (2) France and its principal Latin satellites (Switzerland, Belgium, Italy). Each of these satellite systems itself formed a small monetary chain gang centered around the monetary and trade hegemony of Germany and France. Within these systems the monetary policies of hegemonic economies were compelling. Any changes in monetary practices in the core were quickly exported to the satellite economies. Germany's Northern satellites stayed historically close to German monetary practices principally due to trade dependence. They, like Germany, were on silver standards before the 1870s. At the International Monetary Conference of 1867, the Norwegian delegate Broch made it clear that given Norway and Sweden's dependence on their trade with Northern German states (especially Hamburg), any decision these nations reached on a monetary standard must be conditional upon Germany's selection of the same standard.[143] M. J. Cramer, a U.S. diplomat reporting on the monetary situation among Scandinavian nations following Germany's move to gold in 1871, identified an overwhelming perception that because of Germany's new standard, "a corresponding change in the money system of the Scandinavian North had become an absolute necessity."[144] Holland, too, found the German move compelling. By the mid-1870s Holland found itself locked into the practices of a Central/Northern European gold bloc. As one Dutch Finance Minister noted, as long as German and Scandinavian nations were practicing the gold standard, "we had not the smallest inducement to think of any changes."[145] Compounded by an already large British trade, the Northern nations found themselves in a bloc whose monetary practices were strongly influenced by the preferences of Germany.

The Latin Monetary Union nations showed the same historical conformity in monetary standards. The Union's formation in 1865 merely consolidated an already existent monetary bloc (the franc bloc). In fact, Switzerland, Belgium, and Italy inaugurated the monetary systems of their newly unified or independent nations based exactly upon the French system as legislated in the Law of 1803. In Belgium's case, the Law of 1832 inaugurating a monetary policy was a word-for-word re-creation of the French Law of 1803.[146] By the 1860s, monetary and trade dependence within the Latin constellation had grown so as to discourage any significant deviations from French monetary practices.[147] The Swiss monetary diplomat Kern's statement putting forth his nation's position on monetary unification at the International Monetary Conference of 1867 was representative of the fate of Latin satellites. He said that

Switzerland itself preferred union based on a gold standard, but that its ultimate decision would be conditional upon the preference of France.[148] The Latin Union found itself in a situation in which "as soon as France gave up its double standard and accepted the gold standard . . . [i]t was certain that Switzerland, Belgium, and Italy would express their absolute adherence to such a step."[149]

Hence, the late 1860s and early '70s found the developed world in a nervous environment, and configured in a structure of monetary and trade interdependence that encouraged a conformity in monetary practices (i.e., in a monetary chain gang). Such a situation was ripe for a transition onto gold en bloc once the holding pattern of the 1860s was broken by critical developments in the '70s which increased the urgency of demonetizing silver.

The 1870s

Nations that adopted de jure gold standards in the 1870s did nothing but legally institute that which they had been practicing throughout the 1850s and '60s. Values in the market for metals in these decades had been such that gold displaced silver in circulation (gold was overvalued and silver undervalued at mints). No laws protecting gold circulations were necessary until market conditions changed so as to encourage the displacement of gold. But the overvaluation of gold and undervaluation of silver at mints by the late 1860s were still moderate, and as yet there were no definitive national commitments on the part of major economic powers that threatened the convertibility of silver. The 1870s changed these conditions of watchful waiting into a more intense nervousness. The period of greatest apprehension was initiated by Germany's legal adoption of a gold standard in 1871. Germany's transition can be regarded as the unilateral policy initiative that pulled the monetary chain gang onto gold.[150]

The German move made a crucial impact on the monetary-bloc structure of the international monetary system. Up until the German move in the 1870s, the world had essentially been divided among three major monetary blocs: the gold standard bloc around Great Britain, the bimetallist bloc centering around France, and the silver bloc centering around Germany.[151] That somewhat rough distribution created at least some symmetry in demand conditions among different markets for metals; hence a relatively stable equilibrium in the values of gold vis-à-vis silver was possible. With the shift of Germany and its consequent pull of its Northern European satellites into the gold club, the new bloc structure of the international monetary system upset the equilibrium in the market for metals by increasing the monetary demand for gold and reducing the demand for silver.[152]

Of the nations that eventually made the transition to gold after 1870, Germany was among the most structurally predisposed. Pro-gold ideology was most developed in Germany's elite monetary circles. The agitation of interest groups calling for monetary practices better adapted to industrializing economies was also most visible in Germany. Moreover, politics were strongly conducive to a gold policy, given Bismarck's sensitivity to the liberal economic policy agenda. Also, by the 1870s, Germany was no longer benefiting from the use of silver as much because its major Eastern European trading partners had shifted from silver to paper standards, and its trade was increasingly cleared through London bills. At the proximate level, Germany was anxious not to lag behind a Continental monetary transformation that it perceived as inevitable. The large inflows of silver in 1871, according to Helfferich (1927, pp. 155, 156), wiped out whatever uncertainty still remained in Germany about the exact course of monetary unification. The swelling silver circulation in Germany directly led the government to institute a reduction in the purchase price of silver at the Berlin mint (the largest German mint). When this failed at abating the influx of silver, the purchase of silver from private persons was suspended at the mint. As Helfferich (p. 156) noted, the exact legislation of monetary unification was now "prejudiced by the pressure of events."[153]

The German move had immediate psychological and real impacts on its Northern satellites. These nations immediately faced significant influxes of silver.[154] In 1872, a Joint Scandinavian Monetary Commission was formed to consider the monetary question following Germany's transition to gold. The report of the Commission established the foundations of the Scandinavian Monetary Union. It recommended that these nations follow the German policy and institute gold standards. In December of 1872 an agreement founded on the report was signed by Norway, Sweden, and Denmark. By 1873 all three nations had gold standards. Denmark and Sweden immediately became members of the Union, with Norway deferring membership (but remaining on gold) until 1875. In Holland, the German action caused the King to immediately appoint a monetary commission to consider the question of an appropriate standard for Holland in the wake of the new monetary conditions. The commission concluded that the silver standard had become untenable given the direction of monetary developments in the world. It cited the double standard as theoretically best, but it contended that it was not possible unless Germany instituted such a standard. It recommended that silver coinage be suspended. In December of 1872, the Netherlands Bank stopped purchasing silver. A law instituting a temporary (6-month) suspension of silver coinage was enacted in 1873.[155]

The fall of the German chain gang from silver was consummated by 1873. Fears of the scenario which gained international attention with the International Monetary Conference of 1867 were beginning to be realized. The world was demonetizing silver. The convertibility of silver on a global scale was becoming restricted as Continental mints were closing. Moreover, the entire net silver imports into India from 1870 to the beginning of 1873 were barely more then they had been in the single year of 1869, and they were less than half the net imports of the year 1865. Except for the years 1847–49 and 1854, net imports in the year 1872 were the lowest of the century up to that time (see Table 6.2). The precipitous decline in Indian silver demand in the 1870s was the source of even more pessimistic expectations about the future demand for silver.

On the supply side, the early 1870s experienced a significant increase in silver production and an equally significant decline in gold production. The increase in silver production from 1870 to '71 was the single biggest one-year increase of the century (roughly 20% by most estimates).[156] Moreover, it was believed that the mines in the U.S. were still short of their highest yield potential.[157] Concomitantly, the following year saw the most significant one-year decline in gold since the 1850s.[158] Especially compelling were fears of the supply consequences of Germany's move to gold.

Throughout the '70s the German silver supply was perceived as a major proportion of an increasing global pool of silver chasing fewer and fewer buyers as nations closed their mints. Fears of what France's Leon Say referred to as Germany's "enormous mass of silver . . . [being thrown] upon the metal market" permeated the period.[159] Although this grand conversion of German silver never materialized, it was a crucial factor in discouraging unilateral initiatives to support the price of silver in the 1870s and after. The German silver stock, said one witness before the British Committee on the Depreciation of Silver, was "hanging over the [silver] market" and generating great fear about the future value of the metal.[160] Like most fears, it had a tendency to be exaggerated: a banker testified to the Committee that the depreciation of silver was the result of fears that Germany "would be obliged to sell 50,000,000 to 60,000,000 pounds [sterling]" of the metal.[161]

By 1873 the course of events had brought market conditions to a state that put intense pressure upon Latin Monetary Union nations, which until this time were still in a holding pattern. In 1872 the price of silver breached two important thresholds. On the London market, it had dipped below 60 ppp for the first time since 1849. In September of 1873, the market bimetallic ratio hit the 16-to-1 level for the first time since April of 1845. The resulting influx of silver and outflow of gold from Latin monetary nations assumed "alarming" proportions. The net imports of silver into France in the first three months of 1873 alone reached 52 million francs. Net gold exports more than doubled from 105 million francs in 1872 to 225 million in 1873, and assumed an amount which was greater than one-third the gold holdings of the Bank of France in 1873. In the years 1872 and 1873, no gold was coined in the Latin Monetary Union, with the exception of Italy. The total silver coinage of France and Belgium went from 26,838,370 francs and 10,225,000 francs, respectively, in 1872, to 156,270,160 and 111,740,795 in 1873. Italy, however, experienced only a 20% increase in silver coinage.[162] Switzerland continued its policy of coining little of its own money, but found the influx of silver and the outflow of its foreign gold coin destabilizing. The state of monetary conditions could not continue in this manner.

Latin nations were rapidly losing their gold, and being flooded with silver. Agitation was strong in both Belgium and France to check this unfavorable flow of metals. Belgium was the first among Union nations to begin unilateral actions in response to the alarming developments of 1873 by reviving early in that year an old decree (of 1867) that limited the daily coinage of silver to 150,000 francs for the public, and the same amount for the national bank. Calls for stronger measures followed and the Ministry of Finance addressed the question to a group of monetary authorities, which declared that the Latin Union should move to a gold standard. A law quickly ensued empowering the government to limit or suspend the coinage of 5-franc silver pieces until January 1, 1875. France, in September of 1873, instituted a limit on silver coinage up to 250,000 francs per day (lowered to 150,000 in November). In that same month, the Bank of France stopped making advances on deposits of silver bullion, and practically refused to accept Belgian and Italian 5-franc pieces for deposit. These measures, especially the limitations on coinage which were secret, did little to stem the speculation in France.

A collective Latin response to the problem became inescapable, and in November of 1873 the Swiss issued a request to the French government to call a Latin Union meeting to form a new regime based on gold. The request was founded on a shared belief that since Germany and her Northern European satellites were adopting gold, it would be "folly" for Latin nations to continue their present policy of bimetallism. The meeting of the Latin Union in January 1874 led to the institution of yearly limits on the coinage of the Union's central silver coin, the 5-franc piece. The limits placed Latin nations in a somewhat safer holding pattern from which trends in the market for metals could be assessed before determining an optimal long-term standard for the Union. The measures resulted in a greater flow of gold into Latin nations, thus granting some relief. Although in France, net silver imports in 1874 were substantially larger than those in 1873.[163]

In Holland the temporary suspension of silver coin instituted in 1873 ran out in May of 1874 and the Utrecht mint was again open to silver purchase. The resulting flood of silver into Holland forced the government to once more suspend silver coinage by December of that year.[164] The pressures to make a more complete transition to gold became especially intense in this period, as a suspension of convertibility caused the gulden to depreciate significantly. It was also obvious that as long as market conditions remained the same or worsened, conventional silver and bimetallist standards were not feasible. In June of 1875, Holland established a gold (ten-gulden) coin and continued the provisional suspension of silver until December of 1877 when suspension was made definitive, thus formally instituting a gold standard. In Austria, the mint at Vienna was flooded in the early to mid 1870s as it kept paying out 45 florins per pound of silver. Pressure was unsustainable by 1876. It was in this year that unlimited convertibility of silver was restricted, with ultimate suspension following in 1879.[165]

The Latin Union met again in 1875 to adjust the limits agreed upon for the coinage of 5-franc pieces in 1874. The holding pattern was still viable as a favorable movement of gold which resulted from these measures continued.[166] But it was clear that market conditions were worsening as the value of silver continued to fall.[167] The decline in the price of silver in London was now dramatic. It went from 58 5/16ths ppp in 1874 to 56 7/8ths ppp in 1875. The market bimetallic ratio pushed to its highest level of the century at 16.62-to-1. Indian net silver imports were well below 1874 levels (see Tables 6.2 and 6.3). The belief that the depreciation of silver was not a cyclical phenomenon but secular became more compelling, and monetary authorities were looking for a more definitive standard for the Union.[168] The urgency to move to gold was enhanced by an even more drastic decline in the value of silver in 1876. In July the London price had been quoted as low as 46¾ ppp. The market ratio in that month had surpassed the 19-to-1 level. Following another adjustment of the Latin coinage quotas in early 1876, the silver question finally reached the French Chambers.[169] The result was a law in August of that year suspending both the coinage of 5-franc pieces at the French mint and the further reception of bullion for deposit.[170] The influx of gold into France from both Union and non-Union nations now stepped up. Belgium responded to her loss of gold to France with a law in December providing for complete and indefinite suspension of the 5-franc piece. This policy was extended de jure to the Union as a whole in 1878.[171] The lag in the Union's formal adoption of gold reflects the asymmetrical interdependence in the Latin system. The main force behind the lag was France, whose own preference for watchful waiting through the turbulent market conditions of the 1870s reflected the economic policy agenda of the Ministry of Finance and haute finance. Satellites were calling for gold as early as 1865. Once France formally fell into the gold club in 1876, its Latin allies followed closely behind.

The U.S. was more removed from this specific monetary turbulence of the 1870s, as it continued on an inconvertible paper standard. Hence, events on the Continent did not bring about immediate responses. The U.S. policy evolution toward gold in the 1870s was not of the drastic-reactive type seen in Europe. It was a less frantic and reflective response to compelling developments in the U.S. and the world. Above all, elite concerns gravitated around resuming convertibility with a viable long-run standard. Much of the input into decisions underlying monetary options were considerations of trends in Europe and the general movement of market conditions for precious metals. The management of the money supply and monetary institutions in the U.S. in the 1860s and '70s was configured around stable-money preferences. Behind much of the hard-money assault on bimetallism were fears over events in Europe and prevailing global market conditions. The principal fear was centered around secular trends in the world creating a "depreciated currency" in a bimetallist U.S.[172] Behind the Allison revisions of the Bland Bill of 1877 were sensitivities to the perils of resuming specie payments on bimetallism in a world bent on gold. Allison warned about the growing demand for gold in Europe and the destabilizing flows of silver into France. He affirmed the folly of being the only nation to open its doors to silver in a world which was frantically redeeming its excess silver to increase gold circulations. Each of the concerns manifested itself in the final Bland-Allison Act of 1878, which assured resumption on a gold standard.[173] Although the pull was milder, the U.S. also followed the chain gang onto gold.

By the late 1870s, with the transition to gold consummated, any unilateral initiatives toward silver or bimetallist standards were seen as impossible. Like a Prisoner's Dilemma game in a noncooperative-Nash equilibrium, any unilateral move toward cooperation (opening mints to unlimited silver coinage) exposed the cooperating nation to exploitation. Any newly open mints would be a tempting target for the mass of silver on the world market, just as the Dutch experiment of 1874 showed.[174] With the rapid decline in the value of silver and the now irresistible conviction that silver qua central monetary metal was at a point of no return (barring some grand international agreement), the potential flood of silver was expected to be devastating. Sherman's (1895, p. 541) concern for the U.S. was felt by all recent converts to gold. "The general monetizing of silver now . . . would be to invite to our country, in exchange for gold or bonds, all the silver of Europe. . . ."[175] Nothing better characterized this strategy than France's "expectant policy." It dictated that French policy would only follow the initiatives of the community of developed nations in any attempt to stabilize the price of silver. In essence, it committed France to being a follower, not a leader.[176] All nations still sympathetic to bimetallism (U.S., Holland, France, Italy) shared this view. Any movement back toward silver would have to be en bloc.

It also appeared that the theoretical diatribes against gold and rationales for bimetallism fell into increasing disfavor. Baron de Hock's famous analogy on the dual standard seemed to be accepted by more and more monetary diplomats: that bimetallism was like opium, beneficial in small doses (e.g., to expand the money supply in crisis) but in large amounts could be deadly. No bimetallist regime could be stable where actors believed that gold would go to a premium, because such expectations would fulfill themselves. Even if actors believed that there was no secular pattern to the values of precious metals, if legal ratios diverged from market ratios, national circulations would be subject to destabilizing shortages in central mediums of exchange. The only way to maintain bimetallism in the face of a shifting market ratio was to institute adjustable legal ratios. However, this would never have been seriously considered in the period due to custom (legal ratios had always been fixed) and transaction costs (the burden to the monetary systems was too great to make such changes on a variable basis; in fact, nations tended to make such changes infrequently even though these changes were badly needed).[177]

The International Monetary Conference of 1878, convened by the U.S. as a mandate of the Bland-Allison Act, gave the world a viable forum to discuss the resuscitation of silver. But it was doomed at the outset. The two international conferences which followed fared no better than that of 1878. The supporters of an international agreement, mainly the U.S. and France, significantly lowered their aspirations with respect to the scope of an international regime. Furthermore, moral hazard and the fear of the German surplus and free riding under an international silver-purchase agreement persisted well into the 1890s and destroyed any possibilities of cooperation. None of the core nations came forward to initiate a regime either unilaterally or as a group. Great Britain continued its passive posture toward formal regime building except for the Conference of 1892, where it was most aggressive in attempting to promote a regime in which the burden of supporting the international price of silver fell on the U.S. (the Rothschild proposal).

Not all nations, of course, fell into the gold club by the 1870s, but nations did fall formally out of the bimetallist club, insofar as it was practiced in orthodox fashion (i.e., with fixed legal ratios). The greatest pressure fell on nations that were exchanging gold for silver at legal ratios. For the nations that stayed on silver through the '70s (like Austria) and beyond (like China and India), the greatest pressure from the depreciation of silver was not in the loss of gold but in the depreciation of their exchange rate vis-à-vis gold nations. Actually, nations such as India and China found depreciation not an overwhelming burden to bear, given that they had export-oriented economies (the inflation, of course, was another matter). Some nations that were especially trade dependent on gold nations, like Shanghai, the Philippines, Mexico, Siam, Ceylon, Java, India, Panama, and the Straits Settlements, found an acceptable compromise in a gold exchange standard.[178] Such was a common method of stabilizing exchange rates in colonial blocs. In nations that continued using silver as a central medium of exchange, one means by which mints and monetary authorities could bear the depreciation was through the remuneration of bullion and coin at market value (hence limiting public costs of coinage). China, for example, practiced a bullion rather than formal coin standard, with the purchasing power of silver being determined by the market value rather than the face value of coin. Other nations like Austria and Russia abated the flood of silver in the 1870s and after by limiting the coinage of silver at their mints.[179]

When the scramble for gold began in the first years of the 1870s, it was as much a psychological as a real phenomenon. When Germany turned to gold, market conditions were far from intolerable. The price of silver had declined little, Indian silver demand was only then beginning its precipitous drop, and mints on the Continent remained open to silver. Germany's own move appeared to be structurally driven, with the anticipation of a Continental scramble and some market disturbances enhancing this urge toward gold. Political unification conveniently appeared as a means of realizing its monetary predispositions. Germany's northern satellites were driven by the anticipation of adverse consequences on their trade relations with Germany, as well as disturbances in the flow of precious metals. From 1873 on, however, market conditions became intolerable for any mints fully open to silver. Latin nations found themselves deluged with silver, and Holland's experiment with silver-convertibility resumption in 1874 failed. What was driven by cognitive dispositions at first (i.e., pessimistic projections about conditions in the market for metals) became exclusively sustainable by real conditions as the decade progressed.

There is no question that self-fulfilling prophecy manifested itself in the scramble, specifically in the nervousness of the late 1860s and early 1870s which contributed to the sharp decline in the value of silver in the 1870s.[180] It is also clear, however, that the market itself was in the midst of secular trends that bode poorly for the value of silver. Gold production showed a declining trend after the 1850s, and it would continue until the '90s. Silver production had been secularly increasing across the century, especially sharply after 1850. Also, with the passing of the Civil War and the increasing use of council bills, India would never again be the market for silver that it once was. Compounding these market conditions were, of course, the structural factors driving nations away from silver. The changing nature of economic exchange made silver increasingly archaic as a medium of exchange for large transactions. Growing trade and the internationalization of finance enhanced the desirability of emulating the British standard, which continued to generate appeal on ideological grounds. Shifting political structures created a more hostile environment against an inconvenient and inflationary metal like silver.[181] It is therefore apparent that, self-fulfilling prophecy notwithstanding, the transformation of monetary regimes after 1850 was irresistible. Self-fulfilling expectations merely hastened an inevitable outcome. Structural and market forces had brought the developed world to a state where real disturbances would have eventually threatened national gold circulations, and nations would have reacted (as they did in the 1870s) to these disturbances by demonetizing silver.

The Permissive Foundations of the Gold Standard

Some nations found it easy to follow the structural-proximate compulsion and formally adopt gold standards, while other nations found it more difficult to do so. In this respect, there appear to have been permissive factors which influenced the extent to which structural and proximate catalysts could dictate the choice of a monetary standard. Permissive factors, such as the development of capital markets and central banking institutions, fiscal policies, and the management of money supplies, played important roles in determining whether nations could successfully institute and maintain the gold link. Nations with more developed capital markets and central banking institutions, and which practiced fiscal and monetary restraint (i.e., low inflation and low budget deficits), found it easier to institute and maintain a gold standard. Conversely, nations that did not share these characteristics found it much more difficult to do so.

The development of capital markets affected the capacity for nations to attract liquidity in both normal times and crises. Attracting liquidity in both instances made convertibility more sustainable, but the ability to pull capital in crisis was especially important. Such development meant a greater number of avenues of attraction, as any fully developed capital market had numerous institutions capable of attracting investment in need. We could also expect a good proportion of the capital flows to make their way into central banking institutions as bankers' balances. This enhanced the central pools of liquidity upon which convertibility rested. Furthermore, the most developed markets had the oldest and most respected private financial institutions, themselves generating the confidence which made them low-risk alternatives in tight markets for investment. This was especially important in times of financial distress, when investors naturally reverted to the lowest-risk investment opportunities. Hence, in an international crisis, developed capital markets had a competitive advantage in attracting liquidity, which in turn gave them an advantage in maintaining convertibility over less developed markets.

Central banking institutions enhanced the management of liquidity, which itself determined the ease with which convertibility could be adopted and maintained. Although it cannot be said that central banking institutions across nations mirrored similar goals with respect to inflation, nations with central banks tended to have superior performances in controlling inflation than nations without such institutions. Moreover, there was a relationship between the extensiveness of central banking activity and inflation performance, nations with the most developed and active central banking institutions exhibiting the lowest inflation. Even under the private banking orientations which most of the central banks operated in this period, these results are not surprising. As private institutions, central banks were managed with a view to maintaining convertibility for their customers. Hence, greater control over inflation from central banks was to be fully expected in this period irrespective of how central banks ranked their private versus public functions and goals. Allowing an overly inflationary credit system with respect to convertibility obligations was irresponsible from both a private and public banking mandate. Moreover, there was a great ideological similarity among central bankers of the period irrespective of nationality: they tended to be stable-money ideologues. At times this was not manifest because governments might impose inflationary mandates on them which they could not resist. In general, however, this was far less the case before World War I because monetary management was not seen as a legitimate preserve of governments. This was somewhat less so in the underdeveloped world, where governments were more likely to get directly involved in the management of money supplies.

Trends in the behavior of money supplies, of course, irrespective of the sources, impacted on convertibility. Overissue of notes by central and private banks, for example, made it difficult to maintain convertibility. Hence, inflationary regimes made the gold link difficult to institute and preserve. Silver standards were somewhat easier to institute and defend by inflationary economies, especially at the time when the metal was depreciated. This is the main reason nations seeking to shift from fiat regimes to metal, such as Italy and Austria-Hungary, supported silver or bimetallism. It was much easier to make a transition to convertibility under a depreciated metal, since par was easier to defend with depreciated notes.[182] Under any metallist regime, the value of differing legal-tender monies had to remain in some kind of congruence; otherwise one would be driven out of circulation. If notes, therefore, were issued in excess, gold or even silver would go to such a premium that it would pay arbitragers to take the metal out of circulation and use notes in monetary transactions. The resulting monetary shortage of metal would mean that financial intermediaries would have insufficient means for converting notes.

Fiscal restraint made a dual impact on the capacity of an economy to institute and maintain convertibility. If governments had greater control of the metallic money stock (to use for foreign adventurism or to purchase weapons, for example), the banking system would find itself with insufficient means to keep up with the conversion demands of private actors. This would be all the more inimical to convertibility to the extent that the regime ran up large public debts. In this case, even if governments didn't have control of the money supply, the results could be similar if the governments could obtain advances from central banks or other financiers. This latter scenario would be one of a public drain of the metallic money stock, especially if the advances were needed for foreign payments. If the public authority monetized the debt, the effects on convertibility would of course be through the larger money supply and consequently through depreciated notes driving metal from monetary use. Hence, a lack of fiscal restraint would be inimical to the institution and maintenance of convertibility.

It is no surprise that the scramble for gold was initiated by nations with the most advanced capital markets. They had the capacity to obtain and keep gold. Many less developed nations would have liked a link to gold, but found it difficult to attract sufficient quantities of the metal even when interest rates were raised above those prevailing in developed nations. This appears to be the main reason that the less developed world found it difficult to make and preserve the gold link.[183] Hence, there was an adjustment bias favoring nations with advanced markets.[184] When nations without such markets attempted the gold link, convertibility either failed or experienced a brief life.[185] Even within the smaller context of the developed world, timing of the gold link was consistent with differences in the development of capital markets. Nations such as Russia, Austria-Hungary, and Japan made their link in the 1890s after gold had become more abundant. Their relative financial underdevelopment in the 1870s made it difficult for them to defend convertibility when more advanced markets were in competition for scarce gold supplies. Furthermore, of all those nations that instituted some kind of gold link in the latter 19th century, those that had to break the link by suspending convertibility had less developed capital markets than those that maintained the link. The former were Argentina, Portugal, Italy, Chile, Bulgaria, and Mexico. Moreover, as expected, those that were able to resume convertibility (Italy, Argentina, Bulgaria) had relatively more developed capital markets, in general, than those that did not resume.[186]

Along with more developed capital markets, nations in the gold club tended to have more developed central banking institutions than nations outside the gold club.

One especially crucial function of central banks in maintaining a metallic link was managing gold supplies in periods of financial crisis. Nations found such periods devastating to their gold stocks when they possessed no central institutions to manage the flow of gold so as to maintain convertibility. Those nations with institutions possessing discretionary powers to manipulate gold flows, like the Banks of France, Germany, and England, found convertibility easier to maintain. Nations without such institutions found no means of abating the export of gold in crises. There were various cases, with especially glaring examples in France (1882 and 1889) and Germany (1901), when central banking initiatives kept financial crises from turning into convertibility-ending panics.[187] This differential success in handling crises was visible even in the core of the international system. The U.S. was subject to more frequent and serious financial crises than European gold-club nations because it had less developed central banking institutions relative to other core nations, and had to rely on the Treasury's ad hoc assistance. Without such institutions, the U.S. found that when periodic asymmetries in the regional flow of liquidity combined with international shocks, the results could be severe. Better management of domestic and international capital flows would have put the U.S. in a more resilient financial state, like advanced European nations.[188]

Fiscal and monetary restraint compounded the permissive effects of advanced financial institutions. The early gold club (which made transitions in the 1870s), as a group, comprised nations characterized by prudent fiscal policy and stable money supplies. Budgets tended toward balance, public expenditures were not excessive relative to subsequent periods, and private and public banknotes were not issued in inflationary ways. The nations that jumped on the gold wagon later had relatively inferior performances in these areas. Austria-Hungary and Russia, for example, found the gold link difficult to institute in the 1870s because these nations were plagued by budget difficulties and unstable money supplies. This was especially true of Russia. A link in the 1890s was much more viable given the strides both nations made in abating these problems. Despite strong gold ideologies early in the period, these nations found the gold link difficult to consummate from ideology alone.[189] Of the early gold-club membership, it is not surprising that Italy had the most difficult time with its gold link, having suspended convertibility in 1866, resumed in 1884, and suspended again in 1894. This temporal pattern closely paralleled fiscal and monetary trends. Periods of suspension followed especially large public expenditures which the Italian government monetized. Hence, deficits and a resulting inflation were the catalysts which removed Italy from the gold club. A similar pattern was evident in Argentina's timing in suspension of convertibility and resumption in this period.[190] The fact that the developed world tended to be a gold bloc and the underdeveloped world a paper and silver bloc, is perfectly consistent with differences in fiscal and monetary performance. The former was characterized by much more restrained fiscal policy and stable money supplies, while the latter was not.

Determining which permissive forces dominated is difficult given that these factors commonly overlapped, much like in the case of the structural causes of the gold standard. Furthermore, all of these permissive conditions were clearly linked in a complementary relationship. Fiscal profligacy encouraged inflation, as debts were most easily eradicated through monetization. Central banks, of course, made stable money more likely, while lack of central monetary authorities meant that governments were unconstrained in their issue of notes. Governments which could obtain sizable advances from central institutions or large financial houses had less need to revert to monetizing the public debt. Larger, more developed capital markets necessitated larger central banking institutions for stability. The growth of one encouraged the growth of the other. Nations that had underdeveloped private and public financial institutions tended also to be nations with fiscal and monetary difficulties. Conversely, nations with highly developed financial institutions experienced few such difficulties. All such conditions were most extreme in the least and most developed nations, and unsurprisingly each set of nations gravitated to the expected options in selecting an appropriate standard. To find one dominant factor in this interconnected set of factors is difficult.

In the case of Russia and Austria, it appears that fiscal and monetary conditions were crucial, given that both had relatively advanced central banking structures, although their capital markets could hardly be called developed. In the case of Italy, the level of advancement of the capital market may have been higher than that of central banking institutions, and Italy was also plagued by fiscal profligacy and inflation. In Italy, central banking essentially took the form of an oligopoly of note issue among large private banks, an oligopoly which was poorly conceived from a central perspective and even more poorly executed.[191] But aside from these few crucial cases, much less can be said about the relative effects of permissive factors.

Even more problematic is the prospect of differentiating among the effects of the three sets of factors (i.e., which causes dominated?): structural, proximate, and permissive. Not only did structural, proximate, and permissive factors find complementarities within each set of factors, but there were also clear complementarities across the three sets of factors. Nations that tended to be structurally predisposed toward gold also tended to enjoy the permissive conditions which made the gold link obtainable and sustainable. Nations that experienced industrial and political transformations also happened to be nations with advanced capital markets centering around relatively more developed central banking institutions. In addition, they tended to be nations which practiced fiscal and monetary restraint. The links are fairly apparent. With the growth of the economy came a concomitant growth in capital markets. Growing capital markets required larger and more advanced central banking institutions to survive crises. This general growth of economic activity and finance also created a business and banking class to compete against traditional economic interests in the political hierarchy. With the rise of the bourgeoisie, we saw the monetary debate increasingly resolve itself in favor of stable money, which in turn encouraged fiscal restraint. Hence, it is not surprising that the favorability of structural conditions was paralleled by favorability in permissive conditions. The most advanced economies and most bourgeois political structures tended to have the most developed capital markets, central banks, and prudent macroeconomic policies. The least advanced and least bourgeois nations enjoyed none of these traits. For the former nations, the move to gold was absolutely compelling and possible. For the latter group, the move was neither. We would expect, therefore, that the proximate catalysts that emerged in the 1860s and '70s had greater impact on nations that felt structural compellence and whose financial systems (as well as fiscal and monetary outcomes)

made the link possible, and had less impact on nations facing less favorable structural and permissive conditions. The timing of regime transformation supports this
pattern, but not without anomaly. The more advanced economies with the most developed financial systems made transitions first, but the order of transformation was
not exactly indicative of structural and permissive characteristics. Latin Monetary
nations, for example, with the exception of Italy, made transitions after Northern
European nations which were economically and financially less developed than the
Latin nations. This was primarily a result of lags in French monetary policy which
gave undue influence to bimetallist elements in the monetary hierarchy. France, in
turn, dictated that its Latin neighbors refrain from making immediate transitions to
gold in the 1860s and '70s.

Because of the difficulty of teasing apart the independent impacts of the various
factors contributing to the scramble for gold, a simple definitive model of the regime transformation in the latter part of the 19th century would be difficult to construct. However, the general foundations of the transformation are clear. Specific long-
term forces in the international political economy compelled certain nations away
from silver and bimetallist standards toward the practice of gold monometallism.
These forces were the ideology of gold, economic development and industrialization, and the politics of gold. Although these structural forces predisposed the developed world in favor of a gold link from the mid-century onward, it would not be
until the early 1870s that nations acted to institute formal gold standards. Specific
short-term pressures which manifested themselves in the 1860s and 1870s heightened the urgency of this shift. Once Germany initiated the shift, the rest of the chain
gang of nations fell into the gold club. Finally, nations that were driven to make a
monetary transition to gold found the gold link either easier or more difficult to institute and maintain depending upon specific conditions relating to the nature of their
macroeconomic outcomes and the level of advancement of their financial institutions.

7

The Stability of the Gold Standard

One of the compelling conclusions that emerges from the historiography on the classical gold standard is that the period saw what economic historians call a remarkable level of stability relative to periods before and after.[1] As noted above, however, the historians have marshaled a plethora of diverse properties as testimony to this stability. Defining what constitutes international monetary or economic stability is an exercise in subjectivity. This is to be expected, given the differing views of what constitutes a well-functioning or desirable international monetary regime.[2] One inevitable shortfall of accounting for the performance of differing monetary regimes is, given the variety of definitions, an inability to definitively separate cause from effect. Is the efficiency of the adjustment mechanism to be considered an integral part of a regime's success or a cause of its success? Should international price trends be seen as a property of an international monetary regime or fundamental determinants of the regime's properties (e.g., in terms of their impact on exchange rates and terms of trade)? Should monetary regimes be judged on the performance of real international variables, such as growth in income and employment, or should these real variables be assessed only with respect to their impact on monetary variables such as exchange rates, liquidity, velocity, and inflation? To what extent should national economic performance (fiscal performance, inflation, unemployment) be considered part of the performance of an international monetary regime? The answers to these questions are likely to vary according to the research agendas of differing scholars.

With these caveats in mind, the purpose of this chapter is to explain why the gold standard was successful in maintaining itself throughout most of the developed world in the three and a half decades preceding World War I (i.e., how the gold club was able to persist). This approach looks at stability in a literal sense: a state in which some set of practices and relations remain intact, which in this particular case constituted the ability of a collectivity of nations to maintain the gold link throughout the period. As Bloomfield (1963, p. 29) points out, "No leading country was ever forced to abandon gold." This, in fact, was quite unique over such a long period, since no international metallist regime in the period of a truly global political economy could boast such a life: the interwar attempts to resume convertibility and the active period of Bretton Woods (late 1950s to 1971) produced short-lived international gold standards. Hence, I am more interested in why the international gold standard lasted than in whether this particular regime was good or bad with respect to prevailing visions of what stable monetary relations are or are not. For some, the idea of talking about stability as coterminous with the collective maintenance of gold monometallism would certainly be agreeable, especially for economists who favor fixed exchange rates and disfavor inflation, as the gold link was conducive to stable money and stable exchange rates. Others, however, might see the maintenance of the gold standard as inimical to international monetary stability, especially those inclined to believe that rules-based monetary systems are prone to longer deflationary periods than are discretionary systems.

Irrespective of the disagreement on whether the maintenance of a collective gold link during the period represented an international monetary success or failure, it is clear that an inquiry into the reasons for the maintenance of this set of practices and relations is important in its own right. Furthermore, most economic historians agree that the gold standard period produced outcomes across a spectrum of categories defining international monetary and economic relations that were highly superior to outcomes in other periods in economic history. More important, nations in the gold club themselves generally found the link desirable even though sometimes painful. Hence, although the definition of stability employed here suggests no incentive to change things given what others were doing, it was an equilibrium or status quo that nations in the gold club were fairly happy with. Finally, fundamental adherence to a gold standard had the most widespread implications for those factors or properties which are most often discussed when economists talk about the functioning of international monetary systems. The practice of gold monometallism across developed nations bore directly upon (and was inextricably tied to) the principal categories used in defining an international monetary regime: liquidity, confidence, exchange rates, the structure of adjustment, and the nature of capital controls. Thus, understanding the forces underlying the resilience of the gold standard reveals some essential dynamics of an international monetary regime, both as causes and effects of the fundamental practices and norms characterizing a regime. That these forces are analyzed in causal terms (i.e., being responsible for the collective maintenance of convertibility) should not indicate a purely recursive nature (i.e., one-way effect). The relation between the maintenance of convertibility and the forces delineated here shows such a complex and interactional nature that it challenges those seeking clean and recursive sets of causal paths defining the relational structure among principal variables. My goal, therefore, is oriented more around identifying the forces themselves than a methodologically unproblematic definition of their association with the successful maintenance of convertibility.

The most obvious answer to questions about how the gold link was so successfully maintained would have to revolve around nations' collective ability to adjust.[3] Since convertibility was founded upon some store of metallic reserves, and these metallic reserves were to a large extent reflections of the structure of nations' international transactions (both monetary and real), then it follows rather trivially that the capacity of nations to defend convertibility both domestically and internationally was dependent upon the ability of their international transactions to tend toward balance. This does not mean that external accounts did not vary significantly from balanced payments, only that the international political economy provided an environment sufficiently favorable so that nations could adjust when they needed to.[4] The collective structure of adjustment considered here required that surplus nations be willing to adjust (i.e., surplus nations were not behaving in an overly mercantilistic fashion), since any large and sustained surpluses there would usually mean large and sustained deficits elsewhere. Again, this does not mean that surplus nations would automatically have to move toward balance, only that private economic actors were allowed to engage in actions that resulted in capital outflows whether in the form of investments or payments for imported goods.

As Chapters 3–5 suggest, the collective capacity of the regime to adjust was grounded neither in conventional processes of hegemony nor in cooperation among nations and/or central banks. The stability of the gold standard is attributable to a more diffuse process, one in which numerous factors coalesced to preserve the collective gold link among economically developed nations. The relative ease of adjustment which characterized the regime was the result of a two-tier process. This chapter is divided into two sections according to this two-tier explanation of the stable structure of adjustment (i.e., stability) under the classical gold standard. The first will discuss the most immediate (most direct) influences on the structure of adjustment, i.e., tier 1—the proximate foundations of adjustment. The second section will discuss how the prevailing norms of the period, which were embedded in the greater normative superstructure of liberalism, supported the proximate influences on adjustment, i.e., tier 2—the normative foundations of adjustment.

The stable structure of adjustment, which represented the very basis of regime stability under the gold standard, was most directly founded on a set of political, economic, and social-psychological conditions (tier 1). First, monetary relations were embedded in a set of stable relations in the international political system. That the period of the gold standard was also relatively free from political turmoil (wars, domestic unrest), especially among gold club nations, eliminated a major source of instability. Moreover, the little international violence that did take place did not translate itself into economic warfare. Second, the greater international economy also nurtured the regime: financial crises were few; economic growth remained favorable; trade grew into multilateral networks; and factors, goods, and money moved freely. A third factor accounting for the state of adjustment under the gold standard was the behavior of the four monetary core nations: Britain, Germany, France, and the U.S. These core nations consistently behaved in ways that facilitated adjustment in other nations. Core nations, which had the greatest capacity to generate surpluses (i.e., attract international investment and export goods), continued to export the means of adjustment by importing goods and imposing few controls on capital exports. Hence, the core of the system was quite adept at recycling liquidity through the regime. Great Britain, as the most important player in the international regime (the very core of the core itself) was especially prone to such recycling as it continued to practice the most liberal policies in the world with respect to the flow of goods and capital. A fourth factor proved to be a convergence of macroeconomic performance across gold-club nations. As a fixed-exchange-rate regime, adjustment was disproportionately affected by the structure of macroeconomic outcomes across the member nations. That interest rates, prices, and business cycles paralleled among gold-club nations averted conditions which created biases in the adjustment process (e.g., low-growth nations running up surpluses against high-growth nations). Finally, that adjustment under the gold standard could continue to be principally dependent on private, short-term capital flows made confidence in the regime essential. For these flows to remain elastic (i.e., responsive to the demand for international liquidity), investors had to perceive exchange risk and convertibility risk as low (i.e., maintain inelastic expectations). This in fact was the case under the gold standard. In this respect, convertibility owed a great deal to a process of self-fulfilling prophecy, which in this specific case manifested itself in stabilizing speculation in capital markets. When exchange rates or convertibility were threatened (i.e., adjustment needed to take place), investors readily responded to the higher returns offered in markets in need of liquidity.

These five proximate factors which directly impacted on the adjustment process were themselves dependent upon a set of compelling norms about the management of money, the macroeconomy, and international economic exchanges (tier 2: the normative factors accounting for the stability of the gold standard). The compelling norms, which were essentially of a domestic nature, were themselves embedded in a greater normative superstructure (classical liberalism) which configured the economic philosophies and policies of the day. The mobility of factors, goods, and money dictated by liberal norms was essential to the adjustment process. Such mobility also created a favorable (i.e., nurturing) international economy in which the regime was embedded. The mobility of people lowered the social costs of adjustment. The mobility of goods and money encouraged the growth of global financial and trade networks. The stabilizing actions of core nations were a direct result of following liberal policies with respect to the trans-border flow of goods, factors, and money. Core nations emerged as the most prolific recyclers of liquidity because they continued to resist capital controls and maintained fairly free trade. Furthermore, this freedom of exchange and mobility, as well as limited government intervention in international economic relations, was essential to the synchronous nature of macroeconomies: there was a greater tendency toward the law of one price in the markets for money and goods. Synchronous macroeconomies were reinforced by a liberal orthodoxy which was oriented around fiscal restraint and stable money. But most directly, norms of stable money and balanced budgets reduced the possibilities for two outcomes most inimical to maintaining convertibility: inflation and fiscal deficits. Confidence in the international investment environment was enhanced to the extent that capital could flow freely across borders. The lack of controls kept the perceptions of convertibility and exchange risk low as investors were assured that nations whose exchanges or gold stocks were under pressure could attract the necessary liquidity to preserve the exchange rate and gold link. Liquidity could always be pulled with the right rate, because creditor nations allowed their economic agents the freedom of transferring their wealth out of the country. This was especially important during periods of financial distress when nations required capital to avoid suspensions of convertibility or changes in the exchange rate. Confidence was enhanced all the more by credibility in the norms governing the metallist orthodoxy which was embedded in liberalism—i.e., that authorities would pursue low inflation, fiscal restraint, and resist suspensions of convertibility. In this latter respect, the adjustment process once again exhibited elements of self-fulfilling prophecy.

Finally, the lack of political manipulation of economic processes dictated by liberal norms had a central impact on the adjustment mechanism both at the international and domestic levels. Internationally, it kept political rivalries from spilling over into the international economy. On a domestic level, adjustment was not subject to the vagaries of politics (i.e., the political business cycle). First, manipulating the macroeconomy to generate specific outcomes violated norms of non-involvement. Second, unlike the period following World War I, manipulating the business cycle produced little political utility because governments were not culpable for adverse outcomes in their economies.

Hence, the stable structure of adjustment was the final manifestation (in the causal chain explaining the maintenance of the gold standard) of a chain of forces, each set of forces embedded in another set, all of which sprang forth from the prevailing economic ideology of the day: classical liberalism. The regime proved only as strong as the norms upon which it was founded. When this classical liberal consensus withered away with the coming of World War I, so too was the regime doomed. Failed attempts to resuscitate the regime in the interwar years and the subsequent construction of the Bretton Woods regime (which was configured to be more consistent with the new set of prevailing norms based on domestic growth and full employment) demonstrated just how dependent the prewar monetary regime was on this classical liberal consensus. Any explanation, therefore, of the maintenance of the classical gold standard would have to gravitate around the norms of which this prewar liberalism was composed. In this sense, the gold standard fits well into an explanatory scheme founded on regimes, since the analysis of regimes is oriented around the ways in which shared beliefs (i.e., rules, norms, prescriptions, injunctions) can configure international relations into ordered patterns. In the case of the gold standard, however, the compelling norms or shared beliefs were primarily of a domestic rather than international nature; thus the order in monetary relations was additive (an international order emanated from below—an idea of an international order was missing from the norms themselves) rather than singular (i.e., order from above—some idea of an international order being manifest in the norms themselves).

Tier 1: The Proximate Foundations of Adjustment

The stable structure of adjustment that prevailed during the classical gold standard was most directly conditioned by five fundamental forces: 1) monetary relations during the classical gold standard were embedded in a greater set of international political relations that were themselves fairly stable; 2) the greater international economy within which monetary relations were embedded was also stable and conducive to adjustment; 3) the core of the international monetary system (i.e., the four most influential monetary powers—U.S., Germany, France, and Great Britain) behaved in ways that facilitated adjustment, especially Great Britain; 4) macroeconomic outcomes (inflation, interest rates, and business cycles) showed significant convergence among nations on gold; and 5) investor expectations were stabilizing.

The Stable Supersystem of International Politics

Economic systems can be no more stable than the greater supersystems of international politics in which they are embedded.[5] Strictly in terms of adjustment, the links between political and economic order are fairly evident. Political instability at the domestic level (i.e., revolutions, coups, unrest) will make adjustment more difficult for a variety of reasons. Political instability can restrict normal economic transactions, which in turn can affect the nation's external accounts: home and external trade will be disrupted, and/or foreigners will find the nation a less desirable target for investment. A political regime which is threatened may find high military expenditures necessary. If this encourages a budgetary deficit which is either monetized (by overprinting), leveraged (through borrowing in capital markets), or funded through higher taxes, external effects could be highly adverse. Unstable prices and interest rates may lead to capital flight, higher tax rates may stimulate the same outcome, and expectations about the effects of unstable prices and interest rates on exchange rates might lead to destabilizing speculation. Furthermore, the costs of a military state may exhaust a nation's hard currency, thus leaving it with little slack in its reserves to withstand normal variations in its external accounts. In any case, a metallist regime normally functions as a contingent rule, with people accepting and even expecting the suspension of convertibility in well-understood political emergencies.[6]

When internationalized, political instability carries with it an expanded effect on adjustment, and transforms problems of unilateral adjustment into multilateral problems. Nations at war are naturally thrown into a more mercantilistic mode. The international velocity of money is reduced because hard monies are guarded rather than left to move freely across boundaries. Trade and investment shrink as a result of national controls and political risk. Pressures to finance war cause budgetary problems that tempt authorities to monetize their debts, thus creating problems of convertibility for those nations on metallic standards. If nations are expanding their military conflict into economic conflict, then international relations are further disrupted by nations trying to impose predatory outcomes on one another. Furthermore, wartime naturally restricts the number of international transactions, thus reducing the growth in national economies, an outcome which carries a plethora of adverse consequences for the management of money and macroeconomies.

The monetary consequences of international and domestic conflict are visible across history. France's international exchanges were affected for thirty years after the French Revolution and Napoleonic Wars. British monetary authorities, who viewed convertibility as a sacrament rather than a policy, found it necessary to suspend during the course and aftermath of the Wars (the period of the paper pound, 1797–1821). Sterling was under intermittent pressure throughout the Wars. The Austrian gulden saw some violent swings in these years, i.e., as much as 20% from one day to the next. In 1811 and 1817 the gulden was devalued by 80% and 60%, respectively. Other nations experienced exorbitant depreciations of their currencies from 1796 to 1814: Sweden and Denmark faced depreciations of 70%, while the Russian rouble depreciated by 75%. The Austrian gulden faced its most unstable period through the mid-century as a result of various wars: with Italy and Hungary in 1848–49 (when the premium on metallic money vis-à-vis paper gulden reached 50%), with Italy and France in 1859, and with Prussia in 1866. The three least stable European currencies (the rouble, Italian franc, and peseta) of the 19th century can attribute their most chaotic states to periods of war finance. Several major waves of depreciation in the rouble were set in motion by expenditure to assist Austria versus

Hungary in 1849, the Crimean War in 1854, the Turkish War in 1878, and the Russo-Japanese War in 1904–05. The Austrian War of 1866 forced Italy off gold and initiated a depreciation of the Italian franc (13½% vis-à-vis gold currencies). For Spain, the Spanish-American War in 1898 caused a 50% depreciation in the peseta vis-à-vis gold currencies. Revolutions and war consistently inflated Austria and Russia off their silver standards before 1890. In fact, opponents of a metallist policy in these nations argued that war or domestic instability might be too frequent to ever allow a sustained metallic link.[7] That Austria-Hungary's exchange rate was less erratic than the Russian rate is mainly the result of the greater frequency of war scares and domestic uprisings in the latter relative to the former.[8]

The American Civil War played havoc with the dollar-pound rate: after a brief rise, the dollar found itself depreciating as a result of a shortage of bills to pay for cotton and an inflationary issue of greenbacks. Revolutions on the European Continent had similar effects on national monetary systems and their respective exchanges. France, for example, suspended convertibility in 1830 and 1848 as a result of revolutions, with the franc consequently depreciating on the international market for exchange. In the cases of war or revolution, the common reaction was excessive speculation against the nations involved in anticipation of an inflationary issue of notes and capital controls.[9] The effects of war on monetary relations persisted well after the events. Debt problems emanating from World War I, for example, were a destabilizing element in domestic finance and international relations for decades.[10]

Under the gold standard, whatever hot money flows occurred, notes Bloomfield (1959, p. 21), were most often a reaction to some perceived increase in political risk due to internal or external conditions. In fact, as we approached World War I, the competition among central banks for gold (i.e., competing for a war chest) was growing disproportionately and short-term capital movements were increasingly disturbed. After the Morocco incident, for example, there were large withdrawals of French credits and balances from Germany: the Reichsbank's reserves were drawn down significantly and the Berlin money market was disrupted. One of the most severe cases of abnormal capital flows took place in the aftermath of the Russo-Japanese War, as Russia's deficit-driven increase in the money supply generated intense speculation against the ruble. The Boer War, although small relative to other conflicts, took a great toll on British industry, finance, and external accounts.[11]

International investment appeared to be as politically sensitive in the period of the gold standard as in any other; the difference between this and other periods, however, was that the period of the gold standard was more politically stable than other periods.[12] We can say that the international monetary regime that prevailed in the developed world from 1880 to 1914 was itself embedded in a greater political regime that was relatively stable.[13] The 19th century as a whole, notes Schroeder (1986), was marked by especially stable and peaceful relations. Major powers had limited skirmishes. When they did fight, the wars were relatively quick with minimal damage and minimal reshaping of the European map (unlike great-power wars in the 18th and 20th centuries), with relations being speedily normalized after the conflict. Furthermore, unlike wars in the preceding and succeeding centuries, none of the wars were the outcome of great powers seeking widespread domination over the Continent. From 1815 to 1914, aside from the Crimean War, Russia, Great Britain, Germany, Austria, France, and Italy were involved in war no more than 18 months; hence the label "hundred years' peace" is not much of an exaggeration.[14] Within this hundred years, the period of the gold standard, 1880–1914, was the most stable in terms of both international and domestic political conditions in the developed world. The major wars of the hundred years' peace were fought before 1880 (the Crimean [1854], Franco-Prussian [1870], and Austro-Prussian Wars [1866]). The wars during the gold standard period were limited and localized: Sino-Japanese (1894–95), Spanish-American (1898), Boer (1899–1902), Russo-Japanese (1904–05), Italian-Turkish (1911–12), and the two Balkan Wars (1912–13). Furthermore, depending on whether one chooses to denote Japan as a leading power, it can be asserted that no conflict in the period involved more than one leading power. There were certainly no great power conflicts during the period, as no two of the four core nations ever fought one another.

But even when war did take place between principal players in international politics, it appears that norms regarding the conduct of war limited the adverse economic effects of military confrontation. Unlike war in the 20th century, military conflict did not spill over into economic conflict.[15] That war was not total or all-encompassing conflict kept economic relations on another track, thus minimizing the extent to which economic relations would suffer because nations were fighting one another. These norms regarding the conduct of war produced outcomes that by today's common vision of warfare would seem strange indeed. During the Crimean War, for example, Russian bonds continued to be floated on the London exchange, which essentially meant that British (among other) investors were supporting the Russian war effort against their own compatriots. Before World War I the Treasury and Bank of England continued to resist pressure from the Foreign Office to accumulate more gold for a war chest, even when tension between Britain and Germany was most intense. British houses continued to finance German trade up until the War itself. Lloyd's was even insuring German shipping against wartime accidents.[16]

In terms of domestic political conditions, nations that experienced the most domestic instability, like Russia and Italy, found the metallic link harder to preserve relative to their fellow European nations and the U.S. On the Continent, political and social upheavals were less visible after the mid-century (a peak having been reached in the years 1848–50), while the American Civil War ended in 1865. The gold standard period experienced a domestic tranquility that was generally missing in the developed world in previous decades. Moreover, no international monetary system can be any more stable than its center or core, as destabilizing conditions at the center of a system have a tendency to spread faster than instability in the periphery or outside the immediate core. Domestic stability was, in fact, most visible in the core, especially in Great Britain. The years of the gold standard saw an unparalleled absence of social upheavals in Britain. Convertibility was further enhanced by the relative political stability, with the exception of the Boer War, in the principal regions of gold and silver production.[17]

That the gold regime thrived vindicates one of the basic tenets in the modern study of international political economy: economic systems emerge out of and are conditioned by greater constellations of political relations. The relatively tranquil political environment and the limited nature of warfare relieved national and international monetary systems of the shocks that disrupt the course of normal monetary practices. Monetary stability was a partial manifestation of political stability.

The Stable Supersystem of International Economics

Stable international monetary systems not only require a stable "political equilibrium," but require a stable "economic equilibrium" as well.[18] Not only are such systems embedded in a greater constellation of political relations, they are also embedded in some greater economic system with which they interact over time. Just like the political supersystem of politics showed properties conducive to adjustment, the international economy within which the gold regime was embedded also exhibited a set of favorable conditions that worked to enhance the collective capacity to adjust.

There were no fundamental defects in the international economy during the last four decades before the War: it had no deep-seated maladjustments that required long and painful alterations in economic behavior within and between national economies. Mints (1950) talks of the "soundness" of the international economy of the period. Short-term credit was abundant, goods and capital flowed well, world economic growth was strong, factors (i.e., productive capital and labor) moved freely, and developed economies themselves had become industrialized and economically integrated into the global economy.[19]

That the global economy was in the midst of an industrial revolution made it dynamic and flexible: adjustment could take place with minimal unemployment.[20] The freedom of migration enhanced the global supply of raw materials and productive capacity as people moved from overpopulated areas experiencing declining marginal productivity to underpopulated and raw-material-exporting areas whose productivity was rising on the margin. This had the effect of increasing the supply of food and raw-material inputs to the emergent urban-industrializing economies, it maintained economic growth and wages, it relieved social pressure emanating from unemployment and lack of housing, and the spread of people allowed both a growth and geographic diversification of markets.[21] Furthermore, the superior growth experienced over the period was indirectly instrumental in maintaining the gold link by undermining much of the political support of coalitions favoring inflation and devaluation.[22]

The period was also relatively free of financial crises. After six and a half decades of regular and serious international financial crises, the century closed out in a fairly tranquil manner.[23] Matthews (1982, p. 110) calls the Overend, Gurney crisis of 1866 the last real financial crisis of the 19th century. In the U.S. and Great Britain, no bank failures took place in crisis after 1866 for the rest of the century.[24] In fact, from the time of the Overend, Gurney crisis it would not be until the years 1906–07 that the world would once again experience a significant crisis. And even this distress abated relatively quickly, as the Bank of France pumped liquidity into the London market, which in turn kept liquidity flowing internationally (especially to the U.S.). Hence, the forty years between 1866 and 1906 represented the longest period void of serious and widespread crisis to that date. The crises that did take place during this period were few, geographically restricted, and of short duration.[25] The Baring incident of 1890, by most accounts, appeared relatively innocuous as an international crisis. It was due to the failure of a single firm as opposed to general financial conditions, the international shock effects were limited, and the problem was quickly resolved through the mediating offices of the Governor of the Bank of England. Even on a domestic level for Great Britain, the crisis was not excessive. Bank of England reserves never dipped under 10 million pounds sterling, no other banks fell in the wake of Baring, the financial distress was restricted to London, and interest rates reestablished themselves quickly following the incident.[26] All the more important was the fact that financial crises during the period were especially absent in core nations, since no international monetary system can be more stable than the domestic systems of its leading players.[27] Germany, in fact, was altogether spared of any significant financial crisis. Hence, the very center of the international monetary system experienced limited opportunities to spread its own shocks.[28]

The other major property in the evolution of the international economy in the latter half of the 19th century that contributed to a stable structure of adjustment was the growth of international networks of trade and finance. Both had important implications for adjustment and convertibility: they enhanced the capacity for trade and capital flows to move across borders and allowed nations to adjust as well as economize on the use of gold.[29] Saul (1960, p. 62) identifies the growth of a "world-wide interconnecting network of trade" in the last three decades of the 19th century.[30] The last link in the globalization of trade networks was put in place with the rapid growth of regions of primary production and their increasing demand for the finished products of the U.S. and Europe. The multilateral networks of trade that emerged toward the last decades of the 19th century proved conducive to current account equilibration across nations. Through their multilateral clearing functions they also allowed nations to economize on gold because deficits in one direction of circular trading networks were compensated by surpluses in another direction.[31] The key networks tended to revolve around core nations, especially Great Britain. The British trade deficit with the rest of the world was compensated by a surplus with India, while Great Britain's trade deficit with industrial nations was compensated by its surplus with primary-goods-producing nations. Other principal networks involved Continental Europe, the U.S., and Australia; and the U.S., India, Canada, and Great Britain. (See Figures 7.1 and 7.2.)

Australia ran a surplus against Continental Europe, which, in turn, ran a surplus against the U.S., which ran a surplus against Australia. In the other network, the stable circle of adjustment ran from the U.S. to Canada to Great Britain to India, and back to the U.S. The major network which appeared during the period was truly global in nature. This multilateral network went from the Tropics to the U.S. to the Great plain

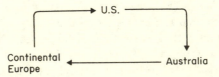

Fig. 7.1 Multilateral trade network under the gold standard: U.S., Australia, Continental Europe (Saul [1960], p. 58).

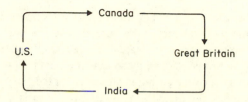

Fig. 7.2 Multilateral trade network under the gold standard: U.S., Canada, India, Great Britain (Saul [1960], p. 58).

nations (Australia, Argentina, and Canada), to Germany, to other Continental European nations, to Great Britain, and back to the Tropics. (See Figure 7.3.)

The latter half of the 19th century saw a concomitant growth and evolution of financial institutions. The growth of finance and the evolution of credit instruments meant that banks and financial houses were accumulating large stores of investable funds (and here the growth in income accompanying the industrial revolution was instrumental) that could flow at relatively low transaction costs all over the globe. The new "cosmopolitan" structure of finance that was growing on the Continent and in the U.S. was marked by an extension of banking business from the province to the city to the nation and finally to the international market.[32] With the growth of banking in this period, the international economy enjoyed a far greater pool of liquidity, and the multiple opportunities for and ease of investment increased the international velocity of money. As Clough (1964, p. 177) observed, "Foreign investments were but an offshoot of banking development." This store of elastic capital which could be easily transported via various credit instruments gave the international system its most important short-term means of adjustment. Shortages of liquidity created by deficits could be effectively abated with the right discount rates. The use of more sophisticated credit instruments insulated national gold stocks from adverse changes in external accounts. Hence, not only did the new cosmopolitan structure of international finance enhance the capacity for collective adjustment, but through its instruments which economized on the flow of gold, the system of collective convertibility enjoyed greater built-in slack which could accommodate shifts in external accounts without affecting gold holdings.

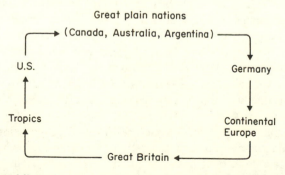

Fig. 7.3 Global multilateral trade network under the gold standard (Kenwood, A. G., and A. L. Lougheed *The Growth of the International Economy, 1820–1980*. London: George Allen & Unwin, 1983, p. 109.

With respect to the general state of the international economy of the period, much has been made of the fact that part of the gold standard period (1873–96) experienced what has become known as the "Great Depression," and that the 1870s initiated a period of rising protectionism; these developments supposedly represented obstacles to the process of collective adjustment. As for the "Depression," studies of economic performance in the period suggest that the term is a misnomer, i.e., the period did not exhibit the kind of overall outcomes that we normally equate with the term depression. According to Rostow (1948, p. 59), "The Great Depression was not a depression."[33] Beales (1934, p. 70) noted that the great depression really embodied three separate slumps and two intervening recoveries: the slumps were 1873–79, 1882–86, and 1890–96; the recoveries were 1879–82 and 1886–90. He added that the recoveries were quite strong in terms of increases in employment; exports; as well as coal, iron, and steel production. Rostow identified the effects of the depression as being restricted to areas outside of a "real" economic domain: the depression witnessed declines in interest rates, prices, equity values, and profit margins; and it witnessed a shift in long-term investment from foreign to domestic.[34] In the area of real performance (employment, agricultural and industrial production, and real growth), the period showed fairly favorable outcomes.

In terms of employment, German unemployment during the period 1887 to 1914 remained consistently under 3%, while during the same period British unemployment generally stayed below 4%. France consistently saw rates under 7% from 1895 to 1914, while U.S. rates achieved high levels from 1892 to 1898 (some reaching above 11.5%), but more moderate levels from 1899 to 1914. All four core nations saw large secular increases in industrial production from 1880 to 1913: British and French production doubled, German production quadrupled, and U.S. production more than quadrupled. Core production of coal, pig iron, steel, and food crops saw especially strong secular performances through this period of so-called depression. British GNP (in constant prices) almost doubled, U.S. GNP more than tripled, and German NNP (net national product) increased 250%. Furthermore, net domestic capital formation as a percentage of net domestic product in core nations was fairly steady or rising through this period.[35]

Although prices were falling in the last two decades of the century, industrial wages in Great Britain, France, and Germany saw strong secular increases from 1880 to 1914. German industrial wages almost doubled in that period. U.S. industrial wages grew a little slower than Great Britain's and France's, but almost tripled their growth rate from 1899 to 1913. Agricultural wages increased secularly in both Great Britain and Germany from 1880 to 1913. Hence, real wage performance, given the decline in prices, was actually quite favorable. Furthermore, price declines were not homogeneous, as they varied by sector, and the greatest declines were over by the 1880s.[36]

As for developments in protectionism, notwithstanding the rising tariffs during this period, trading relations proved generally favorable to the emergence of stable monetary relations. Protectionism did not prove to be a deleterious obstacle to economic relations because it remained fairly moderate and undiversified: protectionism was restricted to tariffs, and these tariffs were generally not excessive. As Ashworth (1952, p. 145) points out, the tariffs of the period were "protective but not prohibitive." The tariffs were generally low to moderate throughout the period.[37] Since they were a major source of revenue for governments (governments of the period relied much more on forms of indirect taxation than they do today), authorities were careful to keep them out of ranges where they would become prohibitive and reduce the tax base (i.e., in typical Laffer-curve reasoning, too high a tax would discourage trade, thus reducing total revenues collected on imports). Furthermore, it was a common practice of commercial policy during the period to use tariffs as bargaining chips. Tariff increases were generally followed by trade negotiations in which concessions would be exchanged bilaterally between specific nations. The French two-tier system of tariffs, for example, operated on just such a principle: French negotiators granted lower-tier tariffs to specific nations for various quid pro quos (France ended up granting its lowest rates to almost all of its trading partners). The German tariff increase of 1906 was quickly followed by treaties with six different nations which granted lower tariff rates. Hence, initial tariff increases withered away or were significantly reduced rather quickly.[38]

That protection was restricted to tariffs (i.e., homogeneous) rather than diversified across devices, including quantitative and qualitative barriers, was important for the growth of trade under the gold standard. Tariffs were less trade-distorting than quantitative and qualitative barriers, because exporters could adjust for their effects by manipulating prices and costs. Moreover, two systematic factors that mitigated the effects of tariffs during this period were the significant fall in transport costs and the great increase of trade finance in the form of bills.[39]

The enormous growth of trade during the last third of the 19th century attests to the nominal effects which the prevailing style of protectionism had on trade flows. Given the significant growth of trade relative to world output during the period, it would be difficult to argue that in fact tariffs were distortive because trade could have achieved significantly higher levels. Neither surplus capacity nor surplus goods—a sure sign of a disjuncture between the ability of a global economy to produce goods and consume goods—proved to be a problem during the period. Furthermore, the structure of trading networks shifted from bilateral to multilateral, normally a characteristic of a more open trading system, which itself served to counteract the effects of tariffs on trade flows.

As in the case of the gold standard's political supersystem, then, the greater economic supersystem in which monetary relations were embedded also proved conducive to a stable monetary regime.

The Gold Standard and Core Nations

The monetary core nations of the gold standard (the four most powerful players in the international monetary system) emerged as a principal factor influencing the structure of adjustment. Insofar as the behavior of the core was conducive to collective adjustment during the period, these large monetary powers emerged as an important source of stability.[40] International monetary regimes exhibit fundamental characteristics of anatomical systems. Just as the health of an organism depends on its heart to maintain some desirable flow of blood, the stability of a monetary regime depends on the capacity of those nations which possess disproportionate ability to attract international capital (through investment and payment for goods) to recycle that capital back into the system.[41] As Strange (1988, pp. 89, 90) observes,

> Credit is literally the lifeblood of a developed economy. Like blood in the human anatomy, money in the predominant form of credit has to reach and renew every part of the economy. It has to circulate regularly and reliably.

The core of the gold standard was the source of greatest trade and capital flows; moreover, these nations had the greatest capacity to attract international capital. This meant that as a group these nations were the principal accumulator of international liquidity. As such, the collective adjustment mechanism would work satisfactorily to the extent that these nations which had an advanced capacity to generate surpluses were willing to adjust. In this respect, the behavior of the core did not disappoint.[42] Core nations remained the largest commodity importers, and France, Great Britain, and Germany were consistently the largest net capital exporters of the period. In terms of net capital exports, France, Great Britain, and Germany showed significant increases over the gold standard period (years of significant growth in income and trade), with increases of 55 to 1,960 million francs, 35.6 to 224.3 million pounds sterling, and 332 to 2,234 million marks, respectively, from 1880 to 1913. The U.S. became a significant net capital exporter in the period from the mid-1890s to 1905. The U.S. was a net exporter for 13 of the 20 years before World War I. The shift in the structure of U.S. capital flows and the enormous increases in net capital exports from France and German made up nicely for a slacking British propensity to export capital in the period from 1891 to 1903.[43]

With respect to trade, the core accounted for 50% of the world's visible trade in 1885, with that figure falling only to 44% by the years 1911–13. Great Britain individually accounted for 19% and 14%, respectively, in those two periods. Core commodity imports increased secularly across the period. Great Britain, Germany, France, and the U.S. saw increases of 411 to 769 million pounds, 2,814 to 10,751 million marks, 5,033 to 8,421 million francs, and 848 to 1,813 million dollars, respectively, from 1880 to 1913.[44]

The external positions of core nations generated surpluses which essentially financed these net capital exports. Current accounts in the core generally moved in an offsetting manner vis-à-vis capital exports.[45] Core current account positions tended to be strong throughout the period (with the U.S. experiencing consistent surpluses after 1896). Some of the surpluses actually reached levels in relation to the size of domestic economies never again seen. The British surplus reached 8% of GNP before the War. The U.S. surplus reached 4% of GNP. Even when in current deficit in this period, core nations never were burdened with highly adverse conditions: the highest current deficit was the United States' 2% of GNP in 1888.[46] Moreover, both the exports and imports of core nations tended to move synchronously, which was an important stabilizing factor in their current accounts: large inflows of goods did not as a result lead to prolonged deficits.[47]

That nations with the greatest capacity for generating surpluses had a tendency toward net capital exportation, and deficit nations had a tendency toward net importation, generated a harmony between lending, borrowing, and the demand for goods.[48] As Robertson (1931, pp. 178, 179) observed, "The needs of exporters, of importers, and of borrowers and lenders walked for the most part hand in hand in apparently pre-ordained harmony."[49] The willingness of surplus nations to export capital created an abundance of liquidity which enhanced the speed and extent of adjustment, but also had more manifold effects on the international economy that were not only stabilizing in themselves but fed back on the adjustment mechanism in a beneficial way.[50] The abundance of liquidity and the speed of adjustment relieved domestic economies in deficit nations of the burden of excessively high discount rates.[51] This was conducive to global economic growth because growth in deficit nations stimulated ongoing demand for the commodities of capital-exporting nations. Since much of the foreign investment went to building infrastructures that facilitated the export of raw materials, both the production potential in the core and export earnings in deficit nations remained high.[52] Also, foreign investment financed imports from the core, which represented a reciprocal extension of the means of adjustment: the capital exports from the core enjoyed positive externalities, as the core was exporting its own means of adjustment. That the structure of capital flow was also coterminous with a movement of liquidity from regions of high savings to regions of low savings served to stabilize the international market for liquidity, as areas of excess supply transferred capital to areas of high demand.

The structure of adjustment within the core, and between the core and other nations, was not without its foreboding possibilities, however. Redistribution of liquidity could take place within the core, and between the core and the non-core nations which included the periphery, as a result of short-term differentials in pulling power, some of which were frequently exploited by central bankers. Various developments, however, limited the possibilities of destabilizing redistribution of liquidity between nations.

First, the structure of European discount rates compensated for differentials in pulling power. The Bank of England historically exhibited one of the lower discount rates among European states.[53] Furthermore, France, which had pulling power over Germany, had a significantly lower discount rate than Germany throughout the period. Second, the structure of monetary and commercial restriction among nations compensated for differentials in pulling power, as the core (especially Great Britain) had more open economies than other nations. Nations that had a competitive advantage in adjustment (i.e., a competitive advantage in drawing short-term capital) were also more likely to follow policies that facilitated reciprocal adjustment: nations with inferior influence over short-term capital found fewer restrictions when trying to attract capital from these nations. Hence, the structure of capital-flow management in the international system compensated for the structure of influence over capital movements. Any international monetary regime exhibiting asymmetrical pulling power, as the classical gold standard did, will be unstable if the core of the regime is overly mercantilistic. The core under the gold standard did not hoard balance-of-payments surpluses, but recycled them.

Third, specifically with respect to adjustment in gold-club nations, the core and the developed world enjoyed a systematic means of adjustment and financial relief in crisis as a result of their capacity to draw short-term capital from the periphery. This capacity to shift part of the burden of adjustment to the periphery, especially in times of greatest need, appeared as a fundamental stabilizing element for gold standard nations. However, as noted in Chapter 2, the conventional image that this has generated (that the stability of the gold standard was achieved by destabilizing the periphery) is somewhat misleading. Capital flows through developed as well as peripheral nations were fairly dynamic: peripheral nations which were subject to an exodus of capital had the capacity to pull more capital in with the right terms for investment (discount rates, commercial credit arrangements, etc.). In essence, what the periphery lost, they could regain at the right price. The burden in terms of the effects of tight credit conditions on economic growth were generally temporary, being most often counteracted by an inflationary management of the money supply. Furthermore, financial crises in gold nations were too infrequent and short to encourage any sustained drain from the periphery in the period. That domestic monetary conditions in peripheral nations were far more turbulent (inflation, crises) cannot justifiably be attributed more to the external drains than to indigenous political and economic factors (i.e., unstable growth in export economies, pro-inflation political groups). After all, turbulent conditions persisted there in periods of both capital inflow and outflow.[54]

Finally, there was a great deal of compatibility among core central banks with respect to their preferences for an optimal stock of gold reserves. Debilitating competition for gold in the face of a fairly stable production was averted by differing perceptions of what constituted an optimal gold stock. The preference of France, Germany, and the U.S. for excessive reserves was satisfied by the Bank of England's moderate reserve targets. It was especially important that Great Britain did not hoard reserves, given the capacity of the London market to attract and keep gold.

Great Britain played a central role within the collective core. To the extent that Great Britain was the best at recycling capital, we can say that it was a stabilizing force within the core as well as the international monetary system. Great Britain's position in both the world economy and the core was crucial: as the period's largest capital market and trader, it was at the very center of the global adjustment mechanism. As the very core of the core itself, it was crucial to the collective adjustment mechanism in the developed world that the willingness to adjust was most pronounced in Great Britain. In this respect the British did not disappoint.[55] Great Britain emerged as the period's largest net capital exporter. This nicely complemented its strong current account performance resulting from earnings on invisibles.[56] As Yeager (1976, p. 300) observes, "Rough equality between payments to and from Great Britain kept the world well supplied with sterling." British capital exports achieved levels relative to the size of Britain's economy never again seen in a core nation. In the four decades before the War, 40% of British savings were invested overseas. In the years just prior to the War, 10% of national income was being accounted for by returns on foreign investment alone. Equivalent figures for the U.S. during the 1950s show returns on U.S. foreign investment accounting for no more than 1% of national income, and the percentage of U.S. savings invested overseas reached only 4%.[57] Even when Britain found itself drawing large amounts of capital in times of financial distress, net capital exports to the nations from which it drew were especially large a year or so after the crisis; hence even recycling from crisis was carried out fairly efficiently.[58]

The timing of capital recycling has gotten much attention in the historiography on the period. Britain's countercyclical timing (i.e., home and foreign investment being inversely related) in its exportation of capital served multiple purposes in the global adjustment mechanism. Directly, it assured nations that were suffering on current account, because of Britain's slacking demand for imports, the means of short-term adjustment in the form of foreign investment. Indirectly, it served as a means of recovery for Great Britain as capital exports stimulated demand for British exports, thus serving to reinvigorate the hub of the global adjustment process.[59] British investment also indirectly facilitated adjustment in foreign current accounts as the capital (especially in regions of primary-goods production) was instrumental in the growth of export sectors.[60] Hence, British foreign investment was at the inner sanctum of collective adjustment in the international economy. It was in this capacity, observes Saul (1960, p. 53), that Britain "made her most vital contribution to the smooth functioning of the world economy."[61] In Bagehot's ([1873] 1921, pp. 12, 13) words, "English capital goes as surely and instantly where it is most wanted, and where there is most to be made of it, as water runs to find its level."

A systematic bias in the flow of international capital emanating from London's superiority as a financial center was somewhat mitigated by the fact that the price Britain offered for credit tended to be somewhat lower than in other financial markets. Not only did the Bank of England discount rate stay consistently below the central bank rates of other developed nations (see Figures A.1–A.3 in Statistical Appendix), but long-term bond and short-term market discount rates also tended to be somewhat lower than in other financial centers. This was an important factor, since much higher rates in London (well above other bank rates) had the capacity to adversely affect the international availability and flow of gold. As Wood (1939, p. 162) observed, "If London had tried to compete for gold by becoming progressively more bearish as other countries, the international standard would have broken down."

In addition, other factors also mitigated a systematic tendency for gold to bottle up in Great Britain. The British gold market was the most open market in the world. It featured the lowest transactions costs of exit in the world (i.e., Britain had the lowest barriers to gold export); hence individuals and central banks could easily obtain gold when in need. This was consistent with Britain's role of net international creditor: making the means of adjustment available to other nations. This free market for gold was complemented by central bank perceptions of what constituted an optimal stock of gold reserves. The Bank of England, mainly for reasons of profitability, never stockpiled gold much beyond essential working balances like other central banks. This mitigated the competition over the fundamental means of convertibility defense: the Bank's reluctance to run up reserves essentially made it easier for other monetary systems to secure the means of maintaining domestic and international convertibility.[62]

The British functioned efficiently as the hub of global adjustment. That they could continue to do so throughout the period owes much to factors which limited the burden of British adjustment. The tendency of British foreign investment to stimulate demand for British manufactures mitigated adverse trends in the British current account. This limited current-account deficits and bolstered British economic growth, which translated into a stable demand for foreign goods: the circle of adjustment was as beneficial to other nations as it was to Britain.[63] Also, that nations running up trade surpluses against Britain were content with simultaneously running up sterling balances in London meant that adverse changes in British trade led to offsetting short-term capital inflows. Furthermore, since British exports and imports covaried positively, any disturbances in the foreign demand for British exports were offset by a decline in imports.[64]

The British Empire also came to play an increasingly stabilizing role for British balance of payments. Just as the Empire came to be a substitute for tariffs in the period, it also provided a source of external surplus which counteracted adverse exchanges with the developed world.[65] Growing difficulties in penetrating markets on the Continent and the U.S. (because of declining competitiveness and tariffs) were compensated for by growing exports to the Empire. From 1899 to 1913 the export of manufactures to Canada, Australia, and South Africa increased by 300%, 30%, and 50%, respectively. By 1912 the percentages of imports taken up by British goods for Australia, New Zealand, India, South Africa, Canada, and the British West Indies were 66%, 66%, 66%, 60%, 45%, and 33%, respectively.[66] The Empire also served as a stabilizing countercyclical force for the British economy and trade. When a global recession diminished the demand for British goods, imperial demand compensated. In the recession years 1872–78, for example, when the exports of British steel, iron, and tin plates to the U.S., Germany, and Holland declined by 82%, 32%, and 32%, respectively, exports of the same goods to India and Australia increased by 300% and 200%, respectively.[67]

India was especially pivotal as a safety valve for the British external position. Britain ran up a growing surplus with India, which in turn ran up a surplus against the rest of the world. Indian goods continued to do well in markets that were becoming less favorable to British exporters. One reason for this was that Indian goods were systematically subjected to less protection than were British goods.[68] Because of this crucial clearing function for the British, de Cecco (1974, p. 122) goes as far as to call India "the largest stabilizing factor" of the international economy during the gold standard.

India's trade (including bullion) balance with Britain, on annual average, went from a deficit of 10.7 million pounds sterling in the period 1880–83 to a deficit of 52.3 million pounds in the three years before the War. Across the same period, India's trade balance with industrially advanced European nations went from a surplus of 10.3 million pounds, on annual average, to a surplus of 32.6 million pounds.[69] By 1910, Britain's balance-of-payments surplus with India (at 60 million pounds) was four times greater than its next-largest bilateral surplus, and was greater than any of its bilateral deficits (its largest deficit in 1910 being with the U.S. at 50 million pounds). In the gold standard years, India was consistently the source of Britain's largest bilateral surplus. It also bolstered Britain's trade balance by providing goods for re-export.

Britain's position as a creditor nation and the center of the international gold and financial markets further proved to be a fundamental source of reducing Britain's burden as the hub of global adjustment. As a creditor, Great Britain had a great advantage in adjustment over debtor nations. When foreign exchanges moved against a creditor nation like Britain, it could adjust by merely abating the exodus of capital. Debtor nations found adverse foreign exchanges far more difficult to counteract, since their only direct and short-term means of adjustment was to attract capital into their financial markets. It was far easier to keep capital in (even if relying purely on market mechanisms rather than capital controls) than to attract capital: given equal foreign and domestic interest rates, investors would (*ceteris paribus*) prefer to keep their money at home, given the lower transaction costs of taking domestic positions relative to foreign positions.[70]

As center of the international gold market, Britain enjoyed an ongoing means of replenishing its gold stock. London itself was a magnet for newly produced gold (especially from South Africa). Bullion was traditionally sold there on Mondays. Any bullion which was not sold automatically went to the Bank of England, which paid the statutory price of 77s and 9d per standard ounce. But the Bank could purchase from the new stock of gold even sooner at a higher price, which it often did after periods of significant depletions in the gold reserve. That this source of replenishment existed throughout the period helped the British to continue the defense of convertibility under conditions (i.e., the thin film of gold) that would have undermined the monetary systems of nations that were less favorably situated in the international gold market.[71]

As the main link between national capital markets, the flow of international liquidity found a principal path through London, which itself provided an ongoing source of adjustment. In fact, given the primary role played by short-term capital flows in the adjustment process during the gold standard, the prominence of the London capital market can be said to have achieved a central status among those factors that mitigated the difficulty of being the main recycler of global liquidity. Individuals readily held sterling in lieu of gold. This took pressure off the slim British gold holdings that had the prodigious dual mandate of defending internal and external convertibility. That sterling was attractive and the London market the focal point of world finance created a situation where Great Britain had a constant and large inflow of short-term funds. The attractiveness of both the market and sterling were rooted in a long and glorious history in which they came to be considered thoroughly established institutions.[72] The market had a very long and impressive history, and by the period of the gold standard it had become the largest, most diversified (in the services offered), and safest haven for investment in the world. The conclusion of the Franco-Prussian War definitively purged the international market of the last viable challenger (Paris). Sterling itself found a similar long distinguished history. Except for the period of the paper pound during the Napoleonic Wars, sterling had been convertible at a stable mint par for two centuries. As Brown (1965, p. 59) observed, "The world had to regard suspension of gold payments and a depreciation of sterling against gold as unthinkable."[73] It was a testimony to the perceptions of low exchange risk attributed to sterling that foreign transactions in sterling normally went unhedged in the futures market for foreign exchange.[74]

Drawing from the U.S. experience in the Bretton Woods regime, monetary economists have emphasized how such a privilege of generating deficits without tears could easily lead the key-currency economy to monetize its external deficit, thus undermining its own power to defend the external convertibility of its currency and encouraging global inflation.[75] Great Britain, however, did not produce the same results visible in the turbulent decades of the 1960s and 1970s. First, the creation of sterling was subject to more rigid rules (with respect to gold holdings), while the Bretton Woods regime saw a much more discretionary management of the American money supply. Second, the U.S. did not enjoy the same stable structure of adjustment created by the factors mentioned above. The American current account deteriorated, unlike its British counterpart a century before, thus precluding the accumulation of surpluses (in the British case created by invisibles and trade with the Empire) that could be recycled. Instead, the American government resorted to the printing press to meet global liquidity needs.

The British economy functioned in a way that imparted stability onto the core specifically and the international system in general. Does this in fact mean that Great Britain hegemonically stabilized the international gold standard (i.e., was the leader or manager of the gold standard)? It is clear that whatever Britain did for the international system was not executed in any way relating to conventional views of hegemony. There were no intentions to stabilize any greater system on the part of monetary or political authorities. The stabilizing actors were not states or state institutions but British citizens and businesses (investors and traders) looking out for the condition of their own ledgers.[76] As Viner (1945, p. 63) noted,

> There can be no doubt that London in the nineteenth century provided a wholly efficient and economical clearing-house for the exchange business of the world. . . . But this was profitable . . . for the London houses . . . , and if London had provided poorer facilities . . . other money markets would have . . . replaced it.

The closest thing we find to mainstream visions of hegemony is the maintenance of laissez-faire policies on the part of the British state, policies which made it possible for British citizens to behave in ways that facilitated the adjustment of other nations. But this was hardly done for the sake of the international system, as British statesmen were pursuing an economic orthodoxy which was perceived to be benefiting British citizens (i.e., competition is good for the British). That these policies were also good for the international gold standard was a fortuitous outcome of the particularistic orientation of British authorities. If indeed one chooses to call this hegemony, then it is non-state in nature (i.e., carried on by non-state actors) and unintended.[77] As Ford (1989, p. 255) observes, "Institutions and financial practices had evolved, albeit accidentally, to meet the needs and effect the management of the prewar gold standard system." The flow of liquidity from the core nations as a whole can be characterized as such: capital flows were predominantly of a private nature, and moved as a result of speculative opportunities in the international monetary system. An exception to this was the inter-central-bank accommodations that took place during the period, but these were relatively few and usually executed in ways that deviated from conventional visions of international hegemony and cooperation.

Synchronous Macroeconomies

Under any system of fixed exchange rates with limited capital controls, a stable structure of adjustment depends upon some convergence (or, conversely, limited divergence) of macroeconomic outcomes among nations whose currencies are linked. As Hawtrey (1947, p. 43) noted, a "gold standard requires all countries that adhere to it to keep pace in their credit movements." More specifically, a stable gold standard is predicated upon a convergence (or limited divergence) among movements of prices, among movements of interest rates, and among movements of business cycles. History has shown that when nations have attempted to link their currencies in the face of diverging macroeconomies, the results have been debilitating for the maintenance of monetary regimes.[78]

The effects of differential macroeconomic performance on the adjustment mechanism under a monetary regime founded on fixed exchange rates can be modeled with a simple two-by-two matrix which produces quadrants corresponding to four bilateral external positions. (See Figure 7.4.) Monetary relations under such regimes can take the form of a static-variable-sum game which exhibits both elements of coordination and Prisoner's Dilemma. The interrelations of macroeconomic variables such as inflation, interest rates, and business cycles across nations in a fixed-exchange-rate monetary regime generate a payoff structure which is a synthesis of both cooperative and noncooperative interaction.[79] Assume a monetary regime made up of two nations in which changes in domestic prices are solely responsible for determining balance-of-payments positions (i.e., interest rates, business cycles, exchange rates, and capital accounts are all held constant, and capital controls are insignificant). In this case outcomes in rates of inflation will have specific effects on the nations' external balances. If Nations 1 and 2 find their rates converging at either high levels (northwest quadrant) or low levels (southeast quadrant), they will enjoy a fairly stable structure of collective adjustment, as limited differentials in price movements are

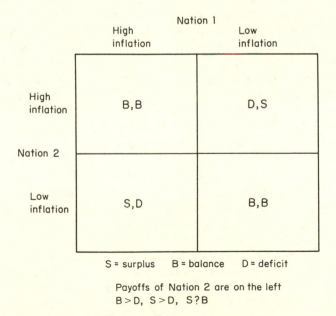

Fig. 7.4 A two-nation balance-of-payments game.

eliminating any pronounced bias in payments between the two nations. In this case, they both remain in balance. If, however, the nations are faced with significant differentials in rates of inflation, the collective structure of adjustment will be less stable, with the lower-inflation nation enjoying an advantage over the higher-inflation nation in the capacity to stay out of deficit.[80] With exchange rates held constant, the lower prices of the low-inflation nation's goods will make its exports more attractive in the other nation's market, and make imports less attractive in its own market. Hence, the low-inflation nation will experience a favorable bias in trade adjustment vis-à-vis the other nation. In the southwest quadrant, Nation 2 is running up surpluses against Nation 1. In the northeast quadrant, Nation 1 is running up surpluses against Nation 2.

We could substitute either interest rates or economic growth (i.e., the business cycle) for the collective structure of inflation in a monetary regime, and also produce similar consequences for external accounts among regime members when all other macroeconomic properties and exchange rates are held constant. Consider a case of two nations whose external accounts are determined principally by interest rates.[81] Where differentials in interest rates appear, the nation with higher rates will experience a tendency to run up surpluses against the other nation. Where no such differentials exist, there will be a collective (in this case bilateral) tendency toward balance. Capital will be drawn, of course, to the nation with higher interest rates, and away from the nation with lower interest rates.[82] Similarly with respect to business cycles, if external positions are determined by the level of economic growth alone, you will have a stable structure of adjustment where business cycles are synchronous (i.e., similar growth levels will limit the redistribution of surpluses). But if one nation is growing slower than the other, it will have a tendency to run up surpluses against the high-growth nation. Low growth will limit the demand for imports, while the demand for imports will be pronounced in the high-growth nation.[83]

Under the classical gold standard, macroeconomic performance across developed nations showed a convergent structure: prices, interest rates, and business cycles were each fairly synchronous.[84] The convergence was even more pronounced among the four core nations, which made the structure of adjustment even more stable since it especially encouraged stability within the core. Thorp's (1926, p. 88) study of business cycles in 17 leading nations showed the strong parallelism in economic growth in the period. Of the 17 nations, 10 simultaneously had recessions in 1890–91, 15 had recessions in 1900–01 and 1907–08, and 12 had recessions in 1912–13. The four core nations were in the same phase of the business cycle 53.5% of the time in the years 1879–1913. The three European core nations (France, Germany, Great Britain) were in the same phase 83.1% of the time during the same period, with the U.S. showing more bilateral parallelism with core business cycles than the 53.5% of overall parallelism in the core (the U.S. exhibited bilateral parallelism 64.9% of the period with Britain, 61.1% with France, and 62.3% with Germany).

With respect to short-term interest rates (market discount rates for European core nations and the U.S. commercial paper rate), the core found itself in the same phase of the interest-rate cycle 48.6% of the period. The three European nations were in the same phase 60.6% of the period. Bilaterally, the U.S. occupied the same phase with European core nations as follows: 72.3% with Britain, 67.8% with France, and

64.1% with Germany. Furthermore, the differentials between the rates were actually declining over the period. Long-term rates also remained synchronous. This parallelism in the developed world, and especially the core, was a unique characteristic of the pre–World War I period, as macroeconomies have shown themselves to be far less synchronous from the interwar period on.[85]

That macroeconomies were synchronized was stabilizing for the structure of adjustment in the developed world, but the classic or conventional depictions of the adjustment mechanism under a gold standard suggest macroeconomies that are producing outcomes which differ quite significantly across nations. The conventional Humian adjustment model would predict prices which were moving in opposite directions. According to the conventional model, when surplus nations experience a growing metallic money supply which serves to inflate prices, deficit nations face declining prices as they lose gold. The latter nations adjust as declining prices make their products more desirable in both domestic and foreign markets. In an expanded model that endogenizes capital flows, the loss of gold diminishes the amount of liquidity in the deficit nations' economies, and this in turn leads to higher interest rates. The higher rates attract capital from abroad and compound the adjustment on the real (i.e., trade) side. Surplus nations which find themselves facing excess liquidity (as gold flows in) require low interest rates in order for financial markets to clear. Again, as with adjustment on the real side, we expect macroeconomic indices (in this case interest rates) which are moving in opposite directions. If business cycles are moving inversely to the credit cycle, then we should also expect diverging trends in economic growth as well. In this case, high interest rates which attract capital create slower growth, which in turn reduces the consumption of imports. Hence, that the gold standard did not work according to the conventional (i.e., Humian) representation was actually a stabilizing development for the adjustment process. In this case a gold standard that worked according to the conventional view would have been subject to less stable balance-of-payments positions across developed nations, including the core.[86]

Synchronous macroeconomies also indirectly contributed to a stable adjustment mechanism by producing other outcomes that affected external positions. With stable exchange rates, synchronous price movements assured fairly stable terms of trade, especially in the core. Kenwood and Lougheed (1983, pp. 169–71) point out that very few nations during the period experienced sustained losses in income due to adverse long-term movements in their terms of trade.[87] Any adverse changes in the prices of imports would be compensated by changes in the prices of exports: paralleling price movements mitigated redistribution of trade surpluses emanating from changes in prices. Essentially, real exchange rates remained stable, thus limiting any redistributional bias in the structure of adjustment.

The reduction of bias in the adjustment process, effected both by synchronous macroeconomies and other factors, served to relieve pressures for the manipulation of nominal exchange rates. This was important as an indicator to investors, whose short-term capital transactions were the principal vehicle of adjustment under the gold standard, that monetary systems were functioning in ways conducive to the maintenance of convertibility. But just as important to the long-run stability of the gold standard was the fact that the limited official manipulation of nominal exchange rates in the developed world allowed exchange rates to be configured by market fundamentals. That real exchange rates were an outcome of the natural (i.e., market determined) value of national currencies vis-à-vis gold and were consistent with national balance-of-payments positions meant that the structure of international exchange in the developed world gravitated closer to purchasing power parity throughout the period, and this emerged as another factor limiting the systematic bias in adjustment. There did not emerge a structure of real exchange rates that conferred an advantage onto the products of certain nations.[88] That the gold standard was not subject to arbitrary exchange parities also limited the potential for beggar-thy-neighbor policies which destabilized the interwar years (i.e., competitive devaluation).[89] As Yeager (1976, p. 308) points out, "Parities, instead of being arbitrarily chosen over short time spans, expressed an equilibrium that had evolved gradually between themselves and national price levels."

Stabilizing Expectations

On several important dimensions, the gold standard was self-sustaining: the stability of the gold link itself owed something to a process of self-fulfilling prophecy. In no other factors affecting the maintenance of convertibility was this more evident than in the effects of investors' perceptions. These perceptions were at the very center of the short-term adjustment process during the gold standard. Equilibrium in external positions in the developed world was maintained largely by short-term capital flows. It is clear, given the synchronous nature of macroeconomic performance, that these large equilibrating capital movements were stimulated by limited differentials between interest rates (as well as limited shifts in exchange rates). That investment could be this price-elastic required certain conditions with respect to the way investors looked at foreign opportunities, conditions which made investors less inhibited about taking advantage of small discrepancies in the nominal returns to investment. These conditions were oriented around perceptions that the international financial system was relatively free of exchange and convertibility risk; this was especially true of perceptions about investment in developed nations (the gold club).[90]

Foreign investment in a monetary system will be *elastic* to the extent that perceptions about the possibilities of convertibility suspension and possibilities for changes in exchange rates are *inelastic*. Any expectations that a national currency will depreciate or that monetary authorities in that nation cannot maintain convertibility of national currencies into gold will inhibit investment in that country. Any divergence in returns to investment that gives that nation an advantage over another nation in attracting capital will have to be increased by some amount (i.e., premium) which promises to compensate the investors for the risk of a depreciation in the exchange rate (exchange risk) and/or the risk that the investors will be unable to liquidate their investments in the money of their choice (convertibility risk). That perceptions of risk require significant premiums in order to encourage foreign investment means that much larger differentials in interest rates will be required in order to stimulate equilibrating capital flows. The need for larger differentials carries further consequences which can be adverse with respect to the stability of monetary relations. It may force interest rates in nations in deficit up to levels that significantly reduce economic growth. Chronic slow growth may encourage beggar-thy-neighbor policies. Furthermore, the divergence in interest rates will be accompanied by greater divergences in inflation and growth, which may serve to overcompensate for an external deficit (i.e., overadjust). The result will be that some nations will have a strong tendency toward surplus (low growth, low inflation, high interest rates) while others will have a strong tendency toward deficit (high growth, high inflation, low interest rates), which in turn will encourage a system of nations prone to an unstable structure of adjustment. Systems where adjustment requires smaller divergences in interest rates will exhibit a more stable structure of balance of payments across nations: more synchronous macroeconomic performance will encourage a systemic predisposition toward balance.

The expectations of investors during the classical gold standard exhibited a highly stabilizing character. Exchange and convertibility risks in gold nations were perceived as extremely low (i.e., inelastic expectations). Machlup (1964, p. 294) observes that in correspondence among investors, references to or rumors of devaluation were generally absent. The most visible manifestation of the low perceived exchange risk was the prevalence of unhedged investment. As Bloomfield (1963, p. 42) notes, "So far as concerned interest arbitrage between countries firmly on a gold basis, the exchange risk as a general rule was not covered because of confidence that the exchange rate would move only within narrow limits approximating the gold points."[91] Similarly, few investors during the period ever questioned the commitment of monetary authorities to preserve the gold link. Investors came to perceive the maintenance of convertibility as a manifestation of a "dogmatic belief in the gold standard," one that "continued to enlist men's strongest loyalties."[92]

The perceptions that national currencies would maintain their values and convertibility into the future essentially created a set of circumstances in which exchange rates and convertibility came to defend themselves through a process characterized by elements of self-fulfilling prophecy.[93] Since investors came to perceive the sanctity of both the gold link and exchange parities, any deviations in financial conditions that potentially threatened the gold link or exchange rates were completely and quickly counteracted by actions which relieved the pressures leading to the deviations. The deviations, of course, opened up possibilities for speculation, and that speculation generally restored the status quo (i.e., stabilizing speculation). Exchange rates which found themselves pushed to the gold points were subject to transactions in the international market for exchange that sent their values back toward their parities. In the case of a depreciation, expectations that the rate would revert back to its parity opened up possibilities for profitable speculation in the form of taking positions in that currency. The greater demand for that currency on international markets stimulated by a depreciation ended up fulfilling the original expectations of speculators. Hence, under such expectations, any shifts in exchange rates which were greater than the transaction costs of investment were subject to a natural negative feedback or self-correcting process.[94] Furthermore, nonspeculative investments, which also generated demand for the depreciating currency, would not be discouraged since investors expected the value of the currency to be restored.

With respect to convertibility, nations facing a shortage of liquidity that threatened convertibility found that under expectations of the sanctity of the metallic link sufficient gold could be attracted by the natural rise in interest rates stimulated by a capital shortage. As long as investors did not equate shortages with suspensions, higher interest rates in foreign markets had little trouble attracting capital.[95] The inelastic expectations about exchange rates compounded the ability of nations to defend convertibility through the attraction of foreign capital, as differentials in interest rates did not have to be augmented by risk premiums to stimulate capital flows.[96] Like the stabilizing speculation in the market for currencies, the defense of convertibility was also subject to stabilizing processes of negative feedback or self-correction.

Given the importance of equilibrating short-term capital flows for the external positions of nations in this period, these expectations were at the very center of the gold standard's stable structure of adjustment. Not only did the natural market reactions to shortages in liquidity (i.e., higher interest rates) and pressures on exchange rates (shifts to the gold points) bring about the means of adjustment, but they did so very quickly. One of the most stabilizing characteristics of adjustment under the gold standard was its speed. As Polanyi (1957, p. 205) observed, "Short-term money moved at an hour's notice from any point of the globe to another."[97] Officer (1989, pp. 4, 5) stresses how quickly exchange rates adjusted to information in the market: any news that affected possibilities for arbitrage were quickly followed by capital flows. Inelastic expectations about exchange rates and confidence in convertibility were central to the speed of reaction to speculative opportunities, as the low risk of foreign investment broke down any hesitancy of transferring funds overseas. The stabilizing expectations also played a crucial role in making the relatively small stock of global gold sufficient for backing a proliferating number of transactions in the international economy. That investors perceived low risks of convertibility and depreciation, made them all the less reluctant to hold foreign exchange rather than gold. This enhanced the use of foreign exchange and allowed nations to economize on their use of gold in international transactions.

Confidence and inelastic expectations became even more necessary for international stability after 1890 when advances in transport and minting technologies caused a tightening of the gold points. Tighter points meant lower returns to speculation. Assuming that speculators' behavior during this period did not diverge significantly from investment behavior posited in theories of modern capital markets, the risk component of any investment had to be low to compensate for a low return (in the form of profits from speculation).[98]

It was also important that the structure of confidence across nations conformed to the structure of capital flow. Those financial centers in which investors had the greatest confidence also belonged to the nations which tended to be the most prolific exporters of capital. All things being equal, investors preferred to hold foreign securities denominated in sterling, marks, or francs. These nations had the most successful traditions of international finance, their financial services were the most advanced in the world, and gold could be obtained most abundantly and consistently from them. This conformity of structures assured a high level of velocity of international capital, since capital naturally gravitated toward nations that were prone to recycle it back into the system.

Tier 2: The Normative Foundations of Adjustment

In all international monetary or economic regimes the nature of relations which characterizes them is normally determined by some configuration of interaction among the members themselves. These outcomes or sets of relations, in turn, usually depend on prevailing beliefs or norms regarding principal economic goals and the most effective means of attaining those goals. As Ruggie (1983) points out, every economic regime is fundamentally embedded in some greater constellation of social relations (themselves driven by prevailing norms) which configure both the nature and course of regime outcomes. Each regime draws strength from these social relations (norms), and when the social relations or norms change in a manner which no longer is consistent with the working of the regime, the regime itself is destined to be changed or transformed. The gold standard was no exception. The five proximate factors which were most directly responsible for creating a stable system of adjustment were themselves outcomes of the liberal norms which dominated latter-19th-century beliefs about the organization of economic systems. The stability of the gold standard, therefore, depended on processes at a deeper level of causation—a level comprising the fundamental economic orientation which shaped the belief systems and policies of the period.

The liberal norm which embodied the belief in the benefits of the unhampered flow of people, money, and goods had effects which permeated all five of the proximate factors which directly impacted on the structure of adjustment. It was the mobility of factors, goods, and money which created such a favorable international economic system within which monetary relations were embedded (i.e., the stable superstructure of international economics). The mobility of people lowered the social costs of adjustment, and was instrumental in maintaining global growth and the supply of raw materials. Maintaining growth across nations, in turn, had even more direct effects on convertibility, through abating fiscal pressures for inflation. The more integrated international economy which was the outcome of the free movement of goods, factors, and money facilitated the expansion of international trading networks which enhanced the collective adjustment mechanism both directly (on the real side) and indirectly (by economizing on gold). The free flow of money facilitated the rise of a global financial system which enhanced the central adjustment mechanism of the gold standard: the movement of short-term capital. This, too, had similar direct and indirect effects on the structure of adjustment.

The freedom of exchange was a fundamental cause underlying the synchronous nature of macroeconomies. That economic agents could exchange goods and money in a fairly unrestricted environment facilitated the law of one price. Under fixed exchange rates and fairly riskless international investment, real and financial commodities will be in greater competition with one another to the extent that agents can have free access to international markets. This will force their prices into greater convergence. This law of one price was most closely approximated in the late 19th century, because of the low barriers to economic exchange.[99] The macroeconomic parallelism was reinforced by the strength of the norms embodied in the orthodoxy of gold monometallism. The orthodox pursuit of low inflation and maintenance of the free flow of metals across borders discouraged interest rates from diverging significantly and kept prices convergent at low levels of inflation.[100] The desire to keep exchange rates fixed further reduced pressures for differentials in prices and interest rates.[101] That prices and interest rates faced strong market pressures to converge also brought business cycles into greater convergence.

The contribution of liberal norms regarding economic exchange to the stable structure of adjustment under the gold standard was most visible in the behavior of the core as capital recyclers. It was all the more stabilizing for the international monetary system of the period that these norms were in fact strongest in core nations. Without the freedom to import goods and make foreign investments, core economic agents could not have facilitated adjustment in other countries. In this case, the freedom to react to market signals was central to the collective adjustment mechanism. When capital (savings) accumulated in core nations as a result of surpluses, a stabilizing structure of collective adjustment required that deficit regions or nations with low savings could attract foreign capital with higher (risk-adjusted) returns to investment. Similarly, deficit nations required the best possible trading opportunities in the core to avoid severe and chronic current account performances. The trading opportunities also facilitated a stable circle of adjustment as deficit nations could use their current earnings to finance their international debts, and, of course, the core's net capital exports would assure that foreign investment maintained the demand for the core's commodity exports.

Great Britain was able to play its special role as the center of the global adjustment mechanism because of the openness it practiced throughout the period. Had the international monetary system's central player followed more mercantilistc norms, outcomes in the system would have likely been quite different. It was all the more fortuitous that the system's dominant player followed the most liberal norms of international exchange: the world and other core nations depended most on British investment and markets.

Confidence in the international investment environment was enhanced to the extent that capital could flow freely across borders. The lack of controls kept the perceptions of convertibility and exchange risk low as investors were assured that nations whose exchanges or gold stocks were under pressure could attract the necessary liquidity to preserve the exchange rate and gold link. Liquidity could always be pulled with the right rate because creditor nations allowed their economic agents the freedom of transferring their wealth out of the country. This was especially important during periods of financial distress when nations required capital to avoid suspensions of convertibility or changes in the exchange rate. Had capital been encapsulated by mercantilistic controls, there would have been far greater reluctance on the part of investors to take foreign positions with their capital. Moreover, that governments followed laissez-faire norms and did not intervene in international financial markets to configure capital flows eliminated a major source of nervousness among investors.[102] On one dimension, investors were always assured recoverability. On another dimension, exchange rates were subject to fewer sources of change: non-interventionist governments meant fewer possibilities for political manipulation of the exchange rate (e.g., competitive devaluation).

The lack of political manipulation of economic processes dictated by liberal norms had a central impact on the adjustment mechanism both at the international and domestic levels. Internationally, it kept political rivalries from spilling over into the international economy. War and international rivalries could be carried on without affecting the adjustment mechanism, as animosities did not stimulate the sorts of mercantilistic controls that have become a common characteristic of modern warfare.[103] Hence, adjustment was not subject to the cycle of international political competition. But neither was adjustment subject to the vagaries of politics (i.e., the business cycle) at the domestic level. First, manipulating the macroeconomy to generate specific outcomes violated norms of non-involvement. Second, unlike the period following World War I, manipulating the business cycle produced little political utility (i.e., there was little bias in favor of the emergence of political business cycles).[104] Norms of government detachment from the economy limited governmental culpability for poor macroeconomic performance. The adverse outcomes of unemployment, slow growth, and disparities in income (which today contribute much in determining success in achieving and maintaining political office) were considered "acts of God" rather than the outcomes of failed political agendas during the period before World War I.[105]

The depoliticized macroeconomy of the gold standard had various consequences for the adjustment mechanism. Political non-involvement in the macroeconomy meant that the synchronous outcomes created by international market forces across economies could go uninterrupted. Monetary authorities found no political obstacles in the orthodox maintenance of a metallist system. There was little pressure to monetize deficits or inflate economies out of recession, both of which would have led to an overexpansion of money supplies which made the maintenance of convertibility more difficult.[106] Strictly on the fiscal side, the manifestations of the depoliticized macroeconomy were small government sectors, typically balanced budgets, and the resilience of a prevailing norm of fiscal restraint.[107] That fiscal prudence had such a strong normative foundation (both in itself and in the norms which depoliticized economic policy) relieved the gold standard from the inflationary pressures that have historically been inimical to metallist regimes. The period of the gold standard appeared to feature just as strong a form of fiscal orthodoxy as monetary orthodoxy.[108] Finally, the limited political rewards to economic performance also minimized the tendencies for economic nationalism resulting in beggar-thy-neighbor policies. Manipulating exchange rates, trade barriers, and interest rates to redistribute or protect external surpluses and employment opportunities was less necessary in a world where the burden of inferior macroeconomic outcomes did not fall on political leaders. In the prewar world of laissez-faire, the domestic political incentives to exploit others was generally absent.[109]

The norms regarding the responsibility of governments for macroeconomic outcomes goes far in explaining how nations could maintain domestic monetary regimes that were oriented around low inflation and some internal adjustment.[110] The structure of political costs and benefits of economic policies did not conflict with the monetary orthodoxy of the period. Stable money and the discipline of the gold link did not generate the pressures for change that we saw after World War I when norms regarding the economic responsibilities of governments changed in a manner which was inimical to the conventional practice of metallism. With the shift in the normative foundations of the gold standard at the domestic level, the monetary orthodoxy it relied upon became more difficult to sustain. As Cleveland (1976, pp. 25, 26) observes, "When, during and after World War I, central banks began to accept regular responsibilities for helping to finance national budgets and to maintain employment and manage demand, the days of the gold standard were numbered." He further (p. 14) points out that the interwar glorification of the automaticity of the prewar gold standard really reflected a reaction to the politicization of the macroeconomy after the War.[111]

In addition to norms of limited government involvement in and responsibility for the economy, free exchange and movement, and fiscal prudence, the final set of norms which supported the period's stable structure of adjustment was embodied in the monetary orthodoxy of the day. Like the other sets of norms, this orthodoxy itself was strongly grounded in a liberal creed. In fact, as Polanyi (1957, p. 135) observed, the gold standard occupied a position as one of the three pillars of 19th-century laissez-faire: the other two being a market for labor (i.e., labor should find its own price on the market) and free trade. It is no accident that the liberal economic agenda gave a central role to gold monometallism (see Chapter 6 on the political rise of gold), since the orthodoxy preached that money creation should be regulated by some impersonal-automatic mechanism, as opposed to meddling authorities who were prone to a more idiosyncratic manipulation of the money supply. This was consistent with the liberal vision of the proper foundations of economic systems: sound money and processes void of public manipulation.[112] The former would be preserved through the discipline of convertibility, i.e., checking inflation through the use of a gold standard. Moreover, the basis of money creation (metal) was itself relatively free of public manipulation as individuals reserved the rights under orthodox metallism to convert their gold into any form desired (coin or bullion) and to import and export it freely across international borders. Hence the goals and means of metallist orthodoxy were consistent with broad liberal tenets.[113]

The metallist norms were instrumental in preserving the essence of the regime by imparting a self-sustaining element onto collective convertibility. Perceptions of the influence of these norms imparted a great deal of credibility onto the gold link and international parities.[114] The self-sustaining element was both direct (in the actual actions of monetary authorities) and indirect (embodied in a process of self-fulfilling prophecy on the part of investors). The metallist norms which were most compelling emphasized the sanctity of the metallic link and the exchange rate. As Polanyi (1957, p. 197) observed, "The supreme directive of [central bankers] was always and under all conditions to stay on gold." If the metallic link became something to be venerated, then certainly the stability of the exchange rate also acquired a sacred quality. Cleveland (1976, p. 26) points out, "The gold parities of leading currencies [became] sacrosanct . . . , their maintenance a public duty that no right-thinking person would question."[115] In essence, the central injunctions of the gold standard had become "article[s] of faith" among monetary authorities.[116] As with most articles of faith, the commitment to a specific behavior mode became quite strong.

In the most direct sense, convertibility protected itself through the orthodox behavior of monetary authorities. Indirectly, both convertibility and exchange rates maintained themselves through a process of self-fulfilling prophecy. The vehicle through which both were preserved was principally short-term capital flows reacting to changes in interest rates and shifts of exchange rates within the gold points. The major protagonists of adjustment were private investors. Any change in interest rates which signaled a shortage of gold or any movement of exchange rates toward the gold points quickly attracted an abundance of capital flows which corrected the initial imbalance. This high-price elasticity of short-term capital, which produced an adjustment mechanism that imparted a self-sustaining quality onto convertibility and exchange parities (i.e., stabilizing speculation), emanated from perceptions at the micro level that monetary conditions would revert to some status quo after a disturbance.[117] Only under such expectations would speculation in the market for exchange and investment reinforce parities and convertibility. Any expectations that convertibility would be threatened or that exchange rates would not revert back to their parities would affect the profit opportunities for speculators. Investors would only respond to much higher interest rates or be reluctant to take a position in a depreciating currency. In the first case, domestic monetary systems short of gold would have greater difficulty attracting enough metal to protect convertibility. In the second case, exchange rates would find greater difficulty in abating their falling values, as the international demand for currencies would not rise as readily after some initial movement toward the gold points. In both cases, investment capital would be far less sensitized to market signals than under more inelastic expectations about exchange rates and convertibility. In the case where investors came to expect the worst (i.e., further depreciation and suspension), their actions would likely contribute to the adverse outcomes; in this case speculation would be destabilizing.

Investors' expectations were partly linked to their perceptions of the practice of monetary orthodoxy. That they came to have inelastic expectations about domestic monetary systems in the gold club fundamentally owes a good deal to their belief in the compelling nature of the norms of metallism. Investors perceived great strength in the injunctions dictating the preservation of the gold link and the exchange rate, but just as important was their perception of the strength of a metallist norm from which those injunctions themselves drew strength—that of stable money. The commitment to keeping the value of national currencies stable was as much a central directive of monetary orthodoxy (and passionately pursued) as the gold link and stable exchange rate were. As Brown (1940, V. I., p. 38) observed, "Every country rejoiced it its success and was alarmed by its failures in keeping intact these familiar landmarks of financial 'soundness.'" Moreover, the pursuit of stable money made the gold link and stable rates possible, as both were successful to the extent that practicing nations could avoid inflation. In a fundamental sense, investors imputed even greater resilience to gold links and stable exchange rates because the underlying process which determined their success was conducive to their perpetuation: investors expected convertibility and stable rates because they perceived the possibilities of inflation as low.[118]

Since investors saw both the gold link and exchange parities as something that authorities maintained with reverence and would defend in the last resort, and since the commitment to the injunctions of stable rates and convertibility was made easier by the compelling nature of the norm dictating stable money, it was profitable to take advantage of any disturbances in exchange rates and gold supplies. In this sense, the stability of the adjustment system under the gold standard was in large part a cognitive outcome in which perceptions of monetary outcomes became linked to perceptions about the compelling nature of monetary norms. As long as the normative foundations of orthodoxy remained unchallenged or constant, microeconomic reactions to market processes remained sufficient means of adjustment for the international monetary system.[119] The causal process, therefore, can be defined as running from the existence of a strong normative foundation regulating the practice of metallism (the metallist orthodoxy gravitating around stable money, convertibility, and stable exchange rates) *to* perceptions of the compelling nature of the metallist orthodoxy *to* the behavior of private investors reacting to possibilities for speculative profits *to* a stable adjustment mechanism *to* the maintenance of collective convertibility. (See Figure 7.5.)

But even this causal path showed reciprocal effects that interjected a feedback loop into the process.[120] That investors behaved based on such confidence in the injunctions of metallist orthodoxy led to a situation that relieved monetary officials from having (with some exceptions) to carry out stabilizing interventions that maintained orthodox practices. As Eichengreen (1989, p. 32) observes, "Their anticipations and consequent actions rendered official intervention largely redundant."[121] Expectations about the resilience of the gold link and exchange rates made such outcomes more sustainable. The actions following from the expectations themselves were usually sufficient to do so. But given the responsiveness of capital to international market signals, when some intervention was necessary, orthodoxy became easier to practice. Outcomes that were consistent with original expectations served

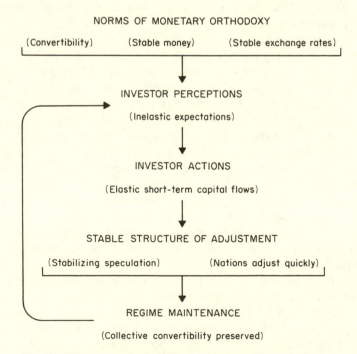

NORMS OF MONETARY ORTHODOXY

(Convertibility)   (Stable money)   (Stable exchange rates)

INVESTOR PERCEPTIONS

(Inelastic expectations)

INVESTOR ACTIONS

(Elastic short-term capital flows)

STABLE STRUCTURE OF ADJUSTMENT

(Stabilizing speculation)   (Nations adjust quickly)

REGIME MAINTENANCE

(Collective convertibility preserved)

Fig. 7.5 The structure of stability under the gold standard.

to reinforce those expectations. In this sense, we can see the emergence of a pattern of mutual reinforcement between outcomes and the perceptions that led to the actions which, in turn, maintained a stable structure of adjustment. As investor perceptions of the sanctity of convertibility and exchange rates continued, so too did nations that came under pressure readily find the requisite short-term capital flows forthcoming as a result of stabilizing speculation. With the relief provided by the capital flows, nations' "track records" or "reputations" as practitioners of orthodox metallism maintained themselves, thus further fueling beliefs in the sanctity of the injunctions underlying metallism.[122] In the words of Ford (1962, p. 189), the entire set of monetary outcomes became "nourished on its past success."[123]

This stabilizing self-fulfilling process that characterized the international regime did not emerge out of thin air with the advent of the gold club in the 1870s. It was actually the result of a long previous history in gold-club nations of success at maintaining metallist regimes. Nations in the gold club had been fairly successful (except for periods of large-scale political disruptions) at maintaining metallist links under silver and bimetallic standards. The stabilizing process characterizing gold convertibility actually had its roots in the pre-gold-standard period. It was not difficult to believe monetary authorities were committed to gold, because outcomes under previous metallist regimes underscored the resilience of other metallic links: why should authorities be any less compelled by a gold link? But even here gold had a distinguished history that imparted even more credibility onto the gold vis-à-vis the silver link. Before the gold club had formed in the 1870s, the only case of a sustained domestic gold standard was Great Britain, and this case produced rather enviable results with respect to the prescriptions of metallism.[124] It is no surprise that nations joining the gold club later in the 19th century imputed a quality to the metal as a basis of a monetary system that other metals didn't have. But gold was more compelling for other reasons as well: Since the status of gold was superior to that of other metals, breaking from a gold link was even more unpleasant than breaking from another metal. Gold was also supported by the dominant political-economic interests of the day. Hence, the gold standard regime was of a more stable character (and therefore different) from other metallist regimes that prevailed among developed nations earlier in the century. Capital flows were more responsive to signals that nations needed to adjust under the gold standard. This partly explains why financial crises were so few and relatively milder under the gold standard than they were under different metallist regimes in previous periods.

It is also not surprising that nations outside of the gold club (i.e., nations that had been unable to institute the link or sustain the link for any significant period) did not experience the same self-stabilizing process with respect to their domestic metallist regimes. These also tended to be nations that demonstrated an historic difficulty in instituting and/or preserving metallist regimes of any kind (most often because these nations had more of a political and economic bias toward inflation). In these nations, the process of self-fulfilling prophecy often worked in a manner unconducive to the preservation of a metallist (including gold) link. This was especially true in periods of financial distress. Sporadic histories of depreciation and suspension diminished confidence in the commitment to orthodox metallism there. Hence, when difficulties presented themselves, they were more likely to be compounded than neutralized (i.e., destabilizing rather than stabilizing speculation). Investors were more likely to withdraw capital in response to external balance problems than to inject new capital into those economies. As Ford (1962, p. 32) observes, the "less successful history meant that the additional threat of a domestic speculative drain was ever present." In some cases, authorities pursuing even heroic efforts to maintain convertibility could not prevent a premium from developing on gold, as was the case in Argentina in 1885.[125] This link between historic track records and the effects of self-fulfilling prophecy more than anything exemplifies the interconnection between perceptions of the commitment of authorities to the injunctions of metallist orthodoxy and nations' successes at preserving the gold link. In the periphery, even when authorities did pursue orthodox practices of metallism, the lack of credibility on the part of domestic and foreign investors led to actions that made it difficult to preserve the link. It is no surprise, therefore, that the gold club was formed and was maintained among nations that experienced relative success at maintaining metallist regimes historically, since their success with gold was partly driven by their track records with silver and bimetallism.

But even within the gold club, questionable commitments to the gold link could not be overcome by relative-historic success in preserving metallism. Investors were not blind to differentials in national attachments to metallism among the more advanced economies, irrespective of track records. Italy, for example, found far less credibility among domestic and foreign investors in its commitment to gold. This followed from a lack of fiscal and monetary restraint which often kept the money supply quite large in relation to the nation's gold base. In this case, perceptions were conditioned by a limited commitment to the injunctions of metallism and rendered speculation far less stabilizing relative to investment in other gold nations. This explains Italy's relatively turbulent experience on the gold standard. Italy showed that a stable structure of adjustment was conditional rather than given, even in the gold club.[126]

In this sense, the gold standard as an economic regime fits well into discussions about the benefits of credible rules for maintaining desired outcomes.[127] Threats to convertibility generated sufficient and quick negative feedback processes (adjustment through stabilizing speculation) to the extent that investors perceived the commitment to the rules of metallism to be credible (i.e., that authorities stood committed to defend the link in the last resort). In nations that had generated such credibility in the sanctity of the rules, no financial crisis appeared too devastating.[128] In nations where the commitment was perceived as less compelling, convertibility was difficult to defend even under milder crises.[129] Hence, rules generated the means of their own preservation wherever commitments were credible (i.e., stabilizing speculation), and generated the means of their own undoing where commitments were not credible. When these norms became less compelling because of the new economic orientations generated by the domestic growth and full-employment concerns after World War I, the rules of metallism became less credible, and consequently the actions of microeconomic actors were no longer of a kind that was conducive to adjustment.[130]

In sum, the stable structure of adjustment upon which the stability of the gold standard was founded was the result of a two-tier process. The first tier comprised five factors which were directly responsible for a stable structure of adjustment. These factors were dependent on prevailing norms which governed economic exchange and money (tier 2). These prevailing norms themselves were embedded in the compelling economic philosophy of the period: liberalism. Hence, in drawing a model of, or specifying the train of forces that resulted in, a stable international monetary regime, we saw a process anchored in the strength of a normative superstructure that generated injunctions which were conducive to the perpetuation of specific monetary practices across nations in the developed world. The success of the gold standard was ultimately and inextricably tied to the success of classical liberalism.[131] (See Figure 7.6.) As long as the philosophy dominated belief systems of the day among gold-club nations, then the regime maintained the inner capacity to generate outcomes that were conducive to the perpetuation of gold monometallism. Freedom of factors, goods, and money to move was fundamental to the adjustment mechanism. That political incentives to manipulate the economy (i.e., limited governmental responsibility for macroeconomic developments) were minimal insulated macroeconomic variables from being subjected to idiosyncratic or predatory manipulation, thus minimizing biases in the structure of collective adjustment among gold-club nations as well as limiting possibilities for inflationary note-issue which directly threatened convertibility.[132] Limited culpability for adverse economic outcomes also made it easier to support an adjustment mechanism that featured an element of internal adjustment. The reluctance to extend warfare into the economic realm maintained economic relations that were conducive to adjustment. Norms of fiscal prudence and small public sectors relieved nations of inflationary pressures inimical to the preservation of the gold link. Finally, the commitment to an organization of money around some impersonal rule dictating growth in the money supply (i.e., metallism) and the free international flow of metals gave nations both the means of adjustment and assured limited inflationary pressures on convertibility.[133]

The international monetary regime of the gold standard found strength in the prevailing economic norms of the day, which, in turn, found strength in the prevailing liberal philosophy of the day. Thus, the gold standard and liberalism were "joined at

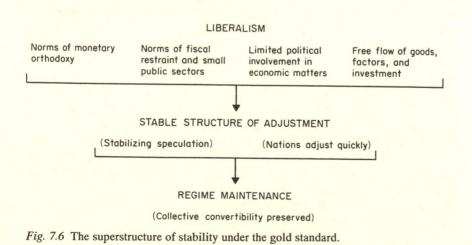

Fig. 7.6 The superstructure of stability under the gold standard.

the hip," with the fate of one paralleling the fate of the other. The gold standard became only as resilient as the liberal philosophy. The injunctions of the gold standard were compelling because the normative superstructure within which they were embedded was compelling. As Yeager (1984, p. 665) notes, "The gold standard is simply a particular set of rules for policy regarding the monetary system; and these rules are no more inherently self-enforcing than any other set of monetary rules." Thus monetary norms were embedded in norms comprising a general economic philosophy: they did not have an independent existence. As long as the philosophy compelled, the regime enjoyed a strong lifeline. And indeed in the gold standard period, the philosophy enjoyed its high point of influence. Polanyi (1957, pp. 135–39) described the status which liberalism achieved with terms such as "evangelical fervor," "crusading passion," "militant creed," and "secular religion." He (pp. 30, 98) noted that "all educated people" were at heart on the side of this "ruling philosophy." Liberalism was in fact the "common matrix" which shaped social relations in and across nations.[134] When the normative foundation of liberalism deteriorated after the War, the lifeline was severed. With the decline of "liberal attitudes and self-restraints" came the decline of the gold standard.[135]

The ultimate downfall of the classical practice of metallism was more the result of changes in economic orientations than the result of specific events like the Boer War or the World War.[136] If indeed the "tree was rotting," as de Cecco (1974, p. 127) argues, then it was not because political crises were shaking confidence in the monetary system. In fact, given the ongoing strength of the normative foundations of the gold standard, the regime had a built-in stabilizing mechanism even in the face of severe crises.[137] Whatever rotting was occurring would have had to be grounded in the weakening of the normative foundations of the regime. To the extent that classical liberalism was losing influence before the War, we can say that indeed the gold standard was weakening as a practice, even though monetary outcomes themselves had not changed significantly in the latter part of the period. Continuing the horticultural analogy of de Cecco, if the soil within which the tree was planted (liberalism) was becoming less fertile, the tree itself can be said to have been dying. But it is unclear just how weak liberalism was becoming before the advent of the War. Although a wave of socialist reform arose over a variety of domestic issue areas in gold-club nations, monetary practices and international economic relations remained encased in a fairly liberal organization. It is conceivable that the challenge to liberalism might not have made serious inroads into the monetary and international economic realms for some time. But all this is problematic given the advent of the War, which served to enhance the rise of the new economic orientation of full employment and government intervention in the macroeconomy. The War interrupted the classical practice of gold monometallism, but it did not necessarily destroy it. The regime found a resurrection difficult because underlying norms about the nature of economic systems and economic relations were transformed in a manner that was no longer conducive to the stable structure of adjustment which existed before World War I. The War hastened the normative transformation, but certainly did not determine it. The gold standard could have survived the War, but it could not (and did not) survive the ultimate demise of classical liberalism.[138]

It is indicative that those economists most familiar with the gold standard look upon possibilities of the return to a gold standard as a matter of not only resuscitating a monetary regime from the past, but resuscitating an entire set of economic belief systems and economic relations on which the gold standard was founded a century ago. The practice of gold monometallism as a set of rules depended on a larger normative support system, all of which was in place before World War I but no longer after the War.[139] In essence, the passing of 19th century (classical) liberalism rang the deathbell for what Yeager (1976, p. 308) refers to as the "good old days" of metallist regimes.

Outcomes connected with attempts at reinstituting forms of the regime (interwar period and Bretton Woods) over the past 70 years have confirmed the demise of this support system. In the interwar period monetary orthodoxy strongly compelled nations to attempt to resuscitate the regime. But its short life reflected that domestic growth and employment were far more important than preserving a time-honored set of monetary practices. Given the new norms, governments could no longer sacrifice their domestic economies on the altar of monetary orthodoxy.[140] Having learned their lessons in the interwar period, national leaders after World War II constructed a new international monetary regime at Bretton Woods that was much more compatible with the new norms. They now promoted an internationalism that was constrained by the imperatives of domestic economic stability. In essence, adjustment would now be sacrificed on the altar of growth and employment.[141]

8

The Gold Standard
and Regime Theory

In returning to the distinction made in Chapter 1 with respect to the typology of regime origin and stability (hegemonic, cooperative, and diffuse regimes), we find that the classical gold standard showed elements of all three, but not in the way that has normally been espoused in the historical work on the period and the general literature on international relations. The origin and stability of the gold standard carry implications for the study of international order under all three regime structures. The first section considers the implications of the regime dynamics of the gold standard with respect to hegemonic regimes, the second section considers the implications with respect to cooperative regimes, and the last considers the implications with respect to diffuse regimes.

Contrary to many visions of the gold standard, the regime dynamics upon which it was founded showed a strongly diffuse character. Moreover, the managerial elements that did show up were quite different from the conventional visions of hegemony and cooperation in the literature on international regimes. The nature of hegemony was much more unintentional and non-state than prevailing theories of hegemonic regimes can account for. The behavior of the British state and Bank of England fell far short of the expectations of proponents of British hegemony under the gold standard. If anything, Great Britain acted more like a weak than a strong nation, and France behaved more hegemonically than Great Britain. But even here the overly domestic orientation of the Bank of France rendered its actions quite distinct from mainstream visions of hegemony. Cooperation, too, fails to explain the origin and stability of the regime. In fact, it was a failure to cooperate that led to the emergence of the regime in the 1870s. The present literature on cooperation has paid very little attention to such default or residual regimes. Interbank lending did emerge as a stabilizing force under the gold standard, but the infrequency of such initiatives and the limited transfers involved are more of a testament to the stability that existed in the regime for other reasons. Furthermore, central bank relations in the period exhibited significant destabilizing elements as well. Moreover, it is not clear that more cooperation would have produced a more stable regime. The lack of cooperative schemes effectively limited the degree to which authorities could allow their macroeconomies to arrive at conditions that would have threatened convertibility (i.e., moral hazard and adverse substitution leading to inflation and fiscal deficits).

In that monetary relations under the gold standard were highly consistent with prevailing national interests, the regime showed a harmonious and self-enforcing nature. The regime remained stable void of significant management because it featured elements that either limited the need for management or that substituted for such management. That the regime formed among a fairly homogeneous and limited set of members, and that it was embedded in a greater international political economy which was itself stable, limited the need for management. In this respect, the gold standard suggests that the state of relations in specific regimes will depend on outcomes in other regimes, and that stability in one regime may be achieved by exporting its problems to other regimes. Both, in turn, suggest that diffuse regimes may be more vulnerable than managed regimes because these interdependencies cannot be manipulated to avert shocks under the former, while they can be manipulated in the latter. In terms of substitution, it was an interlocking set of domestic norms that effectively substituted for international management. In that behavior according to these domestic norms, and the general belief in the sanctity of these norms (i.e., credibility), directly and indirectly protected convertibility suggests the importance of credible rules for the successful functioning of diffuse regimes. To the extent that such credible rules create stable and desirable sets of relations among nations, they may function as a sufficient substitute for cooperation and hegemony in the international political economy.

Hegemonic Regimes[1]

The behavior of Great Britain under the gold standard shows a track record that hardly vindicates conventional visions of monetary hegemony. The Bank of France probably acted more like a hegemon (in the conventional benevolent-hegemonic vision) than did the Bank of England. In fact, it can be said that the Bank of France occasionally played the role of monetary underwriter for the supposed global monetary underwriters (the Bank of England and the London market). So, too, did the French government act more hegemonically than the British government in trying to build a formal regime (i.e., during the Conferences of 1867, '78, and '81). Interestingly, however, this stabilizing behavior came more out of weakness than strength. The Bank of France was always ready to keep the London market liquid because shocks in London adversely affected Paris. Had the Paris market been more resilient to shocks (e.g., had clearly superior pulling power over London), we would have likely seen less benevolence on the part of the Bank of France. The Bank of England was much more passive in bilateral attempts to keep financial markets liquid, but this behavior was not as detrimental to London as to Paris, since the generally superior pulling power of London made the British financial market less vulnerable to international shocks. So, too, in building a regime, the British reluctance to make substantive contributions to construct either a formal union based on gold or a price-support regime for silver reflected a lack of urgency to orchestrate international conditions in a way that fit British interests. This lack of urgency, in turn, seemed to partly reflect a feeling that British finance (including financial conditions in the Empire) was robust enough to withstand whatever developments arose from either the success or failure of multilateral initiatives among the other principal monetary powers.[2]

It was the weaker (vis-à-vis Great Britain) powers—France and the U.S.—which showed a greater willingness to support formal regimes in this period. In these cases the British were somewhat less hegemonic because their domestic monetary system was more resilient to developments in the international monetary system, while the U.S. and the French behaved somewhat more hegemonically because they were more sensitive to such developments. This suggests that conventional structural conditions like rising or declining (absolute or relative) power will have greater difficulty in predicting foreign policy outcomes. In fact, if weakness leads to stabilizing behavior, then it seems that hegemony can arise under conditions that have been heretofore considered conducive to a retraction of hegemony (a retraction meaning a reduction of direct involvement in the international political economy). Hence, hegemons may choose to react to hegemonic decline not by being less but more involved in shaping international outcomes, because they can no longer passively absorb such outcomes in the international system.[3] The idea of a declining hegemon acting more hegemonically is diametrically opposed to the conventional vision of hegemony; such behavior essentially serves to stand the theory on its head because it reverses the purported causal relationship that sees increasing absolute or relative power as motivating greater international involvement. Logically, if one endogenizes dependence as a determinant of power in the international system, then it may be conceivable that truly powerful nations with large domestic demands on their resources may opt for an isolationist position since developments in the international political economy will affect them to a lesser degree than a less powerful (i.e., more dependent) nation. For the former, international involvement may be a luxury, while the latter might very well see it as a necessity. To the extent that such can occur more systematically, the theory of hegemonic regimes needs to redefine its structural independent variables and/or develop variables at other levels of analysis to account for the actions of what in fact truly is a declining but highly active hegemon.

The behavior of the French also suggests that international stability can be something which emanates from several sources rather than a single source. This vindicates the idea of collective hegemony or supportership. The Bank of France's underwriting functions for the Bank of England and London market in times of impending distress in British finance appear as quite an anomaly indeed in the conventional view of hegemony, since another nation helped stabilize the domestic financial market of a nation with hegemonic power.[4] In fact, several financial markets (especially Paris, Berlin, and New York) in the developed world served as major sources of liquidity both for each other as well as for other nations. Given the modest reserves of the Bank of England, it is questionable whether the British could have withstood the burden of hegemony alone; in this case, supportership appears to have characterized the structure of the burden of adjustment under the gold standard.[5] In the origin of the gold standard, successful cooperation in building a formal regime failed because of a lack of support among core nations (i.e., with Great Britain and Germany being the least cooperative).[6]

Scholars such as Kindleberger (1973, p. 299), Cohen (1977, p. 88), Eichengreen (1984 and 1990a), Nevin (1955), and Cleveland (1976) have questioned the stability of a monetary system with several powerful actors. Their arguments center on the capricious flows of capital due either to competition between dominant financial markets, or the erratic shifting of reserve holdings due to changes in confidence between key currencies. The gold standard appears to have avoided such outcomes. The confidence question was never a problem, as absolute and relative confidence in the three key currencies (marks, francs, and sterling) were not subject to significant swings. The problem of competition was mitigated by open capital markets which persisted throughout the period: liquidity shortages could always be replenished for a price. Furthermore, the lack of redistributional consequences for external adjustment (i.e., governments were neither held responsible for adverse economic outcomes, nor were they significantly involved in economic matters) reduced both the motivations and means for competitive redistributions. The fact that the gold standard featured several major participants (i.e., the core) in the international regime actually contributed to stability on various dimensions. Liquidity was greater and more elastic as several key currencies existed and investors faced a competitive market for credit (i.e., there was no monopolistic dispensation of liquidity). The greater number of participants in the international gold market made the market itself less vulnerable to critical domestic developments (e.g., changes in standards, discoveries of gold) in any single dominant player. Finally, as the British themselves became less prolific net capital exporters toward the end of the period, Germany, France, and the U.S. maintained the supply of international liquidity by becoming more prolific net capital exporters.

In the case of the gold standard, part of the short-term burden (i.e., immediate reaction of capital flows to differentials in pulling power) of adjustment fell on the weakest members of the system, a condition that is more consistent with coercive visions of international hegemony than benevolent ones because the costs of the regime are being redistributed to weaker actors. This was especially relevant to the relationship between Britain and India, as the latter served the former as a source of adjustment throughout the period.[7] But the behavior of the more powerful nations in this respect was not altogether consistent, as they themselves continued to shoulder a large part of the burden in the long and short runs by allowing capital to be recycled through their financial markets. In terms of the dual distinction of hegemonic regimes, this showed both elements of benevolence and coercive hegemony.[8]

If one chooses to call the functions of Great Britain in the international adjustment process hegemonic, then surely it is not any kind of conventional hegemony as defined by common views of hegemonic regimes. Furthermore, if one defines actions on the part of dominant monetary powers that are themselves stabilizing for the international system as manifestations of hegemony, then surely hegemony has to be a tautology (i.e., must be present by definition), because it is inconceivable that any international monetary system can itself be stable unless its dominant players act in ways that facilitate adjustment for other nations. Any regime by definition is characterized by the behavior of its parts, and its major players disproportionately configure regime outcomes. During the gold standard, Great Britain and other influential monetary powers exhibited policy orientations (i.e., liberal) that ended up being consistent with the interests of other nations in the system.[9] With respect to the origin of the regime, it was Great Britain's central position in the international economy that strongly contributed to the appeal of gold.

The common view of hegemonic stability suggests that hegemony is marshaled by the state or state institutions based on some public consciousness (i.e., the stability or good of some greater system is acknowledged).[10] In the case of the gold standard, there were no intentions on the part of any political or monetary authorities to stabilize the international monetary system. No state or public institutions intentionally took the burden of stabilization upon themselves. The British state, as well as other gold-club states, in fact had little to do with monetary or economic relations. The one institution that did occasionally act in ways that contributed to the stability of the gold standard (the Bank of England) had a very uneven track record in terms of international stabilization (i.e., it also behaved in destabilizing ways) and its stabilizing functions were principally resultants of particularistic goals and interests.[11] Furthermore, the Bank's management of its own monetary system was extremely suspect, with bouts of weakness coexisting with actions that often destabilized more than they stabilized.

That Britain's propensity to recycle capital through its large net exports was a major stabilizing force can be credited to the acts of individuals and private institutions that found international investment in their interests.[12] The state contributed to this supply of international liquidity only insofar as it maintained a policy of laissez-faire over international transactions. But even here the intentions were not clearly international in nature: laissez-faire compelled for domestic reasons relating to beliefs about the most desirable form of organizing national economies.

British citizens, in this case, were the actual agents of stability rather than the state itself, with the state serving as a permissive factor by pursuing liberal policies in both trade and money. British hegemony under the gold standard was therefore *unintended* and *non-state* in nature. At the collective level, stabilizing behavior by other nations was also of this character. These are two categories which are fairly uncommon in the literature on imposed or hegemonic regimes. Both unintentional and non-state hegemony have been hinted at but not systematically pursued in the literature on hegemony.[13]

The compulsion toward gold that emanated from the desire to emulate the practices of Great Britain suggests that the origin of the regime owed something to the process of hegemonic socialization. The concept of hegemonic socialization or Gramscian hegemony envisions hegemony or domination as a cognitive-normative process. The concept of Gramscian hegemony is pregnant with the Marxian notion of the ideological domination of capitalism: the norms of the dominant class become the dominant norms in society. On an international level hegemons legitimate their domination through the proliferation of norms (i.e., socializing subordinate actors) that are consistent with their own interests.[14] Great Britain exported its standard through, in the terms of Kindleberger (1975, p. 51), "precept and example." Nations came to equate economic advancement in the international political economy with the use of gold. However, the actual process of socialization that manifested itself was much more passive and unintended than mainstream treatments of Gramscian hegemony propose. Under the gold standard Britain did not purposefully attempt to inculcate specific norms in other nations. Nations were in fact attracted to hegemonic practices as a result of learning from history: nations inferred a causal relation between the use of gold and the capacity for industrialization, there was no purposive inculcation on the part of the British state or other British agents. When Britain did have an opportunity to facilitate the proliferation of its monetary practices (the Conference of 1867), it failed to make even the smallest contribution to effect that goal.

But even here socialization wasn't the only hegemonic process at work. The scramble for gold suggests that nations faced a significant amount of structural compellence toward gold because sterling was linked to the metal. Nations traded disproportionately through sterling, and growing banking systems in other nations grew more anxious to obtain access to the London market. This process of influencing outcomes is more consistent with common visions of hegemony: that powerful nations change the incentives facing other nations with respect to selecting policies. However, this influence was not purposive, as it was intended neither by the British state nor state institutions. It is questionable whether socialization alone would have been so compelling without the structural impetus created by the British standard. To the extent that both factors work in a complementary fashion, we would expect that when hegemons do indeed export their practices to other nations, they do so in heterogeneous and complex (through several complementary-interacting factors) rather than strictly simple and homogeneous (i.e., one factor alone) ways.

In sum, hegemony under the gold standard was quite a heterogeneous and anomalous (i.e., vis-à-vis conventional views of hegemony) process. Influence over international monetary relations came from various (especially core nations) sources, rather than one (Great Britain), thus vindicating a supportership or collective view of hegemony.[15] However, the principal stabilizing agents were non-state in nature and policies undertaken by the more powerful nations were generally void of intentions to impart a stabilizing influence over the international regime as a whole. The policies themselves were driven by domestic imperatives with respect to what was perceived as the proper management of national economies. The highly liberal quality of the injunctions driving these policies created a situation which encouraged actions on the part of private actors in powerful nations (i.e., freedom to import goods and invest overseas) that facilitated the external goals of other nations. This unintended and non-state hegemony has been alluded to in the literature on hegemony, but deviates from the more prevalent vision of powerful states engaging in purposive and direct actions to generate outcomes in the international system. That hegemonic behavior was driven by domestic forces is consistent with a prevalent strand in the hegemonic stability literature that sees hegemonic interests deriving from national rather than international-structural (most often the configuration of international power in an issue-area) factors.

Furthermore, the common visions of British hegemony, and unilateral hegemony in general, do not stand up to the actual outcomes under the gold standard. Unlike the hypothetical conventional hegemonic actor, the British state was a regime blocker rather than regime builder at the conferences. In the maintenance of the regime, it received more help in bilateral arrangements between central banks than it gave out. In this way Britain acted more like a weaker power. France acted in a manner closer to the common vision of hegemony at the conferences (i.e., with its willingness to disproportionately support a formal bimetallist regime), in its management of the Latin

Monetary Union (i.e., dictating policy to its Latin satellites), and in the Bank of France's lending to London and the Bank of England. One could make a case for the argument that the real hegemon of the gold standard was the Bank of France, but even here outcomes diverged from common visions of hegemony. France would not unilaterally attempt to build an international bimetallist regime. Hence it did not have what the literature would actually call hegemonic power: it had regional power to manipulate the franc bloc only. Furthermore, the Bank of France's lending to London emanated from a much more restricted goal (i.e., fears of financial spillover from London) than that normally attributed to a hegemon, as well as from relative weakness in its influence over capital flows (as the Bank of France feared that in periods of financial distress, money would be pulled out of Paris and into London).

In the scramble for gold, Britain did vindicate both a vision of structural compellence and hegemonic socialization. The gold standard partly compelled because international trade was financed disproportionately in sterling, nations desired access to the London capital market, and nations drew lessons from the British experience about the relationship between monetary standards and economic development (i.e., overlearning from history). But even here, the outcomes were somewhat different from the treatment in the literature on hegemonic regimes: the British did not purposively contribute to or orchestrate the structural compellence, and the process of socialization was a result of inferences drawn in foreign nations rather than the direct inculcation of norms or injunctions on the part of hegemonic agents.

Cooperative Regimes

The one striking feature of collective attempts at building formal regimes in the last five decades before the War was the failure of nations to effect cooperative schemes that carried significant benefits for them. In this case we had a failure to build formal regimes even when these regimes were "demanded" by almost all developed nations, especially core nations.[16] In 1867 all major players in the monetary system would have liked a gold union. In the years 1878, '81, and '92 some kind of regime to support the price of silver was demanded. The French and Americans acted consistently with expectations about the behavior of nations demanding a regime: they offered to undertake at least a proportional share of the costs. The British reluctance to make even minimal concessions worked to block the emergence of a cooperative regime. But the British themselves were not in principle against gold union in 1867, and in the latter three conferences strongly desired the emergence of a price-support scheme for silver. Although some argument might be marshaled that British reluctance was rational in 1867 (i.e., because of the loss of status in joining a franc-based union, but even here the British sovereign was sure to rise to central status), very little can be marshaled in support of the reluctance at the last three conferences. In this respect, cooperative attempts at both common interests (gold regime in 1867) and common aversions (stop the depreciation of silver in 1878, '81, '92) failed when rational incentives dictated that a regime should have been constructed.[17] These outcomes cut against the rational-game-theoretic approach that sees regimes as the resultants of nations rationally pursuing mutual gains in variable-sum games.[18] The behavior of

Britain was especially troubling to this vision of cooperation, because no other nation had more incentive to cooperate: its concessions would have been relatively small and the benefits potentially great because of the size of its international sector and the Indian problem.

It is also somewhat anomalous, with respect to the literature on the origin of cooperative regimes, that in the rise of the classical gold standard we saw a kind of *default* or *residual* regime, arising from the ashes of failed cooperation directed toward building formal regimes. The literature on international relations commonly sees regimes emerging from successful attempts at cooperation. As Oye (1985, p. 21) points out, "Cooperation is a prerequisite of regime creation."[19] To the extent that default regimes are prevalent, it would appear that failed cooperation is as interesting a subject of analysis as successful cooperation.[20]

Moreover, if regimes do arise because cooperation fails, then it is not necessarily the case that disorder will follow upon the heels of unsuccessful cooperation. During the gold standard, all of the prospective-formal-cooperative schemes that might have emerged at the conferences carried potential elements of international tension in them. A gold regime formed in 1867 would have instituted a national currency as numeraire (the actual proposals falling on the franc), thus instituting seeds of discontent as leading players whose currencies weren't chosen had to live with recognition of their inferior monetary status within the regime. The formation of a price-support regime for silver at any of the last three conferences would have required opening national mints to greater convertibility for silver, a condition which generated an extreme amount of nervousness from the mid-1870s onward. The tension was potentially all the greater under a formal regime, since many of the nations believed that some prospective members (especially Germany) would use any price-support scheme in a highly exploitative manner. If such adverse or exploitative behavior did arise, or the commitments themselves excessively taxed the gold stocks of participating nations, then we might have faced the situation where participation in a formal regime forced certain nations off the gold standard. In the default regime that did arise, questions of status were kept out of confrontational situations: both the British and French could go on believing that each was the very center of international finance without the existence of any formal declarations that one could use to embarrass the other. Moreover, nations found great comfort in guarding their gold circulations by keeping their mints restricted: they were relieved of the tension of having to look over their shoulders for predatory regime members by the fact that they maintained unilateral discretion over silver conversion.

In terms of theories of cooperation, therefore, relations which result from failed cooperation (default or residual regimes) need not invariably be inferior to relations which emanate from successful cooperation. Failed cooperation may signify that a cooperative solution is not stable or simply impossible to institute. The default outcome (i.e., how nations go on in the meantime) may be a collective set of prudent unilateral adaptations to a common problem. While in the best of all worlds (i.e., a world where first-best/cooperative solutions are possible and stable) nations might be able to make themselves substantially better off by constructing a formal regime (i.e., achieve a highly Pareto-superior outcome), but where the most common, formal types of cooperation generate highly adverse externalities (i.e., a second-best world), a superior set of regime outcomes may be achieved through a group of uni-lateral adaptations to pressing problems. In other words, in a second-best world, the residual from failed cooperation may actually generate fairly stable and desirable outcomes.[21]

With respect to regime maintenance, the one form of actual cooperation that manifested itself throughout the period was accommodation among central banks. Cases of accommodation normally reflected defensive behavior on the part of credi-tor banks, as they were preventing adverse financial spillovers into their markets by abating crises at foreign sources. The Bank of France, which was the principal agent of such accommodation during the period, was always ready to lend to London to keep the shock waves between Paris and London minimal. This vindicates the view that interdependence encourages cooperation.[22] However, this cooperation was rare, and it is not clear that central bank relations were ultimately stabilizing in a net sense. There was much competition for gold among principal markets through the use of gold devices and discount rates, especially in times of financial distress. The accom-modations often helped relieve tensions which the banks themselves had created in the first place.

Furthermore, the central bank cooperation under the gold standard deviated some-what from the traditional vision of cooperative regimes in that it tended to be carried on in a bilateral and ad hoc (i.e., according to need) manner. The bilateral context suggests a restricted set of international concerns: the principal focus of cooperation was relations between two banks or two financial markets. This more restricted pub-lic consciousness deviates from the common vision of cooperation which posits a broader (multilateral) consciousness where the outcomes over an entire system or regime are the goals of purposive action. The ad hoc quality of accommodations sug-gests that cooperation arose according to need: this was a form of regime stabiliza-tion where cooperation was activated by extraordinary conditions rather than the more common vision of ongoing and systematic management of relations in both good and turbulent periods (i.e., this could be called a type of part-time cooperation).

The gold standard remained fairly stable, with what amounted to be a kind of cooperation that was fairly low on the managerial continuum. In fact, it is question-able whether it can be called management at all. Can we make any general infer-ences about optimal styles or forms of cooperation in light of the gold standard ex-perience? In a purely hypothetical context, one might argue that indeed to the extent that regimes are threatened by stochastic disturbances within geographically restricted contexts (i.e., bilateral or trilateral), a crisis-intervention function (part-time) based on more particularistic concerns about negative spillovers may be a sufficient sys-tem of regime maintenance. Furthermore, one may argue that if systematic manage-ment generates moral hazard or adverse substitution (because of strong expectations that national problems will be attended to, or because systematic management be-comes a substitute for more responsible policies at the domestic level), the more uncertain form of stabilization embodied in informal, ad hoc arrangements may be superior because nations are driven to take unilateral steps at "keeping their houses in order" (e.g., staying out of debt, maintaining abundant liquidity, keeping budgets balanced): disorderly houses carry potentially adverse consequences for the regime as a whole.[23]

The generalizability of the inferences themselves may rest on just how much people believe that the gold standard has in common with international economic relations of today and the future. Under the gold standard, any conclusions about why moral hazard and adverse substitution were generally absent, and about the consequences of this absence, would be speculative. Clearly, central banks kept their own houses in good order: maintaining themselves in positions of what was perceived as sufficient liquidity to protect their own convertibility. Was this because greater multilateral insurance schemes designed to replenish depleted reserves were missing? Or were the injunctions of metallist orthodoxy principally responsible? No definitive answers can be issued, but it is certain that responsible management of gold stocks was a fundamental source of stability under the gold standard. The ad hoc, bilateral accommodations appeared to be sufficient facilitators of stability under the gold standard because points of friction (wars and financial crisis) themselves were few and geographically restricted. Hence, the magnitude of regime disturbances was commensurate with the low level of management which prevailed in the regime.

In sum, the gold standard showed very little cooperation among national governments in the process of formal regime building. The rise of the gold standard can be seen more as a case of a regime emerging from the failure to cooperate. Such regimes may be pervasive in history, although the literature on regimes has paid little formal attention to them. The cooperation that did take place came in the context of regime maintenance and was restricted to ad hoc rather than systematic accommodations between central banks and financial markets. These cases were fairly infrequent and normally restricted to bilateral arrangements. To the extent that competition among central banks was as extensive as cooperation among central banks, one may question whether relations among central banks had any net positive effects on regime stability over the long run. All this suggests that the gold standard was the product of a greater harmony. Destabilizing stochastic events such as wars and financial crises were few and restricted in magnitude. Monetary orthodoxy gave authorities normative incentives to keep their houses in order. Furthermore, the stable structure of adjustment mitigated the emergence of conditions that required more systematic and pervasive managerial schemes. Both this orthodoxy and stable adjustment under the gold standard derived from the strength of liberalism.[24] Given that these compelling norms dictated domestic policies that encouraged stable monetary relations, it appears that the limited amount of cooperation that took place under the gold standard was well adapted to the general state of relations within the regime itself. Ultimately, the question of the viability of such management for present and future systems turns on the question of just how prevalent we can expect such a state of relations to be in other periods and other issue-areas.

Diffuse Regimes

The classical gold standard does little to vindicate conventional visions of hegemony and cooperation. Much of what we have come to see as the origin and perpetuation of an international monetary order in the last four decades before the War does not fit neatly into either of the two categories, categories which have heretofore been given a great deal of credit for the regime dynamics of the gold standard. Instead, both the origin and maintenance of the regime showed significant elements of a more diffuse process: where the locus of action was spread out over a number of different actors (principally non-state in nature) functioning primarily out of more particularistic concerns, rather than concentrated within a managerial scheme of one or more nations which was oriented around some shared international goals. The regime literature has acknowledged such diffuse processes under various labels: Young's (1983) spontaneous regimes and (1980) tacit or latent regimes, Keohane's (1984) harmonious regimes, Haas's (1980) liberal regimes, Cooper's (1987) free-for-all regimes, and Stein's (1983) no-conflict situations.[25] Under these conceptualizations, a regime can emerge without purposive and managerial action directed at that goal. In fact, parts of the literature suggest that a diffuse process of regime origin may be more the rule than the exception in international politics. Young (1980, p. 350) argues, "There can be no doubt that the evolutionary track will be followed more often than the contractarian track in highly decentralized social systems like the international system."[26] In the case of the gold standard, the crystallization of a regime owed little to either the purposive use of power on the part of dominant nations or more widespread collaboration. The gold standard emerged while both such attempts at formal regime building were failing: i.e., the conferences and Franco-American attempts to build a bimetallist regime. In the words of Kindleberger (1988, p. 134), it "developed more or less unconsciously."[27]

The origin of the gold standard represents only one case of such a process of regime origin, and therefore any inferences for some greater theory of diffuse regimes will be problematic at best. But the origin itself can be illuminating nonetheless by suggesting some possibilities of how diffuse regimes emerge. Several long-term developmental processes (i.e., structural factors) made the move to gold more urgent by the 1870s. This suggests that the emergence of any large-scale regime will be the resultant of various forces which are subject to some kind of historical compatability, i.e., the forces themselves join to have a greater impact in specific combinations and at specific times.[28] The issue of timing was especially important as the eventual members of the gold club faced strong incentives to go to gold over a larger part of the century than that restricted period demarcating the scramble for gold in the 1870s. Changes in coinage laws (if not the practices) might have been put off for a longer period had not crucial events intervened to threaten national gold stocks. In understanding regime origin, therefore, it appears that understanding both long-term incentives and timing (i.e., both the developmental forces and proximate causes) is crucial. But even here, the menu of causes must be expanded. That nations were compelled by long-term and proximate forces toward gold did not, solely, determine the ultimate actions of nations. There were permissive factors which made the developmental and proximate catalysts more or less compelling. Hence, a full understanding of the origins of diffuse regimes requires some reconstruction of the interplay between developmental, proximate, and permissive factors.[29]

The gold standard also vindicates views that regime choice for any group of nations is strongly grounded in domestic factors.[30] In the last half of the 19th century, a greater group than that which ultimately converged into the gold club were subject to similar compelling international forces encouraging a gold link (the depreciation of silver and the status attributed to gold), but not all nations joined. Nations reacted to these common forces in a way that was fairly consistent with their domestic situations. Developments in the market for metals made a gold link more compelling in the developed world as such nations (1) saw gold more as a necessity than a luxury, (2) possessed economies that were more dependent on convenient mediums of exchange, (3) featured political structures which were swinging strongly toward a convenient and non-inflationary monetary standard, and (4) found that the advanced state of their financial institutions and macroeconomic situations were conducive to making and maintaining a gold link. International forces filtered through these domestic structures to create a burning house with a single exit for the most economically developed nations where these domestic conditions were most visible.[31] Nations that tended to stay out of the gold club featured domestic structures that did not compound the compelling aspects of those international developments. In all cases, there was a great deal of conformity between regime choices and domestic structures. Such consistency between domestic structures and regime outcomes seems to be highlighted in many of the case studies on regimes.[32]

Although elements of the literature on regimes are generally not disagreeable to the possibility that diffuse regimes can come into being, the literature as a whole is somewhat more pessimistic about the ability of such regimes to maintain themselves. Such regimes, to use Keohane's (1984, p. 51) definition, represent a state of international relations in which "policies (pursued in their own self-interest without regard for others) *automatically* facilitate the attainment of others' goals." Hence, it is a state of relations where unilateral actions generate positive externalities (i.e., positive spillover effects) for other nations, or at a minimum do not generate significant negative externalities (i.e., adverse spillover effects). Young (1980, p. 348), who has paid most attention to such phenomena in international politics, himself notes that "in the international arena, the pursuit of individual self-interest commonly leads to outcomes that are socially undesirable." Cooper (1987, p. 3) notes that even if such arrangements "finally settle down, the pattern would very likely be far from optimal from the viewpoints of all the participants." Haas (1980, p. 360) avers that liberal regimes are not stable because in complex interdependence there are potentially too many points of conflict. Keohane (1984, p. 50) illuminates Haas's point when he states that "in the absence of cooperation, governments will interfere in markets unilaterally in pursuit of what they regard as their own interests. . . . They will intervene in foreign exchange markets, impose various restrictions on imports, subsidize favored domestic industries, and set prices for commodities." In short, negative externalities potentially abound in diffuse regimes.[33]

Was the gold standard an exception to this rule? The question is a difficult one, because the definition of what constitutes a stable regime is subject to differing assessments of time—i.e., does four decades or so represent a sufficiently long period to qualify under what might be considered regime stability? The answer to this is likely to vary. If we look at the issue in a relative context, no other metallist international regime ever lasted so long and was accompanied by so many favorable regime outcomes as the classical gold standard. However, even such a relative assessment is problematic owing to the few cases (i.e., few observations). From the time a truly global international political economy emerged in the 19th century we have essentially had only three international metallist regimes: the classical gold standard, the failed interwar gold standard, and Bretton Woods (whose effective life was about a decade from the time European currencies became convertible at the end of the 1950s to Nixon's closing of the gold window in 1971). Might the interwar and Bretton Woods cases qualify as extraordinary, and hence not subject to valid comparisons? Or might we assent to the logic that in the turbulent world of international politics, anything that lasts roughly one lifetime may be acknowledged as having demonstrated extraordinary lasting power? Debate over all such questions is unlikely to lead to any definitive consensus. The few cases notwithstanding, the classical gold standard qua international monetary regime in the period of the global political economy is the best (in terms of regime outcomes) and the longest history has to offer, and as such it is deserving of our attention as a possibly suggestive case bearing on the study of diffuse regimes.

Another important question that should preface any analysis of the stability of the gold standard qua diffuse regime is whether the process of diffuse stability qualifies as a continuous or lumpy process. More specifically, can the gold standard be considered a diffuse regime if it included elements of cooperation and hegemony? Again, the question leaves room for disagreement. The managerial elements (in the conventional visions of both cooperation and hegemony) were modest at most: both French hegemonic actions (in lending to London) and central bank cooperation were quite infrequent and restricted to ad hoc crisis intervention rather than ongoing management. The actions of core nations in maintaining open financial systems did account for ongoing stabilization, but these actions can hardly be cited as managerial, since the core had no intentions to stabilize any greater constellations of international monetary relations.

The gold standard, in terms of the collective process of adjustment that was most responsible for its stability (i.e., the collective maintenance of the gold link), generally fits Keohane's (1984) definition of harmony: a group of nations whose actions are fairly consistent with (or at a minimum, not antithetical to) each other's particularistic goals. In the absence of such harmonious relations, various managerial elements would have had to be introduced to render relations stable. Hence, the gold standard, like any other regime with inherently stable elements, benefited from properties that limited the need for management and/or substituted for management. These properties carry important implications for a more general theory of stability in diffuse regimes.

The properties that limited the need for management relate to the gold standard as a geographically restricted regime. First, as a regime with limited membership, the principal interactions within the regime took place among a limited set of participants (advanced-industrial nations). The kind of policy convergence that was at the root of a stable process of adjustment was made easier by the fact that a smaller set of relatively homogeneous nations comprised regime relations. Points of divergence that might create problems for adjustment were circumscribed by the limited and fairly homogeneous nature of monetary relations in the developed world. Furthermore, some of the points of conflict underscored in the international relations literature on diffuse systems were passed out of the regime through the asymmetrical capacity for adjustment that characterized the entire global economy. That financial instability could be partially transferred to the periphery insulated the gold standard from some potentially difficult outcomes. This suggests that stability in restricted regimes may not necessarily imply fair-weather outcomes in the entire global political economy. In fact, stability in one regime (i.e., which is restricted to an issue or a set of nations) may be purchased at the expense of instability in another regime. While harmony characterized relations between developed nations (i.e., the gold club), it was hardly characteristic of relations between the gold and non-gold blocs.[34]

The second element limiting the need for management relates to the gold standard as an embedded or nested regime. This is consistent with an acknowledgment in the international relations literature that regime relations often depend upon outcomes in the greater international regimes in which they are embedded.[35] Monetary relations, like any other economic issue-area, were embedded in the greater international political economy. Nothing better characterizes this than the fact that any metallist regime is dependent on a contingent rule.[36] It has been traditionally understood that convertibility was a practice that could be legitimately suspended (but only temporarily) during extraordinary periods, generally characterized by severe economic or political shocks. Suspension during war was historically tolerated to a far greater extent relative to suspension in normal periods. That the gold standard was relatively free of exogenous shocks suggests a fairly favorable embeddedness in the greater international political economy of the period. Possibilities for a less formal regime like the gold standard were heightened to the extent that exogenous shocks from greater constellations of relations were not forthcoming. The favorability of embeddedness appears especially important for diffuse regimes, since these types of relational systems lack the management to counteract adverse shocks from their greater supersystems.[37] That regimes which evolve in this manner can also avoid an evolution toward a more formal organization depends on avoiding such crises. The gold standard had no such trail of extraordinary events which placed pressure on national leaders to intervene more extensively in national and international monetary systems.[38]

As far as properties that substituted for management, a pervasive set of interlocking domestic norms stand out as the crucial property on which the stability of the gold standard was fundamentally based. This pervasive set of norms, based on a liberal vision of political economy, purged international relations of numerous points of potential tension and conflict which the international relations literature has highlighted as the principal sources of instability in regimes. The norms, in circumscribing potential sources of tension and conflict, substituted for schemes of multilateral or hegemonic management.[39]

A great part of the strategic competition in the international political economy was purged because liberal norms essentially purged both the domestic and international economies of extensive government involvement. In the common visions of the inherently conflictual nature of economic relations, the principal protagonists are national governments conforming to the anarchic structure of international politics by engaging in exploitative behavior. In Keohane's (1984, p. 50) representative view, it is "governments" that intervene in markets unilaterally in their "own self-interest." The pursuit of this self-interest manifests itself in attempts by governments to redistribute wealth to their own citizens through manipulating exchange rates, trade barriers, subsidies, and commodity prices. Under the gold standard, governments were not central players in international finance. Hence, the classic vision of strategic behavior between national governments attempting to make absolute or relative economic gains for their nations at the expense of others was less relevant for monetary relations during this period. When governments did act and compete (militarily), norms about the separation between the state and the economy limited the spillover of geostrategic competition into economic relations.

Furthermore, the motivation and means to engage in redistributional behavior were limited because of these norms. The legitimacy of the separation of the state and the economy relieved governments of the responsibility of adverse outcomes in their own domestic economies. Hence, governments were less compelled to engage in redistributional actions to achieve certain specific macroeconomic outcomes (e.g., raise employment before the next election by raising tariffs or devaluing the currency). The political business cycle was simply not as compelling in the late 19th century. Moreover, separation of state and the economy removed the means of redistribution from governmental control. Governments played little role in managing the money supply and exchange rates, and they did so with extreme discomfort and reservation. Also, the ethic of fiscal restraint gave governments less discretion over the manipulation of government spending to effect redistributional goals (e.g., increase spending to gain a competitive edge in interest rates). So even if the motivation to redistribute existed, the potential for such actions was limited by the lack of means.

In that the normal means of redistribution were guided by prevailing norms rather than governmental discretion ended up rendering the principal structure of game interaction as one of implicit coordination: the common vision of the Prisoner's Dilemma game was less relevant for monetary relations under the gold standard.[40] The prevailing norms of monetary orthodoxy kept the central means of adjustment within convergent structures, thus limiting any adverse redistributional outcomes. Domestic maintenance of nominal parities at low levels of inflation (compounded by open markets for goods and capital) encouraged synchronous prices, interest rates, and business cycles. This made the maintenance of exchange rates much easier. That nations were compelled by domestic practices that allowed their macroeconomic outcomes to gravitate into configurations that mitigated redistributional pressure, fulfilled a minimal requirement for harmony: interactional patterns that minimize negative externalities.[41] At a higher level of harmony, liberal injunctions for freedom of economic exchange facilitated "the attainment of others' goals."[42] The widespread practice of free capital and commodity movements assured the mutual provision of the means of adjustment within the regime (i.e., positive externalities in adjustment). That all such practices were driven by domestic imperatives made the gold standard what Keohane and Nye (1985, p. 273) would call a "self-enforcing" regime, one where favorable interactional patterns are consistent with national interests.[43]

The liberal normative superstructure that drove domestic actions essentially functioned as a set of credible rules.[44] The existence of credible rules had stabilizing effects on three dimensions. First, in the strategic context of relations among public authorities, the belief that injunctions of free exchange were compelling relieved nations of the pressures to consider defensive redistributional positions (e.g., retaliatory exchange controls): when external accounts were moving adversely, there was little threat of public authorities considering mercantilistic responses. As long as nations perceived the sanctity of adherence to laissez-faire, any imbalances could be corrected without extraordinary actions. Second, in the context of the actions of private economic agents (individuals and institutions), perceptions of the sanctity of the normative superstructure were crucial for the prevailing adjustment mechanism characterizing the regime. The effectiveness of short-term adjustment under the gold standard (private short-term capital flows) depended on investors' beliefs that exchange and convertibility risks were minimal. These beliefs were strongly driven by perceptions that monetary authorities valued a stable exchange rate and metallist system, and as time went on these perceptions acquired a self-fulfilling character.[45]

Finally, the prevailing norms of the day bound public authorities to macroeconomic outcomes that relieved pressures at the international level. Some might say that the norms of the 19th and early 20th centuries compelled authorities to follow "responsible policies" (i.e., balanced budgets, low inflation), and that in the politicized macroeconomy of today, there are incentives to follow irresponsible policies, the solution to which may only lie in the form of binding rules.[46] As Poole (1987, p. 44) points out,

> Just as the responsible firm in a pollution-prone industry will be driven out of business by less responsible firms, so also may responsible political officials be driven out of the political marketplace by less responsible officials.

Such responsible policies, for several scholars, would not only place national macroeconomies on a more desirable footing, but would also impart greater stability onto international economic relations. As the *Economist* (1987, p. 56), in representative fashion, argues,

> let [economic ministers] . . . think of co-operation as a boring means to an end, not as a glorious goal in its own right. Because if they all stayed home and adopted sensible domestic policies there would be precious little need for cooperation on trade or exchange rates.[47]

Under the gold standard, exchange rates and convertibility were much easier to maintain, because authorities were driven by injunctions of stable money and fiscal restraint. Furthermore, the convergence of many macroeconomies onto these policies supported the process of implicit policy coordination that characterized the gold standard. Hence, the compellence of macroeconomic orthodoxy kept the structure of adjustment in a collectively favorable state on several dimensions: it reduced investment risk and limited destabilizing divergences in macroeconomic performance across nations in the gold club.

On the level of the individual nation, such macroeconomic outcomes held the key to maintaining its desired domestic monetary standard. Since domestic practices almost exclusively dictated the capacity for maintaining the gold link in any given nation, the gold standard limited the possibilities for moral hazard in macroeconomies. Nations could not count on schemes of collective intervention to stabilize their exchange rates if they engaged in excessive inflation, or if their interest rates were driven up by borrowing which in turn was caused by excessive budget deficits.[48] To the extent that nations valued the gold link, which they did, they were compelled to limit the kind of macroeconomic outcomes that placed pressure on international monetary regimes pursuing fixed exchange rates.[49] It would appear that of the three types of regimes considered in this chapter—hegemonic, cooperative, and diffuse—moral hazard would be least visible in diffuse regimes, because they generally lack the managerial elements that could mitigate the adverse consequences of individual actions (e.g., multilateral lending schemes to counteract biased adjustment structures, multilateral intervention schemes to stabilize inflationary currencies).[50]

In the context of both origin and stability, the classical gold standard was quite consistent with the idea of an additive regime—an idea quite representative of diffuse regimes, since some configuration of individual actions crystallizes into recognizable patterns of international relations. In this sense, the gold standard represents a process of order in parts. An international metallist regime emerged as nations scrambled toward a similar monetary standard. Once crystallized, the pervasive domestic compellence of a liberal normative superstructure kept unilateral actions conducive to a stable structure of collective adjustment, thus imparting stability onto the collective gold link. Hence, the gold standard fits the classic vision of a regime, since it was held together by an intricate set of norms around which expectations converged in the area of money.[51] It diverged from the classic vision of regimes insofar as the norms which held it together were of a domestic rather than international character.

These norms emanated from a liberal vision which itself was a manifestation of a consensual knowledge about the way in which domestic economic systems in general, and monetary systems specifically, should work. Haas (1980, pp. 367, 368) defines such knowledge as "the sum of technical information and of theories about that information which commands sufficient consensus at a given time among interested actors to serve as a guide to public policy designed to achieve some social goal."[52] This consensual knowledge which undergirded liberalism framed the range of political controversy, defined the interests of the state, and set standards for domestic policy.[53] As such, we must acknowledge a strong cognitive element in the rise and the stability of the gold standard. Behavior which had regime consequences was driven by prevailing ideas, and these ideas rendered the collective sets of monetary and macroeconomic policies which comprised the gold standard legitimate.[54]

When the greater liberal normative superstructure within which the gold standard was embedded crumbled, so too did the regime. "Normative evolution's regime effects," as Nye (1987) calls them, demonstrated quite clearly that regimes are no stronger than the greater social relations in which they are nested.

In sum, contrary to many visions of the gold standard, the regime dynamics upon which it was founded showed a strongly diffuse character. Moreover, the managerial elements that did show up were quite different from the conventional categories of hegemony and cooperation in the literature on international regimes. Hegemony was much more unintentional and non-state than prevailing theories of hegemonic regimes can account for. The supposed hegemon of the period, Great Britain, acted more like a weak than a strong nation, and France behaved more hegemonically than Great Britain. But even here the overly domestic orientation of the Bank of France rendered its actions quite distinct from mainstream visions of hegemony. Cooperation, too, fails to explain the origin and stability of the regime. In fact, it was a failure to cooperate that led to the emergence of the regime in the 1870s. The present literature on cooperation has paid very little attention to such default or residual regimes.

In that monetary relations under the gold standard were highly consistent with prevailing national interests, the regime showed a harmonious and self-enforcing nature. The regime remained stable void of significant management because it featured elements that either limited the need for management or that substituted for such management. That the regime formed among a fairly homogeneous and limited set of members, and that it was embedded in a greater international political economy which was itself stable, suggests that the state of relations in specific regimes will depend on outcomes in other regimes, and that stability in one regime may be achieved by exporting its problems to other regimes (these factors limited the need for management). Both, in turn, suggest that diffuse regimes may be more vulnerable than managed regimes because these interdependencies cannot be manipulated to avert shocks under the former. In terms of substitution, it was an interlocking set of domestic norms that effectively substituted for international management. In that behavior according to these domestic norms, and the general belief in the sanctity of these norms (i.e., credibility), directly and indirectly protected convertibility suggests that such credible rules may function as a sufficient substitute for cooperation and hegemony in the international political economy.

Statistical Appendix

Data

All data used were yearly time series. The following series were employed.

Discount Rates of Central Banks

BE	Bank of England
BF	Bank of France
BB	Bank of Belgium
BSW	Bank of Switzerland
BI	Bank of Italy
BG	Reichsbank
BH	Netherlands Bank
BSP	Bank of Spain
BR	Bank of Russia
BA	Bank of Austria

World Price Indices

WDMPI	World Manufactures Price Index
WPPPI	World Primary Product Price Index

British Series

GBRGNP	Real GNP
MB	Money Base
M3	Money Aggregate M3
BBBE	Bankers' Balances at the Bank of England
BERES	Bank of England Gold Reserves
GBDR	Market Discount Rate
GBRP	Retail Price Index
GBPDEF	GNP Deflator
GBGNP	Nominal GNP

Discount rates were taken from U.S. Senate (1910a, pp. 29, 30) and represent yearly averages for the period 1870–1907. I have provided estimates for missing values of the Bank of Switzerland for 1870 and 1871. Rates for the Bank of England 1908–13 were estimated from Goodhart (1972, pp. 605–10).

World primary product and manufactures price indices were taken from Lewis (1978, pp. 280, 281), with 1913 = 100. The primary product index (WPPPI) represents the average of F.O.B. and C.I.F. values for prices of primary products in world trade 1881–1913. The manufactures index (WDMPI) represents F.O.B. prices of manufactured goods in world trade.

Turning points in the global business cycle in Figures A.1–A.5 were estimated from Thorp (1926). (The turning points are represented by arrows at the bottom of Figures A.1–A.5.) The turning points represent the average of individual turning points for the following nations. In the period 1870–89, average turning points were estimated from the national turning points of the U.S., Germany, France, Great Britain, and Austria. In the period from 1889 to 1913, average turning points were estimated from turning points of all the above nations as well as Russia, Sweden, Holland, Italy, Argentina, Brazil, Canada, South Africa, India, Japan, and China.

Except for BERES which was taken from Hawtrey (1938, pp. 297–300), all British series were taken from Capie and Weber (1985, V. I, pp. 52, 53, 82–84, 398, 495, 535). BERES represents the level of the gold reserve at the Bank of England in early December (at approximately the 6th of the month) of each year. Both GBPDEF and GBRP use 1913 (=100) as a base year. The market discount rate (GBDR) represents the average discount rate on 3-month prime bills. Real GNP (GBRGNP) represents nominal GNP (GBGNP) adjusted for inflation by the GNP deflator (GBPDEF). The money base (MB) comprises bankers' balances at the Bank of England, cash in the hands of the public, and bank till money. M3 comprises currency in the hands of the public, total bank deposits (net of interbank deposits and 60% of items in transit), and other deposits at the Bank of England. All British series represent the years 1870–1913.

Estimation Techniques

All equations were estimated using ordinary least squares. Unstandardized beta coefficients were reported with their standard errors, T-statistics, and probabilities. Other statistics reported were: R-squared, adjusted R-squared, standard error of the regression, Durbin-Watson statistic, F-statistic, probability of the F-statistic, log likelihood, sum of squared residuals, standard deviation of the dependent variable, mean of the dependent variable, and a Ramsey RESET F. Additional tests on residuals from the equations have been included so as to carefully scrutinize for possible estimation biases due to autocorrelation or nonstationarities in the series. These tests generated the following statistics: serial correlation F, ARCH test F, White heteroskedasticity test F, Jarque-Bera statistic, Box-Pierce Q, and Ljung-Box Q. The probabilities accompanying the various statistics are in parentheses. All coefficients and statistics designated * are statistically significant at the 5% level, while those designated ** are significant at the 1% level.

The serial correlation F is output from a Breush-Godfrey test for autocorrelated disturbances. Assuming a model $Y = c + b_1X$, this test estimates

$$Y_t = c + b_1X_td_1R_{t-1} \ldots + d_iR_{t-j},$$

where i is a vector of coefficients, R represents residuals, and t–j represents the lags of the residuals. An F-statistic is generated which tests the null hypothesis that the coefficients in the residual vector $d_{1\ldots i}$ are all zero.

The ARCH test F is output from an Engle test for heteroskedasticity. The equation tested is

$$R_t^2 = c + d_1R_{t-1}^2 \ldots + d_iR_{t-j}^2$$

The F-statistic tests the null hypothesis that all the coefficients in the residual vector $d_{1\ldots i}$ are zero. For both the serial correlation and ARCH tests, residuals were tested up to 4 lags.

White heteroskedasticity tests the following equation: assuming a model $Y = c + b_1X + b_2Z$,

$$R^2 = c + e_1X + e_2Z + e_3X^2 + e_4Z^2$$

The F-statistic tests the null hypothesis that all coefficients in the vector $e_{1\ldots 4}$ are zero.

The Ramsey RESET test detects general specification error: omitted variables, incorrect functional form, and correlation between the error term and exogenous variables. The equation estimated is

$$Y = c + f_1X + f_2Z + f_3FIT^2 \ldots + f_iFIT^j,$$

where FIT is the fitted Y value from the original model, i is a vector of coefficients, and j represents the exponential order at which the FIT is estimated. The F-statistic in this case tests the null hypothesis that all coefficients in the vector are zero. Specification error was tested for up to FIT^3.

The Jarque-Bera statistic is a measure of the distribution of the residuals. It tests the null hypothesis that the residuals are normally distributed.

The Box-Pierce Q statistic tests for white noise in the residuals. This test estimates:

$$Q = n\Sigma^p_{j=1}r^2_j,$$

where r_j is the j-th autocorrelation and n is the number of observations. The null hypothesis tested is that all autocorrelations up to j are zero (i.e., the residuals exhibit white noise).

The Ljung-Box Q is a variant of the Box-Pierce Q and also tests for white noise in the residuals. The null hypothesis is the same as in the case of Box-Pierce. Both the Box-Pierce and Ljung-Box Qs tested for autocorrelations up to 4 lags. The Ljung-Box estimate is:

$$Q = n(n + 2)\Sigma^p_{j=1} r^2_j/n{-}j$$

Granger causality tests estimate the following equations. Assume two endogenous variables X and Y, and some set of exogenous (i.e., control) variables W . . . . . . Z. Two equations are generated:

$$Y_t = c + g_1 Y_{t-1} \ldots + g_i Y_{t-j} + h_1 X_{t-1} \ldots + h_i X_{t-j} +$$
$$q_1 W_{t-1} \ldots + q_i W_{t-j} \ldots \ldots + s_1 Z_{t-1} \ldots + s_i Z_{t-j}$$

$$X_t = c + k_1 X_{t-1} \ldots + k_i X_{t-j} + l_1 Y_{t-1} \ldots + l_i Y_{t-j} +$$
$$p_1 W_{t-1} \ldots + p_i W_{t-j} \ldots \ldots + u_1 Z_{t-1} \ldots + u_i Z_{t-j}$$

Output reported is in the form of two probabilities for two F-statistics which test the following null hypotheses. For the first equation, the hypothesis tested is that all coefficients in the vector $h_{1 \ldots i}$ are zero. If they are statistically different from zero, it is said that Y is Granger caused by X. In the second equation, the hypothesis tested is that all coefficients in the vector $l_{1 \ldots i}$ are zero. If they are not, then it is said that X is Granger caused by Y.

All estimations were run using MicroTSP 7.0. For additional information on estimation techniques, refer to *MicroTSP User's Manual* (1990).

Equations

EQUATION 1

LS // Dependent Variable is BE
SMPL range: 1870–1907
Number of observations: 38

Variable	Coefficient	Std. Error	T-Stat.	2-Tail Sig.
C	–1.8090039	1.0669171	–1.6955431	0.1011
BB	0.2259923	0.2290537	0.9866349	0.3323
BF	0.2439514	0.1239100	1.9687790	0.0589
BG	0.5435457	0.1621499	3.3521192	0.0023**
BH	0.2639264	0.1743295	1.5139512	0.1412
BSP	–0.2856505	0.1177964	–2.4249516	0.0220*
BSW	–0.1683582	0.1551463	–1.0851577	0.2871
BI	0.5722133	0.1605143	3.5648743	0.0013**
BR	0.0178932	0.1243982	0.1438377	0.8867
BA	–0.1007640	0.1843452	–0.5466047	0.5890

R-squared	0.789827	Prob(F-statistic)		0.000000**
Adjusted R-squared	0.722272	Ser. Cor. F	2.4400	(.0745)
S.E. of regression	0.359646	ARCH-F	.4984	(.7370)
Log likelihood	–9.257300	Heter. F	.7520	(.7252)
Durbin-Watson stat	1.668133	RESET F	1.4674	(.2477)
Mean of dependent var	3.336316	Jar.-Bera	.2903	(.8649)
S.D. of dependent var	0.682442	Box-Pierce Q	1.57	(.8150)
Sum of squared resid	3.621671	Ljung-Box Q	1.73	(.7850)
F-statistic	11.69154			

EQUATION 2

LS // Dependent Variable is BE
SMPL range: 1871–1907
Number of observations: 37

Variable	Coefficient	Std. Error	T-Stat.	2-Tail Sig.
C	−1.9146898	1.0637733	−1.7999039	0.0835
BB	0.1845780	0.2325326	0.7937723	0.4345
BF	0.1642920	0.1425757	1.1523146	0.2597
BG	0.4815942	0.1667083	2.8888435	0.0077**
BH	0.2691157	0.1795284	1.4990145	0.1459
BSP	−0.2951870	0.1184105	−2.4929120	0.0194*
BSW	−0.0918614	0.1612957	−0.5695219	0.5739
BI	0.5036482	0.1688406	2.9829807	0.0061**
BR	0.0163408	0.1253425	0.1303695	0.8973
BA	0.0191426	0.1982607	0.0965528	0.9238
BE(−1)	0.0945633	0.1245504	0.7592368	0.4545

R-squared	0.807627	Prob(F-statistic)		0.000001**
Adjusted R-squared	0.733637	Ser. Cor. F.	1.7752	(.1698)
S.E. of regression	0.356571	ARCH-F	.4780	(.7515)
Log likelihood	−7.818304	Heter. F	.6830	(.7920)
Durbin-Watson stat	1.817647	RESET F	2.5430	(.0980)
Mean of dependent var	3.342162	Jar.-Bera	.0408	(.9797)
S.D. of dependent var	0.690890	Box-Pierce Q	.45	(.9779)
Sum of squared resid	3.305712	Ljung-Box Q	.51	(.9728)
F-statistic	10.91538			

EQUATION 3

LS // Dependent Variable is BF
SMPL range: 1871–1907
Number of observations: 37

Variable	Coefficient	Std. Error	T-Stat.	2-Tail Sig.
C	1.1623643	1.2111902	0.9596877	0.3461
BF(−1)	0.6130811	0.1319451	4.6464858	0.0001**
BE	−0.1023367	0.2377454	−0.4304467	0.6704
BB	0.4578608	0.2446896	1.8711900	0.0726
BG	−0.0976089	0.2213989	−0.4408735	0.6629
BH	−0.2099571	0.2000168	−1.0496976	0.3035
BSP	−0.1292261	0.1568867	−0.8236905	0.4176
BSW	0.4089204	0.1619322	2.5252571	0.0180*
BI	−0.1756566	0.2106617	−0.8338327	0.4120
BR	−0.0591941	0.1366086	−0.4333113	0.6684
BA	0.0194825	0.2225209	0.0875535	0.9309

R-squared	0.843933	Prob(F-statistic)		0.000000**
Adjusted R-squared	0.783907	Ser. Cor. F.	9.0671	(.0002)**
S.E. of regression	0.393637	ARCH-F	.7581	(.5613)
Log likelihood	−11.47744	Heter. F	5.8760	(.0004)**
Durbin-Watson stat	2.119089	RESET F	2.7002	(.0860)
Mean of dependent var	3.141351	Jar.-Bera	6.0191	(.0493)*
S.D. of dependent var	0.846789	Box-Pierce Q	1.81	(.7699)
Sum of squared resid	4.028697	Ljung-Box Q	1.97	(.7404)
F-statistic	14.05947			

EQUATION 4

LS // Dependent Variable is BB
SMPL range: 1871–1907
Number of observations: 37

Variable	Coefficient	Std. Error	T-Stat.	2-Tail Sig.
C	0.0232319	1.0080339	0.0230468	0.9818
BB(–1)	0.0077005	0.1537938	0.0500702	0.9604
BF	0.1850280	0.1169175	1.5825521	0.1256
BE	0.1118923	0.1697493	0.6591619	0.5156
BSW	0.0853168	0.1344505	0.6345592	0.5313
BI	–0.0228460	0.1646935	–0.1387186	0.8907
BH	0.2768418	0.1473846	1.8783631	0.0716
BG	–0.0124665	0.1620927	–0.0769099	0.9393
BA	0.1625497	0.1626605	0.9993185	0.3269
BSP	–0.1610428	0.1061136	–1.5176454	0.1412
BR	0.2357726	0.0944523	2.4962080	0.0192*

R-squared	0.836630	Prob(F-statistic)		0.000000**
Adjusted R-squared	0.773796	Ser. Cor. F	1.5293	(.2283)
S.E. of regression	0.299528	ARCH-F	.3777	(.8226)
Log likelihood	–1.368303	Heter. F	1.1139	(.4184)
Durbin-Watson stat	2.108606	RESET F	3.2701	(.0541)
Mean of dependent var	3.394595	Jar.-Bera	.9728	(.6148)
S.D. of dependent var	0.629778	Box-Pierce Q	1.36	(.8505)
Sum of squared resid	2.332646	Ljung-Box Q	1.59	(.8106)
F-statistic	13.31482			

EQUATION 5

LS // Dependent Variable is BSW
SMPL range: 1871–1907
Number of observations: 37

Variable	Coefficient	Std. Error	T-Stat.	2-Tail Sig.
C	−1.8322965	1.1356727	−1.6134019	0.1187
BSW(−1)	0.4172917	0.1484843	2.8103425	0.0093**
BE	−0.1184017	0.2054859	−0.5762035	0.5694
BF	0.1259919	0.1511785	0.8333984	0.4122
BB	0.2419621	0.2479388	0.9758943	0.3381
BI	0.2707658	0.1977161	1.3694676	0.1826
BG	0.2667370	0.1963421	1.3585323	0.1860
BH	0.1130730	0.1984485	0.5697851	0.5737
BR	0.1223678	0.1298663	0.9422602	0.3547
BA	−0.0281444	0.2093107	−0.1344624	0.8941
BSP	−0.0110021	0.1430911	−0.0768891	0.9393

R-squared	0.833227	Prob(F-statistic)		0.000000**
Adjusted R-squared	0.769084	Ser. cor. F	1.8770	(.1502)
S.E. of regression	0.380124	ARCH-F	.3156	(.8651)
Log likelihood	−10.18501	Heter. F	.4207	(.9655)
Durbin-Watson stat	1.425378	RESET F	.0386	(.9622)
Mean of dependent var	4.030000	Jar.-Bera	1.9990	(.3680)
S.D. of dependent var	0.791040	Box-Pierce Q	2.88	(.5781)
Sum of squared resid	3.756854	Ljung-Box Q	3.17	(.5302)
F-statistic	12.99009			

EQUATION 6

LS // Dependent Variable is BI
SMPL range: 1871–1907
Number of observations: 37

Variable	Coefficient	Std. Error	T-Stat.	2-Tail Sig.
C	2.3935271	0.8872173	2.6977914	0.0121*
BI(−1)	0.4902029	0.1422180	3.4468412	0.0019**
BE	0.4450085	0.1408215	3.1600885	0.0040**
BF	−0.1089634	0.1101543	−0.9891893	0.3317
BSW	0.1076687	0.1367096	0.7875722	0.4381
BB	0.0809401	0.2003521	0.4039891	0.6895
BG	−0.2466314	0.1541663	−1.5997751	0.1217
BH	−0.1738782	0.1524830	−1.1403121	0.2646
BR	−0.1672536	0.0998049	−1.6758055	0.1058
BA	0.0749781	0.1697398	0.4417236	0.6623
BSP	0.1098831	0.1100962	0.9980638	0.3274

R-squared	0.647530	Prob(F-statistic)		0.000636**
Adjusted R-squared	0.511965	Ser. Cor. F.	.8710	(.4970)
S.E. of regression	0.301708	ARCH-F	.2719	(.8936)
Log likelihood	−1.636591	Heter. F	1.4140	(.2430)
Durbin-Watson stat	1.905776	RESET F	1.6330	(.2146)
Mean of dependent var	4.982432	Jar.-Bera	1.9748	(.3725)
S.D. of dependent var	0.431878	Box-Pierce Q	2.36	(.6707)
Sum of squared resid	2.366721	Ljung-Box Q	2.64	(.6197)
F-statistic	4.776524			

EQUATION 7

LS // Dependent Variable is BG
SMPL range: 1871–1907
Number of observations: 37

Variable	Coefficient	Std. Error	T-Stat.	2-Tail Sig.
C	1.7316102	1.0833235	1.5984239	0.1220
BG(–1)	0.1821037	0.1245546	1.4620384	0.1557
BE	0.5287482	0.1642306	3.2195480	0.0034**
BF	–0.3237742	0.1179398	–2.7452493	0.0108*
BB	–0.0118301	0.2313007	–0.0511460	0.9596
BI	–0.3861002	0.1745106	–2.2124736	0.0359*
BSW	0.2561934	0.1514880	1.6911797	0.1028
BH	0.1695700	0.1808771	0.9374871	0.3571
BA	0.1790009	0.1917080	0.9337166	0.3590
BR	–0.0063135	0.1227614	–0.0514294	0.9594
BSP	0.1171344	0.1285279	0.9113540	0.3705

R-squared	0.787524	Prob(F-statistic)		0.000002**
Adjusted R-squared	0.705803	SER. cor. F	2.5850	(.0652)
S.E. of regression	0.353209	ARCH-F	.7333	(.5769)
Log likelihood	–7.467849	Heter. F	1.8214	(.1138)
Durbin-Watson stat	2.009421	RESET F	1.0013	(.3811)
Mean of dependent var	4.134595	Jar.-Bera	.7913	(.6732)
S.D. of dependent var	0.651198	Box-Pierce Q	6.43	(.1693)
Sum of squared resid	3.243680	Ljung-Box Q	7.32	(.1201)
F-statistic	9.636693			

EQUATION 8

LS // Dependent Variable is BH
SMPL range: 1871–1907
Number of observations: 37

Variable	Coefficient	Std. Error	T-Stat.	2-Tail Sig.
C	0.9109091	1.1773849	0.7736715	0.4461
BH(−1)	0.1409888	0.1481851	0.9514371	0.3501
BG	0.1879618	0.1995641	0.9418619	0.3549
BA	−0.1146900	0.2226807	−0.5150422	0.6109
BSP	0.1177818	0.1451787	0.8112884	0.4246
BR	−0.1055611	0.1281906	−0.8234705	0.4177
BF	−0.1785710	0.1415685	−1.2613753	0.2184
BB	0.3848210	0.2376327	1.6193941	0.1174
BI	−0.2233716	0.1961022	−1.1390573	0.2651
BSW	0.2017103	0.1640708	1.2294096	0.2299
BE	0.3610944	0.1948692	1.8530087	0.0753

R-squared	0.754094	Prob(F-statistic)		0.000010**
Adjusted R-squared	0.659515	Ser. cor. F	1.8511	(.1550)
S.E. of regression	0.373084	ARCH-F	.7940	(.5390)
Log likelihood	−9.493328	Heter. F	.7402	(.7407)
Durbin-Watson stat	1.935623	RESET F	2.9621	(.0694)
Mean of dependent var	3.232973	Jar.-Bera	.0912	(.9553)
S.D. of dependent var	0.639378	Box-Pierce Q	.81	(.9374)
Sum of squared resid	3.618986	Ljung-Box Q	.95	(.9177)
F-statistic	7.973164			

EQUATION 9

LS // Dependent Variable is BR
SMPL range: 1871–1907
Number of observations: 37

Variable	Coefficient	Std. Error	T-Stat.	2-Tail Sig.
C	3.8373111	1.9320874	1.9860960	0.0577
BR(−1)	0.0400041	0.2088692	0.1915270	0.8496
BB	0.8221684	0.3375144	2.4359503	0.0220*
BF	−0.1873247	0.2048932	−0.9142552	0.3690
BG	−0.0126756	0.3132615	−0.0404634	0.9680
BH	−0.2575000	0.2870929	−0.8969223	0.3780
BSP	0.0370084	0.2084251	0.1775622	0.8604
BSW	0.2688749	0.2501814	1.0747197	0.2924
BI	−0.4826275	0.3327252	−1.4505290	0.1589
BA	0.3679439	0.3249873	1.1321794	0.2679
BE	−0.0219134	0.3364938	−0.0651229	0.9486

R-squared	0.665248	Prob(F-statistic)		0.000358**
Adjusted R-squared	0.536497	Ser. Cor. F	2.0572	(.1212)
S.E. of regression	0.564091	ARCH-F	.1184	(.9748)
Log likelihood	−24.78957	Heter. F	3.3285	(.0090)**
Durbin-Watson stat	1.683815	RESET F	.3291	(.7225)
Mean of dependent var	5.765135	Jar.-Bera	.9075	(.6352)
S.D. of dependent var	0.828558	Box-Pierce Q	4.91	(.2267)
Sum of squared resid	8.273171	Box-Pierce Q	5.63	(.2285)
F-statistic	5.166942			

EQUATION 10

LS // Dependent Variable is BSP
SMPL range: 1871–1907
Number of observations: 37

Variable	Coefficient	Std. Error	T-Stat.	2-Tail Sig.
C	0.3448822	1.6510585	0.2088855	0.8362
BSP(–1)	0.2483929	0.2225104	1.1163205	0.2745
BB	–0.3318593	0.3610387	–0.9191793	0.3665
BF	0.1356981	0.1902081	0.7134189	0.4819
BSW	0.1165089	0.2334134	0.4991525	0.6219
BI	0.2716493	0.2787353	0.9745781	0.3388
BG	0.1584203	0.2846171	0.5566083	0.5826
BH	0.2587379	0.2690709	0.9615972	0.3451
BA	0.5318542	0.3376532	1.5751494	0.1273
BR	0.0066336	0.1817427	0.0364999	0.9712
BE	–0.5450464	0.2729629	–1.9967784	0.0564

R-squared	0.635184	Prob(F-statistic)		0.000930**
Adjusted R-squared	0.494871	Ser. Cor. F	2.4363	(.0775)
S.E. of regression	0.518606	ARCH-F	.4084	(.2311)
Log likelihood	–21.67896	Heter. F	1.4413	(.2311)
Durbin-Watson stat	1.929079	RESET F	.9738	(.3910)
Mean of dependent var	4.658919	Jar.-Bera	.9645	(.6173)
S.D. of dependent var	0.729687	Box-Pierce Q	2.58	(.6299)
Sum of squared resid	6.992768	Ljung-Box Q	2.94	(.5681)
F-statistic	4.526890			

EQUATION 11

LS // Dependent Variable is BA
SMPL range: 1871–1907
Number of observations: 37

Variable	Coefficient	Std. Error	T-Stat.	2-Tail Sig.
C	−1.2302133	0.8614797	−1.4280234	0.1652
BA(−1)	0.4335024	0.1059739	4.0906539	0.0004**
BF	−0.0539680	0.1120084	−0.4818207	0.6340
BB	0.3914192	0.1826462	2.1430463	0.0416*
BI	0.1674138	0.1459758	1.1468600	0.2619
BSW	−0.0411046	0.1255771	−0.3273254	0.7460
BR	0.0648309	0.0961092	0.6745543	0.5059
BSP	0.3081007	0.0876337	3.5157777	0.0016**
BG	0.1451477	0.1456778	0.9963611	0.3283
BH	−0.2526607	0.1419667	−1.7797186	0.0868
BE	0.0789346	0.1523633	0.5180683	0.6088

R-squared	0.835736	Prob(F-statistic)		0.000000**
Adjusted R-squared	0.772557	Ser. Cor. F	5.4140	(.0034)**
S.E. of regression	0.277737	ARCH-F	1.1512	(.3532)
Log likelihood	1.426413	Heter. F	3.0909	(.0129)*
Durbin-Watson stat	2.403825	RESET F	1.1549	(.3307)
Mean of dependent var	4.354324	Jar.-Bera	4.2858	(.1173)
S.D. of dependent var	0.582368	Box-Pierce Q	4.77	(.3122)
Sum of squared resid	2.005588	Ljung-Box Q	5.38	(.2504)
F-statistic	13.22813			

EQUATION 12

LS // Dependent Variable is WDMPI
SMPL range: 1881–1913
Number of observations: 33

Variable	Coefficient	Std. Error	T-Stat.	2-Tail Sig.
C	24.429384	17.599446	1.3880769	0.1790
WDMPI(–1)	0.3426660	0.1384268	2.4754307	0.0215*
GBPDEF	0.0821193	0.3243892	0.2531505	0.8025
GBRP	0.0047580	0.2006174	0.0237166	0.9813
MB	0.0091316	0.0884912	0.1031917	0.9187
M3	–0.0094989	0.0293475	–0.3236690	0.7492
BE	1.3967499	2.1017999	0.6645494	0.5132
BERES	0.0090439	0.1324910	0.0682602	0.9462
WPPPI	0.3904334	0.1742460	2.2407026	0.0355*
GBDR	0.2320234	1.9040775	0.1218561	0.9041
GBRGNP	–0.0019046	0.0089817	–0.2120562	0.8340

R-squared	0.963095	Prob(F-statistic)		0.000000**
Adjusted R-squared	0.946320	Ser. Cor. F	1.4506	(.2583)
S.E. of regression	1.437348	ARCH-F	1.1033	(.3777)
Log likelihood	–52.10718	Heter. F	.7990	(.6824)
Durbin-Watson stat	1.538449	RESET F	2.7322	(.0871)
Mean of dependent var	93.32727	Jar.-Bera	.5270	(.7683)
S.D. of dependent var	6.203793	Box-Pierce Q	5.35	(.2535)
Sum of squared resid	45.45130	Ljung-Box Q	6.02	(.1979)
F-statistic	57.41301			

EQUATION 13

LS // Dependent Variable is WPPPI
SMPL range: 1882–1913
Number of observations: 32

Variable	Coefficient	Std. Error	T-Stat.	2-Tail Sig.
C	−62.646511	19.972531	−3.1366336	0.0050**
WPPPI(−1)	0.0911112	0.1422283	0.6405987	0.5287
GBPDEF	0.4795259	0.3978814	1.2051981	0.2415
GBRP	0.5118274	0.2032768	2.5178839	0.0200*
MB	−0.0216558	0.1084078	−0.1997622	0.8436
M3	−0.0312955	0.0357161	−0.8762290	0.3908
BE	−0.3331169	2.4088446	−0.1382891	0.8913
BERES	−0.0671752	0.1480679	−0.4536787	0.6547
WDMPI	0.4813339	0.1923403	2.5025126	0.0207*
GBDR	0.3629859	2.2047796	0.1646359	0.8708
GBRGNP	0.0211262	0.0095841	2.2042939	0.0388*

R-squared	0.970312	Prob(F-statistic)		0.000000**
Adjusted R-squared	0.956175	Ser. Cor. F.	.8507	(.5127)
S.E. of regression	1.615188	ARCH-F	1.7110	(.1819)
Log likelihood	−54.00906	Heter. F	1.1488	(.4219)
Durbin-Watson stat	1.729984	RESET F	.2679	(.7675)
Mean of dependent var	85.01250	Jar.-Bera	1.6631	(.4353)
S.D. of dependent var	7.715453	Box-Pierce Q	3.32	(.5058)
Sum of squared resid	54.78547	Ljung-Box Q	3.87	(.4245)
F-statistic	68.63567			

EQUATION 14

LS // Dependent Variable is BE
SMPL range: 1881–1913
Number of observations: 33

Variable	Coefficient	Std. Error	T-Stat.	2-Tail Sig.
C	0.7387737	2.0513502	0.3601402	0.7223
BE(–1)	–0.0242669	0.0702416	–0.3454775	0.7332
GBPDEF	0.0272649	0.0359393	0.7586355	0.4565
GBRP	–0.0290250	0.0205852	–1.4099907	0.1732
GBRGNP	7.076E–05	0.0010042	0.0704667	0.9445
WDMPI	0.0200159	0.0204754	0.9775568	0.3394
WPPPI	–0.0021311	0.0203562	–0.1046914	0.9176
MB	–0.0105551	0.0122112	–0.8643814	0.3971
M3	0.0007510	0.0032569	0.2305931	0.8199
BERES	0.0114282	0.0149212	0.7659053	0.4523
GBDR	0.8034682	0.0674369	11.914374	0.0000**
BBBE	0.0007456	0.0205245	0.0363250	0.9714

R-squared	0.968411	Prob(F-statistic)		0.000000**
Adjusted R-squared	0.951864	Ser. Cor. F.	.8125	(.5344)
S.E. of regression	0.147600	ARCH-F	.9124	(.4726)
Log likelihood	23.77000	Heter. F	.8379	(.6523)
Durbin-Watson stat	1.945214	RESET F	2.8080	(.0830)
Mean of dependent var	3.402121	Jar.-Bera	1.8030	(.4059)
S.D. of dependent var	0.672750	Box-Pierce Q	2.22	(.6956)
Sum of squared resid	0.457501	Ljung-Box Q	2.52	(.6410)
F-statistic	58.52630			

EQUATION 15

LS // Dependent Variable is BERES
SMPL range: 1881–1913
Number of observations: 33

Variable	Coefficient	Std. Error	T-Stat.	2-Tail Sig.
C	–58.772975	24.606017	–2.3885611	0.0264*
BERES(–1)	0.2506485	0.1942974	1.2900248	0.2111
GBRGNP	0.0383245	0.0110561	3.4663636	0.0023**
GBRP	–0.2648944	0.2962853	–0.8940517	0.3814
GBPDEF	1.3984376	0.4710912	2.9685074	0.0073**
WPPPI	–0.1858305	0.2995751	–0.6203136	0.5417
WDMPI	–0.3419922	0.2877514	–1.1884988	0.2479
MB	0.4528727	0.1550631	2.9205706	0.0082**
M3	–0.1412431	0.0341195	–4.1396575	0.0005**
BE	2.5011003	2.9997166	0.8337789	0.4138
GBDR	–4.3484693	2.4549273	–1.7713230	0.0910
BBBE	–0.3769260	0.2819392	–1.3369052	0.1956

R-squared	0.929123	Prob(F-statistic)		0.000000**
Adjusted R-squared	0.891997	Ser. Cor. F	3.6323	(.0258)*
S.E. of regression	2.066972	ARCH-F	.2997	(.8753)
Log likelihood	–63.32801	Heter. F	1.1557	(.4233)
Durbin-Watson stat	2.355097	RESET F	1.3677	(.2765)
Mean of dependent var	19.65500	Jar.-Bera	22.4419	(.0000)**
S.D. of dependent var	6.289493	Box-Pierce Q	2.66	(.6158)
Sum of squared resid	89.71981	Ljung-Box Q	2.99	(.5588)
F-statistic	25.02606			

EQUATION 16

LS // Dependent Variable is GBRGNP
SMPL range: 1871–1913
Number of observations: 43

Variable	Coefficient	Std. Error	T-Stat.	2-Tail Sig.
C	990.45958	181.38470	5.4605465	0.0000**
GBRGNP(–1)	0.3871925	0.1355353	2.8567646	0.0074**
BE	21.535103	39.956556	0.5389629	0.5935
BERES	6.3300576	2.3082061	2.7424144	0.0098**
MB	–3.6428900	1.9087409	–1.9085304	0.0651
M3	1.9524971	0.3894139	5.0139386	0.0000**
BBBE	0.7325063	3.9988644	0.1831786	0.8558
GBDR	20.230703	33.648026	0.6012449	0.5518
GBRP	8.0249094	3.2391684	2.4774598	0.0185*
GBPDEF	–20.681591	4.6271959	–4.4695732	0.0001**

R-squared	0.994111	Prob(F-statistic)		0.000000**
Adjusted R-squared	0.992504	Ser. Cor. F	1.0352	(.4060)
S.E. of regression	35.92575	ARCH-F	.1569	(.9585)
Log likelihood	–209.3260	Heter. F	1.8399	(.0813)
Durbin-Watson stat	1.706501	RESET F	2.6180	(.0880)
Mean of dependent var	1673.169	Jar.-Bera	2.9136	(.2330)
S.D. of dependent var	414.9534	Box-Pierce Q	5.65	(.2265)
Sum of squared resid	42591.76	Ljung-Box Q	6.36	(.1737)
F-statistic	618.9113			

EQUATION 17

LS // Dependent Variable is MB
SMPL range: 1871–1913
Number of observations: 43

Variable	Coefficient	Std. Error	T-Stat.	2-Tail Sig.
C	29.497446	18.502038	1.5942808	0.1204
MB(−1)	0.2843456	0.0947410	3.0012950	0.0051**
M3	0.1315085	0.0312129	4.2132772	0.0002**
BE	−0.9633360	3.0659764	−0.3142020	0.7553
BERES	0.7049203	0.1560281	4.5179048	0.0001**
GBRGNP	−0.0241204	0.0112643	−2.1413110	0.0397*
BBBE	0.8564053	0.2618582	3.2704925	0.0025**
GBDR	2.4867256	2.5470315	0.9763230	0.3360
GBPDEF	−0.5755446	0.4376938	−1.3149480	0.1976
GBRP	0.5533558	0.2516663	2.1987682	0.0350*

R-squared	0.992989	Prob(F-statistic)		0.000000**
Adjusted R-squared	0.991077	Ser. Cor. F.	.3821	(.8195)
S.E. of regression	2.756379	ARCH-F	.2835	(.8866)
Log likelihood	−98.92194	Heter. F	1.7628	(.0968)
Durbin-Watson stat	2.027999	RESET F	2.5465	(.0937)
Mean of dependent var	171.9047	Jar.-Bera	11.4154	(.0033)**
S.D. of dependent var	29.17972	Box-Pierce Q	1.87	(.7596)
Sum of squared resid	250.7217	Ljung-Box Q	2.05	(.7258)
F-statistic	519.3206			

EQUATION 18

LS // Dependent Variable is M3
SMPL range: 1871–1913
Number of observations: 43

Variable	Coefficient	Std. Error	T-Stat.	2-Tail Sig.
C	−289.01380	57.059437	−5.0651359	0.0000**
M3(−1)	0.3245361	0.1052389	3.0838038	0.0041**
MB	1.7708299	0.5404914	3.2763329	0.0025**
BBBE	−2.5201574	1.1427853	−2.2052763	0.0345*
BERES	−1.1511017	0.7778817	−1.4797902	0.1484
BE	−3.9838339	12.041058	−0.3308541	0.7428
GBRGNP	0.2028206	0.0316484	6.4085583	0.0000**
GBDR	−5.2693479	10.180912	−0.5175713	0.6082
GBPDEF	6.0126404	1.4281358	4.2101321	0.0002**
GBRP	−2.8591004	0.9208212	−3.1049464	0.0039**

R-squared	0.996807	Prob(F-statistic)		0.000000**
Adjusted R-squared	0.995936	Ser. Cor. F	1.2534	(.3107)
S.E. of regression	10.92256	ARCH-F	.1985	(.9374)
Log likelihood	-158.1292	Heter. F	2.0145	(.0547)
Durbin-Watson stat	1.415647	RESET F	.6497	(.5287)
Mean of dependent var	765.1193	Jar.-Bera	.6184	(.7340)
S.D. of dependent var	171.3301	Box-Pierce Q	4.55	(.3372)
Sum of squared resid	3936.978	Ljung-Box Q	4.94	(.2938)
F-statistic	1144.553			

EQUATION 19

LS // Dependent Variable is GBDR
SMPL range: 1871–1913
Number of observations: 43

Variable	Coefficient	Std. Error	T-Stat.	2-Tail Sig.
C	–3.7341284	1.3557738	–2.7542415	0.0095**
GBDR(–1)	–0.0541584	0.0558375	–0.9699296	0.3391
BE	1.0762480	0.0794190	13.551513	0.0000**
BERES	–0.0248049	0.0136659	–1.8150983	0.0786
MB	0.0138784	0.0100498	1.3809637	0.1766
M3	–0.0024435	0.0027732	–0.8811093	0.3846
GBRGNP	0.0005549	0.0008425	0.6586108	0.5147
GBPDEF	0.0084109	0.0351273	0.2394390	0.8122
GBRP	0.0128229	0.0184816	0.6938210	0.4926
BBBE	0.0037922	0.0211281	0.1794860	0.8587

R-squared	0.965508	Prob(F-statistic)		0.000000**
Adjusted R-squared	0.956101	Ser. Cor. F	1.1611	(.3842)
S.E. of regression	0.183426	ARCH-F	.3337	(.8533)
Log likelihood	17.60206	Heter. F	1.8092	(.0871)
Durbin-Watson stat	1.677292	RESET F	2.9776	(.0647)
Mean of dependent var	2.780651	Jar.-Bera	1.6879	(.4300)
S.D. of dependent var	0.875454	Box-Pierce Q	2.39	(.6639)
Sum of squared resid	1.110292	Ljung-Box Q	2.67	(.6146)
F-statistic	102.6376			

EQUATION 20

LS // Dependent Variable is BBBE
SMPL range: 1871–1913
Number of observations: 43

Variable	Coefficient	Std. Error	T-Stat.	2-Tail Sig.
C	–7.8853249	10.101907	–0.7805779	0.4406
BBBE(–1)	0.3317868	0.1184625	2.8007750	0.0085**
BE	0.5509612	1.6567010	0.3325652	0.7416
BERES	–0.1975954	0.0975287	–2.0260239	0.0509
GBRGNP	0.0040927	0.0063699	0.6425072	0.5250
MB	0.2822987	0.0658180	4.2890807	0.0001**
M3	–0.0282454	0.0199953	–1.4126007	0.1671
GBDR	–0.8198301	1.3834392	–0.5926029	0.5575
GBPDEF	0.1938833	0.2364379	0.8200178	0.4181
GBRP	–0.2767501	0.1326871	–2.0857341	0.0448*

R-squared	0.970218	Prob(F-statistic)		0.000000**
Adjusted R-squared	0.962095	Ser. Cor. F.	2596	(.9013)
S.E. of regression	1.466036	ARCH-F	.5191	(.7222)
Log likelihood	–71.77365	Heter. F	1.3889	(.2232)
Durbin-Watson stat	1.904010	RESET F	2.1721	(.1300)
Mean of dependent var	19.18302	Jar.-Bera	1.2936	(.5237)
S.D. of dependent var	7.530064	Box-Pierce Q	.15	(.9972)
Sum of squared resid	70.92565	Ljung-Box Q	.17	(.9967)
F-statistic	119.4494			

EQUATION 21

LS // Dependent Variable is GBPDEF
SMPL range: 1871–1913
Number of observations: 43

Variable	Coefficient	Std. Error	T-Stat.	2-Tail Sig.
C	23.688753	5.2867716	4.4807597	0.0001**
GBPDEF(−1)	0.2082757	0.0716017	2.9088092	0.0064**
BE	1.5945442	1.0215866	1.5608508	0.1281
BERES	0.1862925	0.0631105	2.9518454	0.0058**
GBRP	0.4248319	0.0546867	7.7684761	0.0000**
GBRGNP	−0.0138769	0.0033880	−4.0958891	0.0003**
GBDR	−0.0486194	0.9004801	−0.0539927	0.9573
BBBE	0.0693619	0.1016905	0.6820887	0.4999
M3	0.0531720	0.0100325	5.2999717	0.0000**
MB	−0.1214047	0.0513388	−2.3647741	0.0241

R-squared	0.978001	Prob(F-statistic)		0.000000**
Adjusted R-squared	0.972001	Ser. Cor. F.	.3538	(.8393)
S.E. of regression	0.958345	ARCH-F	.4992	(.7364)
Log likelihood	−53.49394	Heter. F	.9790	(.5105)
Durbin-Watson stat	1.747123	RESET F	2.9630	(.0655)
Mean of dependent var	88.76744	Jar.-Bera	.3601	(.8352)
S.D. of dependent var	5.727283	Box-Pierce Q	9.02	(.0605)
Sum of squared resid	30.30805	Ljung-Box Q	10.14	(.0381)*
F-statistic	163.0043			

EQUATION 22

LS // Dependent Variable is GBRP
SMPL range: 1871–1913
Number of observations: 43

Variable	Coefficient	Std. Error	T-Stat.	2-Tail Sig.
C	−27.657247	11.536639	−2.3973401	0.0223*
GBRP(−1)	0.1321039	0.1199856	1.1009986	0.2789
BE	−3.2751641	1.8912680	−1.7317292	0.0927
BERES	−0.2252671	0.1297073	−1.7367335	0.0918
GBPDEF	1.2871877	0.2153631	5.9768260	0.0000**
GBDR	1.9070372	1.6434893	1.1603588	0.2542
BBBE	−0.3189831	0.1848144	−1.7259645	0.0937
M3	−0.0720397	0.0233927	−3.0795822	0.0042**
MB	0.2512840	0.0987298	2.5451686	0.0158*
GBRGNP	0.0138293	0.0074282	1.8617364	0.0716

R-squared	0.974975	Prob(F-statistic)		0.000000**
Adjusted R-squared	0.968150	Ser. Cor. F	2.0562	(.1126)
S.E. of regression	1.787572	ARCH-F	1.0869	(.3785)
Log likelihood	−80.30037	Heter. F	.8668	(.6171)
Durbin-Watson stat	1.390461	RESET F	1.5411	(.2292)
Mean of dependent var	94.34884	Jar.-Bera	.0085	(.9957)
S.D. of dependent var	10.01638	Box-Pierce Q	18.22	(.0011)**
Sum of squared resid	105.4486	Ljung-Box Q	20.19	(.0005)**
F-statistic	142.8547			

Granger Causality Tests

Granger causality tests were run up to three lagged terms. Assume a Granger causality test on endogenous variables Y and X, with all other variables Z . . . W as exogenous (i.e., control variables). Three pairs of probabilities corresponding to F-statistics on each lag structure were generated (except for the second section, where two lags were tested). The first probability in each pair tested the following: lag 1 tested the significance of the coefficient of X(–1); lag 2 tested the significance of the coefficients of X(–1) and X(–2); lag 3 tested the significance of the coefficients of X(–1), X(–2), and X(–3). The second probability tested the following: lag 1 tested the significance of the coefficient of Y(–1); lag 2 tested the coefficients of Y(–1) and Y(–2); lag 3 tested the coefficients of Y(–1), Y(–2), and Y(–3). Although the selection of a lag structure for Granger tests is a subjective enterprise, introducing several lags generates a stronger statement about the robustness of conclusions about the interactive effects among the endogenous variables. Within each test, all of the variables other than each endogenous pair have entered into the equation as control variables.

Central Bank Discount Rates

The variables used in the following Granger tests were: BE, BF, BB, BSW, BI, BG, BH, BSP, BR, and BA. Tests cover the years 1870–1908.

The probabilities test the following null hypotheses:
Bank of England (Y) rate is not Granger caused by the rate of Bank X
The rate of Bank X is not Granger caused by the Bank of England (Y) rate

Bank of France		Bank of Belgium		Reichsbank	
Lag 1	.2638	Lag 1	.0693	Lag 1	.4152
	.6260		.2717		.2022
Lag 2	.1060	Lag 2	.0256*	Lag 2	.6076
	.1342		.7188		.2559
Lag 3	.7220	Lag 3	.4803	Lag 3	.8895
	.4379		.6233		.5889

Bank of Austria		Bank of Russia		Netherlands Bank	
Lag 1	.1144	Lag 1	.2498	Lag 1	.0001**
	.0959		.0678		.2867
Lag 2	.0345*	Lag 2	.4046	Lag 2	.0008**
	.6090		.7347		.4717
Lag 3	.5346	Lag 3	.6067	Lag 3	.1572
	.4450		.7478		.2774

Bank of Italy		Bank of Spain		Bank of Switzerland	
Lag 1	.0843	Lag 1	.6391	Lag 1	.0029**
	.6927		.0463*		.7136
Lag 2	.2289	Lag 2	.3144	Lag 2	.0067**
	.5396		.0068**		.7839
Lag 3	.6813	Lag 3	.6134	Lag 3	.4608
	.4321		.1499		.2656

World Price Indices and British Series

The variables used in the following Granger tests were: WPPPI, WDMPI, GBRGNP, BERES, BE, MB, M3, BBBE,GBRP, GBPDEF, and GBDR. Only two lags were estimated in these tests due to missing data in the variable WPPPI (before 1881), which resulted in too few observations for lag structures of three and upward. Tests cover the years 1881–1913.

The probabilities test the following null hypotheses:
Price Index ([WPPPI or WDMPI]=Y) is not Granger caused by X
X is not Granger caused by price index ([WPPPI or WDMPI]=Y)

WPPPI—GBRGNP

Lag 1   .3355
        .7451
Lag 2   .2040
        .5605

WDMPI—GBRGNP

Lag 1   .2435
        .2036
Lag 2   .0453*
        .9726

WPPPI—BERES

Lag 1   .5570
        .6825
Lag 2   .5980
        .7623

WDMPI—BERES

Lag 1 .7224
        .0086**
Lag 2 .0824
        .3705

WPPPI—BE

Lag 1   .9987
        .7622
Lag 2   .3112
        .1852

WDMPI—BE

Lag 1   .6051
        .4792
Lag 2   .2015
        .1505

WPPPI—MB

Lag 1   .5901
        .4610
Lag 2   .4661
        .9565

WDMPI—MB

Lag 1   .4432
        .2950
Lag 2   .1599
        .6279

WPPPI—M3

Lag 1   .7998
        .2122
Lag 2   .8269
        .6693

WDMPI—M3

Lag 1   .8636
        .8883
Lag 2   .1589
        .9273

WPPPI—BBBE

Lag 1   .8890
        .1590
Lag 2   .0557
        .4895

WDMPI—BBBE

Lag 1   .8677
        .7955
Lag 2   .1545
        .4419

WPPPI—GBRP

Lag 1   .1605
        .9826
Lag 2   .1019
        .1239

WDMPI—GBRP

Lag 1   .0734
        .2053
Lag 2   .0953
        .2380

WPPPI—GBPDEF

Lag 1   .5730
        .4643
Lag 2   .4426
        .3087

WDMPI—GBPDEF

Lag 1   .3947
        .8925
Lag 2   .9866
        .4333

WPPPI—GBDR

Lag 1   .7328
        .5815
Lag 2   .3019
        .2748

WDMPI—GBDR

Lag 1   .5758
        .4563
Lag 2   .1719
        .2871

Bank of England Discount Rate and British Series

The variables used in the estimates in the next two sections were: BE, BERES, GBDR, MB, M3, BBBE, GBRGNP, GBPDEF, and GBRP. Tests cover the years 1870–1913 for both sections.

The probabilities test the following null hypotheses:
The Bank of England rate (Y) is not Granger caused by X
X is not Granger caused by the Bank of England rate (Y)

GBDR		**MB**		**M3**	
Lag 1	.4620	Lag 1	.4616	Lag 1	.7241
	.3123		.0000**		.0198*
Lag 2	.1484	Lag 2	.7079	Lag 2	.4191
	.3411		.0000**		.3312
Lag 3	.4959	Lag 3	.3593	Lag 3	.9339
	.8462		.0050**		.9975

BERES		**BBBE**		**GBRGNP**	
Lag 1	.3607	Lag 1	.3089	Lag 1	.1789
	.0496*		.1084		.4492
Lag 2	.1182	Lag 2	.0587	Lag 2	.1542
	.3581		.0296*		.6678
Lag 3	.1895	Lag 3	.3003	Lag 3	.7462
	.1552		.5855		.4628

GBPDEF		**GBRP**	
Lag 1	.4890	Lag 1	.1097
	.3511		.5049
Lag 2	.7767	Lag 2	.3804
	.3319		.5635
Lag 3	.8181	Lag 3	.5158
	.5895		.7847

Bank of England Reserves and British Series

The probabilities test the following null hypotheses:
Bank of England reserves (Y) are not Granger caused by X
X is not Granger caused by Bank of England reserves (Y)

GBRGNP		**BBBE**		**GBDR**	
Lag 1	.1325	Lag 1	.9908	Lag 1	.1728
	.4180		.8532		.5735
Lag 2	.2939	Lag 2	.8881	Lag 2	.8163
	.7928		.3324		.3562
Lag 3	.0910	Lag 3	.5886	Lag 3	.4376
	.5695		.7256		.3686

MB		**M3**		**GBPDEF**	
Lag 1	.5926	Lag 1	.1834	Lag 1	.0333*
	.0053**		.0261*		.8631
Lag 2	.7452	Lag 2	.4048	Lag 2	.2254
	.0019**		.3025		.2058
Lag 3	.2956	Lag 3	.4277	Lag 3	.2412
	.0089**		.6638		.1910

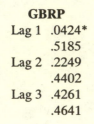

GBRP

Lag 1 .0424*
       .5185
Lag 2 .2249
       .4402
Lag 3 .4261
       .4641

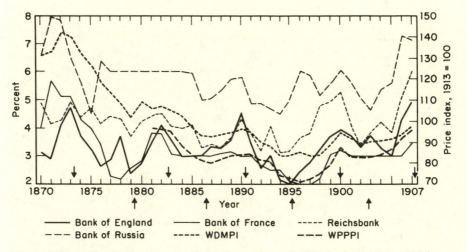

Fig. A.1 Central bank discount rates for leading nations and global prices, 1870–1907 (arrows at the bottom of Figures A.1–A.5 represent turning points in the global business cycle; see text for estimation procedure).

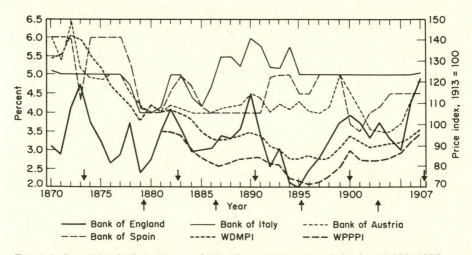

Fig. A.2 Central bank discount rates for leading nations and global prices, 1870–1907.

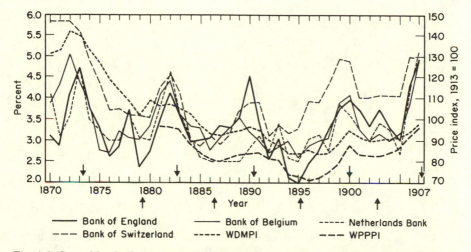

Fig. A.3 Central bank discount rates for leading nations and global prices, 1870–1907.

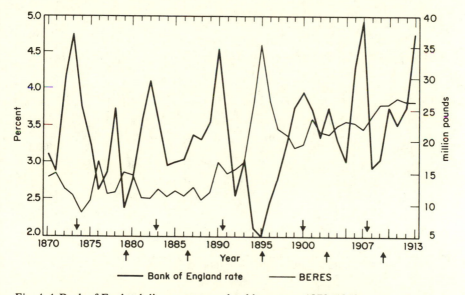

Fig. A.4 Bank of England discount rate and gold reserves, 1870–1913.

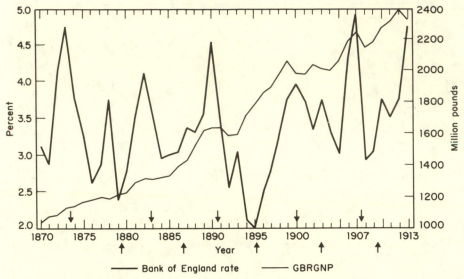

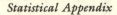

Fig. A.5 Bank of England discount rate and British real GNP, 1870–1913.

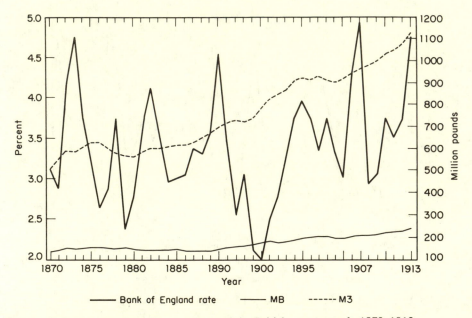

Fig. A.6 Bank of England discount rate and the British money stock, 1870–1913.

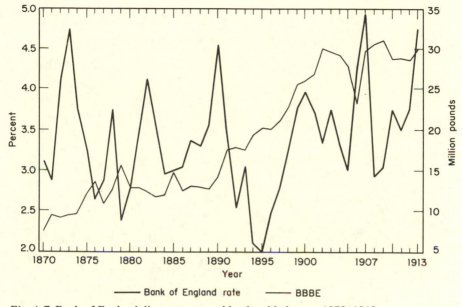

Fig. A.7 Bank of England discount rate and bankers' balances, 1870–1913.

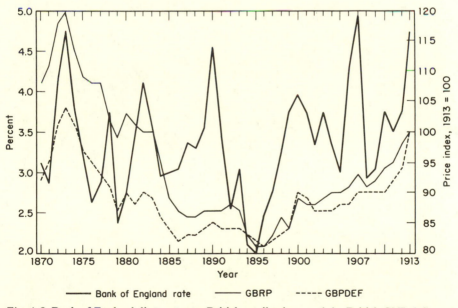

Fig. A.8 Bank of England discount rate, British retail prices, and the British GNP deflator, 1870–1913.

Notes

Chapter 1

1. Bordo and Schwartz (1984) and Eichengreen (1985a). On the monetary non-system, see Corden (1986).

2. See, for example, Bordo (1981), Officer (1989), Meltzer and Robinson (1990), Pope (1990), Garber (1986), Eichengreen (1990b), Grilli (1989), Clark (1984), Diebold et al. (1991), Barsky and De Long (1991), and the collection of articles in Bordo and Schwartz (1984). See Eichengreen (1989) for a survey of the literature on the gold standard over the last three decades.

3. The literature on international regimes has become quite large. The best-known collection on the subject is Krasner (1983a). For critical surveys of the literature, see Young (1986) and Haggard and Simmons (1987).

4. On these different treatments of regimes, see especially Krasner (1983b and 1983c) and Haggard and Simmons (1987).

5. The most common definition of an international regime shows a very strong ideological component: "principles, norms, rules, and decision-making procedures around which actor expectations converge in a given [international] issue area." See Krasner (1983b, p. 1).

6. An exception would be de Cecco (1974), who takes a political-economy approach to the gold standard, but even here explanations of the origin and stability of the regime are underdeveloped.

7. See also Scammell ([1965] 1985) and Wood (1939, p. 162).

8. Young (1983) and Lipson (1983, p. 233).

9. In fact, there was little public intervention at the domestic level as well.

10. Even at the domestic level, central bankers were not the guardians of adjustment that conventional visions of the rules of the game made them out to be.

Chapter 2

1. One might also see it referred to as the international or prewar gold standard. Economic historians are careful to distinguish this set of relations from that which prevailed in the interwar period, where the practice of gold standards resulted in quite a distinct set of outcomes from those that prevailed before the War.

2. The fact that the norms upon which the classical gold standard was founded were primarily domestic in nature places it somewhat outside the mainstream vision of regimes, since this vision emphasizes the relational consequences of international norms.

3. See Keohane and Nye (1985, pp. 67–72), Ruggie (1983), and Cooper (1987). Cohen (1977) refers to it as an order, but his later work on regimes (1983) suggests that the regime approach is perfectly adapted to the gold standard.

4. See, for example, the differing descriptive and evaluational typologies in Cooper (1987), Cohen (1977), and Williamson and Miller (1987).

5. Hence, the use of regime categories in this chapter is primarily descriptive rather than analytical: they provide the most convenient means of understanding the workings of the gold standard. A more analytical use of regimes will be adopted in Chapter 8 where the theoretical implications of the gold standard are considered.

6. See especially Ruggie (1975), Haggard and Simmons (1987), Young (1980), and Krasner (1983a).

7. See especially Cooper (1987) and Cohen (1977).

8. In fact, there was little public intervention at the domestic level as well.

9. Even at the domestic level, central bankers were not the guardians of adjustment that conventional visions of the rules of the game made them out to be.

10. Condliffe (1950) argues that 1897 (the period being 1897–1914) is a valid starting date for the classical gold standard because the monetary question had finally been resolved in the U.S. with the election of McKinley, and Russia and Japan had finally adopted gold standards. Bloomfield's (1959) authoritative history of the gold standard proposes the dates 1880–1914: the transformation of monetary practices had been completed across most of the developed world in the 1870s. One can even make a case for extending the gold standard back to the 1850s, when changes in the market prices of precious metals drove silver out of circulation. Most scholars have accepted Bloomfield's dates, as shall I.

11. The regime literature also refers to this as "consequences of operation." The relevant question in this context is, "What sorts of outcomes (either individual or collective) can the regime be expected to produce?" Quoted from Young (1980, pp. 355, 356).

12. There has been some debate on the stability of prices under the gold standard. Meltzer and Robinson (1989) find that short-term price movements were at least as great before World War I as after. Both Bordo (1981) and Schwartz (1986) concede that the prewar standard may not have been superior in terms of short-run price stability, but note that the period showed far more long-term price stability and predictability (i.e., prices showed a long-run tendency to revert to their mean). Klein's (1975) data show that for the U.S. and Great Britain, short-term variability in wholesale prices was actually greater after the War. Empirical findings generally do agree that inflation was far greater after the War than before. Moreover, movements in short-term prices were less of a problem before the War because they tended to be synchronous (see Chapter 7), and hence they placed less pressure on the adjustment mechanism. Price movements after the War were far less synchronous. On comparative price trends across periods, see also Cooper (1982), Triffin (1964), Bordo (1986), and Eichengreen (1985b).

13. The scope or jurisdictional boundary of a regime, as a descriptive category, is defined in the regime literature as "the coverage of the regime with respect to functional scope, areal domain, and membership." See Young (1980, p. 355) and Haggard and Simmons (1987).

14. But even under the periods of suspension in Italy, laws required banks to hold gold reserves against deposits. On the Italian experience under the gold standard, see Fratianni and Spinelli (1984).

15. Zucker (1975, p. 65).

16. Great Britain came to practice a gold standard de facto from 1717—when Master of the Mint Sir Isaac Newton instituted a legal bimetallic ratio that kept silver underpriced at the mint—and de jure from 1821 (with a temporary suspension of convertibility from 1797 to 1821 due to the Napoleonic Wars). Portugal, whose trade and monetary dependence on Great Britain reached a pinnacle at the mid 19th century (the British sovereign circulated with legal tender in Portugal, and Britain was its largest trading partner), instituted a gold standard in 1854.

17. On the reasons for the scramble for gold, see Chapter 6.

18. Martin (1973) and Laughlin (1886, pp. 79–85) see 1853 as the real end of bimetallism in the U.S., given that the monetary legislation of that year failed to make coinage adjustments that would bring the silver dollar (which had disappeared owing to a higher intrinsic than nominal value) back into circulation, and followed up this so-called (by silverites) "neglect" with a further marginalization of silver coin through changes in weights and legal-tender laws. Legally, however, the silver dollar retained a central monetary status until 1873.

19. The problem of surplus (i.e., inflationary) silver was central to the scramble for gold. See Chapter 6.

20. Gold had actually come to enjoy much greater use from the 1850s, as changes in the relative values of gold and silver (owing to the great discoveries of gold in that decade) caused gold to displace silver in circulation.

21. Spain also remained on paper/silver standards in this period.

22. It is problematic whether the shift from silver and bimetallism to gold constituted a shift within regime (i.e., the practice of metallism continued), or a transformation of regime. Depending on how one defines styles of organizing domestic monetary systems, the answer would vary. It is clear, however, that remaining on silver and bimetallist standards instead of shifting to gold would have generated a far different set of regime outcomes both on the domestic and international levels. Given exogenous developments in the market for metals, silver promised to be a more inflationary standard both at the domestic and international levels. Domestic systems of circulation would have been less conducive to economic growth and the industrial revolution. And exchange rates promised to be far less stable if a silver bloc had been preserved among selected developed nations. It is because of the pervasive effects the transition to gold had on monetary conditions of the period that the transformation from silver and bimetallism to gold shouldn't be considered anything less than a major change in monetary practices and relations. I am grateful to Anna Schwartz's illuminating points on this issue.

23. Given that these nations maintained their legal bimetallic ratios fixed, the situation that naturally resulted from a changing international market ratio was that one of the metals would be overvalued at the mint, while the other would be undervalued. This opened up opportunities for arbitrage as individuals found it profitable, when the changes in the market value of metals were greater than the transaction costs of arbitrage in precious metals, to melt down the coins made of the mint-undervalued metal and sell it in the market for bullion (i.e., in non-monetary use), where it fetched a relatively greater return, and bring the mint-overvalued metal they received in to the mint (i.e., in monetary use), where it fetched a relatively greater return. This arbitrage process represented a form of Gresham's Law: the good money (which had the rising market value) was being driven out of circulation by the bad money (which had the declining market value). See Chapter 6 on the impact of Gresham's Law on the regime transformation of the 1870s.

24. On the experiences of 19th century bimetallist regimes, see Willis (1901) and Laughlin (1886). On the historical instability of bimetallist regimes, see Greenfield and Rockoff (1991) and Redish (1990a).

25. Under a bimetallist regime, the central monetary status is shared among two metals, with a legal bimetallic ratio being instituted as the official price at which one central metal will exchange for the other.

26. Under bimetallism there is dual correspondence for the central monetary unit with respect to each of the central metals.

27. Under the classical gold standard, this was done principally through the regulation of central-bank note issue. This reflected the relative strength of the currency school (which saw effective management of money supplies as dependent on regulating note issue) over the banking school (which saw management of money as dependent on the manipulation of banks' assets and liabilities) during the period before World War I.

28. Most of the more recent rules are versions of a tabular standard originally expressed by Jevons, who saw the most efficient means of combating inflation as the defense of some price index. Another early rule which attracted much attention was Fisher's compensated dollar rule, which called for manipulating the gold content of the dollar to control inflation. On the early rules, see Schwartz (1986). On the more recent rules, see Barro (1986). See Kemmerer (1935) for a good general survey of metallist rules.

29. Seigniorage in these transactions takes the form of a selling price which is slightly higher than the public buying price. In the case of Great Britain under the gold standard, the difference was 1½d (pence): the Bank of England normally bought bullion at 3p 17s and 9d per fine ounce, and normally sold at 3p 17s and 10½d per ounce. These prices were altered to the extent that the Bank was trying to build up or run down reserves.

30. An exception to this is a limping standard, where coins that formerly possessed central money status continue to be accepted at full legal tender. Under the classical gold standard it was not uncommon on the European Continent for nations to limp out of silver.

31. The "rules of the game," a phrase coined by Keynes ([1931] 1952) and used by Sir Robert Kindersley (a Bank of England Director) in his testimony to the Macmillan Committee, referred to the practice whereby central monetary authorities linked the management of the money supply to external gold flows, this in turn allowing the classic specie-flow system of adjustment to operate (see subsection on adjustment below). This required that the authorities avoid sterilizing gold flows. When gold flowed out, the rules of the game dictated that they contract the money supply, thus compounding the deflationary effects of a balance-of-payments deficit, which in turn would facilitate adjustment in the trade balance that would equilibrate external payments. When gold flowed in, authorities should increase the money supply.

32. Bloomfield operationalized the relationship between external gold flows and the money supply by testing the correlation between the direction of yearly change in central banks' international reserves (gold, foreign exchange, silver) and the direction of change in their domestic income-earning assets (securities, discounts, and advances). Given that silver and foreign exchange have been factored into international reserves, his findings do not comment on the pure relationship between gold flows and the money supply. Furthermore, whatever sterilization occurred with respect to assets does not reflect the rather religious adherence of public note creation to changes in the gold stock. This is no surprise, since there were more formal laws restricting the creation of notes, while the manipulation of assets was generally left to the discretion of the central banks themselves. Moreover, the breaking of the rules under the gold standard generally stayed within stable-money parameters in gold-club nations. Inflationary management of note issue and central bank assets combined was much more rampant under gold standards of the interwar and Bretton Woods periods. The management of the money supply vis-à-vis gold (both in the management of assets and note issue) was, in general, much more founded on the rules of metallism during the prewar gold standard than in later international regimes. Hence, the prewar gold standard was a much more orthodox (i.e., inflation-controlling) metallist regime relative to regimes afterward.

33. In normal times, international considerations of central bankers were generally restricted to a concern over having sufficient specie and foreign exchange to facilitate international trade and travel. In crisis periods, they worried about the threat to domestic and international convertibility from a foreign drain.

34. U.S. Senate (1910e, pp. 8, 189, 355, 530) and Bloomfield (1959, pp. 17, 60).

35. Outside of the developed world, the few nations that sought some form of gold regime normally adopted a gold exchange standard—quite a different set of practices vis-à-vis orthodox gold monometallism. Some less developed nations (often colonial possessions) with strong trade dependence on nations practicing orthodox gold standards made a gold exchange

link so as to facilitate trade with their principal trading partners. Siam, Ceylon, India, the Straits Settlement, the Philippines, Java, and Panama all came to practice a gold exchange standard before World War I. This regime called for a theoretical domestic gold par, since authorities did not stand ready to convert domestic claims into gold. The par value of their currencies was maintained internationally through the use of foreign exchange. Money supplies were managed so as to simulate the effects of gold flows through the use of special gold-exchange funds held by central authorities. On the gold-exchange standard, see Kemmerer (1935), Bloomfield (1963, p. 20), and Simkin (1951, p. 76).

36. Dam (1982, p. 31) notes that "the rules that counted most were domestic rules." This brings into question whether the famous "rules of the game" treated widely in the historiography ever occupied the core of a metallist orthodoxy, since they were oriented around the international objective of external payments adjustment. This point is all the more reinforced by the fact that these rules of the game were often violated, while the norms which were more domestic in nature were generally respected.

37. The international effects of the structure of domestic macroeconomic developments have received special attention in the economic diplomacy of the past several decades. A major component of current negotiations among the leading economic powers (G-2, G-3, G-5, and G-7) has concentrated on constructing constellations of macroeconomic outcomes across nations that are consistent with favorable international relations and domestic economic performance. See Funabashi (1988) and Webb (1991).

38. Because of this multilateral effect, it has been common to attribute an international consciousness to the 19th century practice of monometallism. See, for example, Great Britain, *Report of the Macmillan Committee* ([1931] 1985), Willett (1980, p. 8), and Bloomfield (1959, p. 23).

39. This required that foreigners had the privilege of holding domestic balances (reciprocally, this amounted to the privilege that nationals could transfer claims to foreigners), or that nationals had the privilege of transferring funds overseas.

40. There was, however, some competition for central status in national currencies (e.g., the franc versus the dollar), as the French competed for such status at the International Monetary Conference of 1867. On the problem of status in international monetary regimes, see Cohen (1977).

41. Great Britain, *Report of the Macmillan Committee* ([1931] 1985). This may have been a good or bad outcome depending on one's view of the benefits versus costs of the capacity to inflate. Inflation-busting monetarists might favor such constraints against the capacity to randomly increase money supplies, while others may prefer that authorities retain the capacity to stimulate the world economy through the discretionary manipulation of money supplies (i.e., the global Phillips Curve).

42. Those who subscribe to the "engine of growth" idea may take the view that synchronous macroeconomies would be conducive to prolonged global recessions (i.e., there are no high-growth nations to pull the world out of recession). This assumes, of course, that unilateral stimulus is more easily attained than collective stimulus. On the effects of the collective structure of macroeconomies, see Bergsten (1975, pp. 49, 50).

43. An adverse element also arose here, as nations found that their capital was easily pulled by other nations seeking liquidity (i.e., their investors were easily wooed by small differentials in interest rates).

44. The generally unrestricted trade of the period accentuated the law of one price with respect to internationally traded commodities.

45. Cohen (1977, pp. 66–73).

46. Ford (1989, p. 202).

47. On the issue of international inflation control, see Williamson and Miller (1987).

48. In fact, in cases where domestic gold standards experienced turbulent outcomes, one of the principal factors at the root of the problem of maintaining convertibility was excessive note issue. Both Italy and Japan's failed attempts to preserve gold links owed much to this problem. These nations featured unusually decentralized systems of note issue: where note issue was split among several major banks which practiced very little coordination in credit creation, rather than a central bank (which was the common site of public note issue in the gold club). In both cases, excessive note issue resulting from this lack of coordination was compounded by governments which were monetizing their budget deficits. See U.S. Senate (1911, pp. 128–30) and Fratianni and Spinelli (1984, p. 415). Bloomfield (1959, p. 23) notes that cases of erratic credit management during the period often emanated from excessive government involvement in note issue. On comparative regime performance with respect to inflation, see Bordo (1981), Meltzer and Robinson (1989), Schwartz (1986), and Klein (1975).

49. He adds that the Bretton Woods regime was a weaker variant of an international gold standard because only the U.S. fixed the value of its currency to gold.

50. In a regime in which the power structure is skewed, international trends in inflation will depend disproportionately on the domestic trends in the economies of the principal monetary (i.e., key currency) powers. Specifically during the gold standard, the principal key currencies were marks, francs, and sterling. See Lindert (1969).

The stable-money orientations among key-currency economies also suggest that intramarginal rents emanating from seigniorage positions within the monetary regime were somewhat lower during the gold standard given the normative restraints against monetizing external deficits (i.e., deficits without tears). On intramarginal rents, see Cooper (1987, pp. 8, 9).

51. Scammell ([1965] 1985) argues that the gold standard was really a sterling standard with Britain running current account surpluses so it could export sterling to the world. Kindleberger (1984, p. 70) avers, "With sterling bills traded worldwide, serving as a close substitute for money in foreign countries, and their interest rate manipulated in London, the gold standard was a sterling system."

52. This increase was accounted for disproportionately by growth in demand deposits, which increased from 3.3 billion dollars in 1885 to 16.5 billion in 1913. Non-specie currency in the same period more than doubled, from 2.3 billion to 5.9 billion. See also Kindleberger (1984, p. 108).

53. Lindert (1969, pp. 22, 23) and Bloomfield (1959).

54. On the distinction between internal and external stocks, see Ford (1962).

55. When Austria-Hungary and Russia finally joined the gold club in the 1890s, they found it necessary to hold a large amount of foreign exchange reserves to mitigate pressure on their gold stocks. See Hawtrey (1947, p. 60). On the reasons for differing capacities across nations to attract and keep gold, see Chapter 6.

56. Bloomfield (1963, pp. 22, 26). Viner (1937, pp. 270, 271) stressed how central bankers were always looking for ways to economize on the use of gold.

57. Ford (1989, p. 203), Lindert (1969, p. 38), and de Cecco (1974, p. 123).

58. Bills could be differentiated according to the nature of the debt they represented. Commercial or real bills represented a debt incurred as a result of a transfer of goods. Financial bills represented a debt contracted without the transfer of goods. One could also differentiate bills according to geographic scope: inland bills defined domestic debt arrangements, while foreign bills defined international debt arrangements.

59. On the workings of the bill mechanism, see Hawtrey (1947 p. 31), Goschen (1876, p. 2, 3), Yeager (1976, p. 299), and Morgan-Webb (1934, pp. 53, 54). See King (1936) on the London market for bills.

60. The bill holdings were normally of very high quality (i.e., first-class bills) and central banks found discount houses and banks quite willing to rediscount them whenever central banks desired it. In the case of Belgium, for example, the holding of bills reached 25% of central bank reserves in 1900. Discount houses in Belgium were under agreement to rediscount any bills which they originally endorsed. See U.S. Senate (1910f, p. 79).

61. King (1936, p. 31).

62. Commercial banks were opened in London as early as the 1830s to conduct international business. The overseas spread of British finance was given a major boost after 1852 when procedures for chartering overseas banks were relaxed and limited liability banking came into greater use. The number of European bank branches in London went from 4 in 1842 to 105 in 1889. See Williams (1968, p. 270).

63. In fact, challenges from European financial institutions were circumscribed by the fact that deposit banking on the European Continent remained underdeveloped throughout the 19th century. Moreover, the fact that British banks had no legal reserve requirements rendered sterling more elastic than currencies whose banking systems were constrained by such laws. See Bagehot ([1873] 1921, p. 32).

64. The safety came from investors' and traders' perceptions that gold convertibility was least vulnerable in Great Britain. In fact, sterling transactions were usually not hedged in forward markets, suggesting the absence of any perceived exchange risk. And the liquid character came from the fact that the largest sub-market in bills was in sterling. See Yeager (1976, p. 299), Bloomfield (1963, pp. 42, 43), and Wood (1939, p. 161).

65. Morgan-Webb (1934, pp. 53, 54) estimates that sterling financed from 80% to 90% of world trade by the early 19th century. Ford (1962) and Cooper (1982) point out that the propensity for international payments to clear in London imparted a stabilizing element onto the international monetary system because national money supplies and gold reserves in other nations enjoyed greater stability.

66. Yeager (1984, p. 652).

67. See Table 6.1 in Chapter 6. In only Belgium do we find notes significantly dominating gold in the money stock. In Finland, Germany, and Sweden paper was more abundant than gold, but not excessively so. See also Triffin's (1964, p. 56) estimates.

68. Monetary gold stocks tended to be concentrated in central banks during the period. The composition of central bank assets suggests that external assets (specie and foreign exchange) were greater than domestic income-earning assets (discounts, advances, securities). Silver formed a relatively small part of specie reserves in gold-club nations. In terms of domestic assets, discounting dominated advances (against collateral) and securities holdings. Most of the discounting was on commercial (real) bills, with dealings in financial bills growing over time. Securities holdings remained relatively small. Deposits tended to be larger than note issue, with the largest component in deposits being bankers' balances. See Bloomfield (1959, pp. 15–17).

69. Of all the gold-club nations, Finland, Sweden, and Belgium held the highest levels of foreign exchange as a percentage of their total external reserves. See Bloomfield (1963, p. 16).

70. However, foreign exchange reserves as a percentage of total reserves grew at a greater yearly rate than gold reserves in the last decade before World War I (10.8% to 6.3%). Interestingly, both grew at a higher rate than both world trade (which grew at 5.3%) and manufacturing output (3.9%). Gold also enjoyed a higher growth rate than world product in the period. Hence, it appears that the gold standard was not subject to a liquidity shortage: international reserves did not have a problem keeping pace with real economic activity during the period. See Lindert (1969, p. 26, and 1986, p. 490).

71. This suggests that debates over whether the production of gold was sensitive to the liquidity needs of the international system during the period (i.e., the exogeneity versus the endogeneity of the supply of gold) are not definitive comments on the stability of the gold standard. Bordo (1981) and Rockoff's (1984) findings that the supply of gold was responsive in the short run to changes in the real value of the metal suggest that gold production did respond to actual incentives (some of which were in fact manipulated by governments anxious to increase the production of gold). In the longer run, however, the production of gold was fairly stable in the face of strong industrial growth among developed nations, a condition which Friedman and Schwartz (1963) blame for the pronounced deflation during the period. Short- and long-run responsiveness aside, the sensitivity of gold production to the demand for liquidity was less crucial because the demand could be filled by credit, but only to the extent that the credit was considered ultimately convertible. And this credibility was as much (if not more) dependent on perceptions of the compelling nature of the norms of metallism (the commitment to convert) as it was on stocks and flows of gold. In fact, individuals had rather imperfect information about the latter two. Hence, to the extent that individuals remained confident in the sanctity of the gold link, it would appear that the international system had a significant amount of built-in slack with respect to what constituted a sufficient supply of gold in both the short and long runs. Moreover, central bankers remained quite perspicacious in making up for shortages by attracting gold from overseas, and diversifying between internal and external gold stocks.

72. Ford (1989, p. 201). However, there were sharp differences in what central bankers considered to be safe or optimal reserve levels. See Bloomfield (1959).

73. Viner (1924, pp. 177, 178). In some cases, pressures to convert were reduced by agreements between nations to eliminate gold from international payments. This practice was most visible among members of the Scandinavian Monetary Union. See Jonung (1984).

74. Ford (1989, p. 241).

75. Triffin (1964, p. 19).

76. Sweden was especially deft at economizing on internal use of gold so that external convertibility could be maintained. One interesting ploy was the printing of notes in smaller denominations than gold coin so that people would diversify toward paper for smaller transactions. This was an exception for developed nations, which tended to print high-denomination notes. See Jonung (1984).

77. Jonung (1984), Beach (1935, pp. 69, 76, 175), and Triffin (1964). Keynes ([1913] 1971, pp. 50, 51) noted a secular quality to this "centralizing" process across the period. He argued that the needs of official reserves were increasingly displacing gold from circulation.

78. Together, francs, marks, and sterling made up 76% of official foreign exchange reserve holdings in the 35 leading nations of the period (859 out of 1,132.1 million). See Lindert (1969, pp. 10–12, 18, 19).

79. Bloomfield (1968a, p. 13).

80. Edelstein (1982, p. 3) and Feis (1930, pp. 16, 47, 71).

81. Exceptions were China (the target of much foreign direct investment) and the U.S. (the source of much direct investment). See Bloomfield (1968a, p. 3).

82. Bloomfield (1963, p. 91).

83. Bloomfield (1968a, pp. 42–44).

84. Some may question placing the U.S. in the core of the international monetary system, since it was the source of more financial shocks under the gold standard than the three European core nations (Britain, Germany, and France). Eichengreen (1992, pp. 54, 55), for example, places the U.S. in the periphery because of its financial instability relative to European core nations. My definition of an international monetary core, however, comprises nations that have the most influence over outcomes in the international monetary system, whether

this influence is stabilizing for the system or not (i.e., the central players in the system). Clearly the U.S. was one of the central players in the international monetary system in that period. New York was one of the leading financial centers in the world (see Lindert [1969]). A great many central banks, in fact, held large secondary reserves in New York. The U.S. economy was one of the largest and most diversified in the world. In fact, Huffman and Lothian (1984) show that by the end of the period the U.S. economy was affecting the British economy more than the British economy was affecting it. The U.S. was also the largest producer of precious metals throughout the period, and its public-gold holdings were consistently among the highest in the world (see Table 5.1). Together these properties gave the U.S. monetary system and economy a great deal of influence over outcomes in the international monetary system through their influence over international capital flows. Moreover, it is not clear that the U.S. was the source of more destabilizing than stabilizing impulses over a variety of economic processes, especially later in the period. It increased its commodity imports significantly over the period. After the mid-1890s it started running consistent current account surpluses and was consistently a net capital exporter (it was a net exporter in 13 of the 20 years prior to World War I). Furthermore, it kept capital controls low throughout the period. And although the lack of a central bank may have resulted in more domestic financial shocks (and their international impulses) relative to other core nations, the track record of American finance was actually quite strong compared to non-core nations (none of the shocks ever caused it to suspend convertibility after resumption in 1878). Also, the lack of a central bank was somewhat stabilizing internationally in that it made the American money supply more responsive to international demands (i.e., more elastic).

85. Eichengreen's (1990b) findings suggest that net investment positions were quite sensitive to domestic savings rates: nations with greater savings tended to be the larger net capital exporters, while nations with low savings rates tended to be importers. The sensitivity even showed up within nations over time: changes in savings rates within nations over time were correlated with changes in net investment.

86. In the period 1865–1914, 69% of British foreign portfolio investment, for example, was in social overhead projects. See Simon (1968, p. 23).

87. Feis (1930, pp. 51, 73, 74).

88. For the period 1865–1914, the geographic dispersion of British foreign portfolio investment was as follows: North America 34%, South America 17%, Asia 14%, Europe 13%, Africa 11%, and Australia 11%. See Simon (1968, p. 23).

89. Ashworth (1952, p. 174).

90. Some exceptions appeared in German and French investments, which sometimes showed a political motivation, especially German investment under Bismarck.

91. The process was named after David Hume ([1752] 1955), who first articulated this vision of adjustment under a gold standard. Eichengreen (1985b, p. 30) notes that elements of Hume's adjustment process also appear in Cantillon ([1755] 1964).

92. This assumes, of course, no significant differences in price trends between domestically consumed goods and tradables, consumption in both nations is price elastic, and that these elasticities are roughly similar for both nations.

93. On the variants of the Humian process, as well as an extensive survey of principal models of adjustment under the gold standard from Hume to the present, see Bordo (1984). On monetarist contributions to the adjustment literature, see Pope (1993) and Eichengreen (1989).

94. More recent support of the conventional visions of adjustment does not go beyond references to geographically restricted occurrences. Friedman and Schwartz (1963, pp. 98, 99) point to the case of expanded U.S. agricultural exports of the late 1870s leading to a gold inflow that inflated prices, this in turn leading to a reduction of net exports which abated the

gold inflow by 1882. Huffman and Lothian (1984) found that some of the transmission of business cycles between the U.S. and Great Britain was attributable to price changes reflective of a Humian process. Lindert (1969, pp. 43, 44) finds some evidence of more widespread workings of the traditional process, but notes that it was not significant. Grubel (1969, pp. 91–93) is also sympathetic to more general applicability of the classical model. For Great Britain, Pippenger (1984) finds that there was greater adherence to the rules of the game in the long run than the short run. On the workings of the specie-flow mechanism in Italy, Argentina, and Canada, see Fratianni and Spinelli (1984) and Ford (1989, p. 244).

95. Temin (1984, p. 577) points out that econometric tests have shown greater support for the monetarist than the classical approach to adjustment.

96. Triffin (1964, p. 9) and Ford (1989, p. 226).

97. In fact, with respect to regime outcomes (i.e., the consequences of its operation), had the adjustment mechanism worked according to the conventional vision, monetary relations under the gold standard would have likely been far less stable. Adjustment through trade was a slower kind of adjustment than that which actually took place through short-term capital flows. Gold stocks would have been much less stable, thus placing convertibility at greater risk, had adjustment occurred principally through gold flows. Furthermore, the rules of the game called for significant shifts in prices in adjusting external positions, which would have rendered domestic economic growth highly unstable. Moreover, excessive inflation would have threatened the maintenance of convertibility. And the less stable prices that would have prevailed would have placed greater pressure on exchange rates. It appears, therefore, that the mythical gold standard was a potentially far more volatile regime than the one that actually existed. See Grubel (1969, pp. 91–93) and Goodhart (1972, p. 219).

98. More recent country-specific studies of the gold standard issue findings consistent with Bloomfield's (1959). See Rich (1984) on Canada, Jonung (1984) on Sweden, Pope (1993) on Australia, Fratianni and Spinelli (1984) on Italy, Drummond (1976) on Russia, McGouldrick (1984) on Germany, and Dutton (1984) on Great Britain.

99. In accommodating the business cycle, however, a rate which stabilized economic growth was not necessarily inconsistent with assuring sufficient gold stocks. As Schumpeter (1954, p. 1078) noted, "Reacting to the inflow and outflow of gold involved essentially the same behavior as would have reacting to the domestic business situation." When high economic growth drove up imports, thus creating a deficit, the rise in the discount rate served both to induce capital inflows to finance the deficit and prevent the economy from overexpanding. Low economic growth set in motion opposite processes leading to improvement in both the external and internal positions. Furthermore, this was also consistent with the central bankers' profit motives, which were compelling given the private status of central banks. When the economy expanded and demand for money grew, central bankers would naturally follow the market rate up. When the economy contracted and the price of money declined, so would the central bank rate. See Pippenger (1984) and McGouldrick (1984).

100. On the prevailing concerns of central bankers, see McGouldrick (1984), Jonung (1984), and Bloomfield (1959).

101. Eichengreen (1989), Ford (1989), Whale ([1937] 1985), Rich (1984), Goodhart (1972), Triffin (1964), Taussig (1917 and [1927] 1966), Beach (1935), Viner (1924), Angell ([1925] 1965), Williamson (1964), Bloomfield (1968b), and White (1933). Not all the findings in these studies were inconsistent with the traditional models. Taussig and Viner found that terms of trade in Great Britain and Canada did show sensitivity to their external positions. White found that changes in the prices of French imports corresponded to their physical quantities.

102. Bloomfield (1963, pp. 34, 92), Goodhart (1972, pp. 196, 203), Nurkse (1944, p. 29), Grubel (1969, pp. 87, 88), and Ford (1962, p. 48).

103. Ford (1989, pp. 214, 247) notes that this carried disadvantages because central authorities in these nations enjoyed less discretion to smooth the business cycle by sterilizing gold flows. Since real adjustment was relatively more important, it was necessary to compound price changes by following the rules of the game.

104. Lindert (1969, p. 73), *Economist* (1990), and Ford (1989, pp. 238–40).

105. Bloomfield (1968a), Jonung (1984), Scammell ([1965] 1985), and Triffin (1964).

106. Eichengreen (1990a, p. 291; 1992, p. 48; and 1985b, p. 18); Triffin (1964, p. 6); Moggridge (1972, pp. 6, 7); Lindert (1969); Cleveland (1976, p. 25); and Ford (1962). As Cohen (1977) notes, this bears directly on the issue of the distribution of benefits and costs in a monetary regime.

107. Moggridge (1972, pp. 12, 13), Eichengreen (1989 and 1985b, p. 19), Ford (1962, p. 225), Lindert (1969, pp. 45, 46), and Williams (1968, p. 279).

108. See especially Triffin (1964) and Lindert (1969).

109. Simkin's (1951, p. 69) evidence on differentials in the price of government debt suggests that peripheral markets also had to offer a premium on long-term investment in normal times.

110. Actually, a more definitive statement on relative pulling power would require testing the sensitivity of short-term claims and gold shipments (along with the sensitivity of exchange rates) to both market and official discount rates (the two were frequently different in gold-club nations). Three of these variables have been excluded from Lindert's tests due to unavailable or suspect data. Moreover, of Lindert's 20 coefficients measuring sensitivities between financial markets, almost half are statistically insignificant at the 5% level.

111. Lindert's statistical findings render the relative power of London within the core problematic. None of the coefficients linking Amsterdam, Paris, and New York to London are statistically significant. However, qualitative evidence strongly suggests that as the leading financial center in the world, London possessed a competitive advantage over all other financial centers at attracting capital.

112. Both the qualitative and quantitative findings render this three-tier structure of pulling power fairly definitive. The relationship between the periphery and developed world has been constructed principally from the qualitative evidence on the relationship between financial markets under the gold standard. See especially Simkin (1951), Triffin (1964), and Ford (1962). Lindert (1969) does not quantitatively measure the relation between specific peripheral-and developed-nation financial centers.

113. Superior fiscal and monetary outcomes owed much to the fact that fiscally and monetarily prudent nations enjoyed more developed central banking institutions. Furthermore, nations with more developed central banking institutions were, quite unsurprisingly, better at averting and controlling crises. See Bordo (1989) and Ford (1962, p. 214).

114. Bloomfield (1959, p. 42, and 1963, p. 49), Bordo (1984), Keynes ([1913] 1971), and Ford (1962, pp. 213, 214).

115. Capital could always be gotten, especially in the gold club, with the right price. As Bagehot ([1873] 1921, p. 6) pointed out of Great Britain, "It is often said that any foreign government can borrow in Lombard Street *at a price*; some countries can borrow much cheaper than others; but all, it is said, can have money if they choose to pay for it."

116. Saul (1960, p. 66) and Bloomfield (1968a, p. 5).

117. Brown (1940, V. I, p. 173) underscored the importance of stability within the core for the entire international monetary system. He points to the pound-franc-dollar exchange as the very nucleus of the structure of international exchange under the classical gold standard.

118. This, in contrast to a flexible-exchange-rate regime, limited exchange rates as a tool of adjustment, as well as created a situation where macroeconomic developments were more

easily transmitted to other nations. It is no surprise, therefore, that macroeconomic performances across gold nations tended to converge in the period. Einzig (1970, p. 228) notes that
avoiding changes in parities to effect external accounts also gained normative status during
the period, and that the depreciation of currencies was never stimulated by desires to gain an
economic advantage over other nations (i.e., there was little competitive devaluation). See
also Schwartz (1986, p. 58).

119. Gold points, too, were not as perfectly rigid as parities between gold nations, i.e.,
changing according to shifts in mint charges and transport costs, and the use of gold devices.
In fact, they weren't even necessarily identical for all gold arbitragers. Over the 19th century
as a whole, there was a tendency for gold points to shrink as the transaction costs of exchange
were reduced through the evolution of financial instruments and transportation, and the greater
integration of financial markets across the globe. A compelling tendency of this integration
of markets across the century within nations was the greater convergence among exchange
rates quoted in different cities. Although the practice of quoting exchange rates by cities continued, rates toward the end of the century were uniform enough within nations to be quoted
nationally. See Einzig (1970, p. 173) and Bloomfield (1963, p. 39).

120. See also Officer (1989).

121. It was not uncommon for peripheral, especially Latin American, nations to quote
exchanges both in paper and metal currency (e.g., the paper and gold peso). The period was
characterized by fairly erratic swings in their relative values. See Einzig (1970, pp. 197, 198).

122. Bloomfield (1963, p. 20) and Einzig (1970, p. 198).

123. Whatever management did take place was more often to abate a depreciation than
limit an appreciation of currencies. And it frequently took place after political or economic
crises which had forced nations to suspend convertibility or caused a depreciation of currencies. See Bloomfield (1963, pp. 19–27, and 1959, pp. 55–58) and Einzig (1970, pp. 218, 229).

124. For recent evidence see Flood et al. (1990) and Giovannini (1993).

125. In this case, the international market processes and domestic management became
substitutes for intervention. The forces which kept exchange rates aligned worked sufficiently
well so as to reduce the need for intervention within the gold club. Had monetary authorities
been less resolute in their pursuit of prevailing monetary norms, or international financial
markets less favorable in their workings (e.g., pervaded by capital controls), then gold links
would have become much more fragile, and the regime probably much less stable.

The term "management of national money supplies," as it applies to the gold standard,
must be put in perspective. It was quite distinct from the more prevalent modern process of
monetary policy, where central bankers actually pursue targets (i.e., interest rates, monetary
aggregates, exchange rates) for the purpose of achieving some rate of inflation or economic
growth within a specific country. Management of credit under the gold standard was much
more indirect. Central bankers under the metallist standards of the 19th century essentially
managed credit by guarding the gold convertibility of national money supplies. Under the
gold standard, this meant maintaining what was perceived to be a sufficiently large working
stock of gold with respect to projected demands on central banks so as to be able to fulfill
their convertibility obligations (advances, discounts, converting notes, liquidating deposits).
This in turn was generally commensurate with central bankers guarding their own solvency
(like any other bank): i.e., central banks indirectly managed money supplies by looking after
their own solvency. If central banks issued too many notes, made too many discounts, or
arranged too many advances, difficulties might arise when their customers began converting
their claims into gold. In this case, the economy itself would be subjected to a situation where
an increasing pool of credit was chasing a shrinking gold supply (i.e., inflation). The situation might become especially troubling if individuals and institutions made large and simul-
taneous claims on the central bank, as would be the case under conditions of financial dis-

tress. Hence, what turned out to be a prudent orchestration of national credit conditions through a careful management of bank assets and liabilities relative to gold (i.e., the metallist norm of stable money) was perfectly consistent with the dictates or norms of good private banking.

126. The Reichsbank, for example, looked to Germany's exchanges with other nations as an indicator of domestic monetary conditions. See McGouldrick (1984, p. 334). Using such an external target could, however, be insufficient to preserve the domestic link. Two depreciating currencies targeting on one another might mislead monetary authorities into thinking that the growth in their money supplies is not excessive.

127. Even within the gold club, more inflationary regimes found both convertibility and exchange rates more difficult to maintain. Italy's turbulent experience with the gold link (alternating suspensions and resumption), and Russia and Austria-Hungary's delays in making the gold link are attributable to an inability to keep inflation within the necessary boundaries. Interestingly, even under a suspension of convertibility during the period, when they were more successful at controlling the growth in their money supplies, these nations found greater stability in their exchange rates with gold-club nations. See Einzig (1970, p. 223), Yeager (1969), and Fratianni and Spinelli (1984).

128. Sterling was most frequently accepted long without hedges in futures markets, as Great Britain had the best historical track record of preserving convertibility. The existence of such hedging devices suggests that the exchange-rate mechanism during the 19th century was not as simple as some may think. The period, in fact, saw the development of forward exchange markets that functioned similarly to those of the present day. They had evolved from early-century practices of risk-hedging through the use of bills and assignats. Dealings in Russian roubles and Austrian crowns, for example, were often hedged in forward markets. A predominant form of risk-hedging remained pensioning on long bills (foreign customers who obtained discounts on bills promised to buy them back at some specific rate of exchange at maturity), although it increasingly gave way to the use of the forward market in foreign exchange. See Bloomfield (1963, pp. 42, 43) and Einzig (1970, pp. 180, 181).

129. The politics of inflation are discussed in Chapter 6.

130. Both the belief in the sanctity of parities and the few political and financial crises that occurred in the gold club during the period reduced the prospects of hot money flows. Hence the period was little plagued by abnormal capital movements. See Bloomfield (1959) and Einzig (1970).

131. Cooper (1987).

132. Bloomfield (1963, p. 28) underscores how the open market for gold made central bankers less nervous about low reserve levels relative to subsequent periods when international capital markets were permeated by greater impediments.

133. Eichengreen (1985b, p. 18).

134. Einzig (1970, p. 224) notes that capital controls were unpopular even in the early century, but authorities found the imperatives of political and economic crises irresistible.

135. Einzig (1970, pp. 223–25).

136. U.S. Senate (1910e, pp. 26, 27) and Hawtrey (1938, p. 86).

137. This mitigated asymmetries in adjustment, as nations with inferior pulling power had greater means of averting adverse capital flows. See Scammell ([1965] 1985) and Keynes ([1913] 1971, pp. 14, 15).

138. In some cases, the Austro-Hungarian Bank also tried to influence gold flows through manipulating forward discount rates. See Bloomfield (1959, pp. 54–59, and 1963, p. 24) and Keynes ([1913] 1971, pp. 14, 15).

139. Over the period as a whole, however, the gold club consistently featured the most accessible gold and capital markets in the world. See Einzig (1970, pp. 173, 224, 225) and Bloomfield (1959, pp. 58, 59).

140. This contrasted with the openness of the London market, the epitome of this British openness being the floating of Russian bonds on the London market during the time of the Crimean War.

141. Einzig (1970, pp. 163–72) and Feis (1930, pp. 120–22).

142. In this respect some may consider the labeling of gold devices as capital controls to be a misnomer. But given that they represented quasi-public attempts to influence trans-border capital flows (specifically specie in this case), they essentially served functions similar to capital controls. See Giovannini (1988, p. 13).

143. This further cuts against the vision of central bankers of the period standing by like automatons as gold drains depressed prices enough to shift terms of trade in an equilibrating direction. In fact, central bankers were quite cautious about allowing official reserves to drop to excessively low levels. This management of specie, however, was not independent of the banks' private status. Like any other banks under a metallist regime, central banks required sufficient gold to meet their private obligations (i.e., convertibility for their customers), which were quite large given the size of their note issue and the large bankers' deposits they held.

144. The greater reliance on gold devices for both France and Germany is explained by a greater public concern over maintaining stable interest rates in their domestic economies. Sayers (1970, pp. 74–101) and Scammell ([1965] 1985, p. 112) note that the high point of the use of gold devices to supplement the Bank rate in Great Britain was in the period 1890–1907. Sayers accounts for the greater use of gold devices by the Bank of England in this period as a response to increased use of these devices by France and Germany. The devices, Sayers adds, were used less frequently after 1907 because of the success with which the Bank helped manage the crisis of that year through the Bank rate, the prevailing lesson being that the rate was a sufficient tool to manage gold flows. Evidence, however, leads us to be somewhat skeptical about the power of the Bank rate to make itself effective both domestically and internationally throughout the entire gold standard period. See Chapter 5.

145. The symbols p, s, and d represent pounds, shillings, and pence, respectively.

146. Discriminating against foreign bills to abate gold outflows was a tactic used by other central bankers as well. In the years 1899 and 1906–07, for example, U.S. bills faced widespread discrimination throughout Europe because of an effort to abate a redistribution of gold stocks from the Continent to the U.S. Sometimes the discrimination was engineered by manipulating discount rates, as in 1882 when Belgium tried to fight a gold outflow by raising the discount rate on foreign bills to 9%. See Bloomfield (1959, pp. 58, 59).

147. On the British gold devices, see Sayers (1970, pp. 49, 76–85), Yeager (1976, p. 306), Beach (1935, p. 156), and Bloomfield (1959, p. 53).

148. Reversion to the legal privilege of conversion into silver was a strategy used throughout the Latin Monetary Union in periods when gold was scarce.

149. The process recalls the way in which wildcat banks operated in the United States in order to discourage conversion of their notes: they were situated in places of extreme inconvenience (i.e., where only wildcats could go). Sweden, too, actively engaged in the geographic diversification of conversion according to the state of gold stocks. Switzerland showed quite a bit of perspicacity in discouraging conversion. One method was to require banks intent on exporting gold to cede commercial paper to the central bank. Another was quite subtle in the way it manipulated transactions costs of conversion in times when gold was scarce: open up only a limited number of windows for conversion, keep those windows open only for a limited number of hours, and place in those windows rude tellers who counted notes as slowly as possible. See Bloomfield (1959, p. 55) and Jonung (1984). On French gold devices, see Einzig (1970, p. 228), U.S. Senate (1910d, pp. 588, 589), Keynes ([1913] 1971, pp. 14, 15), Bloomfield (1959, pp. 53–55), and Yeager (1976, p. 306).

150. Other nations were also known to use such means, but far less frequently than Ger-

many. In general, this means of influencing gold flows took the form of "hints from head-quarters" and "unofficial pressure." The Bank of France was known to indulge in such tactics from time to time, and in Denmark the preferences of central bankers were easily conveyed through the regular channels of communication between the Bank of Denmark and commercial banks. See Ford (1962, p. 23) and Bloomfield (1959, p. 45).

151. The strategy of suasion extended beyond the management of conversion. Just before the War (1913–14), for example, the government publicized against holding foreign securities unless they were especially remunerative. See Feis (1930, p. 170). On German gold devices, see McGouldrick (1984), Bloomfield (1959, pp. 53–59), U.S. Senate (1910a, p. 127), Yeager (1976, p. 306), and Keynes ([1913] 1971, pp. 14, 15).

152. In this sense, the gold devices functioned like tariffs in trade: importers and exporters can work around them by manipulating costs and prices. Formal quotas on trade cannot be so readily circumvented.

153. The factors underlying the stability of the gold standard are discussed in Chapter 7.

154. These effects are predicated on *ceteris paribus* conditions. Exchange rates in a regime with confidence may still be unstable if nations excessively monetize their external deficits (i.e., deficits without tears). Capital controls may still be in force in nations that have difficulty attracting capital. Furthermore, such nations may still face shortages of liquidity if their inferior pulling power is accompanied by chronic current account deficits.

155. Abnormal capital flows (capital flight and destabilizing speculation) in the gold club during the period were rare, and generally restricted to times surrounding financial crisis or political instability. Bloomfield (1963, p. 87) points out that compared to subsequent periods, these abnormal movements "pale into relative insignificance." He adds that normal movements of capital could also be large and disruptive on occasion, as when capital would shift in a "capricious manner" between financial centers. However, these normal movements didn't threaten convertibility in the larger centers.

156. Bloomfield (1963, p. 42).

157. Yeager (1969) and Fratianni and Spinelli (1984).

158. The importance of the lack of these exogenous events in the gold club cannot be overestimated. Even in Great Britain, for example, significant nervousness about convertibility was generated in the more severe crises of the 19th century. Hawtrey (1938, p. 86) noted how investors reacted to the suspension of the Act of 1844 as a possible signal of the weakness of the gold link.

159. Britain, of course, maintained free trade through this period. See Chapter 7 on the nature of protectionism under the gold standard.

160. For example, if individuals could only hold domestic coins, then it would be costlier to buy foreign gold, as either the buyer or seller would have to incur the mint charges of coining the metal into the domestic coin of the buyer.

161. No doubt much discretionary manipulation went on anyway under the gold standard (i.e., violations of the rules of the game), but the infractions tended to stay (unlike in later periods) within the boundaries of stable money. Hence, although the metallist rule was not inviolable, it was nonetheless compelling. Furthermore, following the metallist rule was consistent with private banking, as any responsible bank in a metallist regime needed to maintain its obligations to convert the fiduciary assets of its customers.

Chapter 3

1. U.S. Senate (1867, p. 86).

2. See, for example, Great Britain, *Gold and Silver Commission* ([1888] 1936), U.S. Senate (1879, p. 81), Sherman (1895, p. 412), and Slater (1886, p. 39). Aside from these references

from elites of the period, no economic historian, to my knowledge, has argued that cooperation among national governments was responsible for the origin of the regime. Willis (1901,
p. 135), however, calls the conference the beginning of a global consensus on the desirability
of a gold standard. See also Russell (1898, pp. 84, 236).

3. Keynes (1930, V. II, pp. 306, 307) argued that through the Bank of England's influence over the London financial market, with the market itself being the center of world finance,
the Bank "could almost have claimed to be the conductor of the international orchestra."

4. Eichengreen underscores the importance of cooperation in crisis (i.e., part-time cooperation) for the stability of the gold standard. See also Eichengreen (1986a, 1986b, and 1991).

5. Jacobson (1984, p. 34).

6. In this case cooperation took the form of coordinating coinage laws.

7. For a comprehensive list see U.S. Senate (1879, p. 779).

8. Nielsen (1933, p. 596).

9. On the formation the Latin Union, see Willis (1901).

10. See the discussion of monetary chain gangs in Chapter 6.

11. Nielsen (1933, p. 598).

12. For the Scandinavian Union, it was Germany.

13. Russell (1898, pp. 34–37, 44).

14. U.S. Senate (1867, p. 20).

15. U.S. diplomat Beckwith, quoted in Russell (1898, p. 38).

16. Quoted in *Ibid.*, p. 43.

17. *Ibid.*, p. 42.

18. He estimated that transaction costs of arbitrage would be greater than the difference
in intrinsic value. See *Ibid.*, p. 57–60.

19. *Ibid.*, p. 43.

20. See the comments of Count d'Avilla in U.S. Senate (1867, p. 31).

21. Russell (1898, p. 37).

22. U.S. Senate (1867, p. 55).

23. Russell (1898, p. 62).

24. This is not surprising since Napoleon III sought the new union as a symbol of France's
growing economic position in the world system.

25. Although the conference documents shed little light on the rationale behind this behavior, French reluctance to consider changes in seigniorage charges appears to have derived
from an intransigence over altering long-honored monetary practices. See Russell (1898,
p. 102).

26. Debate over the legal ratio was especially contentious as supporters of monometallism
felt that the ratio should be done away with in fear that its maintenance would delay transition to gold. Others felt no transition could ever be that rapid, hence there was indeed a need
for a legal ratio.

27. Russell (1898, pp. 69–72).

28. *Ibid.*, pp. 80–88.

29. See Chapter 6 on the reasons for the depreciation.

30. Great Britain, *Gold and Silver Commission* ([1888] 1936, p. 87).

31. Public documents of the period more than bear this out. See, for example, Great Britain, *Gold and Silver Commission* ([1888] 1936).

32. As the world's largest net creditor, the prospect of a depreciation in debt most severely
impacted on Great Britain.

33. Great Britain, *Report of the Commissioners Representing Great Britain at the Paris
Conference* (1878, p. 11).

34. In the Bank of France, for example, specie holdings in 1874 were made up of about

only 20% silver (12.528 million pounds sterling versus a gold stock of 40.484 million pounds). By 1878 silver specie had surpassed gold specie (42.324 million versus 39.344 million in gold). See Russell (1898, p. 260).

35. Even when loans were denominated in both silver and gold, the debtor could always pay in the depreciated metal.

36. Russell (1898, p. 227).

37. These are the words of the Dutch monetary diplomat Mees, quoted in *Ibid.*, p. 223.

38. Great Britain, *Report of the Commissioners Representing Great Britain at the Paris Conference* (1878, p. 14).

39. Russell (1898, pp. 201–203).

40. Great Britain, *Gold and Silver Commission* ([1888] 1936).

41. Russell (1898, p. 203) suggests that there may have been some sinister reasons for this reluctance to negotiate with other nations on the silver question (i.e., perhaps wanting to keep the amount of excess silver a secret). This is dubious given that Germany had shown a moderate trend over the decade in liquidating its silver, and didn't change its style at all even after the conference. Aside from a show of dedication to its recently instituted gold standard in 1871, it is difficult to find any other reason for German intransigence in accounts of the conference.

42. Russell (1898, p. 207).

43. See the comment of Dutch delegate Mees in *Ibid.*, p. 223.

44. *Ibid.*, p. 208.

45. *Ibid.*, pp. 211–14.

46. *Ibid.*, pp. 213–18.

47. In 1867, when Italy was having less trouble with depreciated paper, it advocated a gold standard.

48. U.S. Senate (1879, p. 51).

49. Russell (1898, pp. 243, 244).

50. *Ibid.*, p. 223.

51. Great Britain, *Gold and Silver Commission* ([1888] 1936, p. 208).

52. Russell (1898, p. 225).

53. Great Britain, *Gold and Silver Commission* ([1888] 1936, p. 124).

54. All developments didn't cut the same way, as the demonetization of the silver dollar in 1873 generated some skepticism about U.S. intentions. But more recent events, such as the Bland-Allison Act, served to diminish this skepticism.

55. In this respect, the analysis of Hardin (1982, p. 73) on collective action is relevant. When communities have substitutes for cooperation, they will be less successful in procuring public goods. For example, the existence of high-quality private schools will diminish the collective action in support of better public education, as potential supporters will send their children to private schools (i.e., vote with their feet instead of raising their "voice"). In this case, expectations of unilateral action by the U.S. acted as a substitute for cooperation.

56. Upton (1884, p. 246).

57. Russell (1898, pp. 251–64).

58. It was actually in this loss of gold and growing stock of silver that the conference found its origins. Disturbed by these developments in their monetary stock, French officials began prompting the U.S. government on the possibility of another monetary conference. See *Ibid.*, p. 260.

59. Both in France and in Germany silver was increasingly shunned in business transactions, as shopkeepers and retailers made pronounced efforts to give out change in silver, while buyers were reluctant to accept.

60. Russell (1898, p. 259).

61. *Ibid.*, pp. 269–71.

62. *Ibid.*, pp. 274–78, 298.

63. *Ibid.*, pp. 286, 287, 309, 310.

64. *Ibid.*, pp. 313, 314.

65. U.S. House of Representatives (1881, p. 466).

66. *Ibid.*, pp. 502–05. Now only very few still believed that a viable regime required only the participation of France and the U.S. See Russell (1898, p. 306).

67. Russell (1898, pp. 256–58).

68. *Ibid.*, p. 325.

69. *Ibid.*, p. 265.

70. *Ibid.*, pp. 307, 311, 320, 325, 353 and Goodhart (1972, p. 107).

71. Delegates remembered well how just prior to the conference Germany had taken advantage of an increase in the price of silver orchestrated by British intervention in the market to stabilize the pound-rupee rate. See Russell (1898, p. 254).

72. Russell (1898, pp. 211–14, 249, 292, 303) and Horton (1892).

73. See the statement of Britain's Rothschild in Russell (1898, p. 385).

74. U.S. Senate (1893, p. 10).

75. Russell (1898, pp. 390, 399, 400).

76. *Ibid.*, pp. 391–96.

77. The most obvious example of this are inter-central-bank advances so that central banks in need of gold could maintain international and/or national convertibility. It is this element of cooperation that the advocates of the international-orchestra-of-central-banks argument underscore. As Eichengreen (1992, p. 31) representatively avers, in terms of the stability of the classical gold standard "international cooperation was key." Eichengreen highlights the importance of cooperation in crisis (part-time cooperation). See also Keynes (1930, V. II, pp. 306, 307); Scammell ([1965] 1985); and Eichengreen (1986a, 1986b, and 1991).

78. He (p. 275) quoted a monetary expert of the period, Luzzati: "Today . . . the central banks remain almost inaccessible in their majestic solitude, and only with exception do they communicate with one another."

79. Beyen (1949, p. 29) tells an interesting story which is indicative of the domestic orientation of central bankers during the period. In 1912–13 Directors of the Reichsbank came to Holland. Upon their visit, a Bank of Netherlands official spent a very long lunch with them. Upon his return to the Bank in the afternoon, he was criticized by another official for wasting time on much less important business. "Your work is here," said the latter, "not in coffee-houses."

80. The authoritative works on the Bank of England, Clapham (1944, V. I & II) and Sayers (1970, and 1976, V. I), bear this out. There is a striking absence of references to cooperation between the Bank and foreign monetary authorities. Findings in the Statistical Appendix support this. Equations 2–11 show a statistically significant coefficient for the Bank of England discount rate's effect on the discount rates of the other nine central banks in only two cases (Italy and Germany). The rates of the supposedly weaker central banks of Belgium, Spain, and Italy, in fact, have as many statistically significant effects on other central banks as the Bank of England has (two). In the Granger tests, in only one case (the Bank of Spain) do we find a result suggesting that the Bank of England rate Granger causes another central bank discount rate. In fact, the tests show that the rates of other central banks are more likely to have a Granger causal impact on the Bank of England rate (in the case of Switzerland, Holland, Austria, and Belgium) than the Bank of England rate has on other central bank rates. Neither did the Bank of England influence other central banks indirectly through its effects on the British economy or through its effects on world prices. Equations 16–22 and Granger

tests on the impact of the Bank rate and reserves both on international prices and the British economy show few statistically significant F-values. We would expect much more out of a conductor of the international orchestra than the tests for both direct and indirect influences over other central banks suggest.

81. Beyen (1949, p. 31) and Eichengreen (1986a, pp. 139, 140).

82. The equations in the Statistical Appendix are consistent with this lack of explicit cooperation. In testing for interbank impacts with respect to discount rates (when controlling for the effects of past values of the discount rates themselves, as well as all present values of the rates of other banks), we find relatively few statistically significant coefficients (12). (See equations 2–11.) In seven of the ten equations, we find one or no statistically significant coefficient. In three of the equations (5, 8, 10) we find no independent impact of other discount rates. This latter finding is all the more revealing since we would expect to see some independent impacts of more powerful central banks like the Bank of England or the Bank of France on the rates of these relatively weaker central banks of Holland, Spain, and Switzerland. Granger tests do show an impact by the Bank of England on the Bank of Spain, but not on the Banks of Switzerland and Holland. We see consistent inter-bank effects between England-Germany (equations 2 and 7) and England-Italy (equations 2 and 6). But neither of these relations shows up in the Granger tests.

83. Bloomfield (1959, pp. 57–59), Viner (1937, pp. 273, 274), Kindleberger (1984, p. 64), and Ford (1989, p. 219). Goodhart (1972, pp. 136, 137) notes that some of the most fundamental cooperation was actually between private and central banks on one hand, and foreign governments on another. British banks were most active in carrying on such links, but the goals were grounded in the fiscal objectives of the participating governments rather than the stabilization of any kinds of monetary relations between nations. For example, British banks would help manage foreign nations' public finances, both by making advances and floating government securities on the London market. This was, in fact, very typical of colonial financial management.

84. Polanyi (1957, p. 12).

85. Friedman and Schwartz (1963, p. 111).

86. Bloomfield (1959, pp. 57–59).

87. Morgan (1952, pp. 176, 183).

88. Kindleberger (1984, p. 186).

89. Feis (1930, p. 197). The syndicate that bought U.S. government bonds in exchange for gold in 1895 found the transaction to be quite beneficial as it contracted to buy 30-year, 4% bonds at 104½ and shortly thereafter sold them at 112¼. See Friedman and Schwartz (1963, p. 111).

90. Kindleberger (1984, pp. 124, 125).

91. Bloomfield (1959, pp. 57–59).

92. Kindleberger (1984, pp. 76, 83, 84, 103–106).

93. This suggests that market rates were driving central bank discount rates rather than vice versa. This is perfectly consistent with the private imperatives of central banks, one of which was (as any other bank) to stay competitive with the market price for discounts.

94. U.S. Senate (1910d, p. 301).

95. Viner (1937, p. 273) and Kindleberger (1984, pp. 185–188). Tooke is quoted in Kindleberger (p. 185).

96. Sayers (1970, pp. 102–115) and Kindleberger (1984, p. 188).

97. There were no absolute commitments to lend in last resort, not even from the Bank of England.

98. Viner (1937, p. 274) and Kindleberger (1984, p. 188).

99. Bloomfield (1963, pp. 25, 26).

100. The findings in the Statistical Appendix suggest that interbank impacts were limited even within monetary blocs, however. In the Latin bloc (Italy, France, Switzerland, and Belgium), the only statistically significant impact we find is from the Bank of Switzerland on the Bank of France (see equations 3–6). None of the other Latin members show any independent impact on each other's official discount rates. Surprisingly, the Bank of France appears to have no impact on its satellite banks. In the Northern Europe bloc (Germany, Austria, Holland—equations 7, 8, 11), none appear to have any impact on the others' official discount rates.

101. This was no different from a practice on the part of domestic commercial banks which attempted to influence the central bank discount rate so as to maintain some desired conditions in financial markets. In 1907, for example, the principal joint-stock banks of London transferred 3 million pounds sterling to the Bank of England so it would not have to raise its rate and put upward pressure on their own discount rates. See Hawtrey (1938, p. 117).

102. Ford (1989, p. 219), Sayers (1970, pp. 102–15), and Bloomfield (1959, p. 24).

103. Such a concern was not restricted to the Bank of France. It is therefore not surprising that central banks gave more aid to the Bank of England than they received since financial distress more easily transmitted *from* London than *to* London. Hence the Directors of the Bank could afford to be somewhat more complacent in the face of foreign troubles than other central bankers could in the face of potential crises in London. As British Treasury official Blackett noted, "Foreign countries are too much interested in the stability of the London money market to regard a threatened collapse with equanimity." Quoted in de Cecco (1974, p. 189). See also Viner (1945).

104. U.S. Senate (1910d, p. 301).

105. This bears on Eichengreen's (1992) argument that part-time cooperation (i.e., accommodation in crisis) was crucial to the stability of the regime.

106. U.S. Senate (1909, p. 230) and Beach (1935, pp. 143, 144).

107. Hawtrey (1938, pp. 90–97).

108. Clare (1909, pp. 111–16) and U.S. Senate (1910a, p. 147).

109. In this respect, central bank relations with other central banks mirrored some consistency with the relations between central banks and their own domestic banks. Competition was at least as prevalent as cooperation, especially in the earlier half of the century. When competition created problems for various institutions (usually private banks), schemes of accommodation were promptly forthcoming. See King (1936, pp. 288, 296, 302–20), Beach (1935, p. 150), and Kindleberger (1984, p. 105).

110. Bank for International Settlements (1943, p. 126).

111. Triffin (1964) and Bloomfield (1959). The effects of paralleling macroeconomic outcomes on the regime's stability are discussed in Chapter 7.

112. But, of course, the competition may have been more destabilizing than the paralleling of rates was stabilizing. Paralleling central bank rates may well have owed more to the fact that the various central banks were following domestic market rates, and these latter rates paralleled across nations.

Chapter 4

1. See especially Gilpin (1975 and 1981), Krasner (1976), Keohane (1980), and Kindleberger (1973). See Keohane (1980 and 1984) and Snidal (1985a) for critical surveys. And for more recent work on hegemony, see Russett (1985), Strange (1987), Yarbrough and Yarbrough (1987), Young (1989), James and Lake (1989), and Ikenberry and Kupchan (1990). In the specific area of monetary hegemony, see especially Rowland (1976), Calleo and Rowland (1973), Calleo (1976), and Cohen (1977).

2. Keohane (1984, pp. 140, 141), Block (1977, p. 13), Carr ([1939] 1966, p. 85), Gilpin (1975, pp. 97, 138), Cleveland (1976, pp. 52–55), and Kindleberger (1981b, pp. 267, 268).

3. Snidal (1985a) identifies two main strands in the hegemonic stability literature. One strand conceives of hegemonic behavior as "coercive leadership." In this behavior mode, the hegemon "forces subordinate states to make contributions" to collective outcomes (often conceptualized as public goods) which are generally beneficial to both, but may be disproportionately beneficial to the hegemon (p. 589). This type of hegemon is invariably self-interested, or rational, because the hegemon is expected to receive net benefits from cooperation (although the distribution of gains between hegemon and subordinate states is not clear). In an extreme form of coercive hegemony, the dominant power may be malevolent, imposing extraordinary burdens on subordinate nations to benefit only itself. The other type of hegemony is "benevolent leadership," where a hegemon expends significant resources to bring about collective outcomes that again are likely to be mutually beneficial, although here the benevolence (if morally dictated as Kindleberger [1981a] suggests) may result in a disproportionate benefit for subordinate nations (the group is what collective action theory calls "privileged"), while the hegemon may incur a net loss. Snidal (p. 590) notes that the two strands of hegemony are not logically incompatible, and hence some combination of the two may be conceptualized.

Although Snidal's typology is neither exhaustive nor completely non-arbitrary, it is useful because it integrates so much of the extant literature and ranks behavior based on very intelligible motivations. Hence, notwithstanding its limitations, it will serve as my focal point for assessing British monetary hegemony in the 19th century.

4. The first question bears both on the issues of the regime's origin and the regime's stability. The second bears most directly on the issue of the regime's stability. The third bears most directly on the origin of the regime.

5. The Treasury's limited influence in this period was compounded by its loose relations with the Bank of England.

6. Ziegler (1988, pp. 248, 249).

7. The following observations on Parliamentary monetary debates come from a survey of Great Britain, *Hansard's Parliamentary Debates*, from 1860 to 1914 on the following issues: banks, bimetallism, coinage, currency, international money, mint, money, and international conferences.

8. The survey of *Hansard's* suggests that MPs were relatively uninformed about issues of money in general.

9. Only a handful of such debates actually went beyond a brief exchange among MPs.

10. In matters of grand monetary diplomacy, Parliament showed deference to the Foreign Office as an initiator of international negotiations.

11. For a representative cross section of debates on international monetary issues, see Great Britain, *Hansard's Parliamentary Debates* (December 5, 1867, V. 190, pp. 601, 602; May 12, 1868, V. 192, pp. 107–10; August 6, 1869, V. 198, pp. 1408–22; May 4, 1872, V. 209, pp. 1324, 1325; August 1, 1872, V. 213, pp. 213, 249; August 9, 1872, V. 213, p. 834; June 12, 1882, V. 270, p. 829; May 5, 1885, V. 297, pp. 1645, 1646; June 4, 1889, V. 336, pp. 1869–1923; March 11, 1890, V. 342, pp. 496, 497; February 28, 1893, V. 9 [4th series], pp. 574–688; February 26, 1895, V. 30, pp. 1573–1655; March 17, 1896, V. 38, pp. 1181–1253; March 26, 1901, V. 91, p. 1385; May 14, 1902, V. 108, p. 200; July 30, 1905, V. 126, pp. 894, 895; March 16, 1905, V. 143, p. 187; and March 9, 1909, V. 185, p. 1094).

12. On negotiations between banks, see de Cecco (1974, pp. 150–70).

13. Platt (1968, p. 10).

14. The FO did have a much clearer goal for Continental geostrategic relations: maintain peace and the balance of power. But economic hegemony was never part of this objective.

15. Platt (1968, p. xviii) and Feis (1930, p. 87).

16. It was common to hear of British diplomats overburdened with economic work issue complaints about the "lack of political work." See Platt (1968, pp. xx, xxi).

17. Platt (1968, pp. xviii, 19, 23) and Grenville (1964, p. 437).

18. Platt (1968, p. xxxiv) notes that diplomats deviated from this hands-off approach only under "exceptional circumstances."

19. It is indicative that in Europe money was the last area of economic relations to escape the movement of socialist reform.

20. This representative response was that of Sir Edward Grey to British bondholders protesting a Brazilian default in 1914. Quoted in Feis (1930, p. 110). On the hands-off policy of the Foreign Office, see also Feis (1930, pp. 85, 86, 106, 107, 330) and Platt (1968, pp. 13, 14, 32).

21. Quoted in Platt (1968, p. 42).

22. Undersecretary Earl Percy addressing Parliament as to the Foreign Office's policy with respect to requests for foreign loans. Quoted in *Ibid.*, p. 13.

23. Platt (1968, pp. 12–16).

24. Feis (1930, pp. 107, 110, 113).

25. Foreign Minister Clarendon stated that because this was a matter of ordinary business, it was not something the British government could interfere with easily. See Ziegler (1988, p. 173).

26. It was in these areas that the strongest intervention arose. See Feis (1930, pp. 98, 99).

27. Such might not be the case if the international political economy were functioning so consistently with British interests that British officials felt the best strategy was to do nothing at all. The period of the gold standard was hardly such a period, however. Markets were being increasingly closed to British products, the relative productivity of British industry was declining, and other nations on the Continent and the U.S. were rising to challenge Britain's economic dominance (one of these nations—Germany—was growing more threatening in a geostrategic context).

It is still possible that a hegemonic power could remain inactive if officials do not perceive changes in the international system that adversely impact on the hegemon. This might relate to Friedberg's (1988) argument that actual British perceptions of its relative decline were mixed. However, in this period, the changing opportunities for British trade (that it was becoming increasingly difficult to penetrate other industrial markets) and growing security threats on the Continent (especially Germany) were fairly apparent to officials and groups in Britain. There was certainly enough of a consensus to warrant a stronger foreign policy posture than in fact we saw in the period if Great Britain were acting anything at all like a classic hegemon (either to improve its own position if acting coercively, or improve the state of the world if acting benevolently).

28. Kennedy (1981b, pp. 42, 43) notes how foreign policy orientations were integrated into partisan political competition. Clear and forceful platforms on foreign policy were often valuable in unifying party factions that disagreed on domestic issues.

29. See also Bourne (1970).

30. Curzon saw the Persian Gulf as most vital, while Salisbury and Chamberlain saw the Near East, Africa, and China as most vital. See Grenville (1964, p. 297).

31. *Ibid.*, pp. 162, 163, Ward and Gooch (1923, V. III, pp. 122–126), and Kennedy (1981b, p. 79). Aside from partisan affiliation, some of the disagreement on foreign policy emanated from different perceptions of Britain's relative decline. See Friedberg (1988).

32. Both the Prime Minister and Foreign Minister's preference for intervention could not overcome popular and Parliamentary opposition.

33. Quoted in Swartz (1985, p. 56). Ward and Gooch (1923, V. III, p. 260) see the for-

eign policy of Gladstone and Salisbury as a deviation from the "spirited foreign policy" of the past, and an ascension to a style of "intelligent inaction."

34. Knaplund (1935, pp. 10, 13, 14, 39) and Bourne (1970, pp. 398–400).

35. Grenville (1964, pp. 16–19, 68, 437, 438) and Bourne (1970, p. 148).

36. Bourne (1970, p. 163) and Swartz (1985, pp. 56–60).

37. Kennedy (1981b, p. 43).

38. The pattern in expanding the Empire appeared to be defensive in that vital strategic and economic routes were bolstered rather than extended. Uganda's annexation, for example, was undertaken for the goal of acquiring a position from which to defend the Upper Nile against a potential French threat. The acquisition of Cyprus and the Suez Canal served to secure the route to India. Acquisitions consolidated existing chains rather than starting new ones. See Bourne (1970, p. 153), Knaplund (1935, p. 69), and Platt (1968, p. 357).

39. Knaplund (1935, p. 10) and Kennedy (1981b, p. 92).

40. Ward and Gooch (1923, V. III, p. 6) and Bourne (1970, pp. 123, 124, 154).

41. Although, as suggested by the findings in the next chapter, even as the most influential financial institution in London, the extent of its influence was limited.

42. Since the central banks were not involved in determining international monetary standards (the cases of international monetary unions and the conferences suggest that this duty was the preserve of national governments represented by monetary diplomats), the relevant goal of hegemony with respect to the Bank would have been oriented around stabilizing rather than building monetary regimes.

43. Chancellor of the Exchequer Charles Montegu found that the idea of giving a charter to a corporation offering to lend money to the state and subscribed to by some of the leading financiers of London was the best way to raise money for war in 1694. On the origins of the Bank, see Clapham (1944, V. I, Chapter 1).

44. Great Britain, *Hansard's Parliamentary Debates* (May 18, 1866, V. 183, p. 148).

45. Quoted in Gregory (1964, V. I, p. L).

46. *Ibid.*

47. The specific questions were addressed to the Governor and Directors of the Bank in U.S. Senate (1910e, pp. 8, 11, 17).

48. The Bank had even less to do with the Foreign Office and the Board of Trade. See Feis (1930, p. 86) and Dodwell (1934, p. 65).

49. de Cecco (1974, p. 204).

50. Fetter (1965, pp. 281, 282) and Dodwell (1934, p. 66).

51. Great Britain, *Hansard's Parliamentary Debates* (November 26, 1888, V. 331, pp. 136, 137).

52. Dodwell (1934, pp. 65, 66).

53. Great Britain, *Hansard's Parliamentary Debates* (May 11, 1866, V. 183, p. 841).

54. Keynes himself believed that greater government control over the financial system was the only way for the British system to withstand war. See de Cecco (1974, pp. 138, 139).

55. de Cecco (1974, p. 169).

56. The relevant goal of hegemony in this case would be regime creation rather than regime maintenance.

57. There is, as far as my survey of the literature on hegemony has indicated, a consensus in the work on the subject that hegemons will have more of an international orientation than less powerful nations, simply because their stakes in the international system are greater.

58. Russell (1898, pp. 18–22).

59. Great Britain, *Report From the Royal Commission on International Coinage* (1868, p. 149).

60. *Ibid*, p. 188.

61. Lipson (1983) suggests that hegemons would be more reluctant to start up regimes than maintain them because start-up costs are higher. In this case, it appeared that Great Britain faced limited start-up costs.

62. Germany was a supporter of gold, and France was poised for some kind of union.

63. The literature on hegemonic stability suggests that regimes are most amenable to hegemonic construction when spoilers (nations which have both the strength and motivation to undermine the regime) are absent.

64. The proposal called for a fixed-legal-bimetallic ratio in nations making the transition to gold.

65. All of the literature on hegemony that takes a "supportership" orientation (i.e., regimes are most achievable through collective action of both hegemons and their supporters) suggests that such a circumstance would produced the highest likelihood of success in regime building, and certainly produce the most willingness to contribute to regime initiatives on the part of hegemons. On the supportership strand of the hegemonic-stability literature, see Kindleberger (1981a, p. 252, and 1973), Lake (1983), McKeown (1983, p. 79), Stein (1984, p. 358), Gowa (1984), Keohane (1984, pp. 136–41), Strange (1987, p. 574), Putnam and Bayne (1987, pp. 272, 273), and Young (1989).

66. U.S. Senate (1867, p. 55).

67. Evidence cuts strongly against the existence of any insidious intention to sabotage.

68. Russell (1898, pp. 74, 75).

69. Great Britain, *Report From the Royal Commission on International Coinage* (1868, p. 176). See also his argument in Jevons ([1884] 1909, p. 226).

70. Great Britain, *Report From the Royal Commission on International Coinage* (1868, pp. 68, 71, 114, 127).

71. The literature on hegemony exhibits an active rather than passive vision of hegemony: hegemons are more likely to build regimes than to stop regimes from coming into existence. The closest strand in the literature that appears relevant to the British behavior appears to be the work of James and Lake (1989) where they suggest hegemons can influence international outcomes by either passive or active use of their resources (they emphasize active use, however).

72. In fact, the British delegation voted in the affirmative on various points at the conference, as well as on the final proposal calling for union around gold and the franc. A blocking hegemon would not allow its representatives to provide any such support for a regime. Furthermore, evidence suggests that the British did not carefully consider the consequences of their reluctance. This was apparent in the delegate's comments and communications in public documents.

73. Blank (1978) underscores just how outward (i.e., international) an orientation hegemons will have.

74. In the literature on hegemony, when a hegemon is not charitable, it is almost always rational.

75. France, after all, would be undertaking an even greater burden by minting a new coin (the 25-franc piece) which was expected to be in international demand.

76. Great Britain, *Gold and Silver Commission* ([1888] 1936, pp. 71, 72) and Ellstaetter (1895, p. 39).

77. The inflationary possibilities of silver depreciation were not altogether lamented during the periods of falling prices, but when prices were perceived as having stabilized, concerns ran in an inflation-busting direction. See especially Price (1878, pp. 395–99).

78. Leavens (1939, p. 72), Price (1878, pp. 395–399), and Great Britain, *Gold and Silver Commission* ([1888] 1936, pp. 94–100).

79. Great Britain, *Report of the Commissioners Representing Great Britain at the Paris Conference* (1878, p. 9).

80. This is extremely unusual behavior for what is considered to be a typical hegemon: having to be prodded by colonies and lesser powers to discuss international cooperation which promises to be in the hegemon's interests. See *Ibid.* and Russell (1898, p. 203).

81. Russell (1898, pp. 207, 225).

82. U.S. Senate (1879, p. 51).

83. *Ibid.*, pp. 50–52. The delegation itself was personally of the opinion that some regime should be formed. "We were unanimously . . . of opinion that it was better that the currency of the world should continue to rest upon two metals." See Great Britain, *Report of the Commissioners Representing Great Britain at the Paris Conference* (1878, p. 15).

84. Russell (1898, p. 244) and U.S. Senate (1879, pp. 94, 95).

85. Relevant theoretical literature on regime building suggests that when costs of building regimes are lower, we should expect the hegemon to be all the more willing to initiate some cooperative scheme. See Lipson (1983) and Jervis (1983).

86. Britain, of course, also could influence silver demand in India, which historically dwarfed even what were exaggerated estimates of German excess silver. Discussions in the British Parliament on circulation also suggested that Britain could absorb some silver for small-coin use.

87. British monetary elites were also of the opinion that failure to resuscitate silver would obstruct an escape for the world economy from the deflation of the 1870s.

88. Even prominent ex-Governor Henry Gibbs was advocating bimetallism.

89. This vindicated some of the fears that Germany stood ready to exploit a bimetallic regime by dumping its excess silver on the market when the price of silver rose.

90. Russell (1898, pp. 254–258, 267). It is interesting how the British government was able throughout the period to deflect so much pressure from its society. In this sense it appeared to be a "stronger" state vis-à-vis its society than many have traditionally believed. On the strong-weak state argument, see Krasner (1978).

91. U.S. House of Representatives (1881, pp. 480, 505).

92. *Ibid*, pp. 269, 512.

93. *Ibid.*, p. 481.

94. U.S. Senate (1876, V. II, p. 109).

95. U.S. Senate (1893, p. 9).

96. The intention here was at least consistent with one common vision of hegemony: coercive hegemony.

97. U.S. Senate (1893, pp. 135, 136).

98. It is interesting that behavior generated by a weak disposition had significant influence in obstructing regimes.

99. Outside of the conferences France acted like a typical hegemon in dictating developments in the Latin Monetary Union.

100. In fact, given the support of other powerful nations, a regime did not require hegemonic resources to consummate, only a willingness to make limited commitments by a nation that influenced the international market for metals. Furthermore, aside from itself, prospective regimes had no serious spoilers outside of Germany. But even here a strong British commitment could have neutralized the German threat (i.e., Britain could commit India to converting German silver, or convince Germany to liquidate her excess silver gradually).

101. Russell (1898, p. 375), in fact, called Britain the "great obstruction to international bimetallism" in this period.

102. We would have expected a coercive hegemon to pressure other nations to accept the Rothschild Plan.

103. John Sherman (1895, p. 411) talked about British "pride in its existing coins" as a fundamental source of reluctance.

104. In fact, given the state of British coinage, it appears that some recoinage was necessary irrespective of regime creation, and also that further buying of silver would actually facilitate the circulation of small coin.

Chapter 5

1. Low convertibility risk and highly developed financial institutions gave London an absolute advantage in attracting international capital. And consequently, it came to possess the largest stock of capital (both long and short term) for foreign investment.

2. While the weak form of hegemony may tolerate some limitations in the influence of the Bank over British finance, the strong form would require more absolute control, since the former requires only the creation of domestic conditions, while the latter depends on using domestic conditions to bring about some desired international outcomes. For example, to effect tighter credit in the domestic system, a small increase in the central bank rate may suffice (i.e., since the transaction costs of domestic investment are smaller, domestic capital is more interest elastic with respect to changes in domestic rates). But effecting a state of tight credit on the international level would require even tighter credit domestically (i.e., higher domestic rates) because the lower interest-elasticity of international investment (given higher transaction costs of international investment) would make foreign banks sensitive only to larger changes in domestic rates. Hence, effecting international credit requires greater power over domestic credit because the central bank must be able to bring about even greater changes in domestic market rates.

3. Before the 19th century, not only was there a lack of any sort of central banking theory in Great Britain, but also a lack of banking theory in general. See Fetter (1965, p. 7).

4. The Peel Act of 1844 only split the Bank into two departments (Issue and Banking) and made the issue of banknotes subject to explicit rules. But in terms of the management and goals of the Banking Department, little changed.

5. Hankey (1873) and Sayers (1976, V. I).

6. The administration was carried on by a Court consisting of 24 Directors, as well as a Governor and Deputy Governor. The Governors were normally chosen from the body of directors for two-year terms. The Directors tended to come from the ranks of London's merchant bankers. Bagehot ([1873] 1921, pp. 42, 43, 65, 66) reflected a common view among London's financial elite in seeing the management of the Bank as amateurish: claiming that merchant bankers as a class were normally of inferior knowledge with respect to the art of banking.

7. This is not to say that public responsibility and profitable banking were always incompatible (e.g., lending in crisis could be profitable at penalty rates and short terms), but more often they were.

8. But even this responsibility was never really independent of its own private concerns as it too, like any other private bank, had to maintain its own obligations to convert notes and deposits on demand (i.e., protect its own solvency).

9. Conversely, shareholders often criticized reserve holdings as too high. The Bank was very much involved in the intense competition among joint-stock banks with respect to their dividends. See Beach (1935, p. 162) and Fetter (1965, p. 272).

10. Fetter (1965, pp. 14, 15, 58).

11. *Ibid.*, pp. 154–56, 273; Viner (1937, p. 264); King (1936, p. 159); and Bagehot ([1873] 1921, p. 37).

12. Gregory (1964, V. II, p. 28).

13. Hankey's statements became a special target for those in the London financial community that vilified such public disclaimers by Bank Directors. Quoted in Bagehot ([1873] 1921, pp. 162, 163).

14. Wood (1939, pp. 166, 167).

15. Quoted in Price (1878, p. 534).

16. Acres (1931, pp. 522–25, 565–76).

17. Dodwell (1934). Knowing the size of these balances was crucial to monitoring the pulse of the financial system, since they were the largest and most volatile in the Bank.

18. De Cecco (1974, p. 83) called this the most serious "internal contradiction in the British financial system," adding that it was responsible for causing or at least aggravating every prewar crisis in the British monetary system.

19. Gregory (1964, V. II, p. 55) and Fetter (1965, pp. 152–56, 268).

20. Gregory (1964, V. II, pp. 53, 54) and Wood (1939, pp. 165–68).

21. Some students of the Bank in the 19th century note that there was a tendency for the Bank to be more sensitized to the public when financial conditions were turbulent, and function solely as a profit-maker in good times. See Viner (1945, p. 63) and Clare (1909, pp. 57, 58).

22. It is indicative of the identity crisis of the Bank that Morris himself also made statements suggesting that the Bank had no public responsibilities. Bagehot's ([1873] 1921, pp. 153, 154) claim that the century saw no statements from the Court acknowledging public responsibilities should be qualified, since comments on a dual mandate were occasionally made. The claim is more valid if we search for strong statements of public responsibility, which I have not found. See Gregory (1964, V. II, pp. 19, 20) and Clare (1909, pp. 51, 52).

23. Sayers (1976, V. I, p. 27) and Gregory (1964, V. II, p. 20).

24. Pippenger (1984) and King (1936, p. 38).

25. This works against Rockoff's (1986, p. 165) contention that Court statements denying public responsibility were issued to break down moral hazard in the British financial system. Had the Court actually been thinking about the British system as much as arguments about moral hazard suggest, we would expect the actions of the Bank to have been more consistently in the public interest than they actually were.

26. Wood (1939, p. 5) and Sayers (1970, pp. 26, 27).

27. Scammell ([1965] 1985, p. 110), Sayers (1957, p. 12), and Clare (1909, pp. 8, 9). Even when some distance did appear between the rates, the Bank was not averse to discounting at the market rate for its best customers (this practice began in 1878). This more often occurred when the Bank rate was above that of the market. Hence, even a divergent rate could still restrict the Bank's independence.

Coefficients in equations 14 and 19 (see Statistical Appendix) show a close proximity (BE and GBDR) even in yearly-average movements, although Granger tests over 3 lags are statistically insignificant.

28. Tennant (1865, pp. 319, 320), Wood (1939, p. 141), Sayers (1970, pp. 125, 126), and Andreades (1909, pp. 315, 316).

29. Beach (1935, pp. 91, 110, 111) attributed some of the procyclicity of the ratio to the fact that the Bank allowed more specie into circulation in upswing, which is a different sort of central banking imperative from that of the holder of the national reserve.

30. In several periods of financial distress in London, leading banks discussed forming their own clearing union so as to impose more stable conditions onto the market as a response to the aggressive competition of the Bank of England, which they perceived as compounding the distress. If not for ongoing inabilities to cooperate among private banks, the Bank might have faced stronger competition as London and Britain's central banking facility. See King (1936, pp. 75, 288–95).

31. de Cecco (1974, p. 83). The incentive was especially pronounced in the area of note issue, since the Act of 1844 stated that the note issue privileges of a failed bank would be transferred to the Bank of England.

32. Andreades (1909, p. 266), Gregory (1964, V. II, pp. 30, 31, and 1964, V. I, pp. xxxiii, liii), King (1936, pp. 60, 62), Warren (1903, p. 25), and Morgan (1965, pp. 9, 10).

33. King (1936, p. 289) noted how competition in the London market was especially cutthroat.

34. King (1936, p. 284) noted that restricting rediscounts was more a function of the Bank's concern with its own position than with any concern "for the broad interests of the commercial world."

35. Goodhart (1972, p. 105) and Viner (1932, p. 14).

36. Reprinted in Sayers (1976, Appendixes, p. 23).

37. Irrespective of changes in the influence of the rate, it was consistently considered and treated as the Bank's most powerful weapon by its Directors, especially after 1844 when the Bank Act essentially eliminated discretionary note issue.

38. Quoted in Wood (1939, p. 138).

39. Quoted in Price (1878, p. 534).

40. Quoted in Hawtrey (1938, p. 66). See also the testimony of Gilbart in Gregory (1964, V. I, p. 80).

41. Scammell ([1965] 1985, pp. 108–11), Gregory (1964, V. II, p. 318), Sayers (1970), and King (1936, pp. 312–15).

42. Scammell ([1965] 1985, pp. 112–14) and Sayers (1970). Sayers sees the crisis of 1907 as introducing the period of the effective rate.

43. Scammell ([1965] 1985, p. 110), Gregory (1964, V. I, p. xxxv), and Wood (1939, p. 5).

44. Especially glaring failures in effecting the rate to abate an outflow of gold were visible in 1885, '90, '91, '93, and 1903. The Baring crisis saw the Bank frustrated by an inability to attract gold even after raising the rate to 6%. In 1892 and '93 the Bank's ineffective rate caused the Court to pay out sovereigns rather than bullion so as to discourage the export of gold. See Sayers (1976, V. I, pp. 50, 51), King (1936, pp. 297, 298), Morgan (1965, pp. 202–07), and Beach (1935, p. 140).

45. The link between the Bank and market rates was made even more tenuous by the fact that the Bank might also on occasion discount at a rate higher than the official Bank rate. See Sayers (1970, pp. 52–55) and King (1936, p. 295).

46. Sayers (1976, Appendixes, pp. 22, 23) and de Cecco (1974, p. 197).

47. Beach (1935, pp. 143, 150, 151, 159), King (1936, pp. 308–11), Morgan (1965, p. 222), Gregory (1964, V. I, p. xl), and Sayers (1970, p. 38).

48. Quoted in Clapham (1944, V. II, p. 367).

49. Given the competition between the Bank and major banks of London, de Cecco (1974, pp. 100, 101) calls the period 1890–1914 one of "anarchy" in British finance. In fact, it wasn't until 1911 that formal and ongoing talks were instituted between the Bank and other major banks. Interestingly, this was done at the initiative of the private banks. See Warren (1903, p. 237), Sayers (1976, Appendixes, p. 23), and King (1936, pp. 308–20).

50. de Cecco (1974, pp. 166–68).

51. Wood (1939, p. 139).

52. Hawtrey (1938, p. 67). See also the Samuel Jones Loyd testimony in Gregory (1964, V. I, p. 44).

53. See also Cramp (1962, pp. 3–7) and Beach (1935, pp. 152–54).

54. Eichengreen (1989).

55. Treasury official Blackett noted in a 1914 memo that the amalgamation of London

banking shifted the "center of gravity [in London finance] . . . from the Bank parlour to the Committee of the Clearing House as representing an alliance of all the most important banks." Quoted in de Cecco (1974, p. 197).

56. de Cecco (1974, pp. 21, 22).

57. Sayers (1976, V. I, pp. 9, 10). Yeager (1976, p. 302) estimates that the gold holdings of the Bank gravitated around 2% of the money supply of Great Britain during the period of the gold standard.

58. Bagehot ([1873] 1921, p. 47). See also Goschen (1876, p. 372).

59. It is also apparent that the Bank wasn't even the first line of defense in times of financial distress. When the demand for money was appearing to edge toward excessive proportions, many banks would recall loans from discount houses rather than request discounts or advances from the Bank. See Yeager (1976, p. 302) and de Cecco (1974, pp. 132, 133).

60. See Figure A.7 in Statistical Appendix.

61. See Figure A.4.

62. Goodhart (1972, pp. 112, 113). He also notes (p. 114) that private banks were historically better at hitting the norm of a 15% reserve ratio than the Bank was.

63. Dutton (1984), Pippenger (1984), and Sayers (1976, V. I, p. 8, and 1970, p. 116). Data, however, show that the Bank rate was in fact weakly linked to the Bank's gold reserve. See Figure A.4, equations 14 and 15, and Granger tests on BERES-BE in Appendix. See also Eichengreen's (1989) findings.

64. Lovell (1957) shows that Bank discounting during the 18th century increased in periods of tightness.

65. The private obligations also translated into the maintenance of international convertibility, as foreign governments held sizable interest-bearing assets at the Bank of England which were convertible into gold upon request. See Eichengreen (1992, p. 43).

66. Hawtrey (1932, pp. 119–29).

67. Kindleberger (1984, p. 91).

68. Hawtrey (1932, p. 123).

69. King (1936, p. 110).

70. Gregory (1964, V. II, p. 16).

71. The limitation of discounts to discount houses was especially dangerous given that they functioned as a first line of defense in periods of financial distress. See Yeager (1976, p. 302) and U.S. Senate (1910b, p. 17).

72. King (1936, p. 215).

73. One way it did this was to charge higher rates on longer and inferior bills. See Gregory (1964, V. II, p. 54).

74. Sayers (1970, p. 23) and Morgan (1965, p. 197).

75. Morgan (1965, pp. 173, 174).

76. Sayers (1976, V. I, pp. 18, 19).

77. U.S. Senate (1910e, p. 111).

78. The Baring incident was more a case of crisis prevention owing to the perspicacity of Bank Governor Lidderdale, who orchestrated a banking consortium to back Baring's liabilities (the Bank itself put up a relatively small amount).

79. Governor Morris stated that the Act relieved the Bank "from any obligation" to the public. Quoted in Fetter (1965, p. 261). See also Goschen (1876, p. 133), Gregory (1964, V. II, p. 143), and Viner (1937, p. 229).

80. King (1936, p. 216), Morgan (1965, p. 163), and Gregory (1964, V. II, p. 143).

81. Hawtrey (1938, p. 67) and Bagehot ([1873] 1921).

82. Gregory (1964, V. I, pp. xxvi, xl) and Wood (1939, pp. 146–48). Beach (1935, p. 173) observed that this small reserve pool resulted in a monetary system with little slack; hence

exogenous shocks (e.g., sudden export of gold to the U.S.) could not be absorbed without some kind of pronounced adjustment in the Bank rate.

83. de Cecco (1974, p. 193) and Wood (1939, p. 148). Data show that the Bank rate was much more erratic than the other British series (see Figures A.5–A.8 in Appendix). The rate was especially erratic vis-à-vis real GNP and money aggregates, a condition diametrically opposed to the dictates of conventional central banking functions of managing inflation and the business cycle. When income became more variable after 1885 (see Figure A.5), movements in the rate vis-à-vis GNP were neither procyclical nor countercyclical. In fact, little sensitivity to income was apparent in the behavior of the rate (see Granger tests on BE-GBRGNP and equations 14 and 16).

84. In this sense, the Bank's concern for its proprietors (i.e., the profit motive) was a fundamental source of mismanaging the British economy. See Levy-Leboyer (1982, pp. 68, 69, 80, 93).

85. Sayers (1970, pp. 134, 135) and Clare (1909, pp. 56, 57).

86. King (1936, pp. 288–96).

87. Rockoff (1986), Price (1878, p. 551), Wood (1939, pp. 8, 160), and Morgan (1965, pp. 173, 174).

88. The inconsistency was not always the specific fault of disagreements among Directors, but sometimes a natural outcome of the trade-offs of central banking, as in the case of a central bank accepting slower economic growth so that it can restrain speculation in the stock market or limit inflation.

89. For example, when Bank Governor Lidderdale found in 1890 that Baring's liabilities were dangerously large, he discussed the problem with London's other major banking houses before framing an autonomous solution on the part of the Bank. See Warren (1903, pp. 211, 224, 230).

90. On the Bank's destabilizing behavior in periods surrounding crises before 1847, see Kindleberger (1984, p. 91), Fetter (1965, pp. 14, 15, 60, 113, 114, 165), Andreades (1909, pp. 250–53), King (1936, pp. 35, 36, 95–97), and Bagehot ([1873] 1921, pp. 170, 171).

91. Dornbusch and Frenkel (1984), Acres (1931, pp. 505, 506), Warren (1903, p. 36), Andreades (1909, pp. 334, 335), and Gregory (1964, V. II, pp. 30, 31).

92. Bagehot ([1873] 1921, p. 171) and Warren (1903, pp. 185–94).

93. Probably the most significant strategic mistake made by the Bank in this crisis was a reluctance to buy up new issues of government securities, which were considered the best securities of all in the market.

94. Batchelor (1986, p. 49).

95. Clapham (1944, V. II, pp. 332–34), Ziegler (1988, p. 254), Batchelor (1986, pp. 53, 54), and Sayers (1976, V. I, p. 3).

96. U.S. Senate (1910a, pp. 143, 144).

97. Its behavior in pre-crisis periods was especially assailable.

98. In his definitive work on British monetary orthodoxy during the 19th century, Fetter (1965, p. 255) himself states that he finds no evidence that the "Bank of England or the people of England felt any responsibility for managing the international gold standard." See also Yeager (1976, p. 305).

99. Quoted in Viner (1945, p. 64). See also Mints (1950, p. 107).

100. Gregory (1964, V. I, p. 5).

101. Sayers (1976, V. I, p. 9).

102. Quoted in Morgan (1965, p. 241).

103. Fischer (1982, pp. 166, 167) and Kindleberger (1978, pp. 187, 191).

104. Gregory (1964, V. I, p. 10).

105. Quoted from the testimony of German banker Gamp-Massounen in U.S. Senate (1910d, p. 276). See also Viner (1945, p. 64), Beach (1935, p. 143), and Broz (1989, p. 2).

106. Although the Court perceived such balances to be a problem, it exhibited no systematic policy to limit the convertibility of the balances. When it did act, its response was ad hoc and mostly concerned with balances held directly through the Bank. See U.S. Senate (1876, V. I., pp. 103, 104).

107. In 1913 the gold holdings of the Bank of England were equal to only 14.6% of the foreign exchange holdings of the 35 leading central banks in the world. The Bank also maintained among the lowest ratios of reserves to national imports (along with Holland) in the developed world, perhaps the best reflection of the British system's own precarious existence. See Bloomfield (1963, pp. 31, 32) and Lindert (1969, p. 10).

108. Hawtrey (1938, p. 108).

109. See also Viner (1945, p. 63) and Letiche (1959, p. 23).

110. See also Ford (1989, p. 223) and Mints (1950, p. 108).

111. This ineffective and erratic Bank of England rate is an outcome that cuts sharply against the argument, made by the leader-of-the-international-orchestra proponents, that the Bank of England rate stabilized the regime by providing a focal point for the coordination of central bank discount rates. If it was in fact meant to be a focal point, which it was not, it was neither influential nor stable enough for the purpose.

112. However, Granger tests and equations 2 and 3 suggest no influence either way.

113. Given the Bank's sensitivity to both international and domestic market conditions (because of the competitive posture emanating from the profit motive), we would expect its rate to rise when the demand for money also rose (because prices and/or economic growth were in an upswing), and for its rate to decline when the demand for money declined (i.e., slow growth and/or low prices). In fact, in Granger tests world manufactures prices show more influence on Bank of England reserves than vice versa.

114. In referring to the Bank's so-called leadership of the international banking orchestra, the authors note that this limited power over world credit made the Bank no more than a "second violinist."

115. See, for example, Norman's testimony in Gregory (1964, V. I, p. 7).

116. Morgan (1965, p. 194), Sayers (1970, pp. 24, 25, 133, 134), Ford (1989, pp. 221, 222), Clare (1909, pp. 8, 9) and King (1936, p. 74).

117. Morgenstern's (1959, p. 386) data show excessive variation of the Bank's rate relative to other major central banks on the Continent. In a period of 463 months from January 1876 to July of 1914, the Bank of England changed its rate 393 times (almost a change per month), while changes of the Bank of France and the Reichsbank numbered 277 and 55, respectively. On the variability of the rate see also Clough and Cole (1946, p. 630), Ford (1989, p. 236), U.S. Senate (1910c, pp. 189–96), and Andreades (1909, pp. 315, 316).

118. Beach (1935, p. 140) and Levy-Leboyer (1982, p. 68).

119. The findings show the discount rates of Switzerland, Belgium, Austria, and Holland Granger causing the discount rate of the Bank of England.

120. Gregory (1964, V. I, p. 64).

121. The Bank of England actually made conditions in the U.S. worse when it declared to its own houses that American acceptances were a menace to the stability of the London market.

122. Sayers (1970) and Kindleberger (1978, p. 189).

123. U.S. Senate (1910a, p. 145).

Chapter 6

1. There were some laggards like Japan, Austria-Hungary, and Russia which joined in the 1890s, but the essential nucleus of the regime was formed, as all the most advanced nations in the world had made the gold link before the end of the 1870s. See Chapter 2 for the specific timing of domestic monetary transformations.

2. Laughlin (1886, p. 160).

3. The U.S. too, after the Civil War, undertook extremely painful and unpopular measures to deflate in order to facilitate resumption. See McCallum (1989, pp. 319–21).

4. The quotes are in Yeager (1984, pp. 657–59) and Eichengreen (1989, p. 17).

5. U.S. Senate (1867, p. 51).

6. Hawtrey (1947, p. 78). Besides the ideological attachment to metal, there was also the issue of forgery: coins were much more difficult to forge than notes, hence reducing the problem of counterfeiting. See Fetter (1965, pp. 69–72).

7. Einzig (1970, pp. 221–23).

8. Bloomfield (1963, p. 16).

9. Great Britain began practicing a gold standard de facto in 1717.

10. Fetter (1965, p. 141).

11. *Ibid.*, pp. 141–64, 232.

12. Russell (1898, p. 148).

13. In this period, the term "civilized nations" was commonly used as a synonym for economically developed nations.

14. Russell (1898, p. 239). Other foundations for ideological compellence, such as gold's intrinsic superiority or rarity, seem to have been much less compelling in this period. However, Alexander Hamilton did acknowledge some such sources of attraction in the latter 18th century. See Laughlin (1886, pp. 13, 14).

15. Keynes ([1913] 1971, p. 13).

16. Kindleberger (1975, p. 51) and Clough and Cole (1946, p. 623).

17. Great Britain had looked to the Dutch two centuries earlier when developing its own banking system. See Kindleberger (1984, p. 52).

18. Farmer ([1886] 1969, p. 45). See also Friedman (1990a, p. 1168, and 1990b, p. 94).

19. Great Britain, *Hansard's Parliamentary Debates* (Vol. 30, 1895, p. 1650). On Disraeli, see Slater (1886, p. 45).

20. Russell (1898, p. 400).

21. U.S. Senate (1879, pp. 241, 242).

22. Stern (1977, p. 180).

23. Quoted in Hamerow (1972, p. 60).

24. Rosenburg (1962, p. 14) and Kindleberger (1975). More generally, policies liberalizing exchange were perceived as the reason for the prosperity enjoyed in Great Britain and the U.S. See Hamerow (1972, p. 346).

25. Stern (1977, p. 180).

26. Hamerow (1958, p. 254).

27. See the discussion of permissive factors below.

28. Eichengreen (1989, p. 16).

29. U.S. Senate (1876, V. II, p. 61).

30. Russell (1898, pp. 84, 85) and U.S. Senate (1876, V. II, p. 137).

31. U.S. Senate (1876, V. II, p. 273).

32. For illustrative cases, see Morgan-Webb (1934, pp. 22, 29), Taus (1943, p. 75), Helfferich (1927, p. 118), Kindleberger (1984, p. 23), Hawtrey (1947, p. 66), and Seyd (1868, p. 624).

In a recent paper Redish (1990b, p. 805) asks why the monetary standard of Great Britain (gold as the central monetary metal with token silver), being the most convenient in the early 19th century, was not copied by more nations at that time. Much of the reason, I believe, is to be found in differential rates of economic development. To the extent that monetary institutions are endogenous (i.e., conditions of economic exchange influence monetary institutions), it is only natural to expect Great Britain to be the first to opt for this more convenient monetary standard because it was the first to experience the industrial revolution. Seyd (1868,

p. 624) pointed out how Great Britain in the early 19th century, unlike other European nations, had reached a level of economic performance that disposed it favorably toward gold. Other nations were less compelled in this period, given the nature of their transactions. Their industrial revolutions would come in the mid to latter half of the century. In fact, the French Monetary Commission of 1790 resolved that gold was the natural standard of commercial nations because it was "easy of carriage," but that France at the time had neither the scale of domestic nor international trade to warrant a gold standard. See White (1891, p. 314). Helfferich (1927, p. 125) noted that the German compulsion toward gold in the early 19th century was mitigated by low incomes and the large number of small transactions.

33. Quoted in National Association of Manufacturers (1955, p. 4).

34. Evidence suggests that this bias must be qualified. Both France and Belgium tolerated a displacement favoring silver from 1832 to 1847 when the market ratio caused silver to be overvalued at their mints. In the period 1849–54 Belgium, Switzerland, Naples, Spain, and India instituted policies which diminished the monetary use of gold in response to large gold influxes into circulation. France instituted monetary commissions in 1851 and '57 to discuss solutions to the problems of declining silver circulation. The U.S. in 1853 and Latin Monetary nations in the 1860s reacted to a shrinking silver circulation by altering coinage laws. It should be noted, however, that the greatest concerns relating to the retention of silver in this period were over silver as a subsidiary coin. These practices and policies defending silver were principally stimulated by shortages in small coin. Laughlin's "bias," therefore, is truer of central money metals than metals in general. Developed nations showed a propensity to protect gold as a central monetary metal and protect silver as a subsidiary-coin metal. See Willis (1901, pp. 18, 19), Helfferich (1927, p. 139), and Martin (1973).

35. See the most recent debate over whether the practice of bimetallism in the 19th century led to alternating monometallism (Greenfield and Rockoff [1991] and Redish [1990a]) or in fact maintained both metals in circulation (Rolnick and Weber [1986]).

36. Darwin (1897, p. 144).

37. On the use of the concept of tipping in the selection of money, see Greenfield and Rockoff (1991). My use of tipping does not suggest, as Greenfield and Rockoff's use does, that Gresham's Law might not work (when tipping occurs), but only that people would have found its workings undesirable if these workings resulted in gold shortages.

38. Of course, if the market ratio were kept close to the mint ratio, bimetallism could maintain itself. However, this assumes that people would not systematically discriminate against silver as a medium of exchange, which events in this period suggest is not the case. Furthermore, and as Friedman acknowledges, maintaining bimetallism would require price-support schemes for silver when it was losing its value and threatening to drive gold out of circulation. In the 1870s and '80s, given the severity of events in the silver market and the lack of cooperation among leading monetary powers, it is dubious that nations could have stabilized the price of silver.

39. Milward and Saul (1973, p. 422) and Bouvier (1970, p. 342).

40. Hawtrey (1947, pp. 79, 80).

41. Quoted in Ellstaetter (1895, p. 107).

42. Keynes ([1913] 1971, p. 53).

43. Bordo (1986).

44. de Cecco (1974, p. 116), Kindleberger (1984, pp. 108, 120), and Clare (1909, p. 113).

45. Keynes ([1913] 1971, p. 12) cited the customary traditions of collecting railway fares and paying wages in gold.

46. Hawtrey (1930, p. 208) cited the large denomination as rendering the Bank's notes "intolerably clumsy." Beach (1935, pp. 50, 54, 74, 76) also underscored the limited use of Bank of England notes.

47. Hawtrey (1930, p. 208).

48. Norway appears as an exception. It did not experience an industrial revolution in the 19th century, but pursued monetary practices consistent with the Scandinavian trend. Holland may represent an anomaly in this logic as well. Finally, the U.S. developed as fast as or faster than all of the other early/rapid industrializers except for Great Britain.

49. From 1844 to 1864 the aggregate trade of France, Great Britain, and the U.S. increased threefold from 11.5 billion dollars to 32.7 billion dollars. See U.S. Senate (1876, V. I, pp. 22, 23).

50. Ford (1962, p. 94).

51. Zucker (1975) and U.S. Senate (1868, p. 2).

52. Bordo and Kydland (1990) argue that access to the London market became so precious that even nations that had a great deal of trouble maintaining gold convertibility adopted gold standards.

53. Clough and Cole (1946, p. 688).

54. The popular support for a transformation from silver to gold in the latter part of the 19th century came principally from urban-industrial groups. See also Eichengreen (1992, p. 30).

55. Laughlin (1886, p. 114).

56. *Ibid.* Seyd (1868, p. 624) argued that the perception of gold's greater relative stability vis-à-vis silver was apparent even in the early part of the century.

57. Even in the 1850s, when gold depreciated vis-à-vis silver, French creditors preferred to be paid in gold. However, by the 1870s there was little question regarding creditors' preferences. Whatever ambivalence was created by cheap gold in the 1850s and '60s was gone by the '70s, when silver depreciated precipitously vis-à-vis gold. See Willis (1901, p. 8).

58. In some cases, where the more traditional agricultural classes maintained power, as in Austria-Hungary, a movement toward gold was facilitated by pro-gold groups' success in convincing these entrenched economic interests that a link to gold would actually be more inflationary than the present fiat or silver standards prevailing there. See Yeager (1984, p. 655).

59. See the statement of the Belgian delegate Pirmez in U.S. Senate (1879, p. 124).

60. Monetary authorities in developed nations during this century were far too wedded to metallism to ever consider a paper standard as a long-run option.

61. Laughlin (1886, p. 6). It is consistent with the politics of inflation that those nations that were engaged in attempts to resuscitate silver, like the U.S., Austria-Hungary, and Russia, were also heavily dependent on agricultural exports. See de Cecco (1974, p. 50).

62. Quoted in Hamerow (1972, p. 330).

63. Essentially, he was attempting to sustain a precapitalist political structure in what had become a capitalist society. See Stern (1977, pp. 177–83) and Rosenburg (1962).

64. Hamerow (1972, p. 338).

65. Bohme (1978, p. 54) concurs: the conservative state left the management of the economy "in the hands of manufacturers, bankers, and wholesale merchants."

66. Kindleberger (1984, p. 120).

67. Bismarck himself only became directly involved in monetary unification when it affected political unification. See Stern (1977, p. 180).

68. Even the Conservatives and Progressives in Reichstag gave him relatively little opposition on his initiatives. See Zucker (1975, pp. 69, 74–76).

69. Quoted in Flotow (1941, p. 143).

70. Slater (1886, p. 40).

71. U.S. Senate (1910d, p. 601).

72. Zeldin (1958, p. 2).

73. In 1852, landowners made up 19% of the legislature, while former civil servants and the grand bourgeoisie made up 26% and 24%, respectively. See Plessis (1985, pp. 31–37).

74. Chapman (1962).

75. Schuman, quoted in Clough (1964, p. 210).

76. The Bank of France and haute finance, however, showed strong support for bimetallism well into the 1870s. The Bank's allegiance was founded on a lucrative history of bimetallic arbitrage. Haute finance had their own history of arbitrage, but also found the preferences of the leading institution in French finance to be compelling. The Bank and haute finance's allegiance shifted quickly, however, when the Bank found that remaining on bimetallism threatened to drain its gold stock. Hence, the upper tiers of French finance supported bimetallism until it meant losing gold.

77. Cammaerts (1921, pp. 317, 318).

78. Willis (1901, p. 165).

79. Dandliker (1899).

80. Albrecht-Carrie (1950, p. 192) and Lovett (1982, p. 47).

81. Stromberg (1931, pp. 647–67).

82. Birch (1938, pp. 322–51).

83. Mokyr (1976, p. 83) and Barnouw (1944, p. 185).

84. Barnouw (1944, pp. 187–92).

85. The royal attachment to silver in Holland appears to have been strongly based on ideology—i.e., maintaining monetary tradition. In France, executive advocacy of bimetallism was founded on strong ties to the Bank of France.

86. Derry (1968, p. 177).

87. Milward and Saul (1973, p. 520).

88. As John Sherman (1895, p. 469) noted: "It was not until silver was a cheaper dollar that anyone demanded it, and then it was to take advantage of a creditor."

89. Inflationist groups were able to co-opt urban labor by convincing them that the expanded metallic base assured by bimetallism was more conducive to high wages.

90. Bullock (1900, pp. 106, 107), Sundquist (1983, p. 127), Blaine (1884, V. II, pp. 391, 392, 570, 578), and Frieden (1991). The taxonomy shows numerous anomalies. Western bankers and businessmen commonly advocated bimetallism, and Republicans and Democrats often reversed roles on issues of resumption and the management of greenbacks. Also, Southern urban interests showed a long history of stable-money preferences. These anomalies were often founded on some conflict of interests. Among the capitalist class, it was the bankers and businessmen that had disproportionate ties to agriculture, land speculation, and rural development (i.e., investments in railroads) who were the most likely supporters of inflation. Unger (1964, pp. 158, 159), in fact, argues that such reversals among businessmen over resumption were not rare. The structure of monetary preferences dictated by this taxonomy did, however, manifest itself often enough to maintain its usefulness as a means of categorizing the foundations of competition in monetary politics. See Sherman (1895, pp. 509–20, 540, 570, 1147), Laughlin (1886, pp. 187, 188), Friedman and Schwartz (1963, pp. 45–49), Blaine (1884, V. I, p. 421), Beard and Beard (1927, p. 297), and Clark (1920, pp. 322, 484).

91. Hicks (1931, p. 81).

92. Unger (1964, pp. 71–73, 403) more generally sees partisan monetary preferences in the post–Civil War period as emanating from antebellum differences in class, doctrine, ethnicity, and religion. He highlights the especially strong attraction of soft-money elements to Democratic politics given their deep Jeffersonian and rural roots.

93. Beard and Beard (1927, p. 53).

94. Cochran and Miller (1951, p. 154).

95. Sundquist (1983, pp. 103–15), Unger (1964, p. 72), Blaine (1884, V. II, pp. 240, 241), and Cochran and Miller (1951, p. 160). The bloody-shirt image served to link Democratic politics to those forces that perpetuated "rebellion" and "treason."

96. Friedman and Schwartz (1963, pp. 54, 55, 111) cite the trends in the money stock in the 1870s as reflective of a political balance skewed toward stable money. Later in the 1890s, they add, the political balance was still anti-inflation, given the policy rigidity of maintaining convertibility in the face of financial crisis.

97. Legislation was certainly not insensitive to inflationist interests. As was the political style in Congress, bills often emerged as partisan compromises. However, in the monetary area, it is clear whose preferences prevailed.

98. Sherman (1895, p. 385).

99. The June Act appealed to hard-money interests in its limitation (382 million dollars) on the issue of greenbacks.

100. In Brazil, for example, coffee magnates historically desired depreciation as a means of raising coffee prices vis-à-vis costs. See Eichengreen (1992, p. 60).

101. de Cecco (1974, pp. 58, 59) and Ford (1962, pp. 90, 91).

102. Of course, the structural factor of economic development (i.e., incomes remaining low) discouraged the use of a high-value and more convenient medium of exchange. As for ideology, the evidence suggests that less developed nations desired monetary prestige about as much as any of the developed nations, but the other two structural factors, as well as the permissive factors (see below), worked against both their desire and ability to make and maintain a gold link.

103. de Cecco (1974, pp. 58, 59). Sometimes the political struggle resulted in interesting hybrid systems, such as a paper standard for internal use and a gold standard for foreign transactions.

104. Permissive factors were also relevant in these cases as gold links were rendered precarious by high inflation and lack of fiscal restraint.

105. Schumpeter (1954, p. 770).

106. On the permissive level, discussed below, it was the only core nation not to have a formal central bank, the lack of such an institution making the gold link more difficult to sustain. Also, its financial crises tended to be more severe than those in Europe. See de Cecco (1974, p. 111).

107. All of these nations were dependent on agricultural exports, which created political and economic rigidities against stable money.

108. Williams (1968, pp. 273, 274).

109. Leavens (1939, pp. 113, 114).

110. From a methodological point of view, a variable (in this case, the choice of a monetary standard) cannot be explained by a constant (ideology).

111. Pressnell (1968, p. 170).

112. In his testimony to the U.S. Monetary Commission [see U.S. Senate (1876, V. II, p. 356)], William Sumner argued that Europe was ready to move to gold at any time after 1850.

113. Willis (1901, pp. 18, 19) and McCulloch (1879, pp. 18, 19).

114. Those who argue that bimetallism has the capacity to automatically reverse gold or silver shortages through a stabilizing mechanism that works via the substitution of metal between monetary and non-monetary uses (see Bordo [1987]—such substitution is supposed to automatically bring the market ratio back to the mint ratio) assume that metals are perfectly substitutable as mediums of exchange. If they are not, people will institute coinage laws which prevent their preferred medium from being displaced (as happened in the 1870s).

115. U.S. Senate (1879, p. 190), Russell (1898, pp. 89, 90, 103), Flotow (1941, p. 114), Willis (1901, pp. 38, 105), and Helfferich (1927, pp. 146, 151, 152).

116. This assured that silver would not displace gold in circulation, since it was undervalued and gold overvalued at Latin mints. In this respect, the Union did not intend (in the short run, anyway) to deviate from gold monometallism in practice. See Willis (1901, pp. 40–46) and Redish (1993).

117. Helfferich (1927, p. 143) noted that the conference definitively conveyed that "gold was the standard of the future." Willis (1901, p. 135) regarded it as the beginning of a global consensus on the desirability of a gold standard.

118. U.S. Senate (1879, p. 81). John Sherman (1895, p. 412) expressed the same view.

119. Quoted in Slater (1886, p. 39). See also Russell (1898, pp. 84, 236).

120. Russell (1898, p. 103).

121. Helfferich (1927, p. 149). Interestingly, the Conference of 1867 contributed to the emergence of an international gold regime not because of successful cooperation (its resolution failing to be approved by legislatures), but because it conditioned perceptions that nations were predisposed to make unilateral shifts away from silver-based standards and adopt gold. Nations began fearing the possibility that they would be left with mints open to silver while the rest of the world was demonetizing the metal.

122. Leavens (1939, p. 66).

123. The extraordinary rise in silver imports from 1861 to 1865 owes to the fact that Indian cotton took up the slack of declining U.S. cotton exports caused by the American Civil War.

124. Greater use of notes, a less favorable balance of trade, and the greater use of council bills to clear payments with Great Britain were responsible for a drop-off in silver imports after 1865.

The U.S. Monetary Commission of 1876 cited the drop i the net imports of India as one of the major factors (along with policy changes in Europe and excessive silver production) accounting for the depreciation of silver in the 1860s and '70s. The Commission's conclusion was representative of a widespread belief of this period.

125. The price of silver on the London market changed by only 9/16ths ppp (pence per ounce) from 1865 to 1871 (from $61\frac{1}{16}$ ppp to $60\frac{1}{2}$ ppp) when the net silver imports of India went from 93 million dollars (in 1865) to almost 5 million dollars (in 1870). Furthermore, the price of silver did not change by more than $\frac{3}{16}$ths from 1869 to 1872, years which saw extremely sharp swings in the level of net imports (see Tables 6.2 and 6.3).

126. Council bills were bills of exchange sold by the India Council (the government of India residing in London) for the purpose of making payments to Great Britain for public expenses such as interest on debt and pensions. Since these bills represented claims on silver in India, they increasingly substituted for shipments of silver, as they would be purchased by those in Great Britain who needed to send silver to India in payment for goods. On the effects of council bills on silver flows, see Laughlin (1886, pp. 126, 127, 132).

127. John Sherman (1895, p. 412) attributed the decline in the value of silver in the 1860s solely to the increased production of silver.

128. The market ratio changed from 15.44-to-1 in 1865 to 15.57-to-1 in 1870. The legal ratio in Latin nations was $15\frac{1}{2}$-to-1. After 1866, the market ratio never again dropped below $15\frac{1}{2}$-to-1. See Table 6.3 and Laughlin (1886, pp. 223, 224).

129. India's net imports of silver in 1867 had declined to about ¼th of what they were two years before. Indian net silver imports as a percentage of world silver production had also dropped to about ¼ of what they were in 1865 (see Table 6.2).

130. Russell (1898, p. 33).

131. By the late 1860s a few leading monetary authorities, like Mees of Holland, expressed a belief that silver and bimetallism were at points of no return as standards in principal nations. But in this early period, such beliefs were far less pervasive than they would be a decade later. See Russell (1898, p. 103).

132. Actually, the Latin Union nations might have preempted Germany onto gold if not for the strategic political maneuvers of the French Ministry of Finance, and the Franco-Prussian War. From 1865, Belgium, Switzerland, and Italy had been advocating a Latin Union based on gold monometallism. Even the French delegates at the founding of the Union in 1865 had requested a gold union. French society and the legislature were strongly behind gold. The perpetuation and exportation of a bimetallist standard to the Union in the mid and late 1860s resulted from the deft actions of the Ministry of Finance at keeping the matter out of the legislature and under the jurisdiction of the Ministry. In 1869, for example, Minister Magne responded to a call for assessing France's monetary standard by referring the matter to the Conseil Superier of Agriculture, Commerce, and Industry rather than the Chambers, which was overwhelmingly predisposed to pass a gold bill. The Ministry further protected bimetallism by not making public the Conseil's decision supporting gold over silver and bimetallism (26 to 11) until 1872. With the advent of the Franco-Prussian War and the problem of the indemnity, any meaningful changes would have to wait until after 1873. The Ministry was successful at keeping the matter out of the Chambers until 1876, when a law was passed suspending the coinage of 5-franc silver pieces. A Ministry more sympathetic to gold could have had France and the Latin Union (since Latin Union nations configured their monetary standards to that of France) officially on a gold standard well before Germany.

It is difficult to impute motives other than support for the Bank of France and haute finance to the French Ministry in its defense of bimetallism. Arguments that suggest France was holding out to get into a more advantageous position as leader of a gold bloc on the Continent fail to address the fact that France's intransigence threatened to drive her Latin satellites into a gold union with Germany, certainly an undesirable outcome for the French government and Ministry of Finance. It is clear, however, that French monetary authorities' reluctance to make a quick shift from silver was driven, aside from the profit motives (from bimetallic arbitrage) of haute finance and the Bank of France, by a concern for the large sum of silver still held by French society and the Bank of France (any quick shift might have greatly reduced the value of this metallic stock). See Willis (1901, pp. 105–07).

133. Such contagion was not an issue in the workings of bimetallism before 1860 because perceptions attributed a cyclical rather than secular character to the market for metals.

134. See the testimonies of William Sumner and Joseph Ropes in U.S. Senate (1876, V. II, pp. 312, 355).

135. Quoted in Russell (1898, p. 105).

136. Willis (1901, p. 113), Russell (1898, p. 89), and Helfferich (1927, p. 149).

137. U.S. Senate (1876, V. II, p. 356). The urgency of early liquidation of silver was all the more enhanced by the desire to maximize gold stocks for the impending legal transition to a full gold standard. This necessitated exchanging silver at its maximum purchasing power, which was perceived to be at the beginning of a secular decline.

138. Helfferich (1927, p. 444). Helfferich (p. 149) pointed out that one of the principal considerations driving Germany to gold was a fear of being "isolated" in a world destined to move toward gold monometallism.

139. Great Britain, *Report of the Commissioners Representing Great Britain at the Paris Conference* (1878, p. 5).

140. See O. D. Ashley's letter in U.S. Senate (1876, V. II, p. 61).

141. Willis (1901, p. 163).

142. Great Britain, *Gold and Silver Commission* ([1888] 1936, p. 70).

143. The Swedish rix thaler, in fact, exactly corresponded with the Hamburg rix thaler. See U.S. Senate (1867, p. 35), Russell (1898, p. 58), and Helfferich (1927, p. 144).

144. U.S. Senate (1876, V. I, Pt. 2, p. 170).

145. Great Britain, *Papers Relating to Silver* (1877, p. 433). See also Holmboe's statement in U.S. Senate (1876, V. I, Pt. 2, p. 518).

146. This replication mirrored a very strong trade dependence. See U.S. Senate (1876, V. II, Pt. 2, p. 144) and Willis (1901, p. 15).

147. The monetary dependence of Switzerland and Belgium was particularly acute, owing historically to a large circulation of French coin within their borders. By the end of the 1850s, for example, about 90% of metallic transactions in Switzerland were in French gold. In 1860, 87% of the coins in circulation in Belgium were French. With respect to trade, the Latin monetary satellites were especially dependent given their large trade sectors. Belgium, for example, was consuming only about 1/14th of its total yearly production in this period.

148. U.S. Senate (1867, p. 45).

149. Helfferich (1927, p. 146).

150. Stolper (1940, p. 32) called the German policy initiative one of "extraordinary significance" in moving the developed world toward a monetary transformation. McCulloch (1879, p. 14) saw it as the pivotal-crucial event urging the world to a gold standard. William Sumner's testimony portrayed the German policy change in similar terms. See U.S. Senate (1876, V. II, p. 356) and Friedman (1990b, p. 90).

151. The limited membership in the gold bloc was compensated for by the fact that Great Britain was one of the two major members.

152. See Seyd's testimony in Great Britain, *Report From the Select Committee on Depreciation of Silver* (1876, p. 136).

153. The French indemnity from the Franco-Prussian War was the main cause of the silver inflow given that it was liquidated in a way as to shift French assets to Germany, thus making Germany's international creditor position greater. In the second quarter of 1871, for example, Great Britain exported 2 million pounds' worth of silver to Germany.

Much has been said about the importance of gold transfers from the indemnity in making possible Germany's transition to a gold standard. But in actuality very little gold was transferred. Only 15% (742 million out of 5 billion francs) of the indemnity was actually liquidated in money, and only 5% (273 million francs) was liquidated in gold. It was principally liquidated in stocks, credits, and bills of exchange. Germany, in fact, experienced no net increase in her gold stocks until she began liquidating her excess silver on the world market in 1873. See U.S. Senate (1876, V. I, Pt. 2, p. 79), Willis (1901, p. 110), and Russell (1898, p. 107).

154. The net imports of silver into Sweden increased from 3,129 kilograms in 1870 to almost 28,000 in 1872. Sweden coined more than twice as much silver in 1871 than it did in 1870 (4,361 to 9,975 kilograms). Norway imported more than three times as much specie in 1871 (mostly in silver) than it did the year before. Its silver imports almost quadrupled and the amount of silver in the Bank of Norway almost doubled. See U.S. Senate (1876, V. II, Pt. 2, pp. 516–28) and Great Britain, *Report From the Select Committee on Depreciation of Silver* (1876, pp. 267, 268).

155. Helfferich (1927, p. 175) and White (1893, p. 23).

156. Estimates of Hector Hay and Ernest Seyd show an increase from 51 million dollars to 61 million dollars. See Laughlin (1886, p. 218).

157. Willis (1901, p. 136).

158. By the *Economist*'s estimates global gold production declined from 108 million dollars in 1871 to 87 million dollars in 1872. See Laughlin (1886, p. 218).

159. Because of relatively smaller endowments of precious metals in monetary use, the transition in Germany's Northern satellites caused less concern. The impact of their conver-

sion was mainly psychological, as the realization of an expected trend that would engulf the developed world. See Helfferich (1927, p. 175) and U.S. Senate (1879, p. 57).

160. Great Britain, *Report From the Select Committee on Depreciation of Silver* (1876, p. 77).

161. *Ibid.*, p. 91. More than the actual intentions or actions, it was the uncertainty about the intentions of German monetary authorities and uncertainty about the amount of excess silver that created anxieties in other nations. Estimates of this silver stock in public documents of the period varied greatly: from 8 to 60 million pounds sterling. It didn't help that German authorities were reluctant to make public statements about their future plans, nor about monetary aggregates in their economy. In actuality, the realities fell somewhat short of the fears. In fact, German authorities were careful in liquidating their supply of silver out of fear of depressing the world price of the metal. It wasn't until 1876 that any significant amount of silver was actually liquidated. Up until 1876, most of the territorial coins called in were used for coining Imperial silver coins. From 1873 to 1876, only in the year 1874 was more silver liquidated than assigned to German mints for coinage. Of the estimated 41.9 million pounds (sterling) of surplus silver that Germany needed to dispose of (i.e., that silver stock in monetary use above the subsidiary coin needs of the German population) in 1873, only 10 million had been liquidated by 1876. This latter figure was only 14% of the world's total silver production in that four-year period. See Helfferich (1927, p. 170), Great Britain *Report of the Commissioners Representing Great Britain at the Paris Conference* (1878, p. 17), and U.S. Senate (1876, V. II, Pt. 2, pp. 77, 78).

162. Willis (1901, pp. 89, 90, 115, 116, 301–13).

163. *Ibid.*, pp. 114–51. Interestingly, the governments of Belgium, Switzerland, and Italy all used this agreement to strengthen themselves fiscally. They purchased the requisite silver bullion on the open market, coined the entire amount immediately (thus crowding out private citizens), and deposited the sums with their treasuries.

164. From May to November of 1874, 32 million gulden in silver had been coined.

165. Helfferich (1927, p. 176) and U.S. Senate (1911, pp. 95, 96).

166. In France, net gold imports slightly increased, while net silver imports declined enormously. Substantially more gold was now being coined in both France and Belgium.

167. The interpretation of the British *Gold and Silver Commission* [see Great Britain ([1888] 1936, pp. 141, 142)] that the most destabilizing outcomes in the market for silver came about as a result of the Latin Union delinking from bimetallism may be correct, as this initiated the most precipitous fall in the value of silver. But any suggestion that keeping Latin mints open was desirable or even possible under the intense pressure of the early 1870s is suspect. The influxes of silver appeared simply too great to be absorbed.

168. Willis (1901, pp. 158–60).

169. Up until this year, the Ministry of Finance, erstwhile defender of bimetallism in France, was able to keep it out of the Chambers, where gold had resounding support.

170. Also at the basis of France's unilateral move was a pronounced fear of being preempted onto gold by the Swiss, who had been requesting a gold union for some time, and the Belgians whose upcoming elections were to be contested by Frere-Orban and his pro-gold Liberals. See Willis (1901, pp. 162–165).

171. Except, of course, for Italy, which was exempted for one year.

172. Sherman (1895, pp. 541, 615, 617, 618) and Blaine (1886, V. II, p. 605). See also the various testimonies and letters to the U.S. Monetary Commission [see U.S. Senate (1876, V. I)]. There is some debate on the magnitude of the influence of these external concerns over the demonetization of the silver dollar in the Act of 1873. O'Leary (1960) argues that the principal author of the bill, H. R. Linderman, was compelled by critical developments in Europe and the world market for metals. Friedman and Schwartz (1963, p. 115) are some-

what skeptical about this as being his principal motivation. It is clear, however, that as early as 1872 Linderman did acknowledge the potential dangers of both the increased supply of silver in the world and change of standards in Germany. In fact, Friedman (1990a, pp. 1165–67) more recently appears to converge closer to O'Leary's position.

173. Blaine (1884, V. II, p. 606).

174. Linderman pointed out that any such unilateral initiative by one nation would lead other nations to think, "Here is a good chance . . . to get rid of our silver." See U.S. Senate (1876, V. II, p. 198). Pirmez, the Belgian delegate at the International Monetary Conference of 1878, argued that any viable multilateral return to bimetallism must include all important silver nations; otherwise powerful free riders would use the new union to liquidate their excess silver. See Russell (1898, p. 215).

175. This represented a fairly common response to the U.S. Monetary Commission's question: What would be the consequences of remonetizing silver in the U.S.? See the testimonies of Fitch, Ropes, and Sumner in U.S. Senate (1876, V. II, pp. 35, 313, 345).

The severity of the perceived consequences (among monetary authorities) of incurring the "sucker's payoff" (i.e., opening their mints to silver while other nations did not) leads us to question Friedman's (1990a, p. 1174, and 1990b, p. 91) contention that a unilateral resumption of bimetallism by the U.S. in the mid 1870s could have stabilized the bimetallic market ratio. The events in Latin Union nations and the failure of the Dutch resumption in 1874 made nations extremely reluctant to initiate or support any unilateral actions in this direction. Furthermore, given the propensity of free-riding behavior among core nations, it is likely that a unilateral U.S. initiative would have invited much of the surplus silver from the Continent (i.e., that silver beyond the needs of subsidiary coinage). It is doubtful that the U.S. could have withstood this rapid and large flood of silver.

176. In describing this policy, France's Leon Say underscored the threat which was felt from the large pool of excess silver in Germany yet to be liquidated. See U.S. Senate (1879, pp. 55, 56).

177. Russell (1898, pp. 64, 65) and Darwin (1897, p. 135).

178. Bloomfield (1963, p. 20).

179. Einzig (1970); Russell (1898, p. 253); and Great Britain, *Report From the Select Committee on Depreciation of Silver* (1876, p. 51).

180. Russell (1898, p. 227) identified an element of self-fulfilling prophecy in what he called the "vicious circle" of the 1870s: "States were afraid of employing silver on account of the depreciation, and the depreciation continued because the states refused to employ it."

181. Structural and proximate factors leading to the scramble were inextricably connected. A large component of the nervousness in the 1860s and '70s were fears of unstable money, fears which were nurtured by shifting structures of political power. (*The U.S. Monetary Commission* [see U.S. Senate (1876, V. I, p. 4)] underscored the importance of stable-money interests in bringing about the demonetization of silver in Europe.) The growth in trade and internationalization of finance forged stronger links which bound the monetary chain gang, as did the perception of gold as a political and economic status symbol. Furthermore, the thought of losing one's gold circulation caused grave concern. All these enhanced the nervousness over the anticipation of changes in foreign monetary practices.

182. Ultimately, however, they aspired to a gold standard. Hence, support for bimetallism and silver after the 1870s should not be interpreted as necessarily mirroring anti-gold preferences. See Russell (1898).

183. Ford (1962) and Lindert (1969).

184. Bloomfield (1963, p. 43).

185. de Cecco (1974, p. 58). Although gold could be ultimately attracted with the right interest rates, it might come too late or in insufficient amounts to sustain a stable gold link.

186. Bloomfield (1959, p. 15).

187. Bordo (1989).

188. de Cecco (1974, pp. 56, 114, 115) notes that such an institutional absence in the U.S. made it "constitutionally unstable" in a monetary sense.

189. Yeager (1969).

190. Ford (1962) and Fratianni and Spinelli (1984).

191. Fratianni and Spinelli (1984). Spain, like Italy, appeared to be an anomaly in Western Europe, with underdeveloped private and public financial institutions, as well as unfavorable fiscal and monetary trends.

Chapter 7

1. See, for example, Bordo (1981) and (1986), Klein (1975), Schwartz (1986), Bloomfield (1959, p. 9), Ford (1989, p. 197), Keynes ([1931] 1952, p. 88), Cleveland (1976), Cohen (1977, p. 78), Beyen (1949, p. 25), and Eichengreen (1985b). For debates on the performance of the gold standard, see Meltzer and Robinson (1989), Bordo (1981), and Schwartz (1986).

2. For a sample of differing modes of assessing international monetary stability, see Cooper (1987), Cohen (1977 and 1983), and Williamson and Miller (1987).

3. The ease of adjustment was all the more important in this period given that global liquidity as a proportion of trade was fairly low relative to succeeding periods: in 1913 it was 20%, while in 1965 it was 50%. See Scammell ([1965] 1985).

4. Consistent with the scope of the gold standard (a regime comprising developed nations), the environment did not need to provide the same capacity for the periphery to adjust. In fact, the burden of adjustment partially fell on the periphery as developed nations in need of liquidity found that they could pull capital from less developed economies, while peripheral nations did not have the same pulling power vis-à-vis developed economies.

5. See, for example, Cleveland (1976) and Stein (1984).

6. Bordo (1992).

7. Yeager (1984, p. 652).

8. Yeager (1969, pp. 84–86).

9. Barro (1987) found in his study of fiscal patterns during the 18th and 19th centuries that deficits in this period were most often tied to military expenditures. Furthermore, increases in government spending had the effect of increasing long-term interest rates. Hence, wars were especially destabilizing for convertibility because war finance created conditions ripe for stagflation: monetizing the military debt meant inflationary management of the money supply, while an increase in interest rates slowed growth.

10. Barro (1987) and Beyen (1949, p. 14).

11. Bloomfield (1963, pp. 84, 86) and Beach (1935, p. 38).

12. Eichengreen (1990b, p. 18, and 1992, p. 31).

13. Polanyi (1957, pp. 10–17) saw an essential link that ran in the opposite direction: peace resulted from a stable balance of power which itself was founded on the collusive efforts of "haute finance." Given the disjuncture between monetary affairs/banking and international political goals which prevailed in the developed world during the century, it is dubious that one can posit some fundamental and direct link from some banking oligopoly to questions of international strategic rivalries. Furthermore, the idea of a cooperative "orchestra" of big private banks or central banks has been much exaggerated.

14. Polanyi (1957, p. 5).

15. Polanyi (1957, pp. 16, 17) and Kennedy (1981a).

16. Kennedy (1981a, p. 50).

17. de Cecco (1974, p. 134) and Rockoff (1984, p. 638).

18. Gardner (1956, p. 383).

19. Brown (1965, p. 47) and Haberler (1964, p. 6).

20. Beales (1934, p. 73), Kenwood and Lougheed (1983, pp. 130, 131), and Yeager (1976, p. 307). Although this may be disputed somewhat by those who emphasize that there was no golden age of wage flexibility in this period.

21. Ashworth (1952, pp. 169, 181).

22. Ford (1962).

23. Since threats to convertibility themselves can be characteristics of a crisis, the logic may appear to suggest circular reasoning: convertibility was maintained because it was maintained. The characteristics of crises are, however, varied, and many of them reside at the microeconomic level: e.g., bank failures, shocks in stock markets, failed overseas investment. The argument proposed here is that, aside from the state of convertibility itself and its direct macroeconomic links (e.g., capital flight), the exogenous conditions that can create tensions leading to panics were generally absent during this period. Given that most of these exogenous conditions (both micro or macro) are themselves stochastic or unsystematic causes of crises, we can say that the course of economic and financial "accidents" which condition the state of monetary systems was quite favorable during the course of the gold standard. Hence, the configuration of economic and financial accidents during the period was conducive to a stable structure of adjustment.

24. Gilbert and Wood (1986, p. 5).

25. The years of crisis and principally affected nations were: 1882 in France; 1890 in Britain; 1893 in the U.S.; and 1906–07 in Italy, France, and the U.S.

26. Batchelor (1986, p. 54), Andreades (1909, p. 369), and Matthews (1982, p. 110).

27. Scammell ([1965] 1985).

28. As noted, the U.S. financial system was the most turbulent of the core, but even this was relatively mild compared to the state of financial systems outside the core. The U.S. in fact never suspended convertibility under the gold standard period.

29. Bloomfield (1963, p. 28) underscores how important it was, given the relatively stable production of gold across the period, for nations to economize on the use of gold. With the growth of incomes, capital flows, and trade, the period required a concomitant rise in liquidity for the collective adjustment mechanism to function smoothly.

30. See also Kenwood and Lougheed (1983, pp. 130, 131).

31. Furthermore, since trade was financed disproportionately in British bills, much of the clearing went on in the books of London houses without the need of gold flows, which in turn enhanced central banks' ultimate means of defending convertibility.

32. Bouvier (1970, p. 368).

33. For Lewis (1978, p. 40) the depression may have been long but was not deep.

34. See Figures A.1–A.3 in Statistical Appendix on the behavior of prices and central bank discount rates.

35. Rostow (1948), Lewis (1978), Warren and Pearson (1935), Saul (1960), Beales (1934), and Mitchell (1980).

36. *Ibid.*

37. See also Moggridge (1972, p. 6).

38. Ashworth (1952, pp. 145, 146) and Stein (1984). Ashworth notes that in fact much of the government intervention in trade during the period actually encouraged trade: they paid excessive rates to merchants for mail carriage, subsidized exports, and limited taxes on the railway carriage of products destined for export.

39. Cottrell (1975, p. 29) and Haberler (1964, p. 5). Tariffs may even have had some stabilizing effects in terms of domestic economic growth. Polanyi (1957, p. 214), for example, argued that tariffs helped relieve some of the adverse effects of fixed exchange rates on employment.

40. This does not, however, support prevailing theories of hegemonic stability, since the stabilizing behavior of the core nations was quite unintended. Furthermore, the stabilizing actions themselves emanated primarily from non-state actors (investors, traders, private banks) rather than state actors. See Chapter 8 on unintended and non-state hegemony.

41. This is an essential element in Gardner's (1956, p. 383) preconditions of a stable international monetary system: policies (especially in the largest monetary actors) that facilitate adjustment in other nations.

42. In drawing comparisons between the stability of the classical gold standard and subsequent periods, Triffin (1964, pp. 7, 8) and Eichengreen (1990b, p. 8) underscore the importance of the willingness of surplus nations to adjust in the period before the War, a willingness that appeared to be absent, and a major source of instability, in the interwar period. See also Bank for International Settlements (1943); Great Britain, *First Interim Report of the Cunliffe Committee* ([1918] 1985, pp. 192, 193); and Bloomfield (1959, p. 23).

43. On net capital export trends in the core, see Bloomfield (1968a, pp. 8, 9).

44. Ashworth (1952, p. 166) and Mitchell (1980, pp. 510–17).

45. Triffin (1964, pp. 7, 8) points out that nations with the strongest current account positions also tended to be the largest net capital exporters.

46. Outside of the core, some nations did experience highly adverse current balances, such as Canada, whose current account deficit averaged 8% of GNP from 1883 to 1913.

More recently, core balances of payment have not showed as favorable a set of outcomes. After World War II, current account positions have exhibited much less stability, with nations fluctuating in and out of deficits. Current account surpluses have not reached the British levels of pre–World War I (Japan and Germany reaching as high as 4% of GNP in the mid-1980s). Deficits have reached greater levels, with Great Britain reaching 4% of GNP in 1974 and 1989, and the U.S. reaching 4% in the mid-1980s. See The *Economist* (1990) and Ford (1989, pp. 238–40).

47. Ford (1989, p. 240).

48. de Cecco (1974, p. 123) points out that only a trickle of gold ever flowed from deficit to surplus nations.

49. He adds that this harmony was no longer evident in the interwar period with European-reconstruction borrowing.

50. Of course, the main protagonists in the adjustment process were individual investors and traders, as opposed to states or state institutions. Hence, when we speak of nations' willingness or capacity to adjust in this period, it means that economic actors in those nations had the freedom to engage in economic transactions that were conducive to adjustment.

51. Capital imports in the period were positively correlated with economic growth in the long run. See Bloomfield (1968a) and Moggridge (1972, p. 13).

52. Bloomfield (1968a) and Saul (1960, p. 66). Eichengreen (1990b) adds that global growth was enhanced by the fact that major net importing regions were newly industrializing areas where productivity was higher.

53. It was consistently lower than discount rates in Germany, Switzerland, Austria-Hungary, and the Scandinavian countries. The British rate, however, was consistently above that of France. See Figures A.1–A.3 in Statistical Appendix.

54. It would appear, upon careful reflection, that the core and the periphery probably shouldered most of the burden of adjustment during the classical gold standard, with non-core developed nations being an intermediary that experienced more limited sacrifices. Thus the regime was characterized by a structure of adjustment in which the main burdens of adjustment were falling both on relatively weaker nations and the world's economically strongest nations. One can make a case for the argument that this is an inherently stable configu-

ration because the weak cannot as readily destabilize the regime and the strong can more easily bear such costs.

55. Again, as in the general case of the core, the stabilizing agents were British traders and investors, not the state or public institutions.

56. While its invisibles earnings accounted for 55 million pounds (on average) during the 1860s, average invisibles earnings in the period 1900–10 were 164 million pounds. Invisibles represented 130.42% of net foreign investment in the period 1856–1914. In the last four years before the War, they accounted for 7.15% of nominal GNP. These earnings were basically recycled in the form of foreign investment. See Ashworth (1952, p. 167), Cottrell (1975, pp. 45–48), Bloomfield (1968a, p. 8), and Ford (1962, pp. 63, 64).

57. Yeager (1976, p. 300). One domestic institutional feature that enhanced the international supply of sterling was the lack of legal minimum reserve requirements in British banking; this gave British banks far greater discretion in decisions to lend capital targeted for foreign investment. See Ford (1989, p. 202).

58. Ford (1962, p. 38).

59. The periods 1860–73, late 1880s–1891, and 1902–12, for example, were all boom periods with respect to British foreign investment in Latin America. Each of the periods coincided with large increases in British commercial exports to Latin America. Two of the biggest sources of British investment were Argentina and Brazil, which in turn imported most of their goods from Great Britain. See Platt (1973, pp. 275, 280) and Cottrell (1975, pp. 24, 41–43).

Cairncross's (1953, p. 188) findings suggest that it was booms in foreign rather than domestic investment that pulled Great Britain out of depression in the period. British foreign investment was especially instrumental in generating demand for British goods after 1870 as a result of a shift in the flow of British capital from less productive (e.g., bonds to finance war and foreign adventurism) to more productive (public and private enterprises that stimulated demand for British manufactures) uses. Investment in railways, for example, generated a large demand for British iron. On the relation between capital and trade flows to the Empire, see de Cecco (1974, pp. 36, 37).

60. Cottrell (1975, p. 44).

61. On the strategic importance of British adjustment and countercyclical lending, see Brown (1965, p. 58), Schwartz (1984, p. 16), Cairncross (1953, p. 187), Ford (1965, pp. 23, 24), Yeager (1976, p. 300), Williamson (1968, p. 79), and Kenwood and Lougheed (1983, p. 164).

62. Eichengreen (1986a, pp. 144, 145).

63. Brown (1965, p. 58), Cottrell (1975, p. 50), Eichengreen (1992, p. 48), and Ford (1965, p. 23).

64. Eichengreen (1992, pp. 46, 47).

65. de Cecco (1974, p. 29) and Gallarotti (1985, p. 177).

66. Bowden et al. (1937, p. 640).

67. Saul (1960, p. 100), de Cecco (1974, p. 238), and Bowden et al. (1937, p. 640).

68. Saul (1960, pp. 59–64).

69. *Ibid.*, p. 204.

70. Keynes ([1913] 1971, p. 13) and Ford (1962, p. 137). Moreover, Cottrell (1975, p. 45) stresses how fortuitous it was for Britain to be the world's largest creditor in a period of low global inflation.

71. Tennant (1865, p. 829), Sayers (1970, p. 74, and 1957, p. 13), and Ford (1962, p. 33).

72. Brown (1965, p. 59).

73. Warren (1903, p. 196), moreover, underscored how quickly confidence returned to British finance after crises.

74. Cleveland (1976, p. 21) and Bloomfield (1963, p. 42).

75. See, for example, Willett (1980, pp. 54–59) and Ford (1989, p. 234).

76. When a conventional institution of hegemony like the Bank of England did act in a stabilizing way, such as refusing to hoard gold, it did so for its own profit motive (i.e., maintain the dividend).

77. See Chapter 8.

78. Brittain (1976). The most recent problems of the EMS show the difficulty of maintaining exchange-rate boundaries in the face of significantly divergent macroeconomies and low capital controls.

79. The game discussed below shows both incentives to exploit the other player (the Prisoner's Dilemma element) and incentives to coordinate with the other player by copying his/her strategy (the coordination element).

80. The complete ordinal structure of the payoffs cannot be defined because it is unclear whether a nation prefers surplus to balance. (It is reasonable to posit, however, that balance and surplus will be preferred to deficit.) To the extent that nations prefer surplus, the game will feature a stronger Prisoner's Dilemma than coordination element. To the extent that nations prefer balance, the coordination element will prevail.

81. Here we must assume economic growth, inflation, and exchange rates constant, and that capital controls are insignificant.

82. This, of course, assumes that the differentials in rates is greater than the transaction costs of foreign investment, and that Fisher effects (i.e., expectations of higher interest rates coupled with expectations of higher inflation) do not prevail.

83. There are numerous possibilities for external outcomes not to conform to the differentials discussed. For price differentials to effect trade flows, both imports and exports have to be price elastic, and nations have to exhibit similar elasticity structures with respect to their products. In a case where a nation's exports are price inelastic, low inflation may worsen its trade account as its terms of trade worsen without a concomitant rise in exports. Similarly, for interest rates to have the expected effects on external positions, the interest elasticity (i.e., the elasticity with respect to the price of credit) of foreign investment must also be significant and convergent across nations, and Fisher effects must be absent. Under the category of growth, upturns in the business cycle are normally accompanied by increases in imports, but such need not always be the case (e.g., income-inelastic imports).

Furthermore, I underscore the *ceteris paribus* assumption in all three games. For example, adverse external developments due to high inflation may be compensated for by slow growth (i.e., stagflation works both for and against a favorable external position).

84. Cleveland (1976, p. 16), Ashworth (1952, p. 184), and Ford (1989, pp. 226, 227, and 1962, p. 27) stress the importance of this factor for the regime's stability.

85. Morgenstern (1959), Cooper (1982, pp. 8, 9), Triffin (1964), Bloomfield (1959, p. 37), and The *Economist* (1990).

86. That the limited divergences in interest rates were able to effect adjustment was attributable to the high interest elasticity of foreign investment during the period (this is discussed in the next subsection). If foreign investment had been less elastic, overly synchronous macroeconomic outcomes might have had highly adverse effects on adjustment given the stability in exchange rates. As it was, the gold standard featured an ideal macroeconomic-based process of adjustment: limited but sufficient (to effect adjustment) divergences in macroeconomic outcomes. For a somewhat different view of the stability of synchronous macroeconomies in general, see Bergsten (1975, pp. 49, 50).

87. Moggridge (1972, p. 5) points out that nations also enjoyed synchronous export and import performance, as well as synchronous production-cost structures, all of which compounded the stabilizing effects of synchronous macroeconomies.

88. Goodhart (1972, p. 220), Brown (1929, p. 17), Yeager (1976, p. 308), Diebold et al. (1991), McCloskey and Zecher (1976), and Cohen (1977, p. 87).

89. Brown (1929, p. 17) saw the unstable structure of adjustment during the interwar years as an outcome of a set of exchange rates which emanated from the discretionary privilege of monetary authorities, a defect, he adds, which the prewar international economy was unburdened by.

90. Exchange risk can be seen as the assessment of the probability that any given exchange rate or set of exchange rates will change. Convertibility risk can be seen as an assessment of the probability that any given nation or set of nations will no longer convert national currencies into gold. The two risks are related but not necessarily synonymous. A higher exchange risk may indicate a higher convertibility risk, e.g., a nation is depreciating its currency because it cannot cover its trade deficit out of existing reserves. But the risks can also function independently of one another, e.g., convertibility suspension may not be accompanied by perceptions that an exchange rate is threatened.

91. Barsky and DeLong (1991) and Brown (1940, V. I, p. 38) suggest that these inelastic expectations about exchange rates were partially driven by low expectations of inflation: investors perceived one fundamental cause of depreciation (inflation) as being unlikely because of monetary authorities' commitment to the stable-money orthodoxy inherent in the practice of gold monometallism during the period. Officer (1989, p. 24) stresses how unique such inelastic expectations were to the classical gold standard period. He underscores the extent to which monetary relations during the interwar and Bretton Woods years suffered from destabilizing speculation because investors lost faith in the sustainability of exchange rates.

92. Polanyi (1957, p. 198). Bloomfield (1963, p. 26) points out that the convertibility of leading currencies was never really questioned.

93. Eichengreen (1985b, pp. 9, 24, and 1992, p. 30), Flood et al. (1990), Giovannini (1993), Beyen (1949, p. 28), Grubel (1969, p. 88), and Brunner (1984, p. 446). As methodologically troubling as it is to specify causal paths in situations of self-fulfilling prophecy (i.e., Do the expectations or the actual behavior receive causal priorness?), these situations are nonetheless prevalent in many economic processes (i.e., processes whose existence becomes self-sustaining). Markets have a tendency to generate the outcomes that they expect. The rational-expectations approach to the effects of market expectations has been historically concerned with how these processes render policies neutral. In the case of the gold standard, it was actually the investors' faith in the commitment of authorities to norms of monetary orthodoxy (i.e., orthodox metallism) that led to actions that solidified convertibility and exchange parities. Hence, the causal process was somewhat less self-contained. But even so, the outcomes brought about by the actions of investors (behaving from specific perceptions about these outcomes) fed back onto the perceptions to reinforce the resilience of convertibility and exchange rates in the gold club. This is further discussed in the next section.

94. Kindleberger (1963, p. 353) and Ford (1989, p. 210).

95. Edelstein (1982) points out how the period of the gold standard generally experienced no natural bias against foreign investment in favor of home investment. Investors saw international investment opportunities as comprising one market, rather than geographically encapsulated markets. In this respect, the period came closer than any other period to a single international financial system within the developed world.

96. The workings of stabilizing speculation in exchange rates also depended on perceptions that convertibility would be maintained, as investors would be reluctant to take positions in inconvertible currencies.

97. See also King (1936, p. 270).

98. Keynes's solution to the problem of slow adjustment during the interwar period, for example, was the institution of wider gold points which would allow the possibility for greater

returns to speculation in the market for foreign exchange. See Kindleberger (1963, p. 353).

99. Triffin (1964, p. 10) and Moggridge (1972, p. 5).

100. Fetter (1968, p. 76) and Clough and Cole (1946, p. 625). On the tendency of low inflation across nations to reduce inflation differentials, see Emminger (1976, p. 12).

101. In this respect, fixed exchange rates, as is normally the case, contributed to synchronous macroeconomic outcomes. Hence both these processes became linked in a relationship of mutual support.

102. Clark (1984), in fact, found that when violations of the gold points did occur, it was usually as a result of ill-fated government intervention.

103. Central banks did, as the War approached, engage in greater competition for war chests, but this was hardly done under political duress, as central bankers throughout the period maintained ultimate discretion over the operations of their banks, especially in the core. The profit motive served throughout the period as a force limiting the size of public gold stocks, as large stocks carried excessive opportunity costs. This was most visible in Britain, where, in fact, the separation of politics and economics was greatest. Thus, the private nature of central banking also entered into the matrix of stability, as private incentives conferred greater velocity onto the world's gold stock. See Bloomfield (1959, p. 23).

104. Willett (1980, pp. 12, 13), Eichengreen (1990a, p. 291), Polanyi (1957, pp. 193–96), and Cleveland (1976, p. 28). For representative discussions of the political business cycle, see Nordhaus (1975) and MacRae (1977).

105. Beyen (1949, pp. 11, 28) underscores the extent to which changes in norms about governmental responsibility after the War fundamentally altered the role played by governments in economic life both in character and scope.

106. The sacrifices of breaking from the metallist orthodoxy continued to be perceived as greater than the sacrifices imposed by unemployment and slow growth. See Polanyi (1957, p. 193) and Wood (1939, pp. 158, 159).

107. Ashworth (1952, pp. 140–42), Eichengreen (1990a, p. 289), and Bloomfield (1959, p. 16).

108. Yeager (1984, pp. 664, 665) stresses the fact that fiscal prudence was a goal that nations pursued for its own sake. This "ideology of fiscal restraint," as he refers to it, created a situation in which governments agonized over even small budget deficits. Lehrman (1976, pp. 83, 84) highlights the central role which the quest for balanced budgets played in the liberal agenda of the period. Grilli (1989) and Fratianni and Spinelli (1984) show that the few problems of convertibility that occurred in the developed world during the gold standard were frequently the result of inflation emanating from a lack of fiscal restraint. *The Cunliffe Report* [see Great Britain ([1918] 1985)], in fact, stressed the importance of avoiding such situations if Great Britain was going to return successfully to the gold standard.

109. But even existing incentives to redistribute growth and employment had a limited impact on policies, given prevailing norms that discouraged government manipulation of prices, interest rates, and exchange rates. Even if governments had the desire, they lacked the effective means of predation. Any Prisoner's Dilemma incentive structures that existed during the period were mitigated by limited freedom to make defecting (i.e., exploitative) moves. Hence, because of these domestic norms, economic relations in this period were not as inherently unstable as conventional visions of the nature of international economic relations suggest.

110. As noted, the adjustment mechanism functioned differently from conventional accounts of the gold standard. Nations were often spared the full burden of internal adjustment through prudent discount policies on the part of central banks and short-term capital movements. The internal adjustment mechanism did, however, play more significant a role than it would in the period after World War I.

111. Grubel (1969, p. 38) notes that in the age where governments became committed to domestic growth and full employment, the gold standard became archaic. Schumpeter (1954, p. 771) observed that with the shift in economic priorities, the gold standard "was losing its popularity like a naughty child that tells embarrassing truths."

112. Lehrman (1976, pp. 83, 84). Polanyi (1957, p. 24) noted that "men and women everywhere appeared to regard stable money as the supreme need of human society." The liberal aversion to inflation reflected a more fundamental fear of the idiosyncratic-discretionary manipulation of money supplies.

113. Schumpeter (1954, p. 770) pointed out that "the credo of economic and political liberalism prevailed in the field of monetary policy throughout the period . . . [and] of all the articles of that credo, the gold standard was the last to go." See Polanyi (1957, p. 147) on how liberalism was challenged in other issue-areas.

114. See Eichengreen (1992, p. 30) on credibility and the self-sustaining character of convertibility and parities.

115. Yeager (1984, pp. 665, 666) notes how any deviation from the London par could be extremely embarrassing.

116. Moggridge (1969, p. 11).

117. Eichengreen (1985b, p. 24, and 1989, pp. 29–32); Giovannini (1993); Flood et al. (1990); Brunner (1984, p. 446); Grubel (1969, p. 88); and Nurkse (1944, p. 29).

118. Barsky and De Long (1991).

119. It was in later periods, when the credibility of authorities' commitment to the gold standard had deteriorated because of a change in the normative foundations of monetary orthodoxy, that the adjustment mechanism broke down. See Eichengreen (1985b, p. 24) and Nurkse (1944, p. 29).

120. This is methodologically troubling because questions of causal priorness are difficult to resolve (i.e., which are in fact the independent variables?). Such self-sustaining or self-fulfilling processes, however, are quite prevalent in the economic world, and social scientists have placed more emphasis on understanding the circular effects than on trying to identify neat recursive causal paths. On self-fulfilling prophecies in economic systems, see Krugman (1991).

121. See also Eichengreen (1992, p. 65) and Giovannini (1993).

122. Eichengreen (1989, p. 31).

123. Hence, I include the arrow denoting feedback from regime maintenance to the inelastic expectations of investors in Figure 7.5.

124. Having joined the gold club in the mid 19th century, Portugal had actually come to gold rather late relative to Great Britain, which began practicing a gold standard de facto in the early 18th century.

125. Ford (1962, p. 134).

126. Fratianni and Spinelli (1984).

127. Much of this debate has occurred in the context of the effects of monetary rules on inflation performance. The literature is cited and discussed in Barro (1986) and Bordo (1992). This issue is further discussed in Chapter 8.

128. Friedman and Schwartz (1963, p. 105) underscore how even the severe conditions in the U.S. in the 1890s did not lead to capital outflows that necessitated suspension because of investors' beliefs that authorities would never break the gold link.

129. Ford (1962).

130. Eichengreen (1985b, p. 24), Grubel (1969, p. 38), and Nurkse (1944, p. 29) underscore how the normative transformation in the way governments viewed the macroeconomy after World War I had consequences that made the orthodox practice of metallism nonviable.

131. Classical liberalism is distinguished from embedded liberalism, the latter being a type of liberal philosophy that emerged after World War I and embodied certain socialist (i.e., domestic growth, welfare, and full-employment) concerns. On embedded liberalism, see Ruggie (1983).

132. Predatory manipulation of macroeconomic variables would create an intended bias in adjustment between specific nations (i.e., trying to export unemployment). Idiosyncratic manipulation would create an unintended bias in adjustment by causing macroeconomic outcomes to be less synchronous across nations.

133. As Friedman and Schwartz (1963, p. 10) observe, "The blind, undesigned, and quasiautomatic working of the gold standard turned out to produce a greater measure of predictability and regularity—perhaps because its discipline was impersonal and inescapable—than did deliberate and conscious control exercised within institutional arrangements intended to promote monetary stability."

134. See also Kindleberger (1975), Grubel (1969, p. 91), and Beyen (1949, p. 11).

135. Yeager (1984, p. 665).

136. de Cecco (1974, pp. 115–25) underscores the degree to which confidence in sterling was shaken by the Boer War, but the confidence was quickly restored, and sterling and other key currencies continued to be held in lieu of gold.

The competition for gold did increase after 1900 as nations actively accumulated war chests. In the U.S., demand for gold stocks increased as a result of the Treasury taking on more responsibilities of a central bank to the U.S. financial community. But even this greater competition was marshaled upon a greater global supply of gold (as a result of the great discoveries of the mid 1890s), and nations in the gold club still refrained from administering capital controls (gold could still be gotten at a price). Furthermore, Britain did not join in the scramble for war chests.

137. Dutton (1984, p. 173) identifies this capacity to withstand crises as providing the basis for a much longer life for the regime. He notes "the system might have operated reasonably well for decades longer." Even on the eve of the War, British bankers and monetary authorities were discussing how gold convertibility could be managed during hostilities. Lindert (1969, p. 1) points out that the most stable period of the gold standard was actually after 1900, when all principal nations had finally completed the link. Einzig (1970, p. 199) argues that if anything, the period was becoming more stable with respect to the foreign exchanges. Even historically unstable currencies like the rouble, the krone, and the Italian franc had stabilized by the end of the century, and more peripheral nations were going to a gold exchange standard.

138. Grubel (1969, p. 38), Eichengreen (1985b, p. 24), Nurkse (1944, p. 29), and Yeager (1984, p. 665). Gold orthodoxy did not die a sudden death with the War, as evidenced by the anxious state of monetary officials in the 1920s (especially in Britain) to resume the link. But instituting and maintaining gold standards under the normative transformation became difficult, and with the failures came the gradual realization that the monetary orthodoxy of the 19th century had essentially outlived its usefulness. Writing shortly after World War II, Triffin (1947, p. 54) pointed out how the new norms of full employment and government intervention in the economy undermined the "ideological and institutional framework" of the gold standard.

139. Schwartz (1984), Bordo (1981), and Eichengreen (1985b).

140. Eichengreen (1992) demonstrates that in fact attempts at renewing the gold link compounded the depressions which nations were experiencing in this period.

141. On the creation of Bretton Woods and the embedded-liberal compromise, see Ruggie (1983) and Gardner (1956).

Chapter 8

1. Young (1986, p. 112) and Keohane (1984, p. 37) note that the hegemonic vision of order has long dominated the study of regimes.

2. In its vacillation between passive and free-riding behavior, in fact, the British state acted in a fashion diametrically opposed to conventional benevolent visions of hegemony (which posit hegemonic powers as providers of public goods). It was, to use Keohane's (1984, p. 142) terms, a "passive, tightfisted hegemon." Such behavior effectively blocked rather than facilitated the construction of formal institutions. This style of hegemony (i.e., hegemons as an obstructive rather than constructive force) has received little formal treatment in the literature on hegemony, even though such phenomena are not uncommon in history: e.g., the U.S. and the International Trade Organization (ITO), and the U.S. and the League of Nations.

3. To the extent that this is the case, regimes may remain resilient in the face of changing power structures—something quite inconsistent with the mainstream view of hegemony. On resilient regimes, see Young (1983), Puchala and Hopkins (1983, p. 89), Keohane and Nye (1985, pp. 49–52), and Keohane (1980).

4. But even here the Bank of France's concerns were not very international, given that it was principally concerned with the bilateral spillover of crisis from London to Paris.

5. No incident better reflected the Bank's need for support in helping stabilize financial markets than the Baring crisis where Governor Lidderdale solicited support from various sources to keep Baring solvent. This would be consistent with collective bargaining notions of hegemony: Young's (1989 and 1991) "institutional bargaining," Maier's (1978) notion of "consensual hegemony," and Whitman's (1975) idea of leadership through "compromise and persuasion." Such a process envisions hegemony as being effected through a group of large powers. Moreover, the burden also fell partly on the weakest monetary players in the world monetary system: peripheral nations.

6. On articulations of a supportership (i.e., collective) vision of hegemonic regimes, see Lake (1983), Kindleberger (1981a, p. 252), Gilpin (1981, p. 227), McKeown (1983, p. 79), Keohane (1984, pp. 37, 38, 136–41), Snidal (1985a, p. 595), Strange (1987, p. 574), Stein (1984, p. 358), Whitman (1975, p. 160), Putnam and Bayne (1987, pp. 272, 273), and Young (1989).

7. That the burden of adjustment in the gold club was partially undertaken (albeit reluctantly) by peripheral nations adds a somewhat new twist to the idea of supportership. Conventional views of collective hegemony posit that hegemons are helped by other powerful (although not as dominant) nations: there are few categories in the literature for weak supporters. At most the latter may qualify as regime breakers, but normally they are not even that, usually being classified as "price takers" (i.e., powers whose actions have little effect on the regime).

8. The literature on hegemony does not normally synthesize the two, although Snidal (1985a) underscores their compatibility.

9. These policies, which were fundamentally of a domestic nature, were essential to the stability of the gold standard. That domestic forces determined actions which had an effect on the international monetary system supports the view that domestic factors are principal catalysts for hegemonic behavior, although even here more purposive hegemonic action is posited in the literature on hegemony than actually took place under the gold standard. On domestic sources of hegemonic behavior, see Gowa (1984), Strange (1987), Keohane (1984), Maier (1978), Krasner (1978), and Block (1977).

10. Kindleberger (1973, p. 28), and Gilpin (1975, p. 48, and 1981, p. 144).

11. The reluctance to hoard gold, which made gold less scarce internationally, was based on a concern for profit.

12. Similarly, in the collective provision of liquidity, it was private investors in the gold club and peripheral nations that were the actual agents of stability in the regime.

13. On references to unintentional and non-state hegemony, see Gilpin (1975, pp. 97, 138, 139), James and Lake (1989, p. 8), Keohane (1984, pp. 140, 141), Young (1980, p. 355), Cleveland (1976, pp. 52–55), and Kindleberger (1981b, pp. 267, 268).

14. The classic statement of this kind of logic was in Carr ([1939] 1966), although neither Carr nor his logic was Marxist. For more recent expressions, see Cox (1980) and Ikenberry and Kupchan (1990).

15. But even here, support came from very weak nations as well, an outcome which diverges from common visions of supportership (although it fits visions of coercive hegemony).

16. Keohane (1983 and 1984) argues that in the absence of hegemony, collective demand on the part of several key players in an issue-area is sufficient to create a regime. Jervis (1983) concurs: one necessary condition for the rise of regimes is that powerful nations want them.

17. Stein (1983) argues that games of common aversion are more conducive to cooperation than games of common interests, yet only in the Conference of 1867 did negotiations end in a consensus declaration about the desirability to construct a gold union. The cases of common aversion were apparently less successful than the case of common interests, although even in the latter national legislatures did not turn the declaration into law.

18. See, for example, Stein (1983).

19. The literature does at least allude to the possibility of residual or default regimes: Keohane (1984, p. 14) states that "regimes arise against the background of earlier attempts, successful or not, at cooperation."

20. We see a classic case of a default regime in the GATT, which went from a temporary mode of organizing trade relations to the institutional center of the post–World War II trade regime when the International Trade Organization (ITO) failed to gain U.S. support.

21. The GATT, as a residual regime, has generated a great deal of criticism, but one rarely sees convincing arguments that alternative regimes would be either more viable or stable. On the adverse effects of cooperation, see Gallarotti (1991).

22. Haas (1980, p. 360) and Waltz (1979, p. 209).

23. On moral hazard and adverse substitution, see Gallarotti (1991).

24. In this sense, stability under the gold standard was primarily an outcome of a normative process: prevailing norms encouraging actions that added up to form a fairly harmonious set of relations.

25. A formal theory of such regimes has not been fully articulated as yet in the literature on international relations. On broadly related work in the greater field of the social sciences, see the citations in Young (1983, pp. 98, 99).

26. The literature is, however, much less enthusiastic about the stability of such regimes. See below.

27. Bagehot ([1873] 1921, p. 14), in fact, identified international finance in the latter 19th century as the "unconscious organization of capital." See also Strange (1988, p. 99), Ford (1989, p. 255), Bloomfield (1963, p. 77), and Viner (1945, p. 63).

28. That the regime emerged from the interplay of both forces on the international and domestic levels suggests that regime formation was the resultant of the convergence of forces from different levels of analysis.

29. This would also pertain to hegemonic and cooperative regimes, with the focus of analysis falling only on the key players which are orchestrating the regime (i.e., regime makers), rather than the more extensive set of participants as in a diffuse regime.

30. On the primacy of domestic factors in determining international outcomes, see Katzenstein (1978). Both Milner (1992) and Haggard and Simmons (1987) underscore the importance of domestic factors in influencing regimes.

31. Within the developed world, nations that didn't make or successfully maintain the link, or delayed (Italy, Spain, Austria-Hungary, Russia), featured domestic structures that were less conducive to a gold link.

32. See, for example, Jervis (1983), Ruggie (1983), and Lipson (1983).

33. See also Snidal (1985b, p. 939), Kindleberger (1976, p. 16), Keohane and Nye (1985, p. 274), and Gilpin (1975, p. 40).

34. Although, even here, the norms of liberalism in developed financial systems gave the periphery the means to adapt to the asymmetrical pulling power. Hence, the exportation of instability between blocs under the gold standard was limited.

35. On embedded regimes, see Keohane (1984, pp. 90, 91), Aggarwal (1985), Ruggie (1983), Cohen (1983, p. 317), and Polanyi (1957).

36. Bordo (1992).

37. Young (1983) points out that regime stability is generally dependent on the absence of such exogenous shocks. This suggests that diffuse regimes will, *ceteris paribus*, be more fragile than managed regimes (hegemonic or cooperative) because adaptation to adverse outcomes from outside the regime cannot be as readily orchestrated.

38. Young (1983, p. 103) notes that regimes frequently evolve from one form into another. Puchala and Hopkins (1983, p. 89) add that in fact regimes will evolve toward more formal modes of organization in response to crises. In this sense, the informality in the organizational form of a regime may signal strength rather than weakness if, in fact, formal organization is a response to adverse outcomes.

39. As Keohane and Nye (1985, p. 273) point out, "Issues lacking serious conflicts of interest may need very little institutional structure."

40. Both Eichengreen (1986a) and Giavazzi and Giovannini (1988) underscore the fact that implicit macroeconomic policy coordination will be a natural outcome of a gold standard as long as the nominal parities are being maintained in orthodox fashion.

41. The literature on cooperative regimes points out that coordination games require far less regulation than more conflictual interactional settings like Stag Hunts or Prisoner's Dilemmas. Snidal (1985b, p. 932) argues that "the simple coordination problem is almost certain to result in a decentralized solution." See also Keohane and Nye (1985, p. 273) and Stein (1983).

42. This draws again from Keohane's (1984, p. 51) definition of harmony.

43. This fits one of Young's (1983) principal conditions for regime stability: that regimes possess limited inconsistencies between required behavior and national interests. Under the gold standard, few such inconsistencies manifested themselves in the structure of adjustment.

44. The literature on credible rules has been principally concerned with macroeconomic stabilization policies. Most of the arguments have been articulated in the context of monetary rules. See Kydland and Prescott (1977), Bordo and Kydland (1990), and Bordo (1992).

In a strategic-international-relations context, rules could serve to assure players in strategic games that other players will not defect from some desired equilibrium. The rules in this case might make a Pareto-optimal equilibrium more robust by either limiting opportunities for predation or by introducing focal points which make coordination games easier to solve. Strategic interactions can attain desired collective outcomes to the extent that actions become more predictable; rules are one way to enhance this predictability. See Finlayson and Zacher (1983, p. 314), Young (1989, pp. 369, 370), and Wagner (1983). On focal points in coordination games, see Schelling (1981).

45. Several contributions to the regime literature note the special role of self-sustaining mechanisms in stable regimes. The role of such processes appears all the more important in diffuse regimes, given the scarcity of managerial elements in such systems. This may suggest another reason why diffuse regimes would be fragile: once the self-sustaining processes in a

regime break down, the restoration of such properties might be a long and painful process in the absence of management. On self-sustaining processes in regimes, see Jervis (1983), Young (1982, p. 16), and Krasner (1983c, p. 361).

46. Probably the most visible manifestation of this thinking is in Buchanan's (1989) call for a constitutional amendment for stable money.

47. Corden (1977, pp. 139, 140) observes that "if countries make adequate use of policy instruments available to them, there is no need for coordination of policies. . . . And if their policies are intelligent and speedy, they will achieve whatever stabilization they wish to achieve." See also Feldstein (1988), McCallum (1989, p. 296), Tumlir (1985), Emminger (1976), and Volcker (1976).

48. The U.S. used the recent Plaza Accord in 1985 to do collectively (intervene to bring the dollar down) what it hesitated to do unilaterally (bring the dollar down by reducing the budget deficit). Such intervention schemes would reduce the pressure on nations running high deficits to reduce them, since one of the major adverse consequences of such deficits (an overvaluation of the offender's currency) would be mitigated. See Gallarotti (1991, pp. 210, 211).

49. Jervis (1983) identifies a limited capacity for moral hazard as a crucial condition for the stability of any regime. See also Cohen (1983, p. 319).

50. But although such regimes have a built-in bias against moral hazard, they also lack the external discipline possessed by cooperative and hegemonic regimes to compel nations to refrain from behaving in ways that might destabilize the regime. The discipline in diffuse regimes must be internal. Under the gold standard, it was—in the form of domestic norms.

51. As such, it vindicates Cooper's (1987, p. 3) argument that even diffuse regimes are not systems without rules.

52. Ruggie (1975, pp. 569, 570) uses the term "epistemes": sets of shared symbols and references which condition behavior in the greater international political economy. The social goals, symbols, and references under the gold standard were almost exclusively on a domestic level.

53. See Adler and Haas (1992, p. 375).

54. Krasner (1983c, p. 360) underscores the dependence of regimes on cognitive legitimacy. Haas (1980) cites consensual knowledge as a fundamental precondition for the emergence of regimes. On consensual knowledge and regimes, see also Haas (1989 and 1992).

References

Acres, W. Marston. 1931. *The Bank of England From Within*. London: Oxford University Press.

Adler, Emanuel and Peter Haas. 1992. "Conclusion: Epistemic Communities, World Order, and the Creation of a Reflective Research Program." *International Organization* (Winter), 46:367–90.

Aggarwal, Vinod. 1985. *Liberal Protectionism: The Politics of Organized Textile Trade*. Berkeley: University of California Press.

Albrecht-Carrie, Rene. 1950. *Italy From Napoleon to Mussolini*. New York: Columbia University Press.

Andreades, A. 1909. *History of the Bank of England*. Translated by Christabel Meredith. London: P.S. King & Son.

Angell, J. W. [1925] 1965. *The Theory of International Prices*. New York: Augustus M. Kelley.

Ashworth, William. 1952. *A Short History of the International Economy*. London: Longmans, Green and Co.

Bagehot, Walter. [1873] 1921. *Lombard Street: A Description of the Money Market*. New York: E. P. Dutton.

Bank for International Settlements 1943. *Thirteenth Annual Report*. (Autumn). Basel: Bank for International Settlements.

Barnouw, A. J. 1944. *The Making of Modern Holland: A Short History*. New York: Norton.

Barro, Robert. 1986. "Rules Versus Discretion." In Colin Campbell and William Dougan, eds., *Alternative Monetary Regimes*, pp. 16–30. Baltimore: Johns Hopkins University Press.

Barro, Robert. 1987. "Government Spending, Interest Rates, Prices, and Budget Deficits in the United Kingdom, 1701–1918." *Journal of Monetary Economics*, 20:221–47.

Barsky, Robert and J. Bradford De Long. 1991. "Forecasting Pre-World War I Inflation: The Fisher Effect and the Gold Standard." *Quarterly Journal of Economics* (August) 106:815–36.

Batchelor, Roy. 1986. "The Avoidance of Catastrophe: Two Nineteenth-century Banking Crises," in Forrest Capie and Geoffrey Wood, eds., *Financial Crises and the World Banking System*, pp. 41–73. New York: St. Martin's Press.

Beach, W. 1935. *British International Gold Movements and Banking Policy, 1881–1913*. Cambridge: Harvard University Press.

Beales, H.L. 1934. "The 'Great Depression' In Industry and Trade." *Economic History Review* (October) 5:65–75.

Beard, Charles and Mary Beard. 1927. *The Rise of American Civilization*. Vol. II. New York: Macmillan.

Bergsten, C. Fred. 1975. *The Dilemmas of the Dollar: The Economics and Politics of United States International Monetary Policy.* Washington: Council on Foreign Relations.

Beyen, J. W. 1949. *Money in a Maelstrom.* New York: Macmillan.

Birch, J. H. S. 1938. *Denmark in History.* London: John Murray.

Blaine, James G. 1884. *Twenty Years of Congress From Lincoln to Garfield.* Vols. I & II. Norwich: Henry Bill.

Blank, Stephen. 1978. "Britain: The Politics of Foreign Economic Policy, the Domestic Economy, and the Problem of Pluralistic Stagnation." In Peter J. Katzenstein, ed., *Between Power and Plenty: Foreign Economic Policies of Advanced Industrial Sates*, pp. 89–138. Madison: University of Wisconsin Press.

Block, Fred. 1977. *The Origins of International Economic Disorder.* Berkeley: University of California Press.

Bloomfield, Arthur. 1959. *Monetary Policy Under the International Gold Standard: 1880–1914.* New York: Federal Reserve Bank of New York.

Bloomfield, Arthur. 1963. *Short-Term Capital Movements Under the Pre–1914 Gold Standard.* Princeton Studies in International Finance, no. 11. Princeton: Princeton University Press.

Bloomfield, Arthur. 1968a. *Patterns of Fluctuation in International Investment Before 1914.* Princeton Studies in International Finance, no. 21. Princeton: Princeton University Press.

Bloomfield, Arthur. 1968b. "Rules of the Game of International Adjustment?" In C.R. Whittlesey and J.S.G. Wilson, eds., *Essays in Money and Banking in Honor of R.S. Sayers*, pp. 26–46. Oxford: Oxford University Press.

Bohme, Helmut. 1978. *An Introduction to the Social and Economic History of Germany: Politics and Economic Change in the Nineteenth and Twentieth Centuries.* Translated by W.R. Lee. Oxford: Oxford University Press.

Bordo, Michael. 1981. "The Classical Gold Standard: Some Lessons for Today." *Federal Reserve Bank of St. Louis Review* (May) 63:2–17.

Bordo, Michael. 1984. "The Gold Standard: The Traditional Approach." In Michael Bordo and Anna Schwartz, eds., *A Retrospective on the Classical Gold Standard*, pp. 23–120. Chicago: University of Chicago Press.

Bordo, Michael. 1986. "Explorations in Monetary History: A Survey of the Literature." *Explorations in Economic History* (October) 23:339–415.

Bordo, Michael. 1987. "Bimetallism." *The New Palgrave.* London: Macmillan.

Bordo, Michael. 1989. "The Lender of Last Resort: Some Historical Insights." *NBER Working Papers* No. 3011 (June).

Bordo, Michael. 1992. "The Gold Standard and Other Monetary Regimes." *NBER Reporter* (Spring).

Bordo, Michael and Finn Kydland. 1990. "The Gold Standard as a Rule." *NBER Working Papers* No. 3367 (May).

Bordo, Michael and Anna Schwartz, eds. 1984. *A Retrospective on the Classical Gold Standard.* Chicago: University of Chicago Press.

Bourne, Kenneth. 1970. *The Foreign Policy of Victorian England 1830–1902.* Oxford: Oxford University Press.

Bouvier, Jean. 1970. "The Banking Mechanism in France in the Late 19th Century." In Rondo Cameron, ed. *Essays in French Economic History*, pp. 341–69. Homewood: Irwin.

Bowden, Witt, Michael Karpovitch, and Abbott Usher. 1937. *An Economic History of Europe Since 1750.* New York: American Book Co.

Brittain, W. H. Bruce. 1976. "The Relevance of Political Leadership to Economic Order: Evidence From the Interwar Period." In Benjamin M. Rowland, ed., *Balance of Power* or Hegemony: The Interwar Monetary System, pp. 61–82. New York: New York University Press.

Brown, A. J. 1965. "Britain in the World Economy." *Yorkshire Bulletin of Economic and Social Research* (May) 17:46–60.

Brown, William Adams Jr. 1929. *England and the Gold Standard 1919–1926*. New Haven: Yale University Press.

Brown, William Adams Jr. 1940. *The International Gold Standard Reinterpreted 1914–34*. Vol. I. New York: NBER.

Broz, J. Lawrence. 1989. "The Rise of the United States, International Monetary Instability, and the Origins of the Federal Reserve Act of 1913." Paper delivered at the Annual Meeting of the American Political Science Association.

Brunner, Karl. 1984. "Comment." In Michael Bordo and Anna Schwartz, eds., *A Retrospective on the Classical Gold Standard*, pp. 446, 447. Chicago: University of Chicago Press.

Buchanan, James. 1989. "Reductionist Reflections on the Monetary Constitution." *Cato Journal* (Fall) 9:295–300.

Bullock, Charles. 1900. *Essays on the Monetary History of the United States*. London: Macmillan.

Cairncross, A. K. 1953. *Home and Foreign Investment 1870–1913*. Cambridge: Cambridge University Press.

Calleo, David P., ed., 1976. *Money and the Coming World Order*. New York: New York University Press.

Calleo, David P. and Benjamin M. Rowland. 1973. *America and the World Political Economy: Atlantic Dreams and National Realities*. Bloomington: Indiana University Press.

Cammaerts, Emile. 1921. *A History of Belgium*. New York: Appleton.

Cantillon, Richard. [1775] 1964. *Essai Sur La Nature Du Commerce En General*, ed. by H. Higgs. New York: Augustus M. Kelly.

Capie, Forrest and Alan Weber, eds., 1985. *A Monetary History of the United Kingdom, 1870–1982*. Vol I. London: George Allen & Unwin.

Carr, Edward Hallett. [1939] 1966. *The Twenty Years' Crisis 1919–1939*. New York: St. Martin's Press.

Chapman, Guy. 1962. *The Third Republic of France: The First Phase 1871–1894*. New York: St. Martin's Press.

Chevalier, Michel. 1859. *On the Probable Fall in the Value of Gold*. Translated by Richard Cobden. New York: Appleton.

Clapham, John. 1944. *The Bank of England: A History*. Vols. I & II. Cambridge: Cambridge University Press.

Clare, George. 1909. *A Money-Market Primer, and Key to the Exchanges*. London: Effingham Wilson.

Clark, Champ. 1920. *My Quarter Century in Politics*. Vol.I. New York: Harper and Brothers.

Clark, Truman. 1984. "Violations of the Gold Points, 1890–1914." *Journal of Political Economy* (October) 92:791–823.

Cleveland, Harold van B. 1976. "The International Monetary System in the Interwar Period." In Benjamin M. Rowland, ed., *Balance of Power or Hegemony: The Interwar Monetary System*, pp. 1–60. New York: New York University Press.

Clough, Shepard. 1964. *France: A History of National Economics 1789–1939*. New York: Scribner's.

Clough, Shepard and Charles Cole. 1946. *Economic History of Europe*. Boston: Heath.

Cochran, Thomas and William Miller. 1951. *The Age of Enterprise: A Social History of America*. New York: Macmillan.

Cohen, Benjamin J. 1977. *Organizing the World's Money: The Political Economy of International Monetary Relations*. New York: Basic Books.

Cohen, Benjamin J. 1983. "Balance-of-Payments Financing: Evolution of a Regime." In Stephen D. Krasner, ed., *International Regimes*, pp. 315–36. Ithaca, NY: Cornell University Press.

Condliffe, J. B. 1950. *The Commerce of Nations*. New York: Norton.

Cooper, Richard. 1982. "The Gold Standard: Historical Facts and Future Prospects." *Brookings Papers on Economic Activity*. Washington, D.C.: Brookings Institution.

Cooper, Richard. 1987. "Prolegomena to the Choice of an International Monetary System." In Cooper, *The International Monetary System: Essays in World Economics*. Cambridge: MIT Press.

Corden, W. Max. 1977. "The Coordination of Stabilization Policies Among Countries." In Albert Ando, Richard Herring, and Richard Marston, eds., *International Aspects of Stabilization Policies*. Conference Series no. 12. Boston: Federal Reserve Bank of Boston.

Corden, W. Max. 1986. "Fiscal Policies, Current Accounts and Real Exchange Rates: In Search of a Logic of International Policy Coordination." *Weltwirtschaftliches Archiv*, 122:423–38.

Cottrell, P. L. 1975. *British Overseas Investment in the Nineteenth Century*. London: Macmillan.

Cox, Robert. W. 1980. "The Crisis of World Order and the Problem of International Organization in the 1980s." *International Journal* (Spring) 35:370–95.

Cramp, A. B. 1962. *Opinion on the Bank Rate, 1822–60*. London: G. Bell and Sons.

Dam, Kenneth. 1982. *The Rules of The Game: Reform and Evolution in The International Monetary System*. Chicago: University of Chicago Press.

Dandliker, Karl. 1899. *A Short History of Switzerland*. Translated by E. Salisbury. London: Swan Sonnenschein.

Darwin, Major Leonard. 1897. *Bimetallism: A Summary and Examination of the Arguments for and Against a Bimetallic System of Currency*. London: John Murray.

de Cecco, Marcello. 1974. *Money and Empire: The International Gold Standard, 1890–1914*. Totowa: Rowman and Littlefield.

Derry, T. K. 1968. *A Short History of Norway*. Westport: Greenwood.

Diebold, Fransis X., Steven Husted, and Mark Rush. 1991. "Real Exchange Rates Under the Gold Standard." *Journal of Political Economy* (December) 99:1252–71.

Dodwell, David William. 1934. *Treasuries and Central Banks*. London: P. S. King & Son.

Dornbusch, Rudiger and Jacob Frenkel. 1984. "The Gold Standard and the Bank of England in the Crisis of 1847." In Michael Bordo and Anna Schwartz, eds., *A Retrospective on the Classical Gold Standard, 1821–1931*, pp. 233–64. Chicago: University of Chicago Press.

Drummond, I. 1976. "The Russian Gold Standard." *Journal of Economic History* (September) 36:663–88.

Dutton, John. 1984. "The Bank of England and the Rules of the Game Under the International Gold Standard: New Evidence." In Michael Bordo and Anna Schwartz, eds., *A Retrospective on the Classical Gold Standard*, pp. 173–95. Chicago: University of Chicago Press.

Easton, Stephen T. 1984. "Real Output and the Gold Standard Years, 1830–1913." In Michael Bordo and Anna Schwartz, eds., *A Retrospective on the Classical Gold Standard, 1821–1931*, pp. 513–38. Chicago: University of Chicago Press.

Economist. 1866. October 27.

Economist. 1987. September 26.

Economist. 1990. "The State of the Nation-State." December 22.

Edelstein, Michael. 1982. *Overseas Investment in the Age of High Imperialism*. New York: Columbia University Press.

Eichengreen, Barry. 1984. "Central Bank Cooperation Under the Interwar Gold Standard." *Explorations in Economic History* (January) 21:64–87.

Eichengreen, Barry, ed. 1985a. *The Gold Standard in Theory and History*. New York: Methuen.

Eichengreen, Barry. 1985b. "Editor's Introduction." In Eichengreen, ed., *The Gold Standard in Theory and History*, pp. 1–36. New York: Methuen.

Eichengreen, Barry. 1986a. "International Policy Coordination in Historical Perspective: A View From the Interwar Years." In Willem Buiter and Richard Marston, eds., *International Economic Policy Coordination*, pp. 139–83. Cambridge: Cambridge University Press.

Eichengreen, Barry. 1986b. "Conducting the International Orchestra: The Bank of England and Strategic Interdependence Under the Classical Gold Standard." *Brookings Discussion Papers in International Economics* No. 43 (March).

Eichengreen, Barry. 1989. "The Gold Standard Since Alec Ford." *NBER Working Papers* No. 3122 (September).

Eichengreen, Barry. 1990a. "Hegemonic Stability Theories of the International Monetary System." In Eichengreen *Elusive Stability: Essays in the History of International Finance, 1919–1939*, pp. 271–311. Cambridge: Cambridge University Press.

Eichengreen, Barry. 1990b. "Trends and Cycles in Foreign Lending." *NBER Working Papers* No. 3411 (August).

Eichengreen, Barry. 1991."The Gold Standard and the Great Depression." *NBER Reporter*. (Spring).

Eichengreen, Barry. 1992. *Golden Fetters: The Gold Standard and the Great Depression*. New York: Oxford University Press.

Einzig, Paul. 1970. *The History of Foreign Exchange*. London: Macmillan.

Ellstaetter, Karl. 1895. *The Indian Silver Currency: An Historical and Economic Study*. Translated by J. Laurence Laughlin. Chicago: University of Chicago Press.

Emminger, Otmar. 1976. "Contribution." In Robert Mundell and Jacques Polak, eds., *The New International Monetary System*, pp. 3–24. New York: Columbia University Press.

Farmer, E. J. [1886] 1969. *Conspiracy Against Silver or a Plea for Bimetallism in the United States*. New York: Greenwood.

Feis, Herbert. 1930. *Europe: The World's Banker*. New Haven: Yale University Press.

Feldstein, Martin. 1988. "Let the Market Decide." *Economist*, December 3.

Fetter, Frank. 1965. *Development of British Monetary Orthodoxy 1797–1875*. Cambridge: Harvard University Press.

Finlayson, Jock A. and Mark W. Zacher. 1983. "The GATT and the Regulation of Trade Barriers: Regime Dynamics and Functions." In Stephen D. Krasner, ed., *International Regimes*, pp. 273–314. Ithaca, NY: Cornell University Press.

Fischer, Wolfram. 1982. "Comment." In Charles Kindleberger and Jean-Pierre Laffargue, eds., *Financial Crises: Theory, History, and Policy*, pp. 166–67. Cambridge: Cambridge University Press.

Flood, Robert P., Andrew K. Rose, and Donald J. Mathieson. 1990. "An Empirical Exploration of Exchange Rate Target Zones." *NBER Working Papers* No. 3543 (December).

Flotow, Ernst. 1941. "The Congress of German Economists, 1858–1885: A Study of German Unification." Ph.D. dissertation: American University.

Ford, A. G. 1962. *The Gold Standard 1880–1914 Britain and Argentina*. Oxford: Clarendon.

Ford, A. G. 1965. "Overseas Lending and Internal Fluctuations: 1870–1914." *Yorkshire Bulletin of Economic and Social Research* (May) 17:19–30.

Ford, A. G. 1989. "International Financial Policy and the Gold Standard, 1870–1914." In Peter Mathias and Sidney Pollard, eds., *Cambridge Economic History* Vol. VIII, pp. 250–314. Cambridge: Cambridge University Press.

Fratianni, Michele and Franco Spinelli. 1984. "Italy in the Gold Standard Period." In Michael Bordo and Anna Schwartz, eds., *A Retrospective on the Classical Gold Standard, 1821–1931*, pp. 405–41. Chicago: University of Chicago Press.

Friedberg, Aaron L. 1988. *The Weary Titan: Britain and the Experience of Relative Decline, 1895–1905*. Princeton: Princeton University Press.

Frieden, Jeffry A. 1991. "Greenback, Gold and Silver: The Politics of American Exchange Rate Policy 1870–1973." *UCLA Center for International Business Education and Research Working Paper* (April).

Friedman, Milton. 1960. *A Program for Monetary Stability*. New York: Fordham University Press.

Friedman, Milton. 1990a. "The Crime of 1873." *Journal of Political Economy* (December) 98:1159–94.

Friedman, Milton. 1990b. "Bimetallism Revisited." *Journal of Economic Perspectives* (Fall) 4:85–104.

Friedman, Milton and Anna Schwartz. 1963. *A Monetary History of the United States*. Princeton: Princeton University Press.

Funabashi, Yoichi. 1988. *Managing the Dollar: From Plaza to the Louvre*. Washington, DC: Institute for International Economics.

Gallarotti, Giulio. 1985. "Toward a Business-Cycle Model of Tariffs." *International Organization* (Winter) 39:155–87.

Gallarotti, Giulio. 1991. "The Limits of International Organization: Systematic Failure in the Management of International Relations." *International Organization* (Spring) 45:183–220.

Gallarotti, Giulio. 1993. "The Scramble for Gold: Monetary Regime Transformation in the 1870s." In Michael Bordo and Forrest Capie, eds., *Monetary Regimes in Transition*, pp. 15–67. Cambridge: Cambridge University Press.

Garber, Peter. 1986. "Nominal Contracts in a Bimetallist Standard." *American Economic Review* (March) 76:1012–30.

Gardner, Richard. 1956. *Sterling-Dollar Diplomacy: Anglo-American Collaboration in the Reconstruction of Multilateral Trade*. Oxford: Oxford University Press.

Giavazzi, Francesco and Alberto Giovannini. 1988. "Can the European Monetary System Be Copied Outside? Lessons From Ten Years of Monetary Policy Coordination in Europe." *NBER Working Papers* No. 2786 (December).

Gilbert, R. Alton and Geoffrey E. Wood. 1986. "Coping With Bank Failures: Some Lessons From the United States and United Kingdom." *Federal Reserve Bank of St. Louis Review* (December), pp. 5–14.

Gilpin, Robert. 1975. *U.S. Power and the Multinational Corporation: The Political Economy of Foreign Direct Investment*. New York: Basic Books.

Gilpin, Robert. 1981. *War and Change in World Politics*. Cambridge: Cambridge University Press.

Giovannini, Alberto. 1988. "How Do Fixed-Exchange-Rates Regimes Work: The Evidence From the Gold Standard, Bretton Woods and the EMS." *NBER Working Papers* No. 2766 (November).

Giovannini, Alberto. 1993. "Bretton Woods and Its Precursors: Rules Versus Discretion in the History of International Monetary Regimes." In Michael Bordo and Barry Eichengreen, eds., *A Retrospective on the Bretton Woods System: Lessons for International Monetary Reform*, pp. 109–47. Chicago: University of Chicago Press.

Goodhart, C. A. E. 1972. *The Business of Banking, 1891–1914*. London: London School of Economics.

Goschen, George J. 1876. *The Theory of Foreign Exchanges*. London: Effingham Wilson.

Gowa, Joanne. 1984. "Hegemons, IOs, and Markets: The Case of the Substitution Account." *International Organization* (Autumn) 38:661–83.

Great Britain. *First Interim Report of the Cunliffe Committee on Currency and Foreign Exchanges After the War*. [1918] 1985. Reprinted in Barry Eichengreen, ed., *The Gold Standard in Theory and History*, pp. 169–83. New York: Methuen.

Great Britain. *Gold and Silver Commission*. [1888] 1936. Reprinted in Ralph Robey, ed., *The Monetary Problem Gold and Silver*. New York: Columbia University Press.

Great Britain. *Hansard's Parliamentary Debates*.

Great Britain. *Papers Relating to Silver*. 1877. In *British Parliamentary Papers: Monetary Policy Currency*, Vol. 6, pp. 377–745. Shannon: Irish University Press.

Great Britain. *Report From the Royal Commission on International Coinage*. 1868. In *British Parliamentary Papers: Monetary Policy Currency*, Vol. 3, pp. 57–452. Shannon: Irish University Press.

Great Britain. *Report From the Select Committee on Depreciation of Silver*. 1876. In *British Parliamentary Papers: Monetary Policy Currency*, Vol. 6, pp. 9–376. Shannon: Irish University Press.

Great Britain. *Report of the Commissioners Representing Great Britain at the Paris Conference*. 1878. In *British Parliamentary Papers: Monetary Policy Currency*, Vol. 4, pp. 9–20. Shannon: Irish University Press.

Great Britain. *Report of the Macmillan Committee on Finance and Industry*. [1931] 1985. Reprinted in Barry Eichengreen, ed., *The Gold Standard in Theory and History*, pp. 185–99. New York: Methuen.

Greenfield, Robert and Hugh Rockoff. 1991. "Gresham's Law Regained." Rutgers University, unpublished manuscript.

Gregory, T. E., ed., 1964. *Select Statutes, Documents & Reports Relating to British Banking 1832–1928*. Vols. I & II. New York: Augustus M. Kelley.

Grenville, J. A. S. 1964. *Lord Salisbury and Foreign Policy: The Close of the Nineteenth Century*. London: Athlone Press.

Grilli, Vittorio. 1989. "Managing Exchange Rate Crises: Evidence From the 1890's." *NBER Working Papers* No. 3068 (August).

Grubel, Herbert G. 1969. *The International Monetary System: Efficiency and Practical Alternatives*. New York: Penguin.

Haas, Ernst B. 1980. "Why Collaborate? Issue-Linkage and International Regimes." *World Politics* (April) 32:357–405.

Haas, Peter M. 1989. "Do Regimes Matter? Epistemic Communities and Mediterranean Pollution Control." *International Organization* (Summer) 43:377–404.

Haas, Peter M., ed., 1992. Special Issue of *International Organization* (Winter) 46.

Haberler, Gottfried. 1964. "Integration and Growth of the World Economy in Historical Perspective." *American Economic Review* (March) 54:1–22.

Haggard, Stephan and Beth A. Simmons. 1987. "Theories of International Regimes." *International Organization* (Summer) 41:491–517.

Hall, Robert E. 1980. "Monetary Policy for Disinflation, Remarks Prepared for the Federal Reserve Board." Stanford University, unpublished manuscript.

Hamerow, Theodore. 1958. *Restoration, Revolution, Reaction: Economics and Politics in Germany 1815–1871*. Princeton: Princeton University Press.

Hamerow, Theodore. 1972. *The Social Foundations of German Unification 1858–1871: Struggles and Accomplishments*. Princeton: Princeton University Press.

Hankey, Thomson. 1873. *The Principles of Banking, Its Utility and Economy; With Remarks on the Working and Management of the Bank of England.* London: Effingham Wilson.

Hardin, Russell. 1982. *Collective Action.* Baltimore: John Hopkins University Press.

Hawtrey, R. G. 1930. *Currency and Credit.* London: Longmans, Green and Co.

Hawtrey, R. G. 1932. *The Art of Central Banking.* London: Longmans, Green and Co.

Hawtrey, R. G. 1938. *A Century of the Bank Rate.* London: Longmans, Green and Co.

Hawtrey, R. G. 1947. *The Gold Standard in Theory and Practice.* London: Longmans, Green and Co.

Helfferich, Karl. 1927. *Money.* Vols. I & II. Translated by Louis Infield. New York: Adelphi.

Hicks, John. 1931. *The Populist Revolt: A History of the Farmers' Alliance and the People's Party.* Minneapolis: University of Minnesota Press.

Horton, S. Dana. 1892. *Silver in Europe.* New York: Macmillan.

Huffman, Wallace and Lothian, James. 1984. "The Gold Standard and the Transmission of Business Cycles, 1833–1932." In Michael Bordo and Anna Schwartz, eds., *A Retrospective on the Classical Gold Standard*, pp. 455–507. Chicago: University of Chicago Press.

Hume, David. [1752] 1955. *Of the Balance of Trade.* Reprinted in E. Rotwein, ed., *Writings on Economics.* Madison: University of Wisconsin Press.

Ikenberry, G. John and Charles A. Kupchan. 1990. "Socialization and Hegemonic Power." *International Organization* (Summer) 44:283–316.

Jacobson, Harold. 1984. *Networks of Interdependence: International Organization and the Global Political System.* 2nd Edition. New York: Knopf.

James, Scott C. and David A. Lake. 1989. "The Second Face of Hegemony: Britain's Repeal of the Corn Laws and the American Walker Tariff of 1846." *International Organization* (Winter) 43:1–30.

Jervis, Robert. 1976. *Perception and Misperception in International Politics.* Princeton: Princeton University Press.

Jervis, Robert. 1983. "Security Regimes." In Stephen D. Krasner, ed., *International Regimes*, pp. 173–94. Ithaca, NY: Cornell University Press.

Jevons, W. Stanley. [1884] 1909. *Investigations in Currency and Finance.* London: Macmillan.

Jonung, Lars. 1984. "Swedish Experience under the Classical Gold Standard, 1873–1914." In Michael Bordo and Anna Schwartz, eds., *A Retrospective on the Classical Gold Standard, 1821 1931*, pp. 361–99. Chicago: University of Chicago Press.

Katzenstein, Peter J., ed., 1978. *Between Power and Plenty: Foreign Economic Policies of Advanced Industrial States.* Madison: University of Wisconsin Press.

Kemmerer, Edwin Walter. 1935. *Money.* New York: Macmillan.

Kennedy, Paul. 1981a. "Strategy Versus Finance in Twentieth-Century Great Britain." *International History Review* (January) 3:44–61.

Kennedy, Paul. 1981b. *The Realities Behind Diplomacy: Background Influences on British External Policy, 1865–1980.* London: Fontana.

Kenwood, A. G. and A. L. Lougheed. 1983. *The Growth of the International Economy 1820–1980.* London: George Allen & Unwin.

Keohane, Robert. O. 1980. "The Theory of Hegemonic Stability and Changes in International Economic Regimes." In Ole Holsti, Randolph Siverson, and Alexander George, eds., *Change in the International System*, pp. 131–62. Boulder: Westview Press.

Keohane, Robert O. 1983. "The Demand for International Regimes." In Stephen D. Krasner, ed., *International Regimes*, pp. 141–72. Ithaca, NY: Cornell University Press.

Keohane, Robert O. 1984. *After Hegemony: Cooperation and Discord in the World Political Economy.* Princeton: Princeton University Press.

Keohane, Robert O. and Joseph S. Nye, Jr. 1985. *Power and Interdependence: World Politics in Transition.* 2nd Ed. Glenview, IL, Scott, Foresman.

Keynes, John Maynard. [1913] 1971. *Indian Currency and Finance* in *The Collected Writings of John Maynard Keynes*. London: Macmillan.

Keynes, John Maynard. 1930. *Treatise on Money*. Vol. II. London: Macmillan.

Keynes, John Maynard. [1931] 1952. *Essays in Persuasion*. London: Rupert Hart-Davis.

Kindleberger, Charles. 1963. *International Economics*. 3rd Edition. Homewood: Richard D. Irwin.

Kindleberger, Charles. 1973. *The World in Depression 1929–1939*. Berkeley: University of California Press.

Kindleberger, Charles. 1975. "The Rise of Free Trade in Western Europe, 1820–1875." *Journal of Economic History* (March) 35:20–55.

Kindleberger, Charles. 1976. "Systems of International Economic Organization." In David P. Calleo, ed., *Money and the Coming World Order*, pp. 15–40. New York: New York University Press.

Kindleberger, Charles. 1978. *Manias, Panics and Crashes: A History of Financial Crises*. New York: Basic Books.

Kindleberger, Charles. 1981a. "Dominance and Leadership in the International Economy: Exploitation, Public Goods, and Free Rides." *International Studies Quarterly* (June) 25:242–54.

Kindleberger, Charles. 1981b. "Quantity and Price, Especially in Financial Markets." In Kindleberger *International Money: A Collection of Essays*. London: George Allen & Unwin.

Kindleberger, Charles. 1984. *A Financial History of Western Europe*. London: George Allen & Unwin.

Kindleberger, Charles. 1988. *The International Economic Order: Essays on Financial Crises and International Public Goods*. Cambridge: MIT Press.

King, W. T. C. 1936. *History of the London Discount Market*. London: Routledge.

Klein, Benjamin. 1975. "Our Monetary Standard: The Measurement and Effects of Price Uncertainty, 1880–1973." *Economic Inquiry* (December) 13:461–84.

Knaplund, Paul. 1935. *Gladstone's Foreign Policy*. New York: Harper & Brothers.

Krasner, Stephen D. 1976. "State Power and The Structure of International Trade." *World Politics* (April) 28:317–47.

Krasner, Stephen D. 1978. "United States Commercial and Monetary Policy: Unravelling the Paradox of External Strength and Internal Weakness." In Peter J. Katzenstein, ed., *Between Power and Plenty: Foreign Economic Policies of Advanced Industrial States*, pp. 51–88. Madison: University of Wisconsin Press.

Krasner, Stephen D., ed., 1983a. *International Regimes*. Ithaca, NY: Cornell University Press.

Krasner, Stephen D. 1983b. "Structural Causes and Regime Consequences: Regimes as Intervening Variables." In Stephen D. Krasner, ed., *International Regimes*, pp. 1–22. Ithaca, NY: Cornell University Press.

Krasner, Stephen D. 1983c. "Regimes and the Limits of Realism: Regimes as Autonomous Variables." In Stephen D. Krasner, ed., *International Regimes*, pp. 355–68. Ithaca, NY: Cornell University Press.

Krugman, Paul. 1991. "History Versus Expectations." *Quarterly Journal of Economics* (May) 106:651–67.

Kydland, Finn and Edward Prescott. 1977. "Rules Rather Than Discretion: The Inconsistency of Optimal Plans." *Journal of Political Economy* (June) 85:473–91.

Lake, David. 1983. "International Economic Structures and Foreign Economic Policy, 1887–1934." *World Politics* (July) 35:517–43.

Laughlin, J. Laurence. 1886. *The History of Bimetallism in the United States*. New York: Appleton.

Laughlin, J. Laurence. 1931. *Money, Credit and Prices*. Vols. I & II. Chicago: University of Chicago Press.

Leavens, Dickson H. 1939. *Silver Money*. Bloomington: Principia.

Lehrman, Lewis E. 1976. "The Creation of International Monetary Order." In David P. Calleo, ed., *Money and the Coming World Order*, pp. 71–120. New York: New York University Press.

Letiche, John M. 1959. *Balance of Payments and Economic Growth*. New York: Harper & Brothers.

Levy-Leboyer, Maurice. 1982. "Central Banking and Foreign Trade: The Anglo-American Cycle in the 1830s." In Charles Kindleberger and Jean-Pierre Laffargue, eds., *Financial Crises: Theory, History, and Policy*. Cambridge: Cambridge University Press.

Lewis, W. Arthur. 1978. *Growth and Fluctuations 1870–1913*. London: George Allen B. Unwin.

Lindert, Peter. 1969. *Key Currencies and Gold 1900–1913*. Princeton Studies in International Finance, No. 24. Princeton: Princeton University Press.

Lindert, Peter. 1986. *International Economics*. 8th Edition. Homewood: Irwin.

Lipson, Charles. 1983. "The Transformation of Trade: The Sources and Effects of Regime Change." In Stephen D. Krasner, ed., *International Regimes*, pp. 233–72. Ithaca, NY: Cornell University Press.

Lipson, Charles. 1985. *Standing Guard: Protecting Foreign Capital in the Nineteenth and Twentieth Centuries*. Berkeley: University of California Press.

Lovell, Michael C. 1957. "The Role of the Bank of England as Lender of Last Resort in the Crises of the Eighteenth Century." *Explorations in Entrepreneurial History* (October) 10:8–21.

Lovett, Clara. 1982. *The Democratic Movement in Italy*. Cambridge: Harvard University Press.

Machlup, Fritz. 1964. *International Payments, Debts, and Gold*. New York: Charles Scribner's Sons.

MacRae, C. Duncan 1977. "A Political Model of the Business Cycle." *Journal of Political Economy* (April) 85:239–63.

Maier, Charles S. 1978. "The Politics of Productivity: Foundations of American International Economic Policy After World War II." In Peter J. Katzenstein, ed., *Between Power and Plenty: Foreign Economic Policies of Advanced Industrial States*, pp. 23–50. Madison: University of Wisconsin Press.

Martin, David. 1973. "1853: The End of Bimetallism in the United States." *Journal of Economic History* (December) 33:825–44.

Matthews, R.C.O. 1982. "Comment." In Charles Kindleberger and Jean-Pierre Laffargue, eds., *Financial Crises: Theory, History, and Policy*, pp. 110–13. Cambridge: Cambridge University Press.

McCallum, Bennett T. 1984. "Some Issues Concerning Interest Rate Pegging, Price Level Determinacy, and the Real Bills Doctrine." *NBER Working Papers* No. 1294 (March).

McCallum, Bennett T. 1989. *Monetary Economics: Theory and Policy*. New York: Macmillan.

McCloskey, Donald N. and J. Richard Zecher. 1976. "How the Gold Standard Worked, 1880–1913." In Jacob A. Frenkel and Harry G. Johnson, eds., *The Monetary Approach to the Balance of Payments*, pp. 184–208. London: Allen & Unwin.

McCulloch, Hugh. 1879. *Bimetallism*. New York: G.P. Putnam's Sons.

McGouldrick, Paul. 1984. "Operations of the German Central Bank and the Rules of the Game, 1879–1913." In Michael Bordo and Anna Schwartz, eds., *A Retrospective on the Classical Gold Standard*, pp. 311–49. Chicago: University of Chicago Press.

McKeown, Timothy. 1983. "Hegemonic Stability Theory and Nineteenth-Century Tariff Levels in Europe." *International Organization* (Winter) 37:73–92.

Meltzer, Allan and Saranna Robinson. 1989. "Stability Under the Gold Standard in Practice." In Michael Bordo, ed., *Essays in Honor of Anna J. Schwartz*, pp. 113–202. Chicago: University of Chicago Press.

MicroTSP User's Manual. 1990. Program by David M. Lilien. Manual by Robert E. Hall, Jack Johnston, and David M. Lilien. Version 7.0. Irvine: Quantitative Micro Software.

Milner, Helen. 1992. "International Theories of Cooperation Among Nations: Strengths and Weaknesses." *World Politics* (April) 44:466–96.

Milward, Alan and S.B. Saul. 1973. *The Economic Development of Continental Europe 1780–1870*. Totowa: Rowman and Littlefield.

Mints, Lloyd W. 1950. *Monetary Policy for a Competitive Society*. New York: McGraw-Hill.

Mitchell, B. R. 1980. *European Historical Statistics*. 2nd Edition. New York: Facts on File.

Moggridge, Donald E. 1969. *The Return to Gold*. Cambridge: Cambridge University Press.

Moggridge, Donald E. 1972. *British Monetary Policy 1924–1931: The Norman Conquest of $4.86*. Cambridge: Cambridge University Press.

Mokyr, Joel. 1976. *Industrialization in the Low Countries, 1795–1850*. New Haven: Yale University Press.

Molière. 1947. *Le Bourgeois Gentilhomme*. With an introduction and notes by Ronald A. Wilson. Boston: D. C. Heath.

Morgan, E. V. 1952. *Studies in British Financial Policy, 1914–25*. London: Macmillan.

Morgan, E. V. 1965. *The Theory and Practice of Central Banking 1797–1913*. New York: Augustus M. Kelley.

Morgan-Webb, Charles. 1934. *The Rise and Fall of the Gold Standard*. New York: Macmillan.

Morgenstern, Oskar. 1959. *International Financial Transactions and Business Cycles*. Princeton: Princeton University Press.

National Association of Manufacturers. 1955. *The Gold Standard*. New York: National Association of Manufacturers.

Nevin, Edward. 1955. *The Mechanism of Cheap Money: A Study of British Monetary Policy, 1931–1939*. Cardiff: University of Wales Press.

Nielsen, Axel. 1933. "Monetary Unions." *Encyclopedia of the Social Sciences* (June) 10:595–601.

Nordhaus, William. 1975. "The Political Business Cycle." *Review of Economic Studies* (April) 42:169–90.

Nurkse, Ragnar. 1944. *International Currency Experience*. Geneva: League of Nations.

Nye, Joseph S. Jr. 1987. "Nuclear Learning and U.S.-Soviet Security Regimes." *International Organization* (Summer) 41:371–402.

Officer, Lawrence. 1989. "The Remarkable Efficiency of the Dollar-Sterling Gold Standard, 1890–1906." *Journal of Economic History* (March) 49:1–41.

O'Leary, Paul. 1960. "The Scene of the Crime of 1873 Revisited: A Note." *Journal of Political Economy* (August) 68:388–92.

Oye, Kenneth A. 1985. "Explaining Cooperation Under Anarchy: Hypotheses and Strategies." *World Politics* (October) 38:1–24.

Pippenger, John. 1984. "Bank of England Operations, 1893–1913." In Michael Bordo and Anna Schwartz, eds., *A Retrospective on the Classical Gold Standard*, pp. 203–22. Chicago: University of Chicago Press.

Platt, D. C. M. 1968. *Finance, Trade, and Politics in British Foreign Policy 1815–1914*. Oxford: Oxford University Press.

Platt, D. C. M. 1973. *Latin America and British Trade 1806–1914*. New York: Harper & Row.

Plessis, Alain. 1985. *The Rise and Fall of the Second Empire, 1852–1871*. Translated by Jonathan Mandelbaum. Cambridge: Cambridge University Press.

Polanyi, Karl. 1957. *The Great Transformation*. Boston: Beacon Press.

Poole, William. 1987. "Monetary Control and the Political Business Cycle." In James Dorn and Anna Schwartz, eds. *The Search for Stable Money: Essays on Monetary Reform*, pp. 31–46. Chicago: University of Chicago Press.

Pope, David. 1993. "Australia's Payments Adjustment and Capital Flows Under the International Gold Standard, 1870–1913." In Michael Bordo and Forrest Capie, eds., *Monetary Regimes in Transition*, pp. 201–37. Cambridge: Cambridge University Press.

Pressnell, L. S. 1968. "Gold Reserves, Banking Reserves, and the Baring Crisis of 1890." In C. R. Whittlesey and J. S. G. Wilson, eds., *Essays in Honor of R. S. Sayers*, pp. 167–228. Oxford: Oxford University Press.

Price, Bonamy. 1878. *Chapters on Practical Political Economy*. London: C. Kegan Paul & Co.

Puchala, Donald and Raymond Hopkins. 1983. "International Regimes: Lessons From Inductive Analysis." In Stephen D. Krasner, ed., *International Regimes*, pp. 61–92. Ithaca, NY: Cornell University Press.

Putnam, Robert D. and Nicholas Bayne. 1987. *Hanging Together: Cooperation and Conflict in the Seven-Power Summits*. Cambridge: Harvard University Press.

Redish, Angela. 1990a. "Bimetallism in Nineteenth Century France: A Razor's Edge." University of British Columbia, unpublished manuscript.

Redish, Angela. 1990b. "The Evolution of the Gold Standard in England." *Journal of Economic History* (December) 50:789–805.

Redish, Angela. 1993. "The Latin Monetary Union and the Emergence of the International Gold Standard." In Michael Bordo and Forrest Capie, eds., *Monetary Regimes in Transition*, pp. 68–85. Cambridge: Cambridge University Press.

Rich, Georg. 1984. "Canada Without a Central Bank: Operation of the Price-Specie-Flow Mechanism, 1872–1913." In Michael Bordo and Anna Schwartz, eds., *A Retrospective on the Classical Gold Standard, 1821–1931*, pp. 547–75. Chicago: University of Chicago Press.

Richardson, J. Henry. 1936. *British Economic Foreign Policy*. New York: Macmillan.

Robertson, Dennis H. 1931. "The Transfer Problem." In A.C. Pigou and Dennis H. Robertson, eds., *Economic Essays and Addresses*, pp. 170–82. London: P.S. King.

Rockoff, Hugh. 1984. "Some Evidence on the Real Price of Gold, Its Costs of Production, and Commodity Prices." In Michael Bordo and Anna Schwartz, eds., *A Retrospective on the Classical Gold Standard, 1821–1931*, pp. 613–44. Chicago: University of Chicago Press.

Rockoff, Hugh. 1986. "Walter Bagehot and the Theory of Central Banking." In Forrest Capie and Geoffrey E. Wood, eds., *Financial Crises and the World Banking System*, pp. 160–80. New York: St. Martin's Press.

Rolnick, Arthur and Warren Weber. 1986. "Gresham's Law or Gresham's Fallacy?" *Journal of Political Economy* (February) 94:185–99.

Rosenberg, Arthur. 1962. *The Birth of the German Republic 1871–1918*. New York: Russell & Russell.

Rostow, W. W. 1948. *British Economy of the Nineteenth Century*. Oxford: Oxford University Press.

Rowland, Benjamin M., ed., 1976. *Balance of Power or Hegemony: The Interwar Monetary System*. New York: New York University Press.

Ruggie, John Gerard. 1975. "International Responses to Technology: Concepts and Trends." *International Organization* (Summer) 29:557–83.

Ruggie, John Gerard. 1983. "International Regimes, Transactions, and Change: Embedded Liberalism in the Postwar Economic Order." In Stephen D. Krasner, ed., *International Regimes*, pp. 195–232. Ithaca, NY: Cornell University Press.

Russell, Henry. 1898. *International Monetary Conferences*. New York: Harper and Brothers.

Russett, Bruce. 1985. "The Mysterious Case of Vanishing Hegemony: or, Is Mark Twain Really Dead?" *International Organization* (Spring) 39:207–32.

Sargent, Thomas J. and Neil Wallace. 1975. "Rational Expectations, the Optimal Monetary Instrument, and the Optimal Money Supply Rule." *Journal of Political Economy* (April) 83:241–54.

Saul, S. B. 1960. *Studies in British Overseas Trade 1870–1914*. Liverpool: Liverpool University Press.

Sayers, R. S. 1957. *Central Banking After Bagehot*. Oxford: Oxford University Press.

Sayers, R. S. 1970. *Bank of England Operations*. Westport: Greenwood Press.

Sayers, R. S. 1976. *The Bank of England 1891–1944*. Vols. I, II, & Appendixes. Cambridge: Cambridge University Press.

Scammell, W.M. [1965] 1985. "The Working of the Gold Standard." In Barry Eichengreen, ed., *The Gold Standard in Theory and History*, pp. 103–20. New York: Methuen.

Schelling, Thomas. 1981. *The Strategy of Conflict*. Cambridge: Harvard University Press.

Schlesinger, Arthur Jr. 1945. *The Age of Jackson*. Boston: Little, Brown.

Schroeder, Paul W. 1986. "The 19th-Century International System: Changes in the Structure." *World Politics* (October) 39:1–26.

Schumpeter, Joseph. 1954. *History of Economic Analysis*. New York: Oxford University Press.

Schwartz, Anna. 1984. "Introduction." In Michael Bordo and Anna Schwartz, eds., *A Retrospective on the Classical Gold Standard, 1821–1931*, pp. 1–20. Chicago: University of Chicago Press.

Schwartz. Anna. 1986. "Alternative Monetary Regimes: The Gold Standard." In Colin Campbell and William Dougan, eds. *Alternative Monetary Regimes*, pp. 44–72. Baltimore: Johns Hopkins University Press.

Seyd, Ernest. 1868. *Bullion and Foreign Exchanges*. London: Effingham Wilson.

Sherman, John. 1895. *John Sherman's Recollections of Forty Years in the House, Senate and Cabinet*. Vols. I & II. Chicago: Werner.

Simkin, C. G. F. 1951. *The Instability of a Dependent Economy: Economic Fluctuations in New Zealand 1840–1914*. Oxford: Oxford University Press.

Simon, Matthew. 1968. "The Pattern of New British Portfolio Foreign Investment, 1865–1914." In A.R. Hall, ed., *The Export of Capital From Britain 1870–1914*, pp. 15–44. London: Methuen.

Skidelsky, Robert J.A. 1976. "Retreat From Leadership: The Evolution of British Economic Foreign Policy, 1870–1939." In Benjamin M. Rowland, ed., *Balance of Power or Hegemony: The Interwar Monetary System*, pp. 147–94. New York: New York University Press.

Slater, M. H. 1886. *Money: A Brief Treatise on Bimetallism in Plain Words*. Washington: National Bimetallic Coinage Association.

Snidal, Duncan. 1985a. "The Limits of Hegemonic Stability Theory." *International Organization* (Spring) 39:579–614.

Snidal, Duncan. 1985b. "Coordination Versus Prisoners' Dilemma: Implications for International Cooperation and Regimes." *American Political Science Review* (December) 79:923–42.

Stein, Arthur A. 1983. "Coordination and Collaboration: Regimes in an Anarchic World." In Stephen D. Krasner, ed., *International Regimes*, pp. 115–40. Ithaca, NY: Cornell University Press.

Stein, Arthur A. 1984. "The Hegemon's Dilemma: Great Britain, the United States, and the International Economic Order." *International Organization* (Spring) 38:355–86.

Stern, Fritz. 1977. *Gold and Iron: Bismarck, Bleichroder, and the Building of the German Empire*. New York: Knopf.

Stolper, Gustav. 1940. *German Economy 1870–1940*. New York: Reynal & Hitchcock.

Strange, Susan. 1987. "The Persistent Myth of Lost Hegemony." *International Organization* (Autumn) 41:551–74.

Strange, Susan. 1988. *States and Markets*. New York: Basil Blackwell.

Stromberg, Andrew. 1931. *A History of Sweden*. New York: Macmillan.

Sundquist, James. 1983. *Dynamics of the Party System: Alignment and Realignment of Political Parties in the United States*. Washington: Brookings Institution.

Swartz, Marvin. 1985. *The Politics of British Foreign Policy in the Era of Disraeli and Gladstone*. New York: St. Martin's Press.

Taus, Ester Rogoff. 1943. *Central Banking Functions of the United States Treasury, 1789–1941*. New York: Columbia University Press.

Taussig, F. W. 1917. "International Trade Under Depreciated Paper, a Contribution to Theory." *Quarterly Journal of Economics* (May) 21:380–403.

Taussig, F. W. [1927] 1966. *International Trade*. New York: Augustus M. Kelley.

Taylor, John B. 1985. "What Would Nominal GNP Targeting do to the Business Cycle?" In Karl Brunner and Allan Meltzer, eds., *Understanding Monetary Regimes*, Vol. 22, pp. 61–84. Amsterdam. North-Holland.

Temin, Peter. 1984. "Comment." In Michael Bordo and Anna Schwartz, eds., *A Retrospective on the Classical Gold Standard, 1821–1931*, pp. 576–81. Chicago: University of Chicago Press.

Tennant, Charles. 1865. *The Bank of England: and the Organization of Credit in England*. London: Longmans, Green.

Thorp, Willard Long. 1926. *Business Annals*. New York: NBER.

Triffin, Robert. 1947. "National Central Banking and the International Economy." *Review of Economic Studies* 14:53–75.

Triffin, Robert. 1964. *The Evolution of the International Monetary System: Historical Reappraisal and Future Perspectives*. Princeton Studies in International Finance, No. 12. Princeton: Princeton University Press.

Tumlir, Jan. 1985. *Protectionism: Trade Policies in Democratic Societies*. Washington, DC: American Enterprise Institute.

Unger, Irwin. 1964. *The Greenback Era: A Social and Political History of American Finance, 1865–1879*. Princeton: Princeton University Press.

United States Congress: House of Representatives. 1881. *International Monetary Conference*. 49th Congress, 1st Session.

United States Congress: House of Representatives. 1903. *Stability of International Exchange*. 58th Congress, 2nd Session.

United States Congress: Senate. 1867. *International Monetary Conference of 1867*. 40th Congress, 2nd Session.

United States Congress: Senate. 1868. *Report of the Committee on Finance on Bills, Reports, and Memorials Relating to International Coinage*. 40th Congress, 2nd Session.

United States Congress: Senate. 1876. *U.S. Monetary Commission*. Vols. I & II, 44th Congress, 2nd Session.

United States Congress: Senate. 1879. *International Monetary Conference of 1878*. 45th Congress, 3rd Session.

United States Congress: Senate. 1893. *International Monetary Conference of 1892*. 52nd Congress, 2nd Session.

United States Congress: Senate. 1909. *The Evolution of Credit and Banks in France* by Andre Liesse. 61st Congress, 2nd Session. National Monetary Commission.

United States Congress: Senate. 1910a. *The Bank of France In Its Relation to National and*

International Credit by Maurice Patron. 61st Congress, 2nd Session. National Monetary Commission.

United States Congress: Senate. 1910b. *The Discount System in Europe* by Paul M. Warburg. 61st Congress, 2nd Session. National Monetary Commission.

United States Congress: Senate. 1910c. *The English Banking System* by Hartley Withers, R.H. Inglis Palgrave, and Other Writers. 61st Congress, 2nd Session. National Monetary Commission.

United States Congress: Senate. 1910d. *German Bank Inquiry of 1908*. 61st Congress, 2nd Session. National Monetary Commission.

United States Congress: Senate. 1910e. *Interviews on the Banking and Currency Systems of England, Scotland, France, Germany, Switzerland, and Italy*. 61st Congress, 2nd Session. National Monetary Commission.

United States Congress: Senate. 1910f. *The National Bank of Belgium* by Charles A. Conant. 61st Congress, 2nd Session. National Monetary Commission.

United States Congress: Senate. 1911. *Banking in Russia, Austro-Hungary, The Netherlands and Japan*. 61st Congress, 2nd Session. National Monetary Commission.

United States Department of Commerce. 1910. *Statistical Abstract of the United States*.

Upton, J. K. 1884. *Money in Politics*. Boston: D Lothrop.

Viner, Jacob. 1924. *Canada's Balance of International Indebtedness 1900–1913*. Cambridge: Harvard University Press.

Viner, Jacob. 1932. "International Aspects of the Gold Standard." In Quincy Wright, ed., *Gold and Monetary Stabilization*, pp. 3–42. Chicago: University of Chicago Press.

Viner, Jacob. 1937. *Studies in the Theory of International Trade*. New York: Harper & Brothers.

Viner, Jacob. 1945. "Clapham on the Bank of England." *Economica* (May) 12:61–68.

Volcker, Paul. 1976. "Contribution." In Robert Mundell and Jacques Polak, eds., *The New International Monetary System*, pp. 25–36. New York: Columbia University Press, 1976.

Wagner, R. Harrison. 1983. "The Theory of Games and the Problem of International Cooperation." *American Political Science Review* (June) 77:330–46.

Waltz, Kenneth. 1979. *Theory of International Politics*. Reading, Mass.: Addison-Wellesley.

Ward, A. W. and G. P. Gooch, eds., 1923. *The Cambridge History of British Foreign Policy 1783–1919*. Vol. III. New York: Macmillan.

Warren, George F. and Frank A. Pearson. 1935. *Gold and Prices*. New York: John Wiley & Sons.

Warren, Henry. 1903. *The Story of the Bank of England*. London: Jordan & Sons.

Webb, Michael C. 1991. "International Economic Structures, Government Interests, and International Coordination of Macroeconomic Adjustment Policies." *International Organization* (Summer) 45:309–42.

Whale, P. Barrett. [1937] 1985. "The Working of the Pre-War Gold Standard." In Barry Eichengreen, ed., *The Gold Standard in Theory and History*, pp. 49–62. New York: Methuen, 1985.

White, Harry Dexter. 1933. *The French International Accounts 1880–1913*. Cambridge: Harvard University Press.

White, Horace. 1891. "Bimetallism in France." *Political Science Quarterly* (June) 6:311–37.

White, Horace. 1893. *The Gold Standard*. New York: Evening Post Publishing Co.

Whitman, Marina V.N. 1975. "Leadership Without Hegemony: Our Role in the World Economy." *Foreign Policy* (Fall) 20:138–61.

Willett, Thomas D. 1980. *International Liquidity Issues*. Washington, DC: American Enterprise Institute.

Williams, David. 1968. "The Evolution of the Sterling System." In C. R. Whittlesey and J. S. G. Wilson, eds., *Essays in Honor of R.S. Sayers*, pp. 266–97. Oxford: Oxford University Press.

Williamson, Jeffrey G. 1964. *American Growth and the Balance of Payments 1820–1913.* Chapel Hill: University of North Carolina Press.

Williamson, Jeffrey. 1968. "The Long Swing: Comparisons and Interactions Between British and American Balance of Payments." In A. R. Hall, ed., *The Export of Capital From Great Britain 1870–1914*, pp. 55–83. London: Methuen.

Williamson, John and Marcus H. Miller. 1987. *Targets and Indicators: A Blueprint for the International Coordination of Economic Policy.* Washington, DC: Institute for International Economics.

Willis, Henry Parker. 1901. *A History of the Latin Monetary Union: A Study of International Monetary Action.* Chicago: University of Chicago Press.

Wood, Elmer. 1939. *English Theories of Central Banking Control 1819–1858.* Cambridge: Harvard University Press.

Yarbrough, Beth V. and Robert M. Yarbrough. 1987. "Cooperation in the Liberalization of Trade: After Hegemony, What?" *International Organization* (Winter) 41:1–26.

Yeager, Leland B. 1969. "Fluctuating Exchange Rates in the Nineteenth Century: The Experiences of Austria and Russia." In Robert Mundell and Alexander Swoboda, eds., *Monetary Problems of the International Economy*, pp. 61–89. Chicago: University of Chicago Press.

Yeager, Leland B. 1976. *International Monetary Relations: Theory, History, and Policy.* New York: Harper & Row.

Yeager, Leland B. 1984. "The Image of the Gold Standard." In Michael Bordo and Anna Schwartz, eds., *A Retrospective on the Classical Gold Standard, 1821–1931*, pp. 651–70. Chicago: University of Chicago Press.

Young, Oran R. 1980. "International Regimes: Problems of Concept Formation." *World Politics* (April) 32:331–56.

Young, Oran R. 1982. *Resource Regimes: Natural Resources and Social Institutions.* Berkeley: University of California Press.

Young, Oran R. 1983. "Regime Dynamics: The Rise and Fall of International Regimes." In Stephen D. Krasner, ed., *International Regimes*, pp. 93–114. Ithaca, NY: Cornell University Press.

Young, Oran R. 1986. "International Regimes: Toward a New Theory of Institutions." *World Politics* (October) 39:104–22.

Young, Oran R. 1989. "The Politics of International Regime Formation: Managing Natural Resources and the Environment." *International Organization* (Summer) 43:349–76.

Young, Oran R. 1991. "Political Leadership and Regime Formation: On the Development of Institutions in International Society." *International Organization* (Summer) 45:281–308.

Zeldin, Theodore. 1958. *The Political System of Napoleon III.* London: Macmillan.

Ziegler, Philip. 1988. *The Sixth Great Power: A History of One of the Greatest of all Banking Families, the House of Barings, 1762–1929.* New York: Alfred A. Knopf.

Zucker, Stanley. 1975. *Ludwig Bamberger: German Liberal Politician and Social Critic.* Pittsburgh: University of Pittsburgh Press.

Index

/